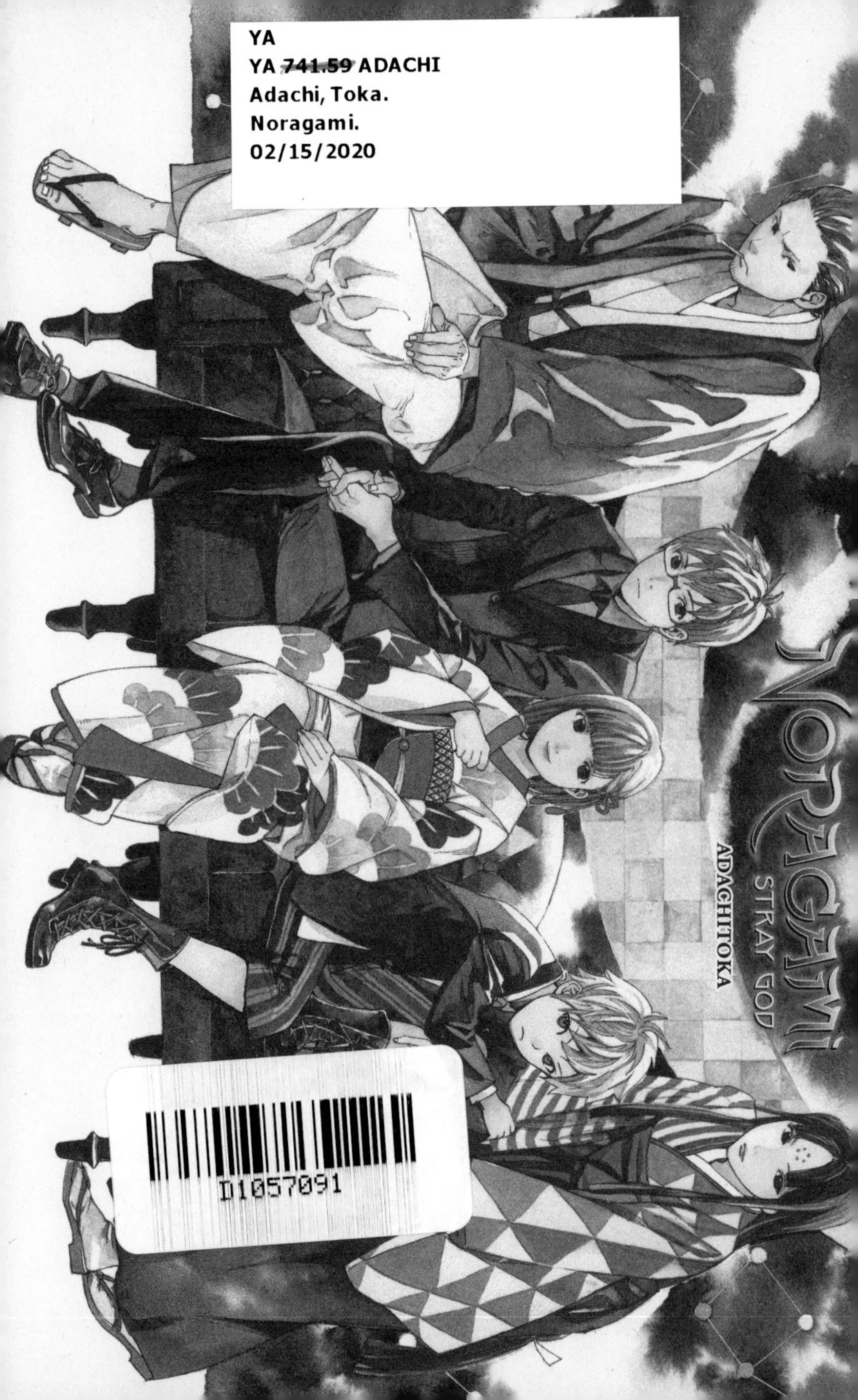
NORAGAMI
STRAY GOD
ADACHITOKA

characters

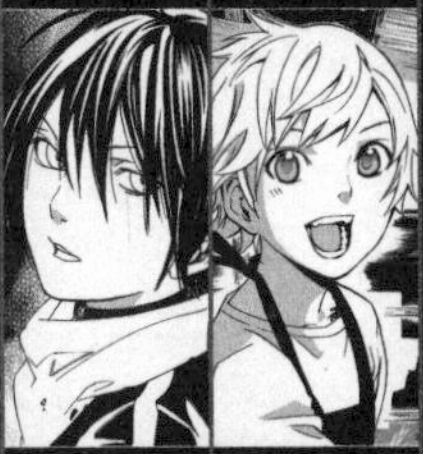

YATO
A minor deity who always wears a sweatsuit.

YUKINÉ
Yato's shinki who turns into swords.

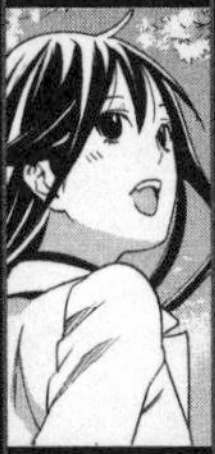

HIYORI IKI
A high school student who has become half ayakashi.

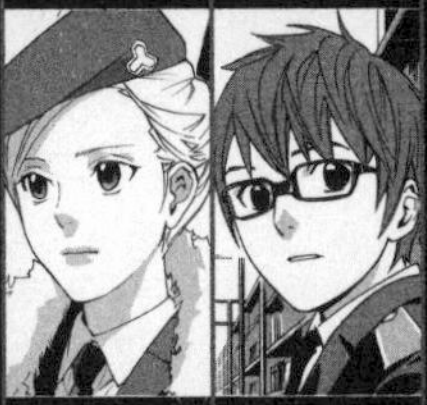

BISHAMONTEN
A powerful warrior god, one of the Seven Gods of Fortune.

KAZUMA
A navigational shinki who serves as guide to Bishamon.

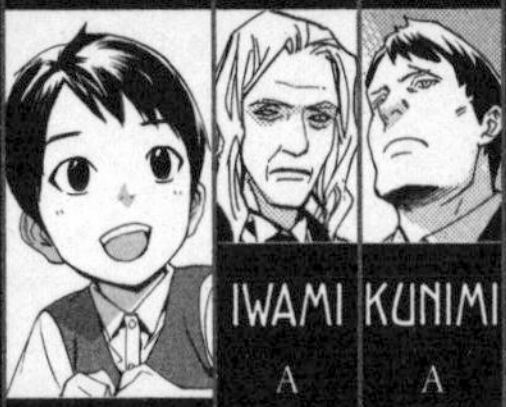

EBISU
A business-god in the making, one of the Seven Gods of Fortune.

IWAMI
A shinki who knows Ebisu's history.

KUNIMI
A shinki who enhances Ebisu's motor skills.

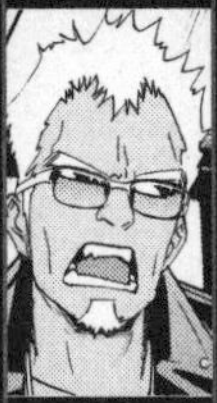

ÔKUNINUSHI (DAIKOKUTEN)
Number one of the Seven Gods of Fortune.

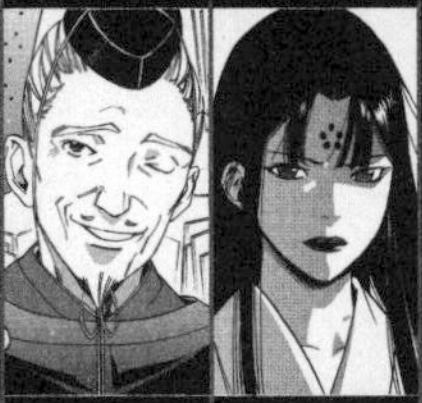

TENJIN
The god of learning, Sugawara no Michizane.

TSUYU
A spirit of the plum tree, Tenjin's attendant.

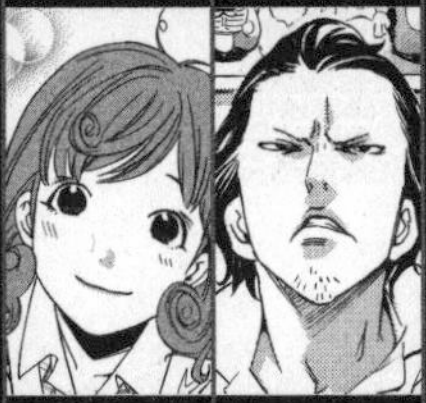

KOFUKU
A goddess of poverty who calls herself Ebisu, after the god of fortune.

DAIKOKU
Kofuku's shinki who summons storms.

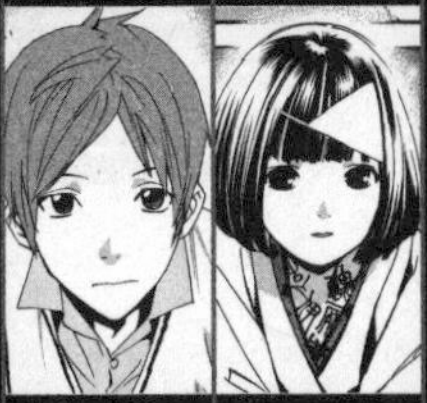

KÔTO FUJISAKI
Yato's "father."

STRAY
A shinki who serves an unspecified number of deities.

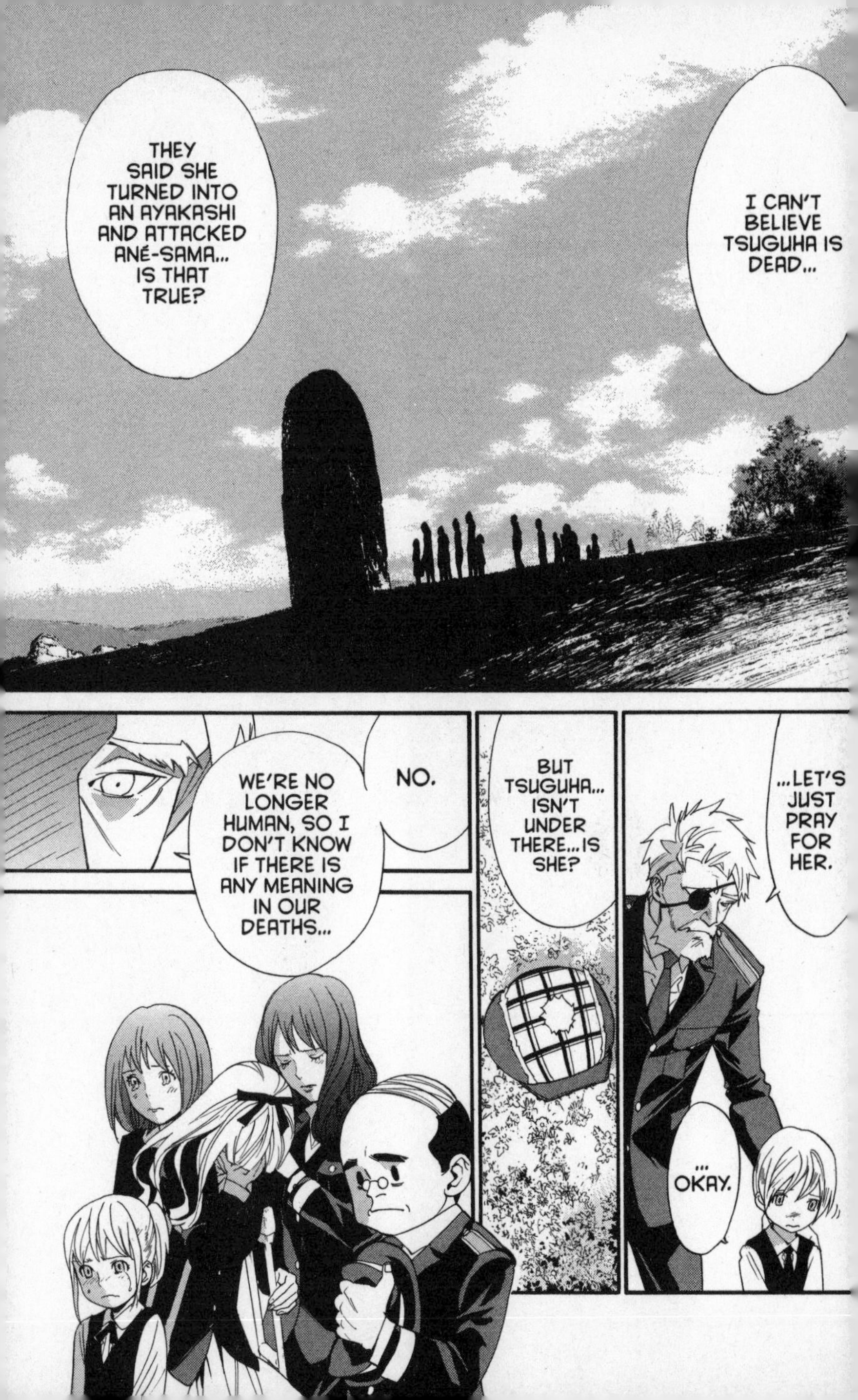
I CAN'T BELIEVE TSUGUHA IS DEAD...
THEY SAID SHE TURNED INTO AN AYAKASHI AND ATTACKED ANÉ-SAMA... IS THAT TRUE?
...LET'S JUST PRAY FOR HER.
...OKAY.
BUT TSUGUHA... ISN'T UNDER THERE...IS SHE?
NO.
WE'RE NO LONGER HUMAN, SO I DON'T KNOW IF THERE IS ANY MEANING IN OUR DEATHS...

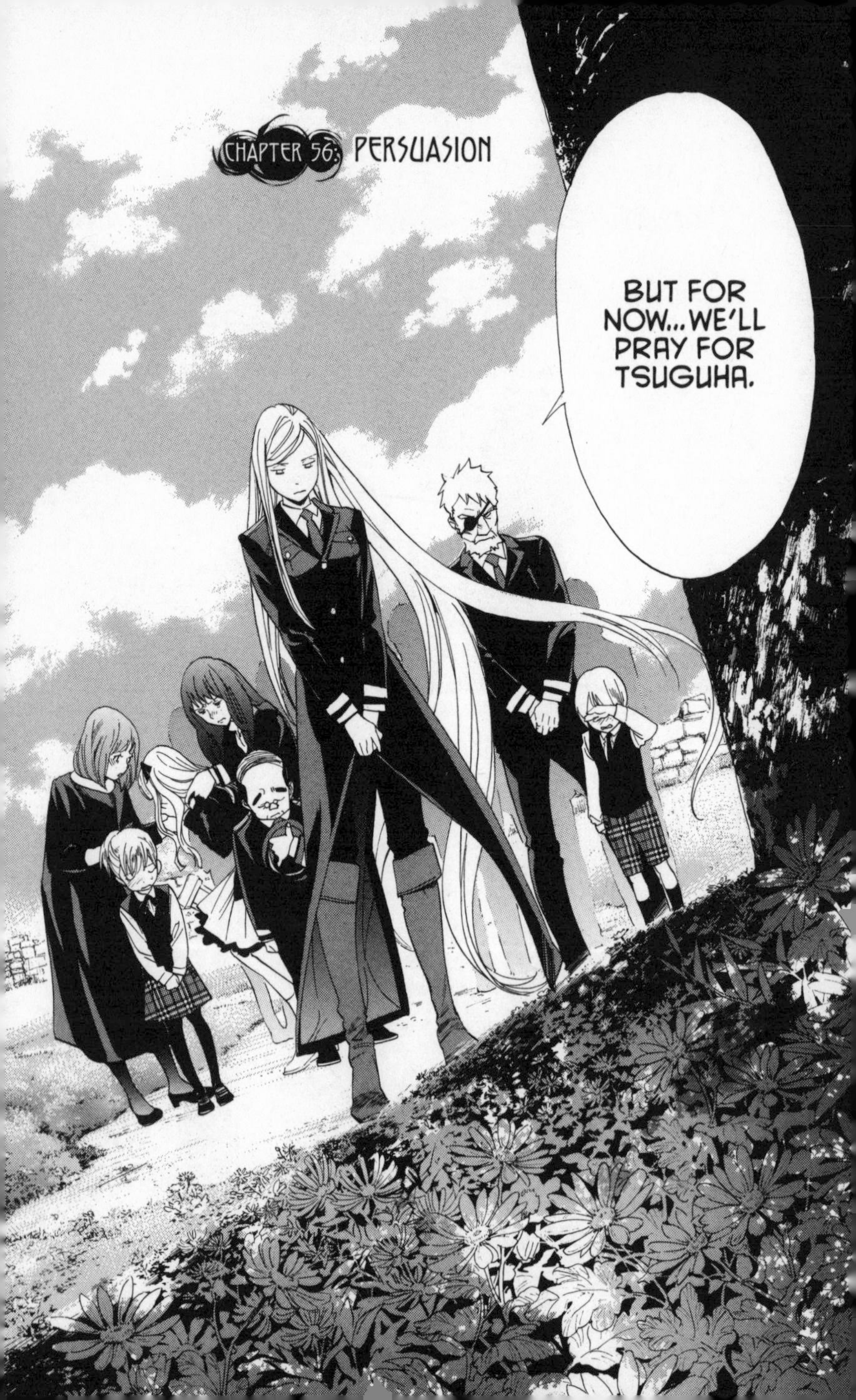
CHAPTER 56: PERSUASION
BUT FOR NOW... WE'LL PRAY FOR TSUGUHA.

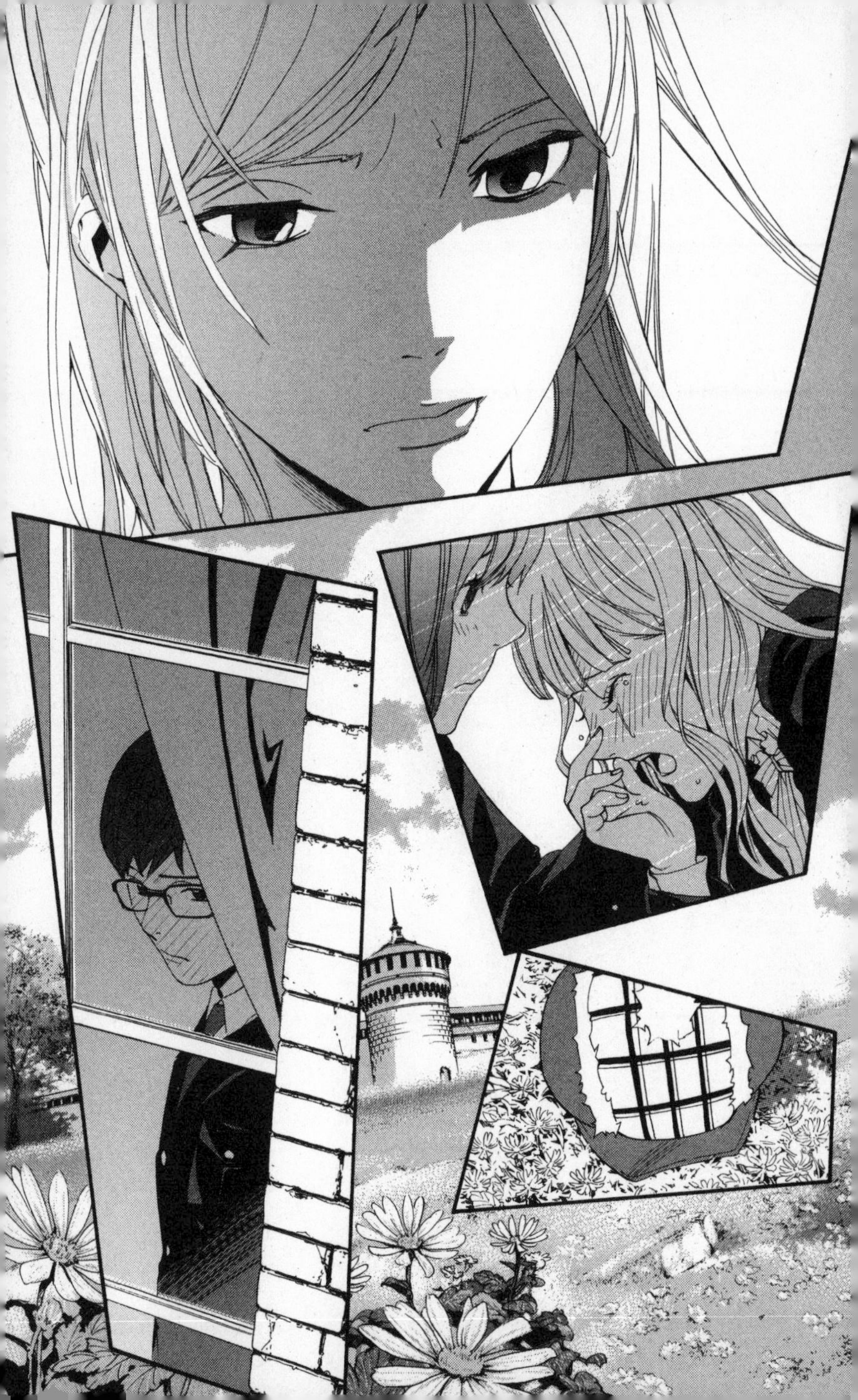

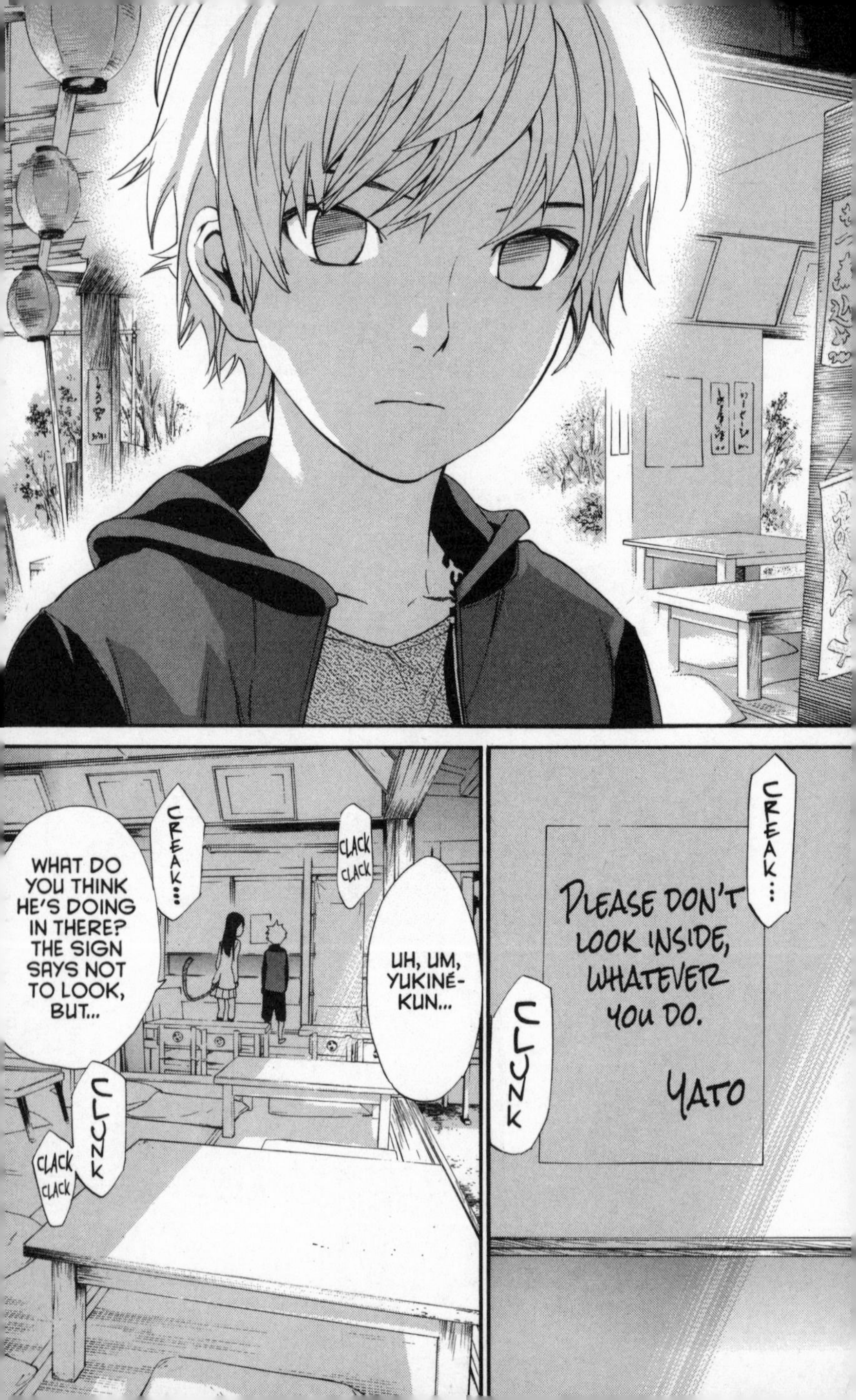
CREAK...
PLEASE DON'T LOOK INSIDE, WHATEVER YOU DO.
YATO
CLUNK
CLACK CLACK
CREAK...
UH, UM, YUKINÉ-KUN...
WHAT DO YOU THINK HE'S DOING IN THERE? THE SIGN SAYS NOT TO LOOK, BUT...
CLUNK
CLACK CLACK

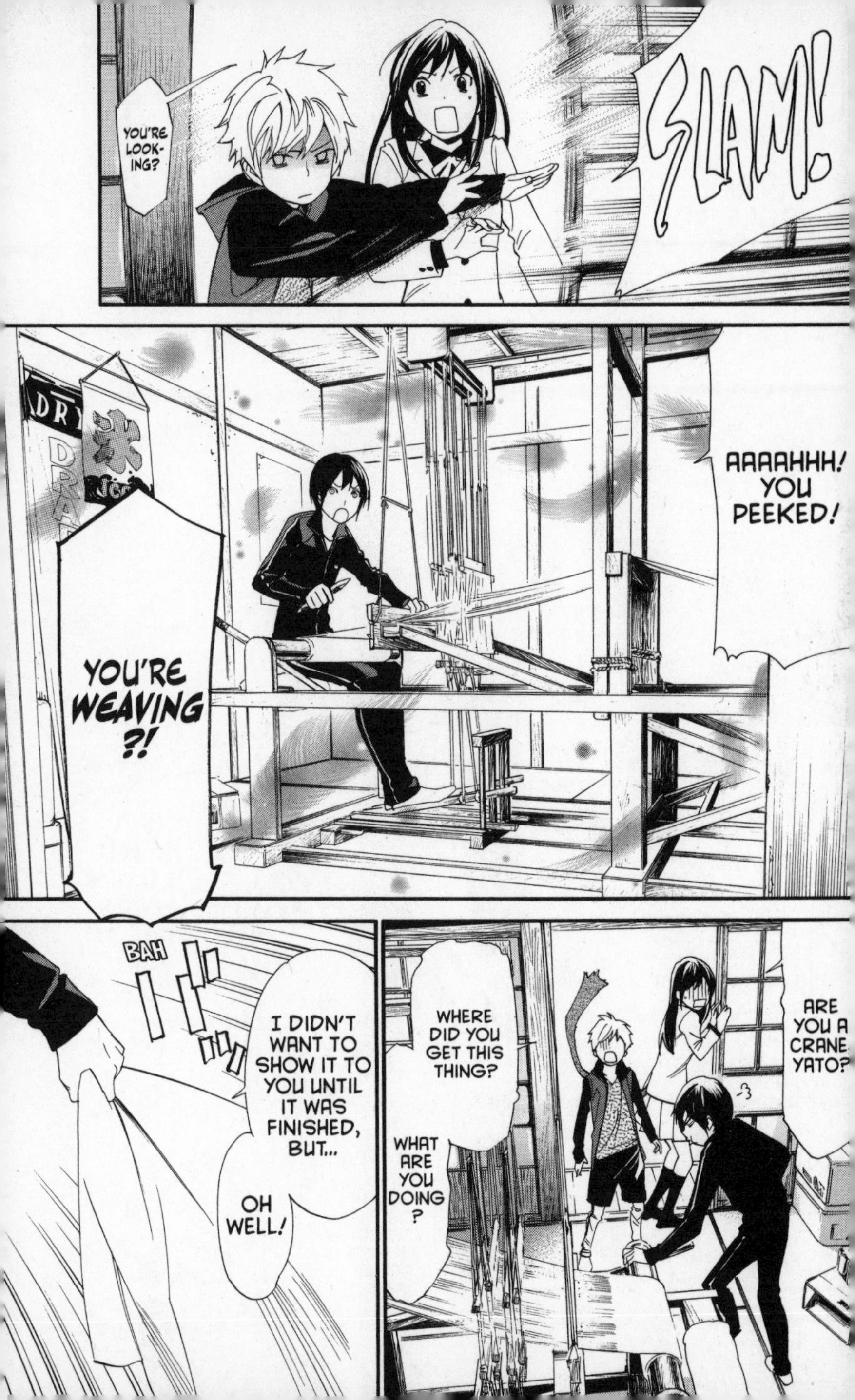
SLAM!
YOU'RE LOOK-ING?
AAAAHHH! YOU PEEKED!
YOU'RE WEAVING?!
ARE YOU A CRANE YATO?
WHERE DID YOU GET THIS THING?
WHAT ARE YOU DOING?
BAH
I DIDN'T WANT TO SHOW IT TO YOU UNTIL IT WAS FINISHED, BUT...
OH WELL!

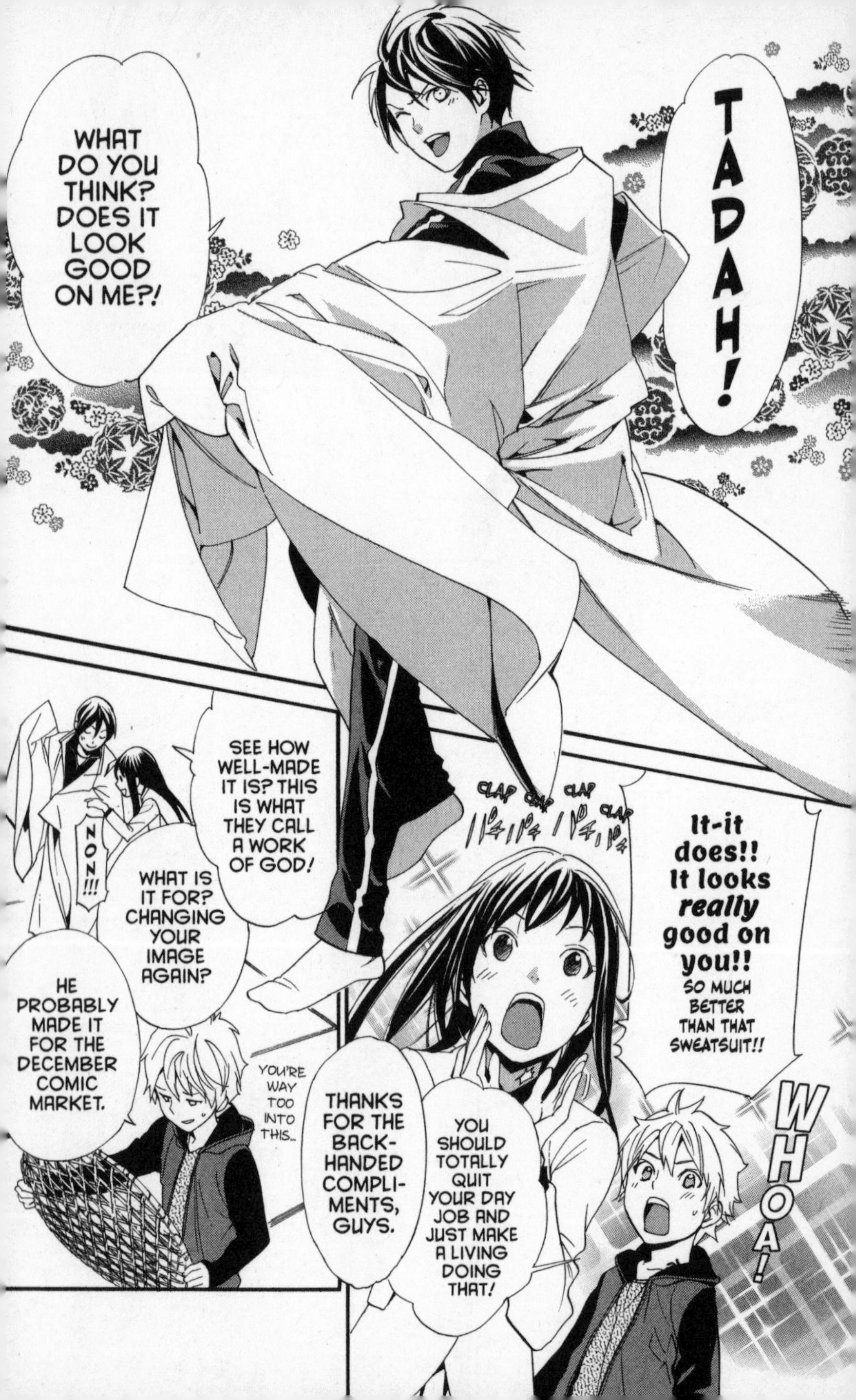
TADAH!
WHAT DO YOU THINK? DOES IT LOOK GOOD ON ME?!
CLAP CLAP CLAP CLAP
It-it does!! It looks *really* good on you!! SO MUCH BETTER THAN THAT SWEATSUIT!!
WHOA!
YOU SHOULD TOTALLY QUIT YOUR DAY JOB AND JUST MAKE A LIVING DOING THAT!
THANKS FOR THE BACK-HANDED COMPLI-MENTS, GUYS.
SEE HOW WELL-MADE IT IS? THIS IS WHAT THEY CALL A WORK OF GOD!
NON!!!
WHAT IS IT FOR? CHANGING YOUR IMAGE AGAIN?
HE PROBABLY MADE IT FOR THE DECEMBER COMIC MARKET.
YOU'RE WAY TOO INTO THIS...

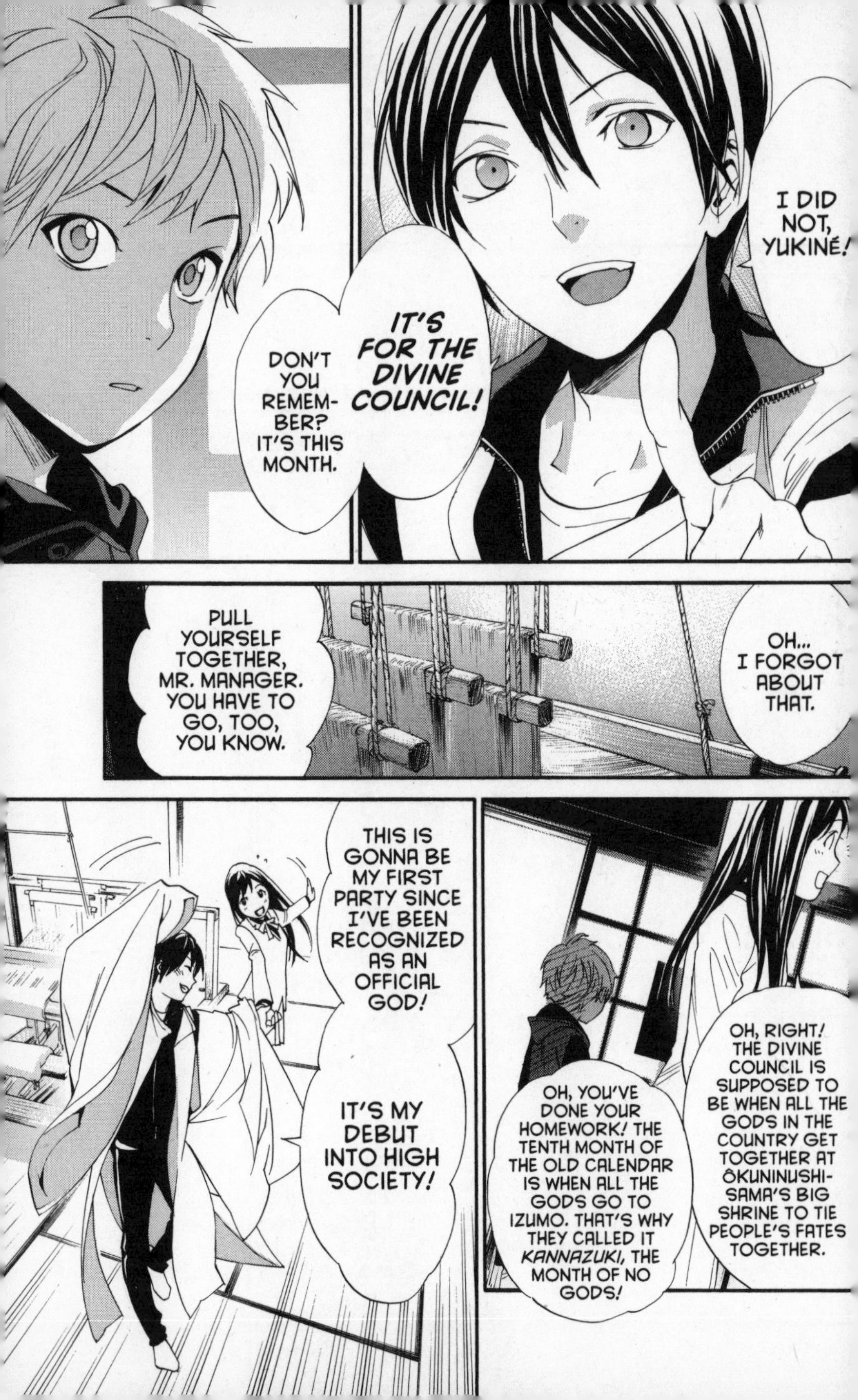
I DID NOT, YUKINÉ!
IT'S FOR THE DIVINE COUNCIL!
DON'T YOU REMEMBER? IT'S THIS MONTH.
OH... I FORGOT ABOUT THAT.
PULL YOURSELF TOGETHER, MR. MANAGER. YOU HAVE TO GO, TOO, YOU KNOW.
OH, RIGHT! THE DIVINE COUNCIL IS SUPPOSED TO BE WHEN ALL THE GODS IN THE COUNTRY GET TOGETHER AT ÔKUNINUSHI-SAMA'S BIG SHRINE TO TIE PEOPLE'S FATES TOGETHER.
OH, YOU'VE DONE YOUR HOMEWORK! THE TENTH MONTH OF THE OLD CALENDAR IS WHEN ALL THE GODS GO TO IZUMO. THAT'S WHY THEY CALLED IT *KANNAZUKI*, THE MONTH OF NO GODS!
THIS IS GONNA BE MY FIRST PARTY SINCE I'VE BEEN RECOGNIZED AS AN OFFICIAL GOD!
IT'S MY DEBUT INTO HIGH SOCIETY!

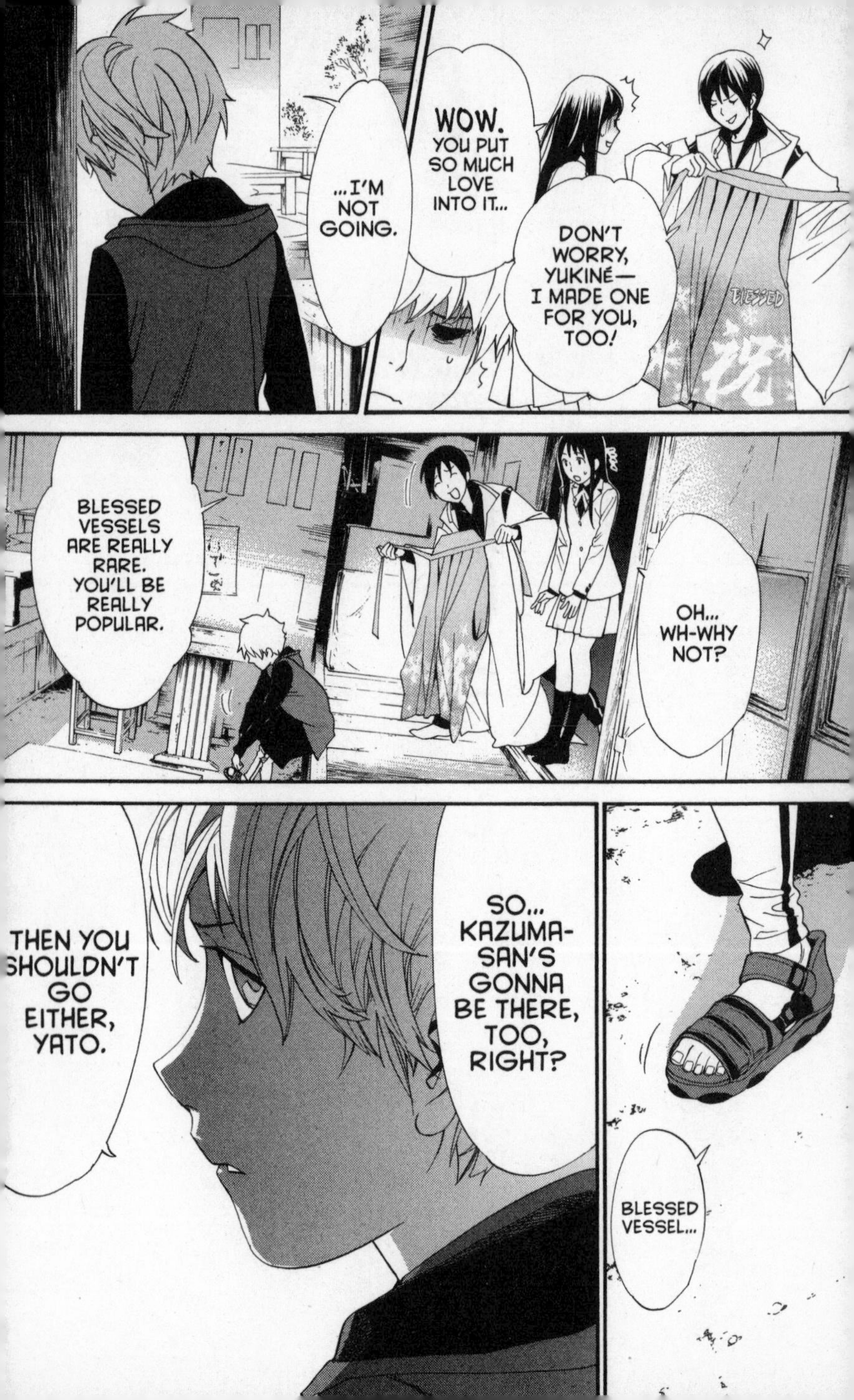

WOW. YOU PUT SO MUCH LOVE INTO IT...
DON'T WORRY, YUKINÉ— I MADE ONE FOR YOU, TOO!
BLESSED
...I'M NOT GOING.
OH... WH-WHY NOT?
BLESSED VESSELS ARE REALLY RARE. YOU'LL BE REALLY POPULAR.
BLESSED VESSEL...
SO... KAZUMA-SAN'S GONNA BE THERE, TOO, RIGHT?
THEN YOU SHOULDN'T GO EITHER, YATO.

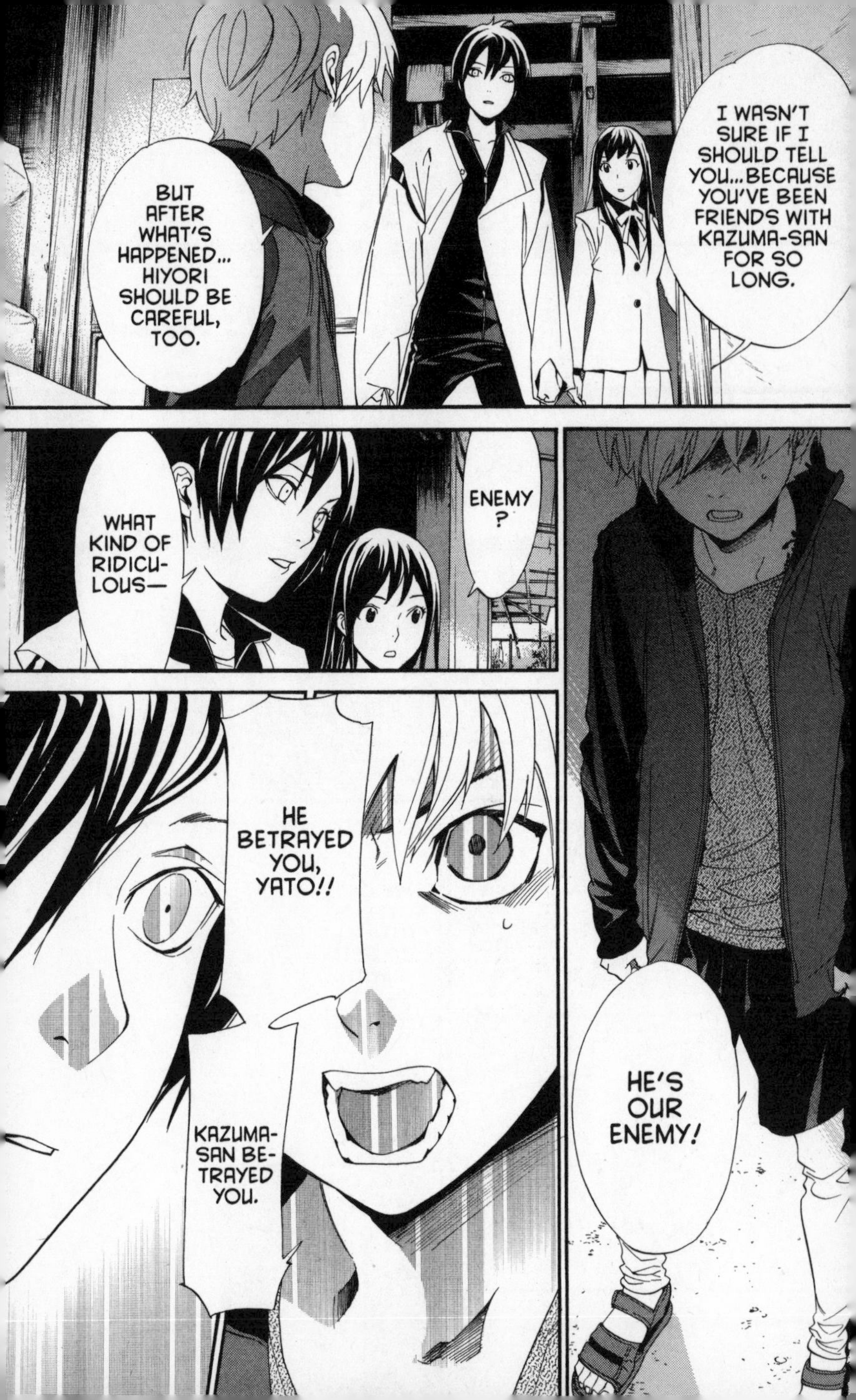
I WASN'T SURE IF I SHOULD TELL YOU...BECAUSE YOU'VE BEEN FRIENDS WITH KAZUMA-SAN FOR SO LONG.
BUT AFTER WHAT'S HAPPENED... HIYORI SHOULD BE CAREFUL, TOO.
HE'S OUR ENEMY!
ENEMY?
WHAT KIND OF RIDICU-LOUS—
HE BETRAYED YOU, YATO!!
KAZUMA-SAN BE-TRAYED YOU.

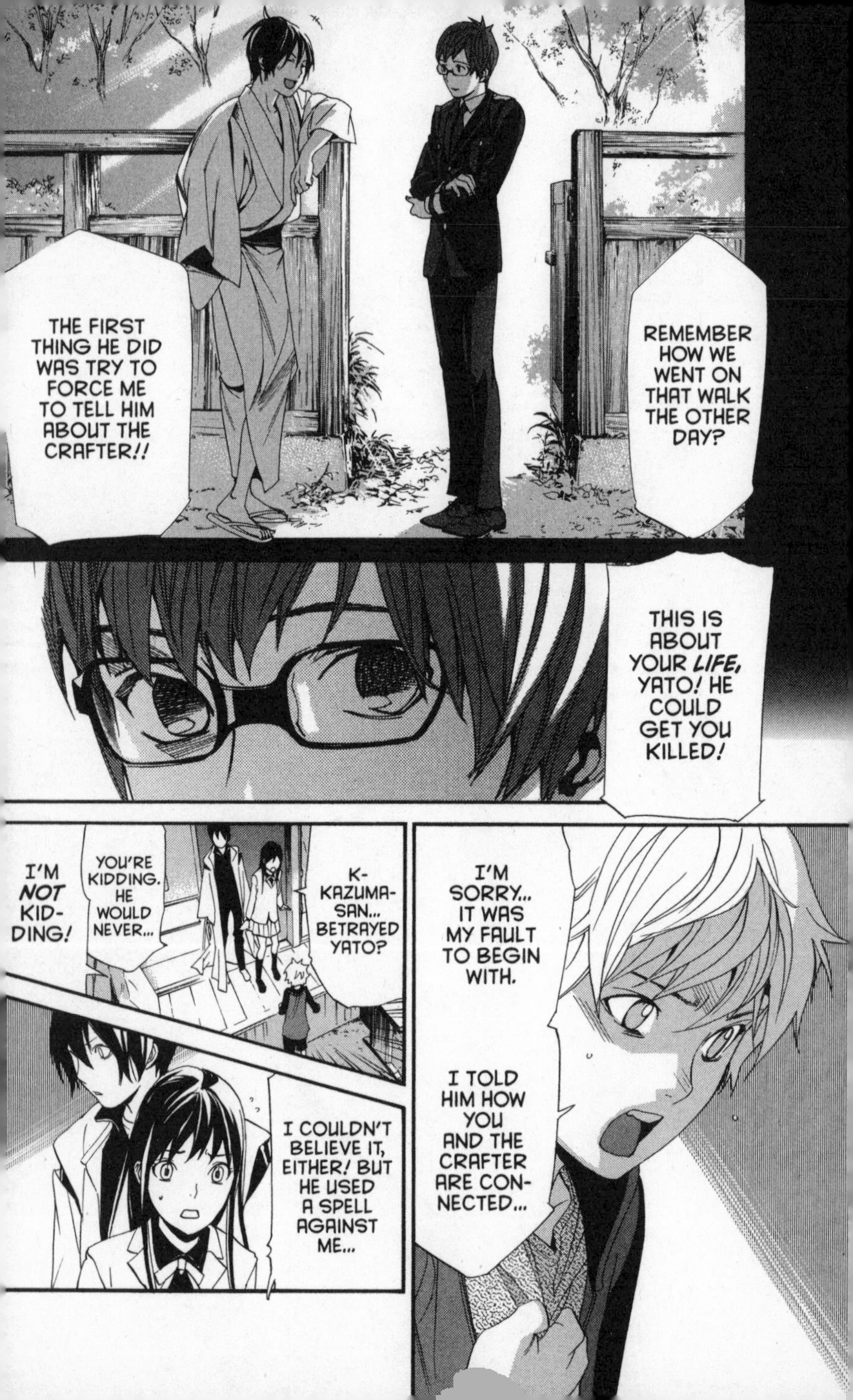
REMEMBER HOW WE WENT ON THAT WALK THE OTHER DAY?
THE FIRST THING HE DID WAS TRY TO FORCE ME TO TELL HIM ABOUT THE CRAFTER!!
THIS IS ABOUT YOUR *LIFE*, YATO! HE COULD GET YOU KILLED!
I'M SORRY... IT WAS MY FAULT TO BEGIN WITH.
I TOLD HIM HOW YOU AND THE CRAFTER ARE CONNECTED...
K-KAZUMA-SAN... BETRAYED YATO?
YOU'RE KIDDING. HE WOULD NEVER...
I'M *NOT* KIDDING!
I COULDN'T BELIEVE IT, EITHER! BUT HE USED A SPELL AGAINST ME...

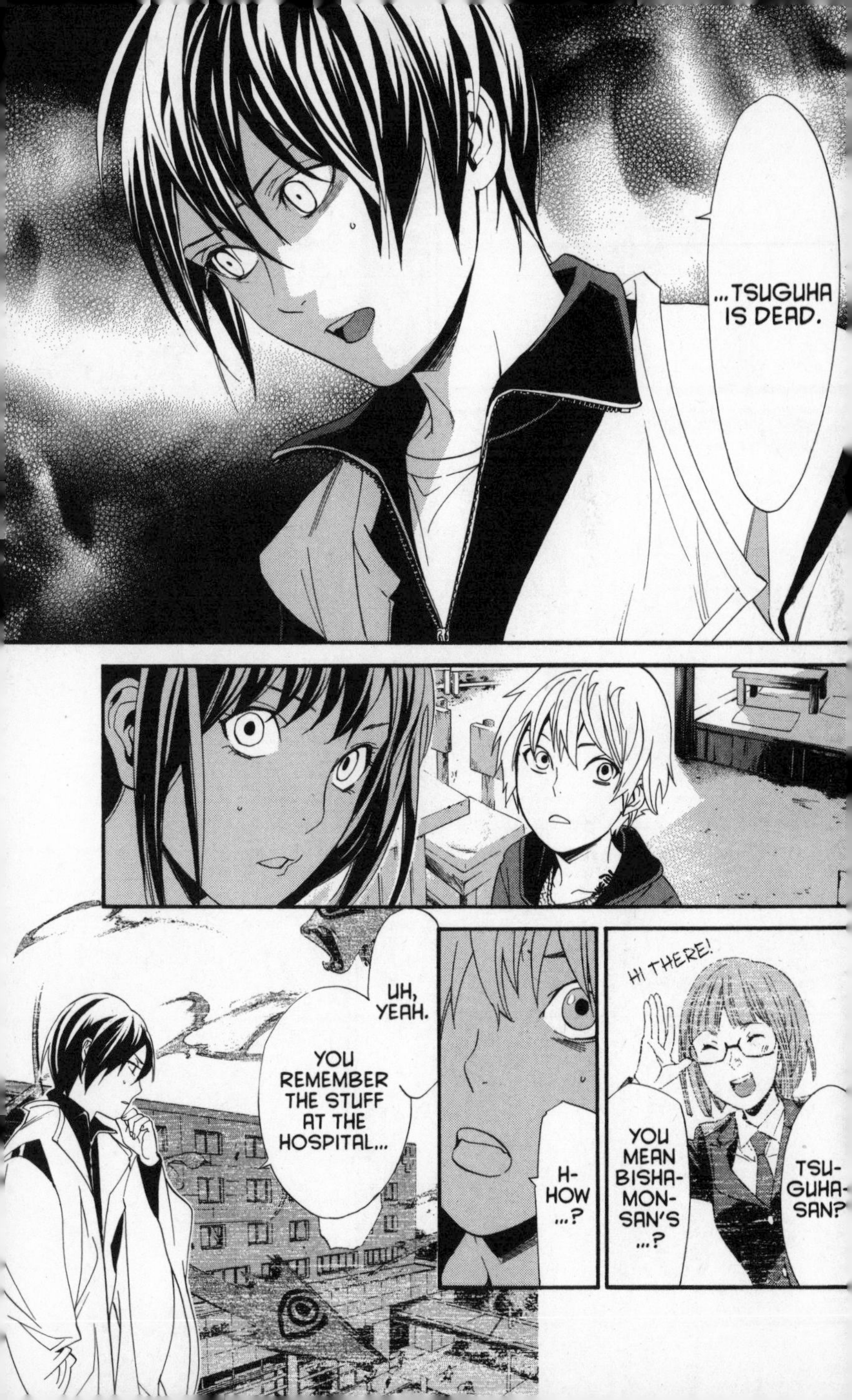
...TSUGUHA IS DEAD.
HI THERE!
TSU-GUHA-SAN?
YOU MEAN BISHA-MON-SAN'S ...?
H-HOW ...?
UH, YEAH.
YOU REMEMBER THE STUFF AT THE HOSPITAL...

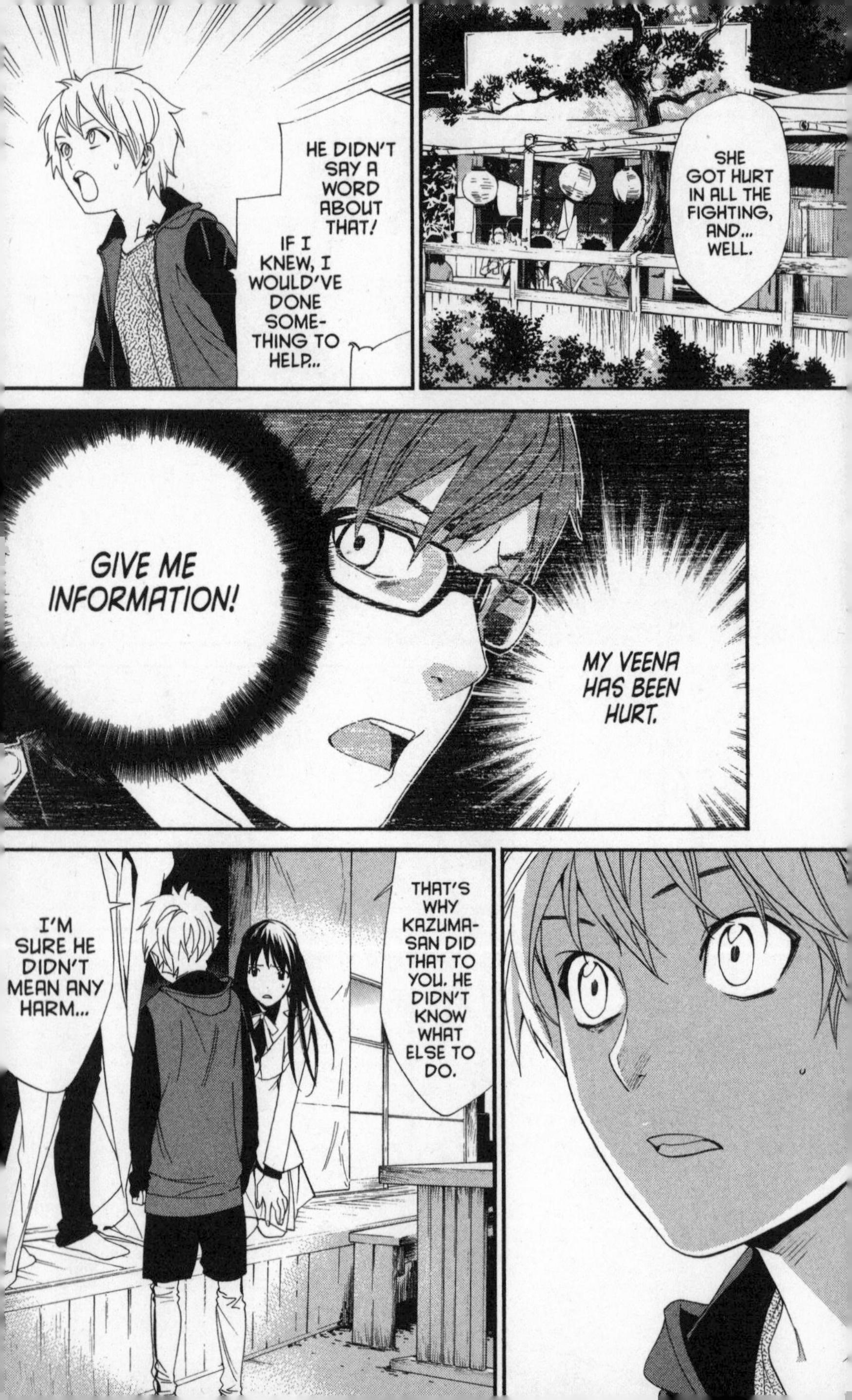
SHE GOT HURT IN ALL THE FIGHTING, AND... WELL.
HE DIDN'T SAY A WORD ABOUT THAT!
IF I KNEW, I WOULD'VE DONE SOMETHING TO HELP...
MY VEENA HAS BEEN HURT.
GIVE ME INFORMATION!
THAT'S WHY KAZUMA-SAN DID THAT TO YOU. HE DIDN'T KNOW WHAT ELSE TO DO.
I'M SURE HE DIDN'T MEAN ANY HARM...

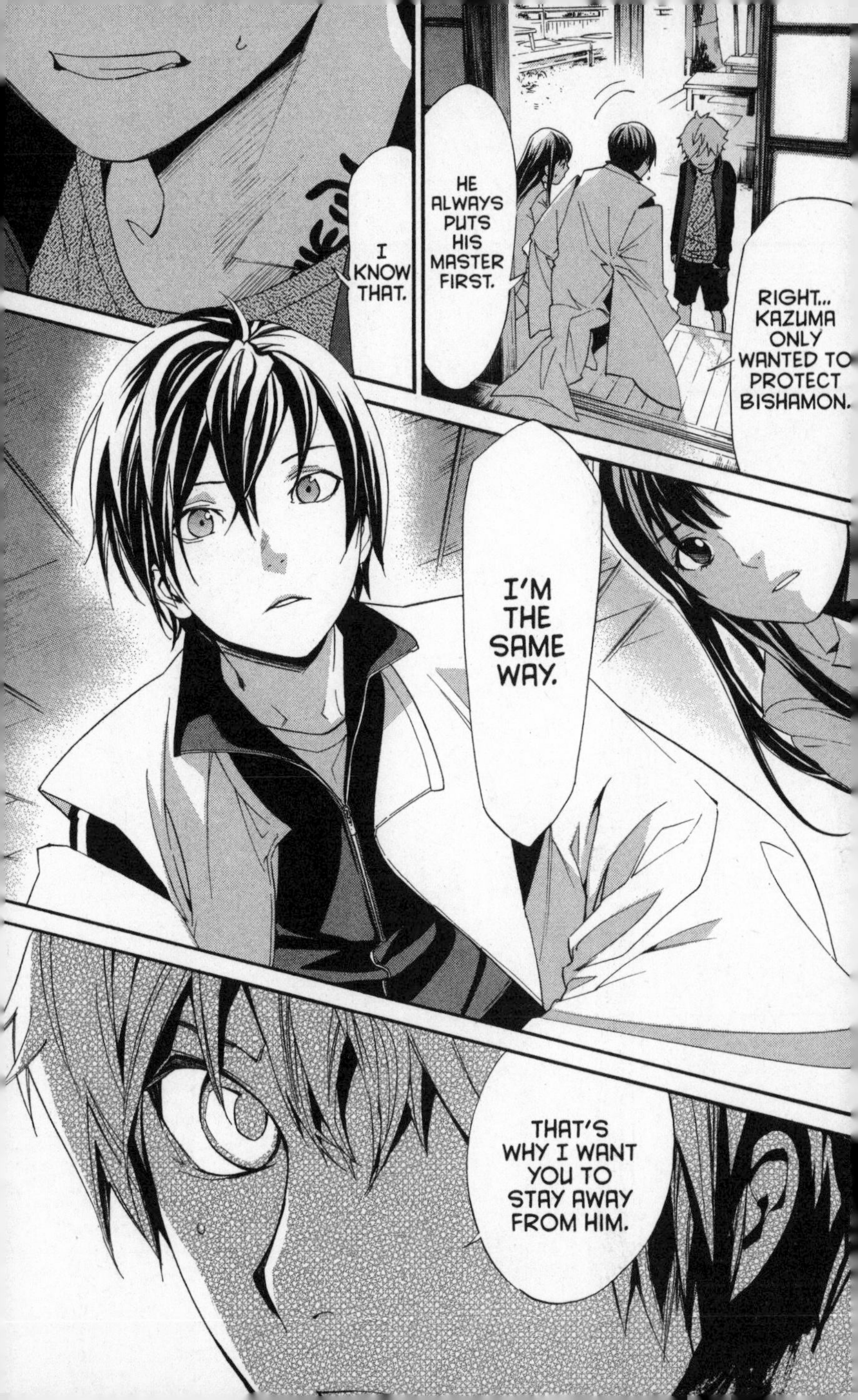
RIGHT... KAZUMA ONLY WANTED TO PROTECT BISHAMON.
HE ALWAYS PUTS HIS MASTER FIRST.
I KNOW THAT.
I'M THE SAME WAY.
THAT'S WHY I WANT YOU TO STAY AWAY FROM HIM.

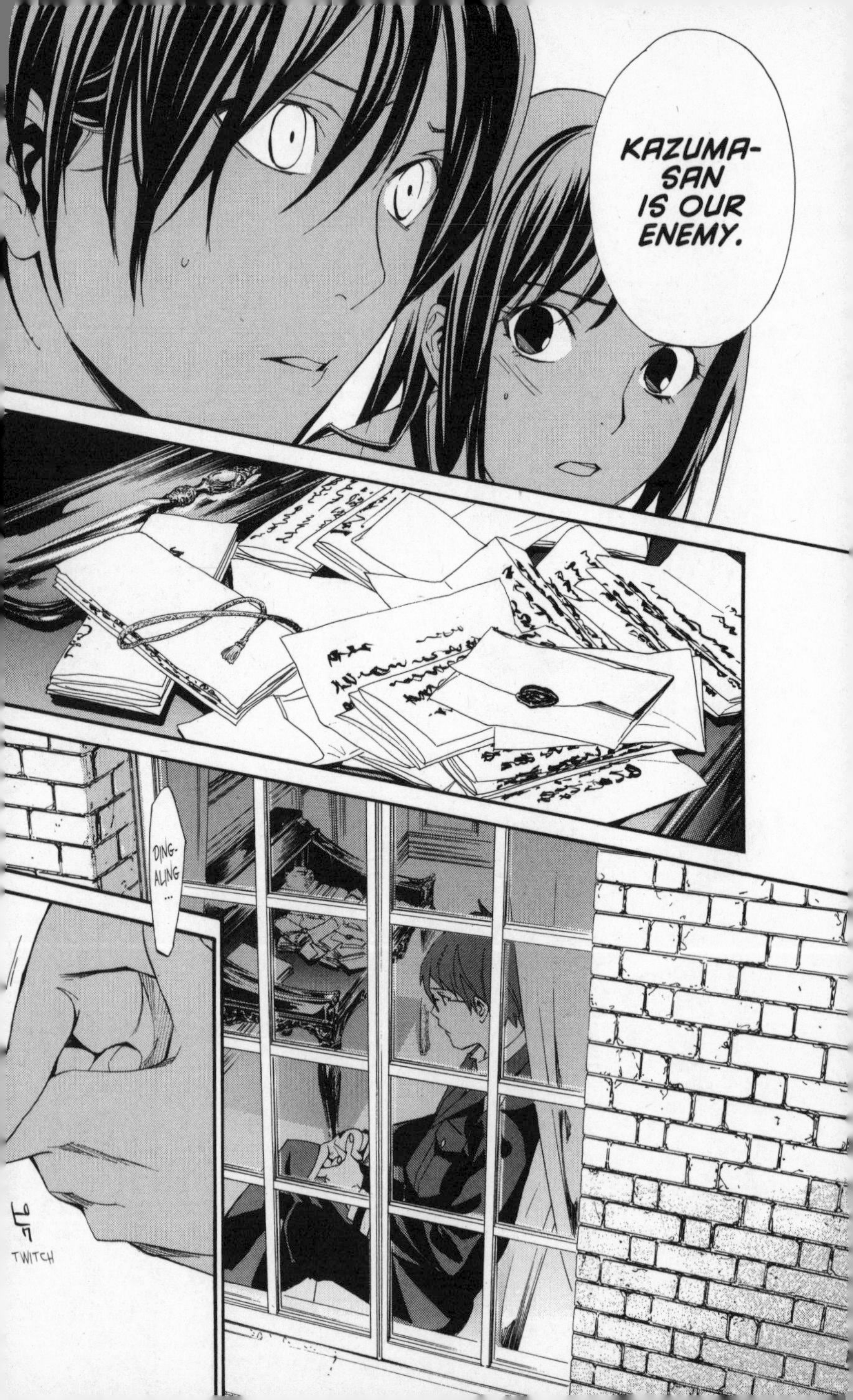
KAZUMA-SAN IS OUR ENEMY.
DING-ALING...
TWITCH

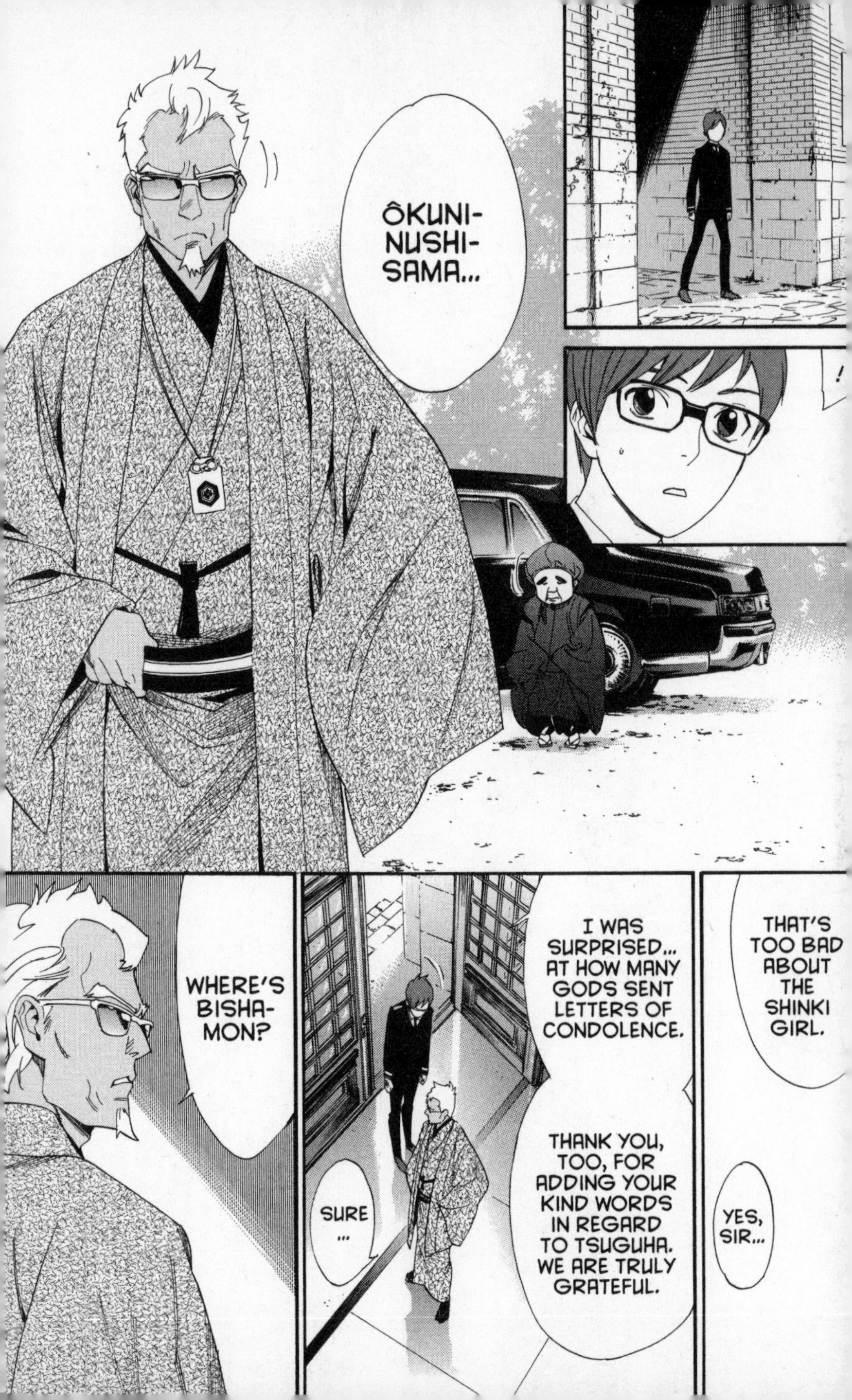
!
ÔKUNI-NUSHI-SAMA...
THAT'S TOO BAD ABOUT THE SHINKI GIRL.
YES, SIR...
I WAS SURPRISED... AT HOW MANY GODS SENT LETTERS OF CONDOLENCE.
THANK YOU, TOO, FOR ADDING YOUR KIND WORDS IN REGARD TO TSUGUHA. WE ARE TRULY GRATEFUL.
SURE ...
WHERE'S BISHA-MON?

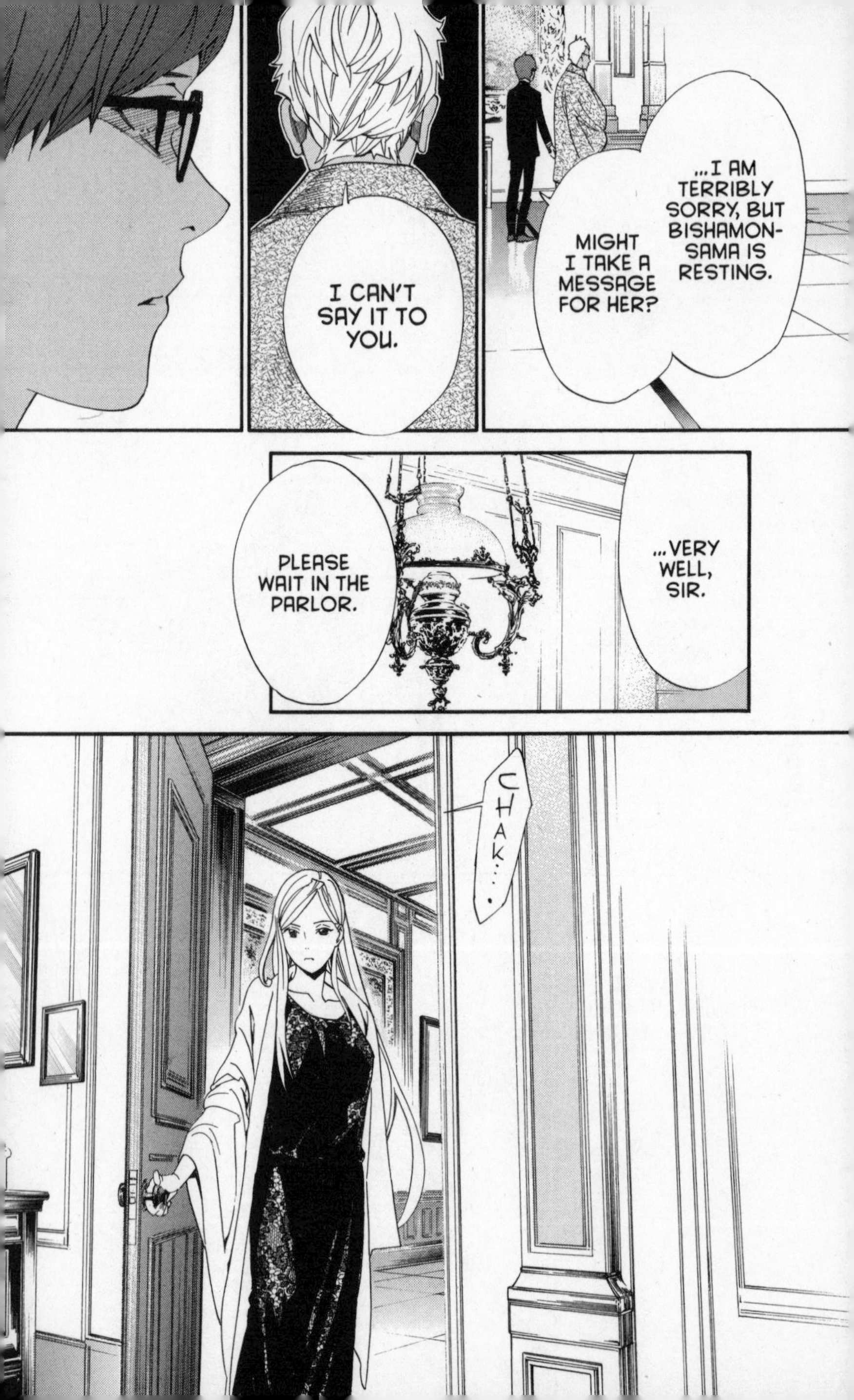
...I AM TERRIBLY SORRY, BUT BISHAMON-SAMA IS RESTING.
MIGHT I TAKE A MESSAGE FOR HER?
I CAN'T SAY IT TO YOU.
...VERY WELL, SIR.
PLEASE WAIT IN THE PARLOR.
CHAK...

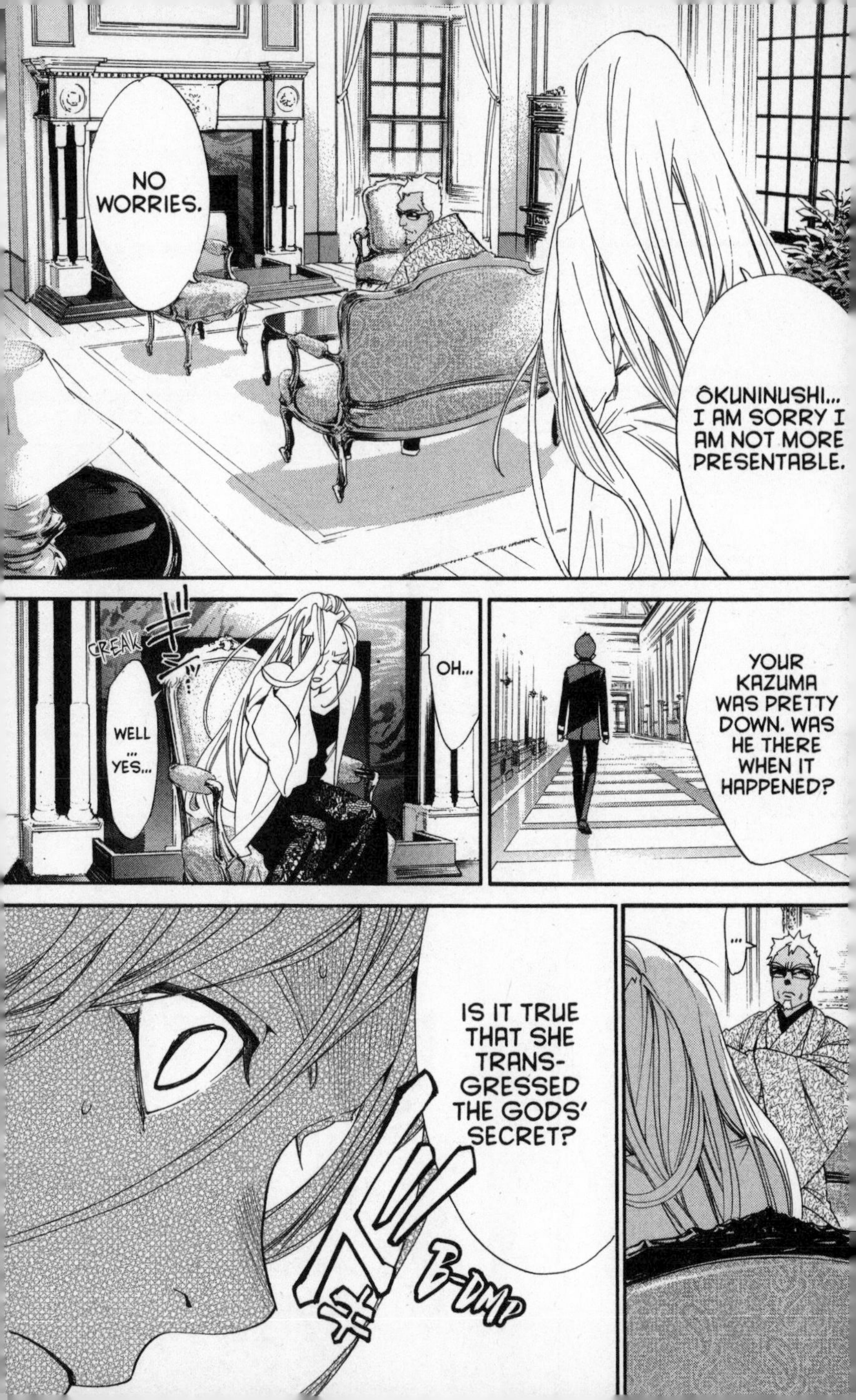
ÔKUNINUSHI... I AM SORRY I AM NOT MORE PRESENTABLE.
NO WORRIES.
YOUR KAZUMA WAS PRETTY DOWN. WAS HE THERE WHEN IT HAPPENED?
OH...
CREAK
WELL ... YES...
...
IS IT TRUE THAT SHE TRANS-GRESSED THE GODS' SECRET?
B-DMP

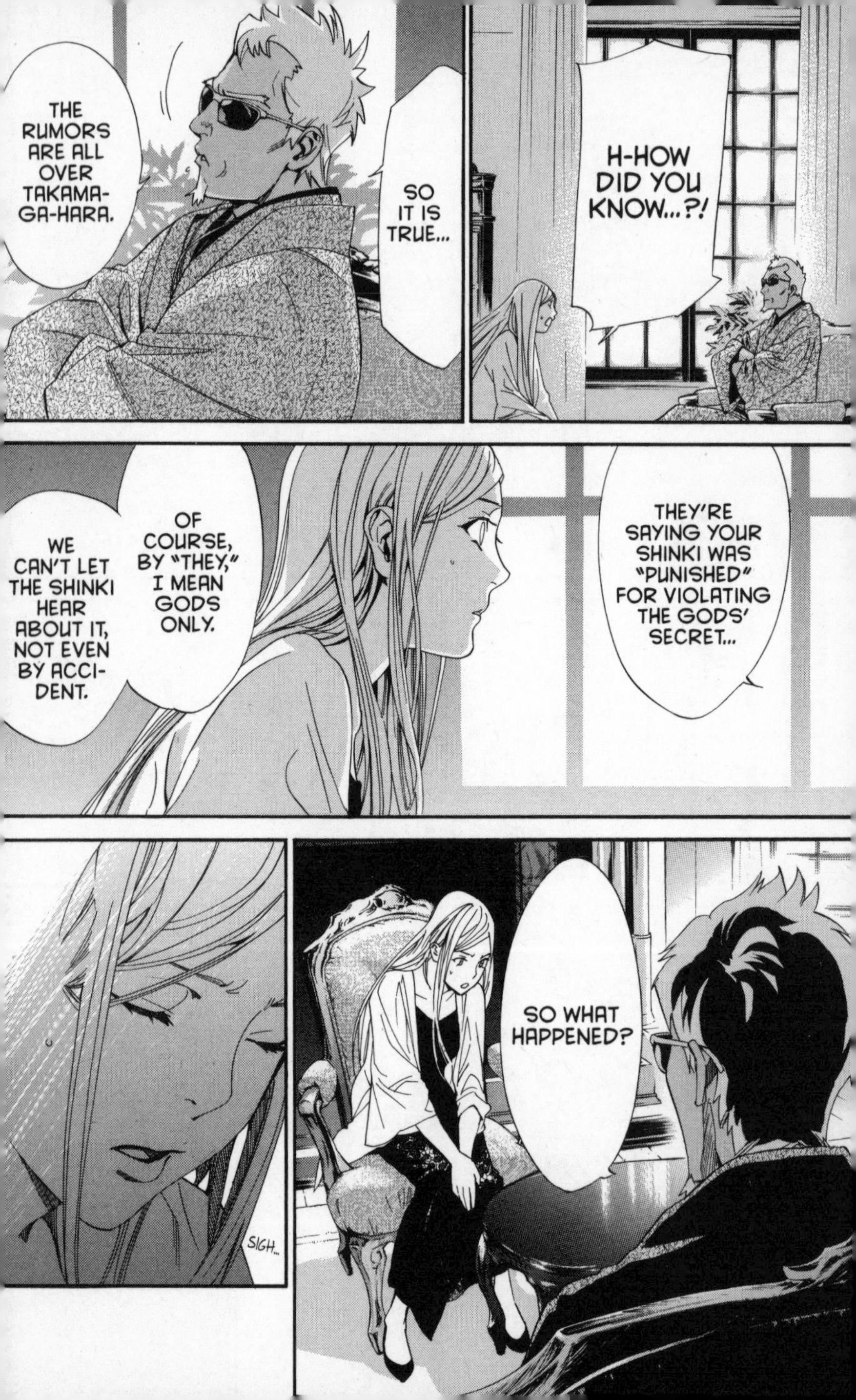
H-HOW DID YOU KNOW...?!
SO IT IS TRUE...
THE RUMORS ARE ALL OVER TAKAMA-GA-HARA.
THEY'RE SAYING YOUR SHINKI WAS "PUNISHED" FOR VIOLATING THE GODS' SECRET...
OF COURSE, BY "THEY," I MEAN GODS ONLY.
WE CAN'T LET THE SHINKI HEAR ABOUT IT, NOT EVEN BY ACCI-DENT.
SO WHAT HAPPENED?
SIGH...

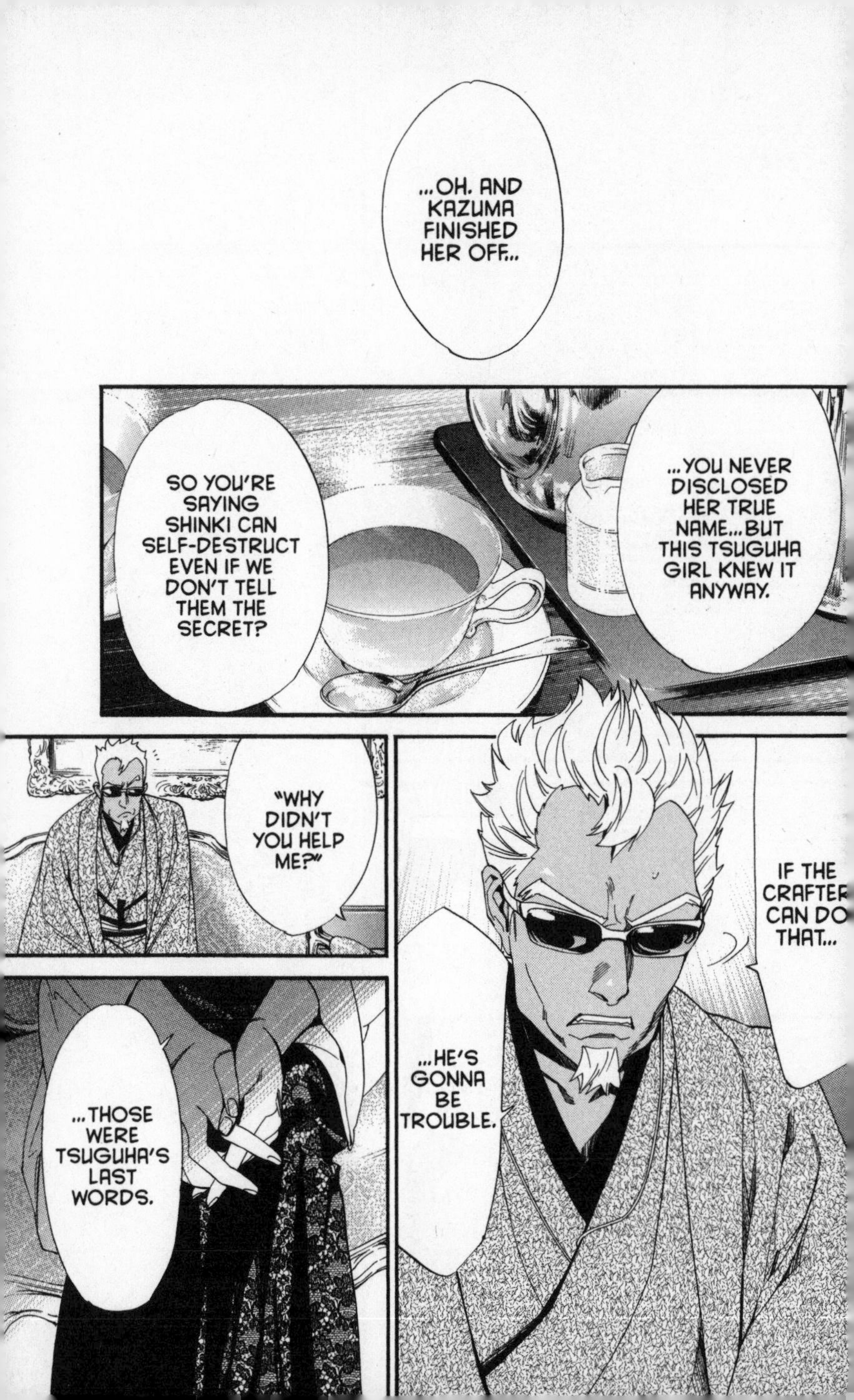
...OH. AND KAZUMA FINISHED HER OFF...
...YOU NEVER DISCLOSED HER TRUE NAME...BUT THIS TSUGUHA GIRL KNEW IT ANYWAY.
SO YOU'RE SAYING SHINKI CAN SELF-DESTRUCT EVEN IF WE DON'T TELL THEM THE SECRET?
IF THE CRAFTER CAN DO THAT...
...HE'S GONNA BE TROUBLE.
"WHY DIDN'T YOU HELP ME?"
...THOSE WERE TSUGUHA'S LAST WORDS.

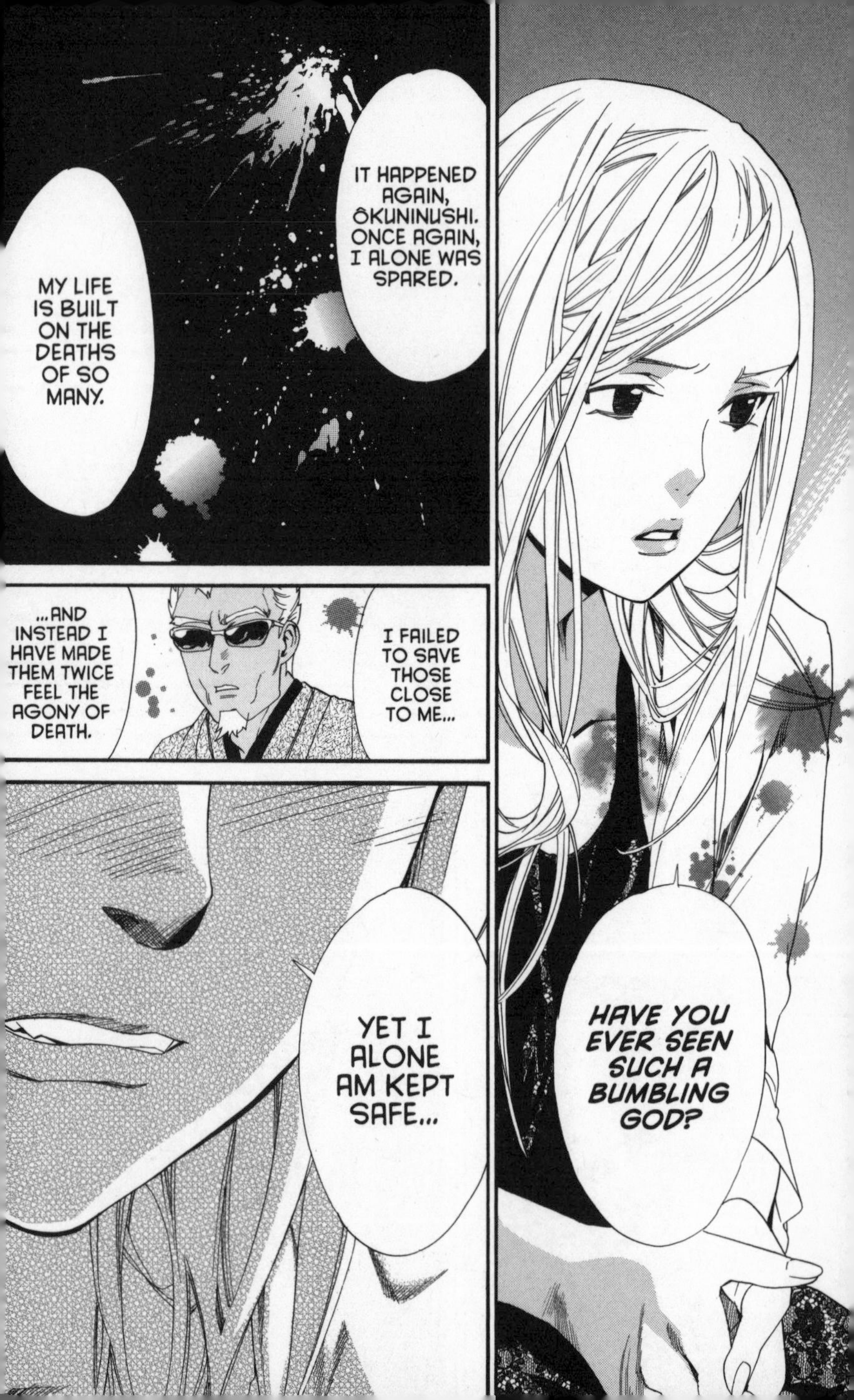
HAVE YOU EVER SEEN SUCH A BUMBLING GOD?
IT HAPPENED AGAIN, ÔKUNINUSHI. ONCE AGAIN, I ALONE WAS SPARED.
MY LIFE IS BUILT ON THE DEATHS OF SO MANY.
I FAILED TO SAVE THOSE CLOSE TO ME...
...AND INSTEAD I HAVE MADE THEM TWICE FEEL THE AGONY OF DEATH.
YET I ALONE AM KEPT SAFE...

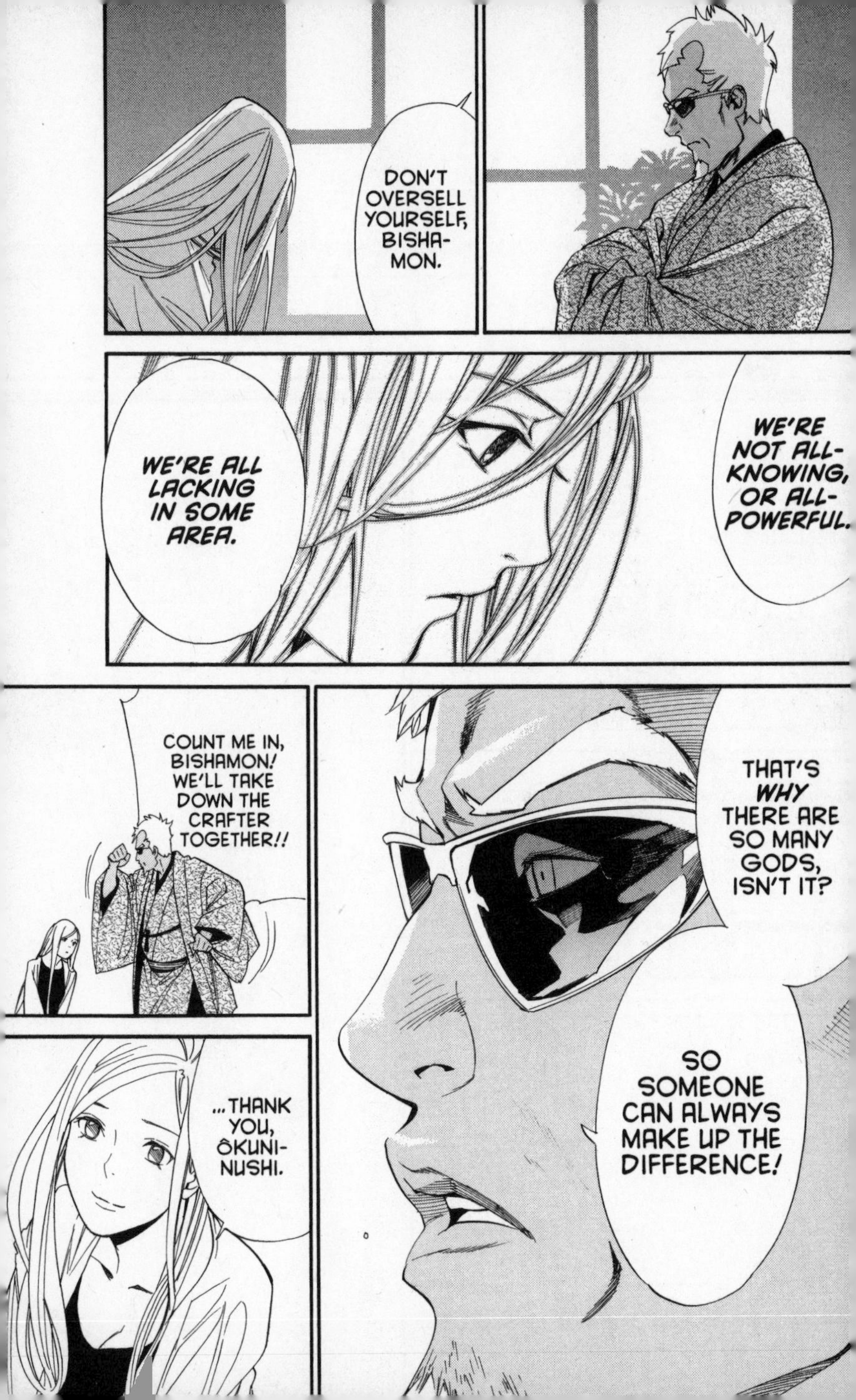
DON'T OVERSELL YOURSELF, BISHAMON.
WE'RE NOT ALL-KNOWING, OR ALL-POWERFUL.
WE'RE ALL LACKING IN SOME AREA.
THAT'S WHY THERE ARE SO MANY GODS, ISN'T IT?
SO SOMEONE CAN ALWAYS MAKE UP THE DIFFERENCE!
COUNT ME IN, BISHAMON! WE'LL TAKE DOWN THE CRAFTER TOGETHER!!
...THANK YOU, ÔKUNINUSHI.

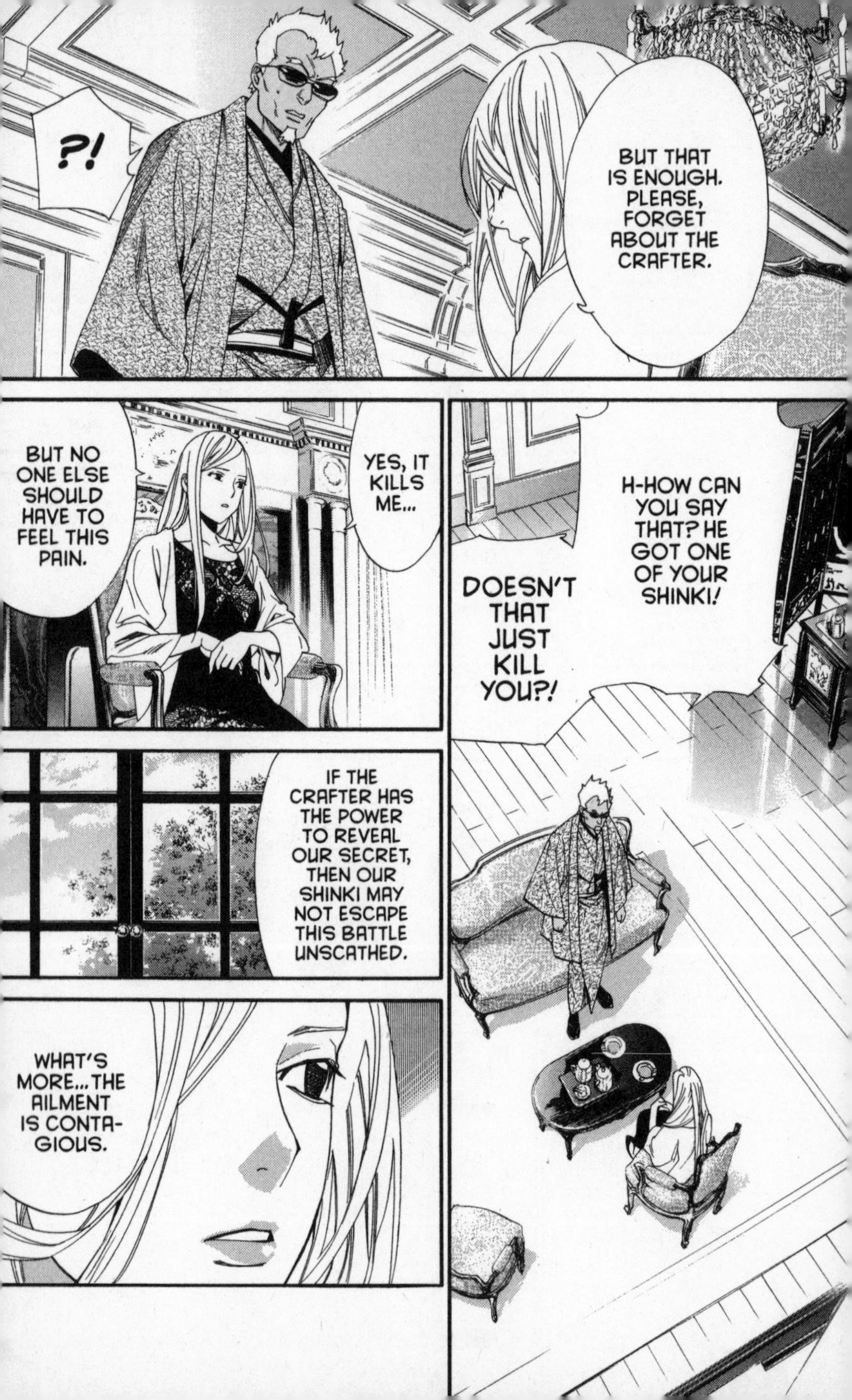
BUT THAT IS ENOUGH. PLEASE, FORGET ABOUT THE CRAFTER.
?!
H-HOW CAN YOU SAY THAT? HE GOT ONE OF YOUR SHINKI!
DOESN'T THAT JUST KILL YOU?!
YES, IT KILLS ME...
BUT NO ONE ELSE SHOULD HAVE TO FEEL THIS PAIN.
IF THE CRAFTER HAS THE POWER TO REVEAL OUR SECRET, THEN OUR SHINKI MAY NOT ESCAPE THIS BATTLE UNSCATHED.
WHAT'S MORE... THE AILMENT IS CONTA-GIOUS.

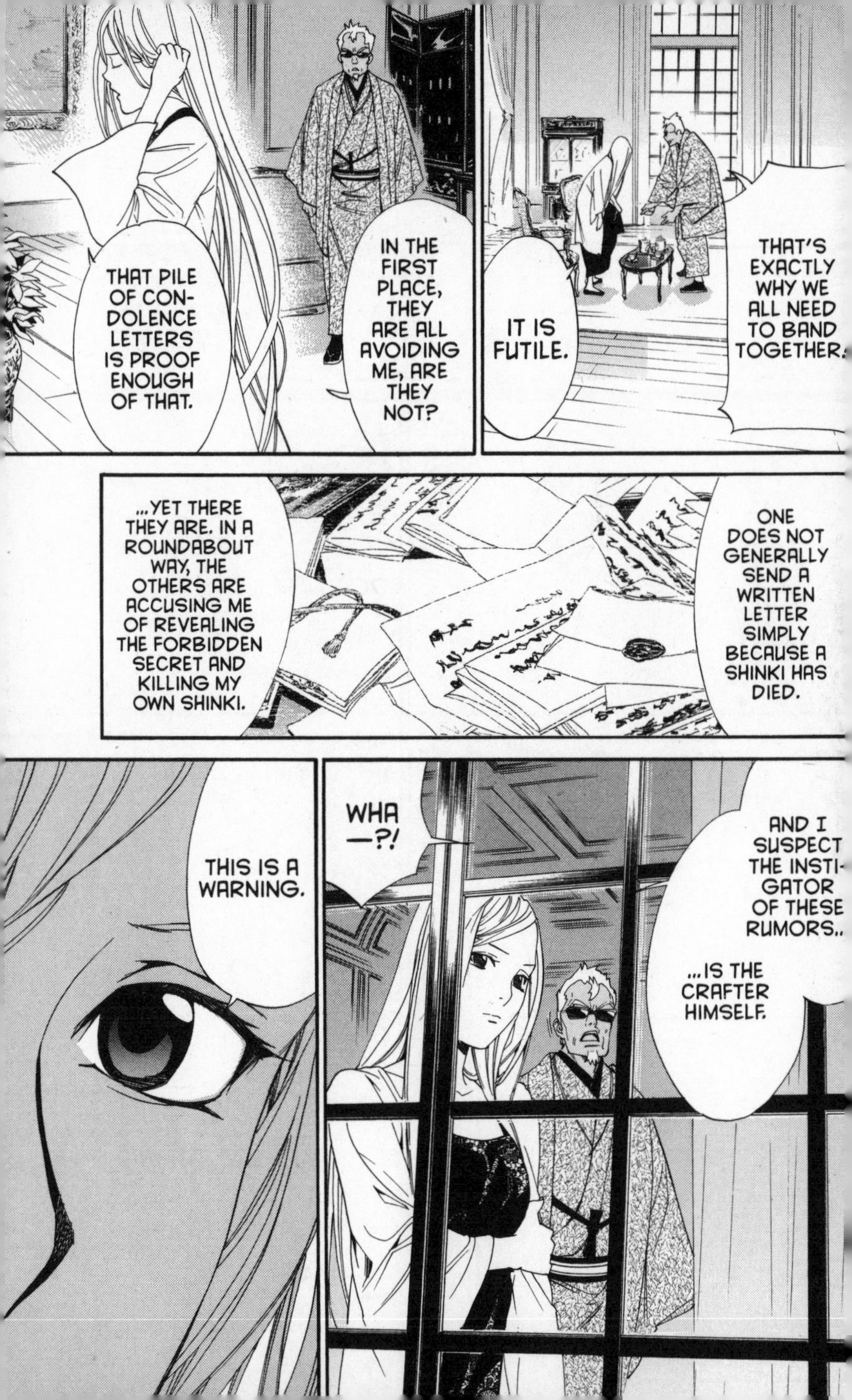
THAT'S EXACTLY WHY WE ALL NEED TO BAND TOGETHER.
IT IS FUTILE.
IN THE FIRST PLACE, THEY ARE ALL AVOIDING ME, ARE THEY NOT?
THAT PILE OF CON-DOLENCE LETTERS IS PROOF ENOUGH OF THAT.
ONE DOES NOT GENERALLY SEND A WRITTEN LETTER SIMPLY BECAUSE A SHINKI HAS DIED.
...YET THERE THEY ARE. IN A ROUNDABOUT WAY, THE OTHERS ARE ACCUSING ME OF REVEALING THE FORBIDDEN SECRET AND KILLING MY OWN SHINKI.
AND I SUSPECT THE INSTI-GATOR OF THESE RUMORS..
...IS THE CRAFTER HIMSELF.
WHA—?!
THIS IS A WARNING.

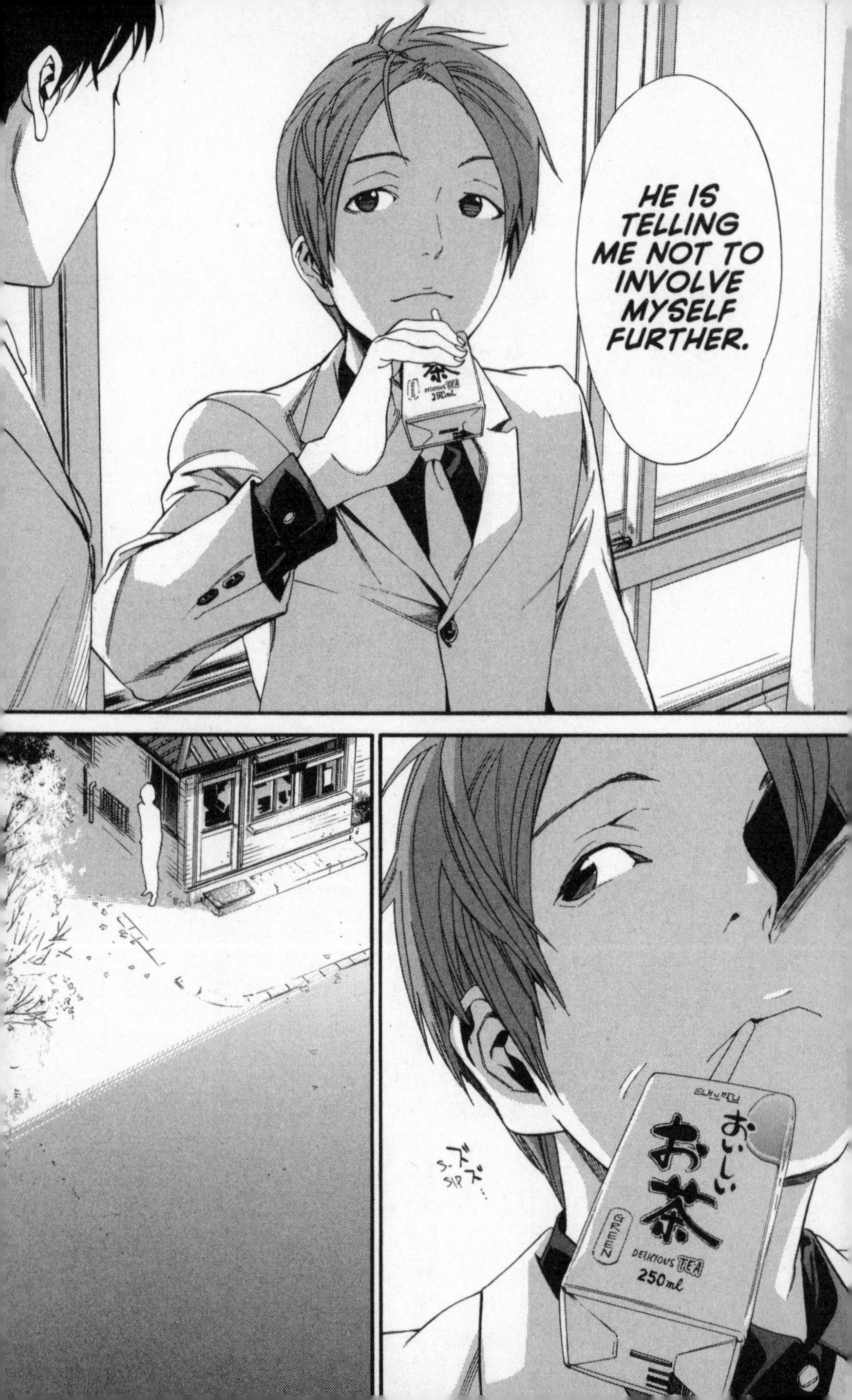
HE IS TELLING ME NOT TO INVOLVE MYSELF FURTHER.
ズズ…
S- SIP…
おいしいお茶
GREEN
DELICIOUS TEA
250ml

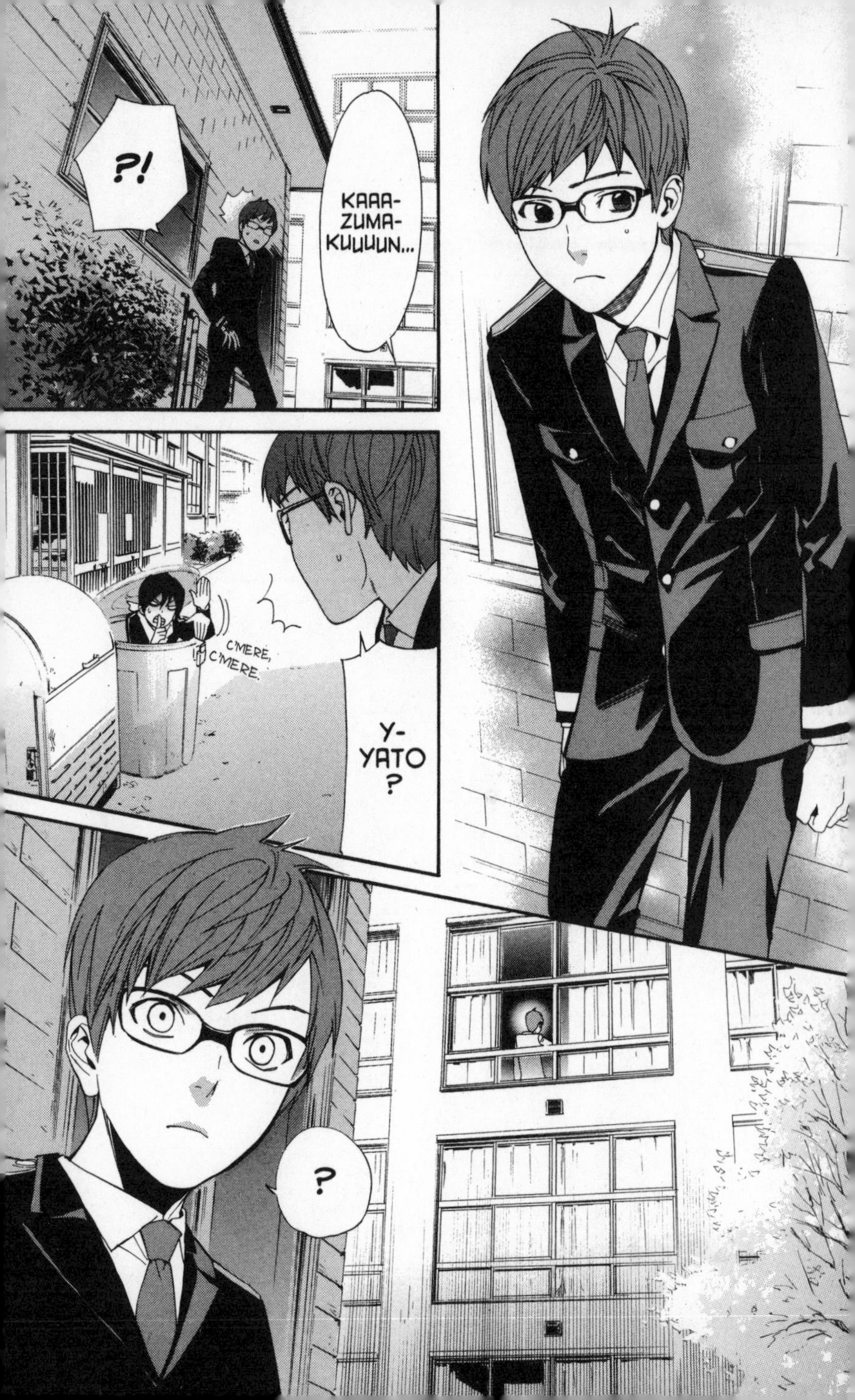
KAAA-ZUMA-KUUUUN...
?!
Y-YATO?
C'MERE, C'MERE.
?

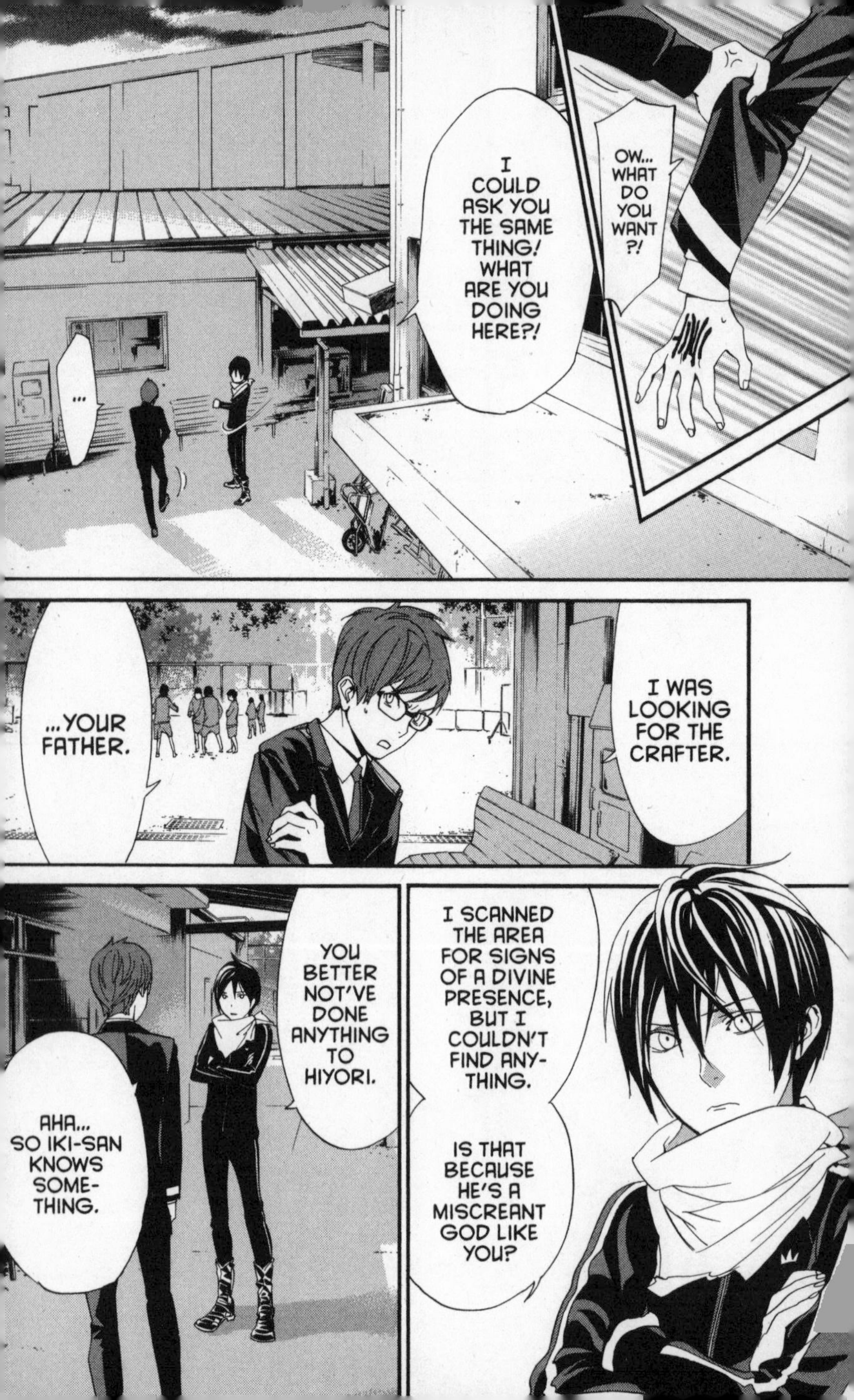
OW... WHAT DO YOU WANT?!
I COULD ASK YOU THE SAME THING! WHAT ARE YOU DOING HERE?!
...
I WAS LOOKING FOR THE CRAFTER.
...YOUR FATHER.
I SCANNED THE AREA FOR SIGNS OF A DIVINE PRESENCE, BUT I COULDN'T FIND ANY-THING.
IS THAT BECAUSE HE'S A MISCREANT GOD LIKE YOU?
YOU BETTER NOT'VE DONE ANYTHING TO HIYORI.
AHA... SO IKI-SAN KNOWS SOME-THING.

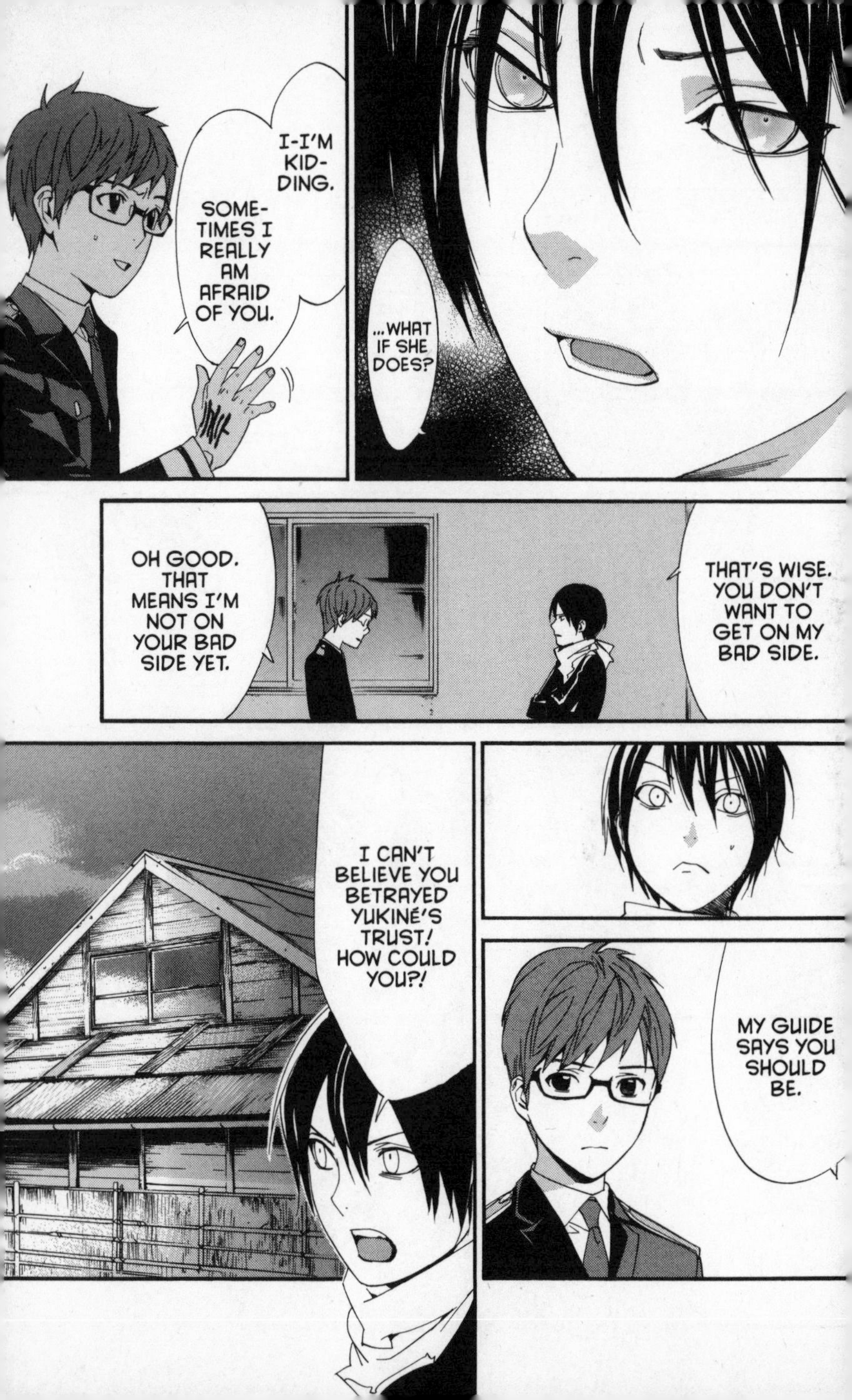
...WHAT IF SHE DOES?
I-I'M KID-DING.
SOME-TIMES I REALLY AM AFRAID OF YOU.
THAT'S WISE. YOU DON'T WANT TO GET ON MY BAD SIDE.
OH GOOD. THAT MEANS I'M NOT ON YOUR BAD SIDE YET.
MY GUIDE SAYS YOU SHOULD BE.
I CAN'T BELIEVE YOU BETRAYED YUKINÉ'S TRUST! HOW COULD YOU?!

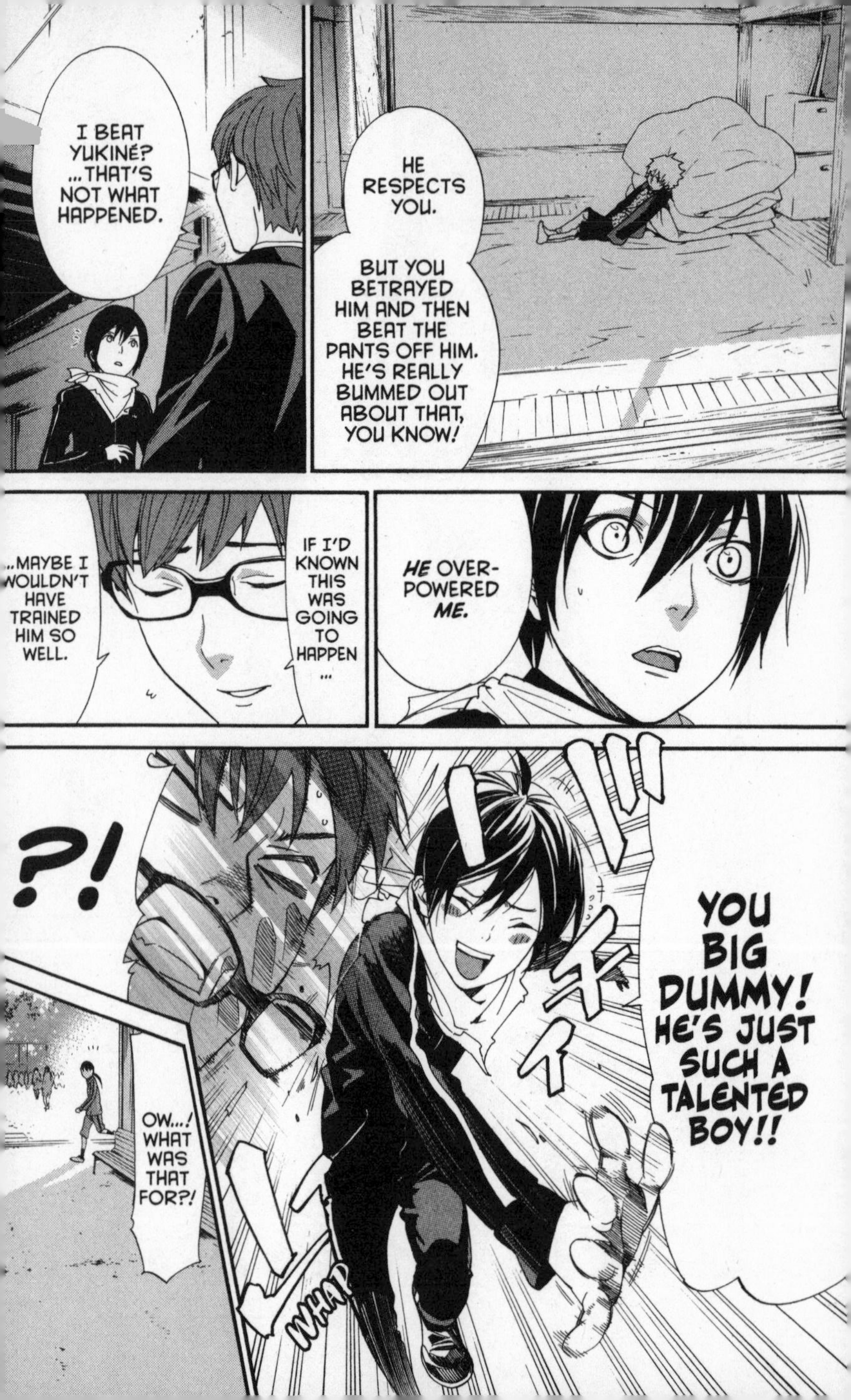
HE RESPECTS YOU.
BUT YOU BETRAYED HIM AND THEN BEAT THE PANTS OFF HIM. HE'S REALLY BUMMED OUT ABOUT THAT, YOU KNOW!
I BEAT YUKINÉ? ...THAT'S NOT WHAT HAPPENED.
HE OVER-POWERED *ME.*
IF I'D KNOWN THIS WAS GOING TO HAPPEN...
...MAYBE I WOULDN'T HAVE TRAINED HIM SO WELL.
YOU BIG DUMMY! HE'S JUST SUCH A TALENTED BOY!!
?!
WHAP
OW...! WHAT WAS THAT FOR?!

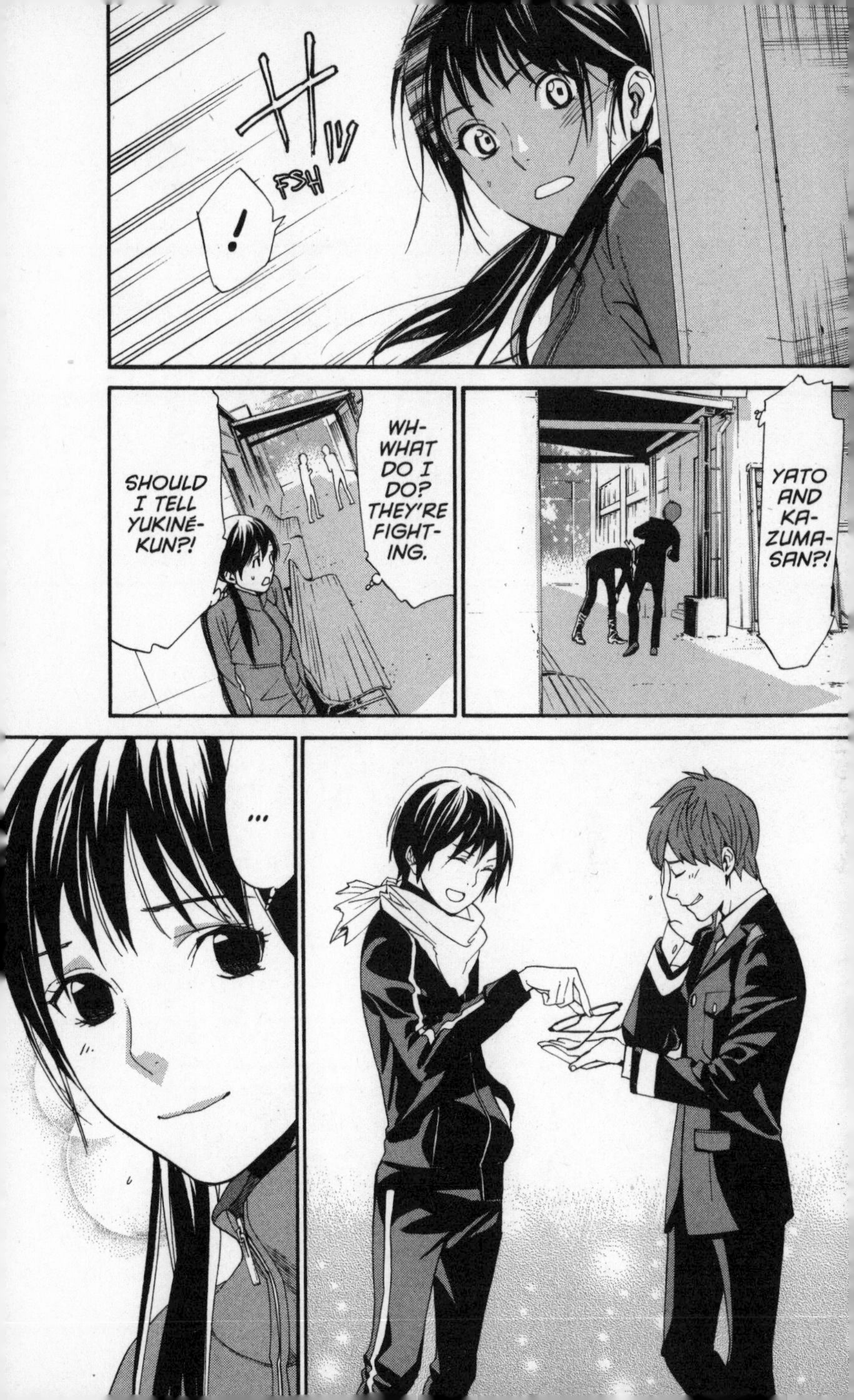
FSH
!
YATO AND KA-ZUMA-SAN?!
WH-WHAT DO I DO? THEY'RE FIGHT-ING.
SHOULD I TELL YUKINÉ-KUN?!
...

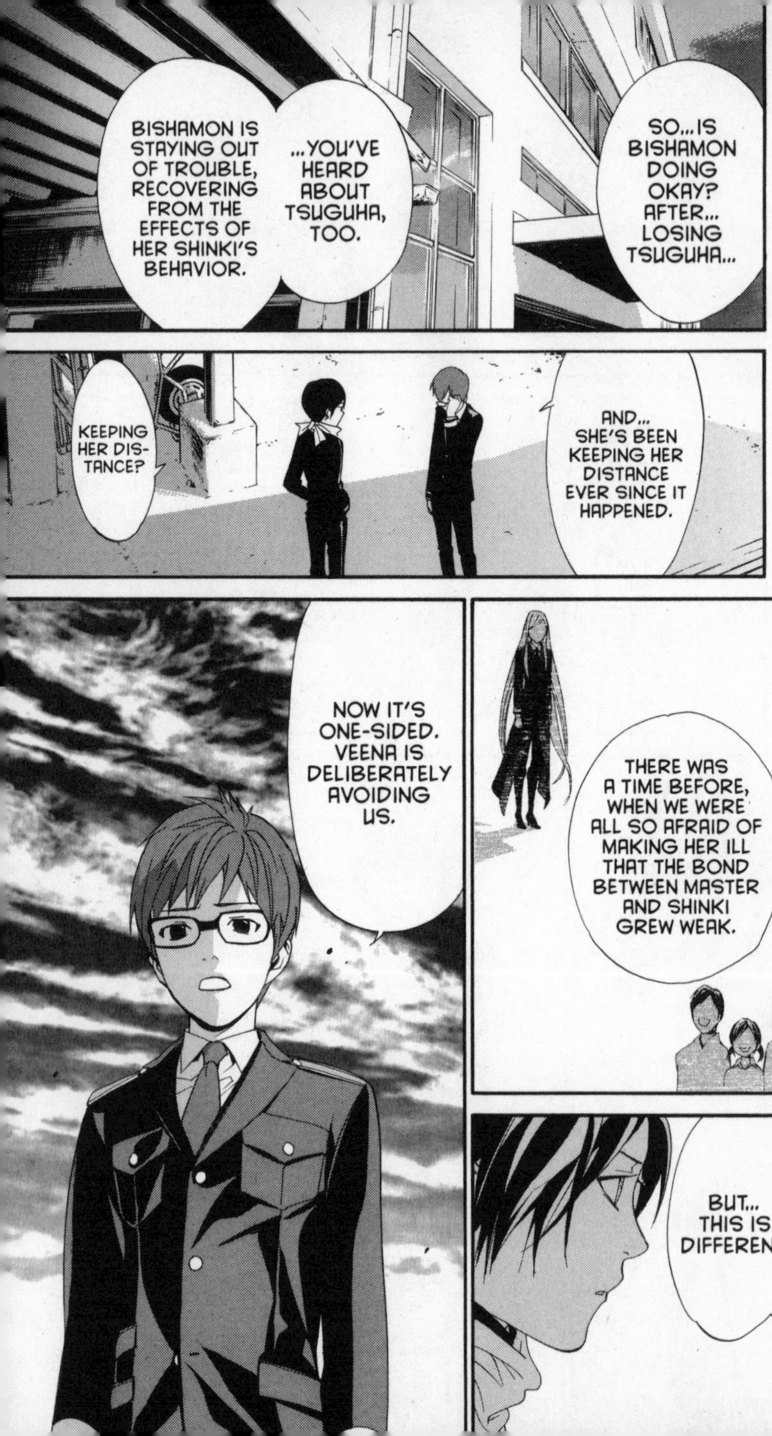
SO...IS BISHAMON DOING OKAY? AFTER... LOSING TSUGUHA...
...YOU'VE HEARD ABOUT TSUGUHA, TOO.
BISHAMON IS STAYING OUT OF TROUBLE, RECOVERING FROM THE EFFECTS OF HER SHINKI'S BEHAVIOR.
AND... SHE'S BEEN KEEPING HER DISTANCE EVER SINCE IT HAPPENED.
KEEPING HER DIS-TANCE?
THERE WAS A TIME BEFORE, WHEN WE WERE ALL SO AFRAID OF MAKING HER ILL THAT THE BOND BETWEEN MASTER AND SHINKI GREW WEAK.
BUT... THIS IS DIFFERENT.
NOW IT'S ONE-SIDED. VEENA IS DELIBERATELY AVOIDING US.

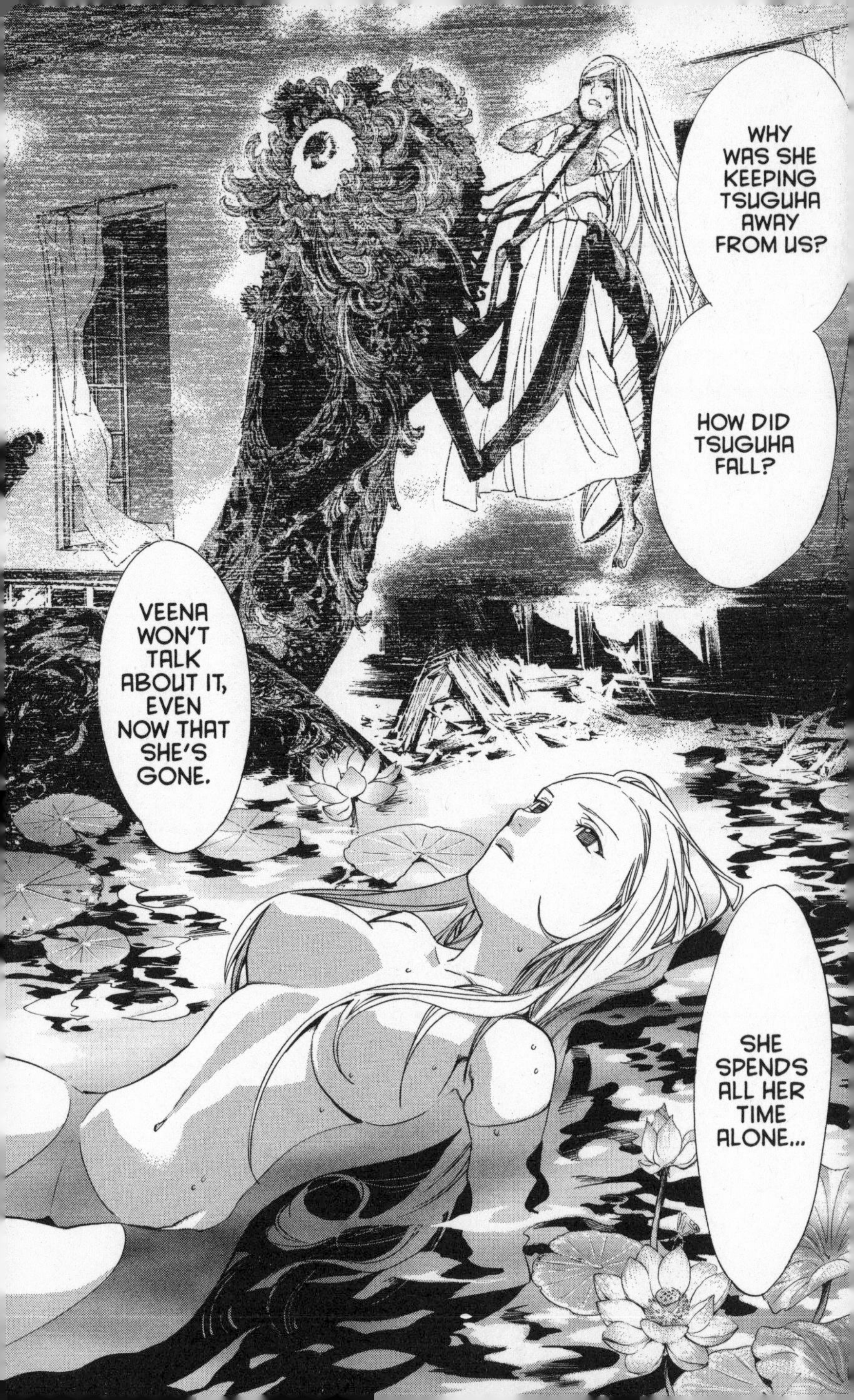
WHY WAS SHE KEEPING TSUGUHA AWAY FROM US?
HOW DID TSUGUHA FALL?
VEENA WON'T TALK ABOUT IT, EVEN NOW THAT SHE'S GONE.
SHE SPENDS ALL HER TIME ALONE...

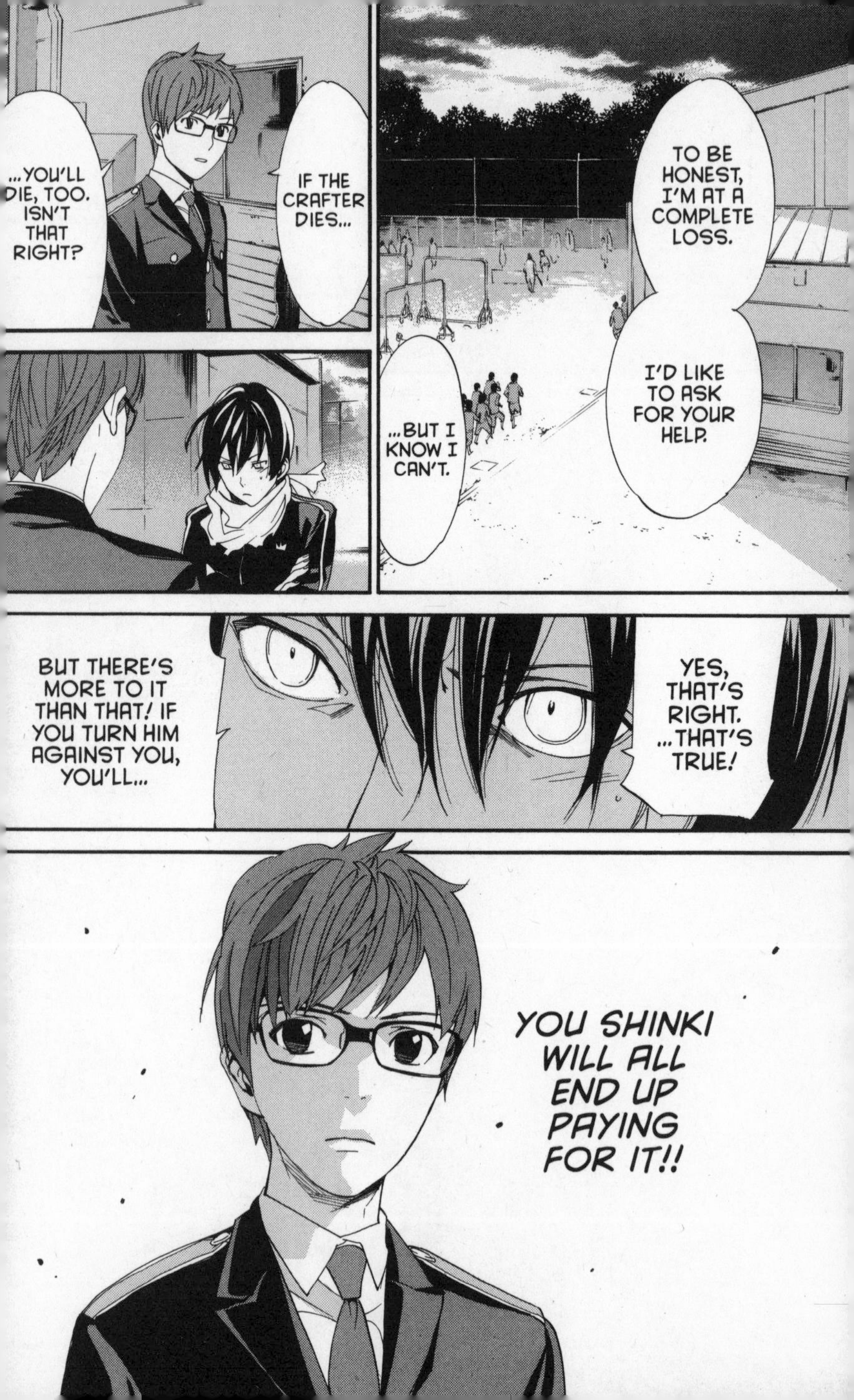
TO BE HONEST, I'M AT A COMPLETE LOSS.
I'D LIKE TO ASK FOR YOUR HELP.
...BUT I KNOW I CAN'T.
IF THE CRAFTER DIES...
...YOU'LL DIE, TOO. ISN'T THAT RIGHT?
YES, THAT'S RIGHT. ...THAT'S TRUE!
BUT THERE'S MORE TO IT THAN THAT! IF YOU TURN HIM AGAINST YOU, YOU'LL...
YOU SHINKI WILL ALL END UP PAYING FOR IT!!

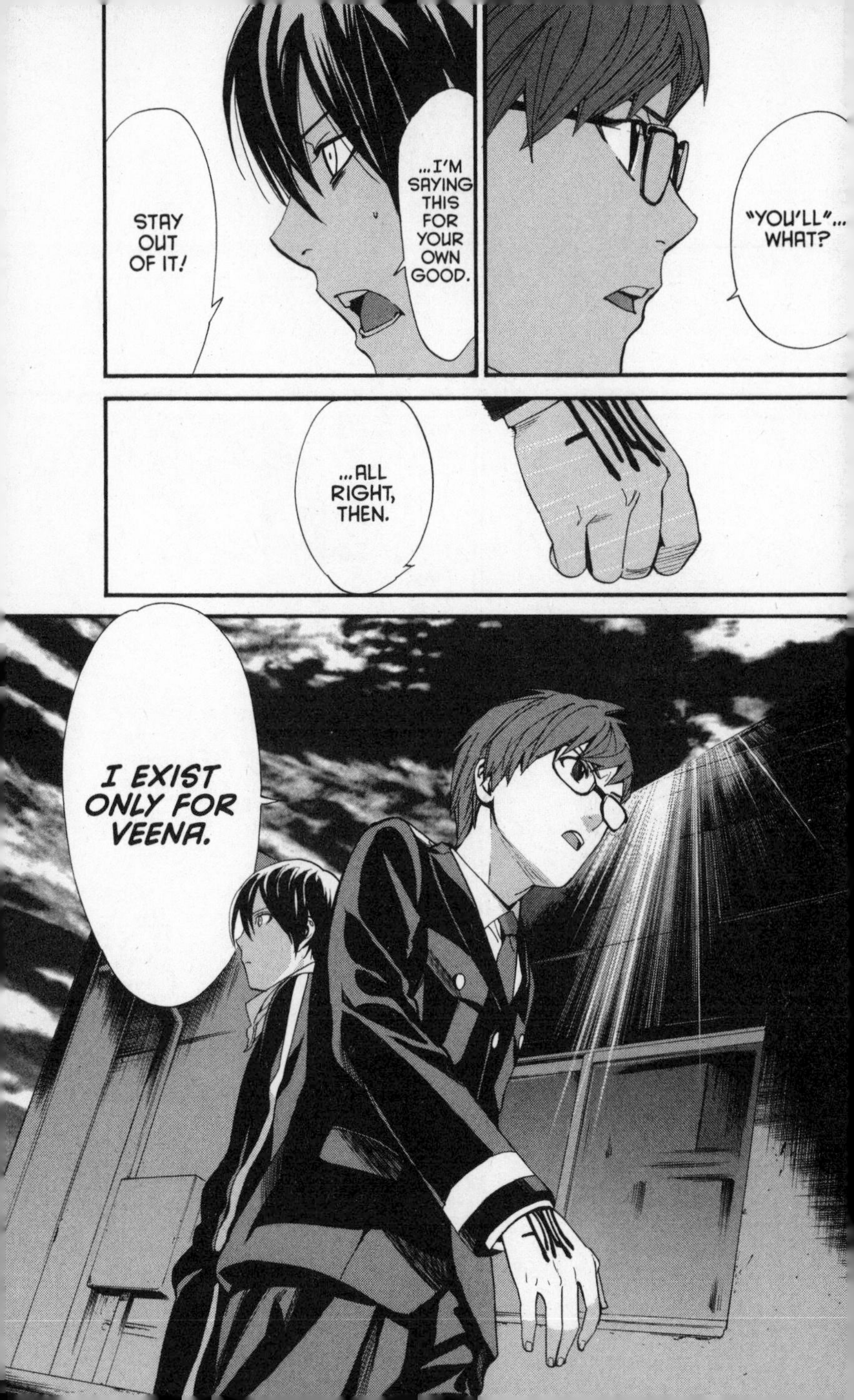
"YOU'LL"... WHAT?
...I'M SAYING THIS FOR YOUR OWN GOOD.
STAY OUT OF IT!
...ALL RIGHT, THEN.
I EXIST ONLY FOR VEENA.

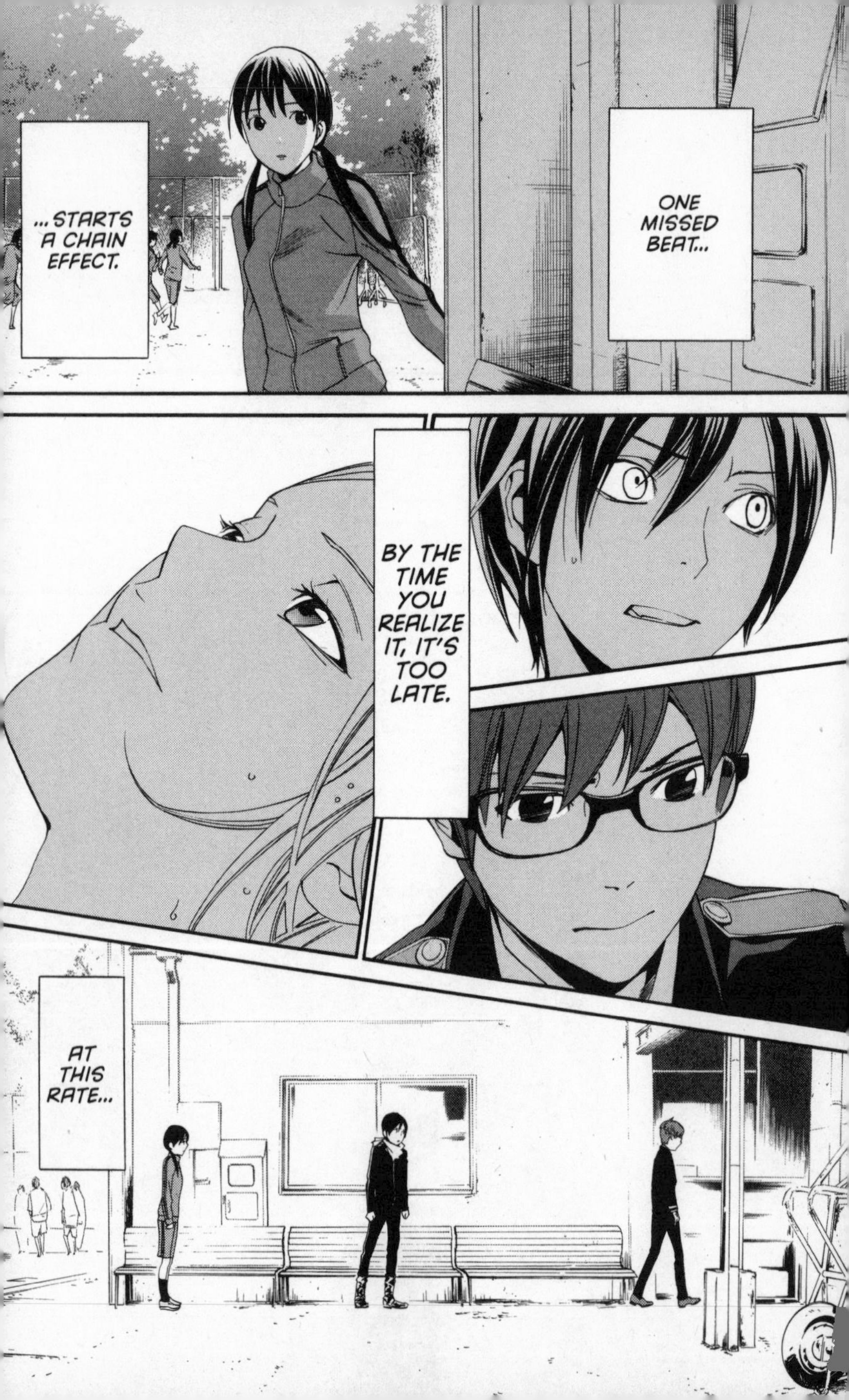
ONE MISSED BEAT...
...STARTS A CHAIN EFFECT.
BY THE TIME YOU REALIZE IT, IT'S TOO LATE.
AT THIS RATE...

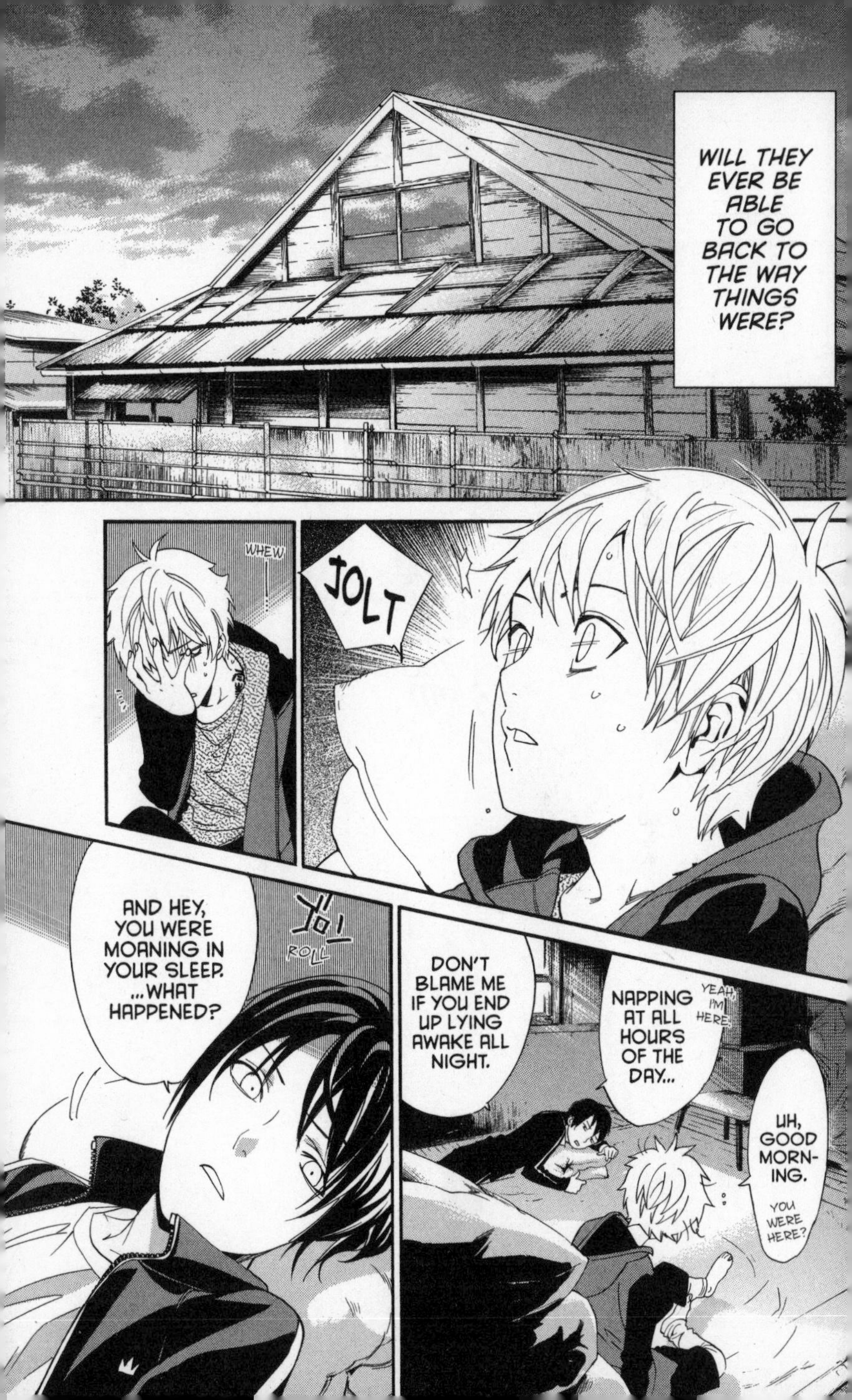
WILL THEY EVER BE ABLE TO GO BACK TO THE WAY THINGS WERE?
JOLT
WHEW
UH, GOOD MORNING.
YOU WERE HERE?
YEAH, I'M HERE.
NAPPING AT ALL HOURS OF THE DAY...
DON'T BLAME ME IF YOU END UP LYING AWAKE ALL NIGHT.
ROLL
AND HEY, YOU WERE MOANING IN YOUR SLEEP. ...WHAT HAPPENED?

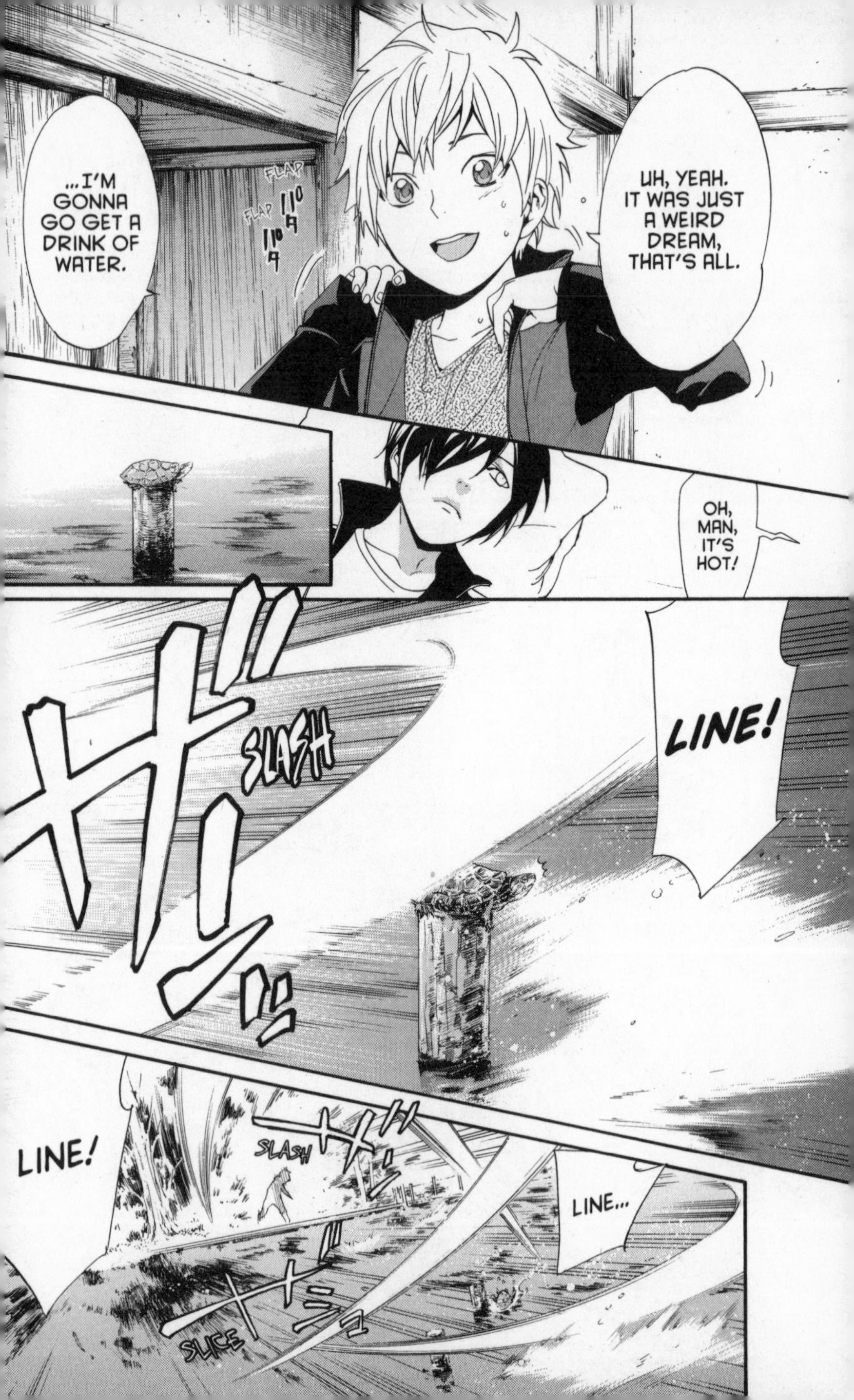
UH, YEAH. IT WAS JUST A WEIRD DREAM, THAT'S ALL.
FLAP FLAP
...I'M GONNA GO GET A DRINK OF WATER.
OH, MAN, IT'S HOT!
LINE!
SLASH
LINE...
SLASH
SLICE
LINE!

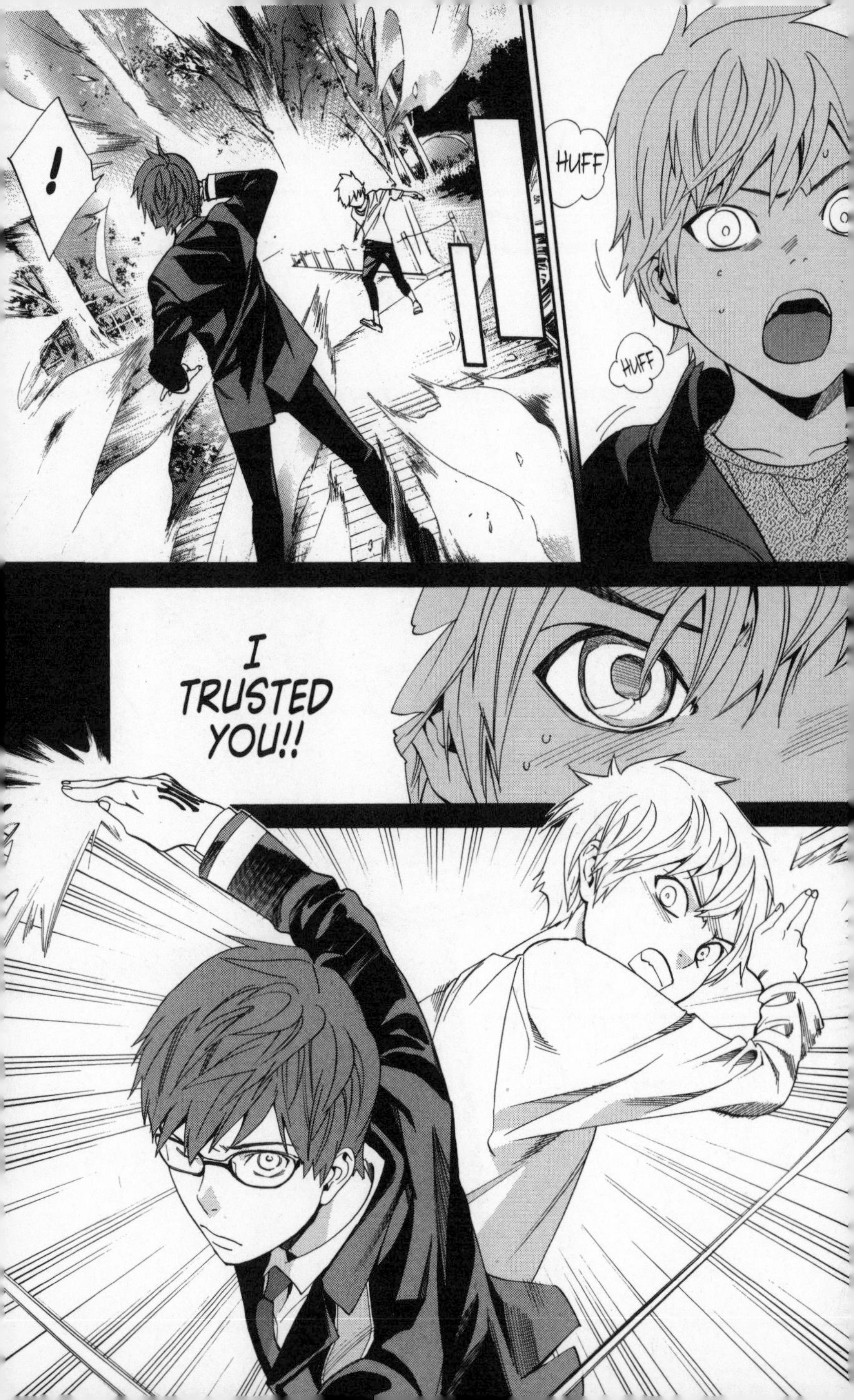
HUFF
HUFF
!
I TRUSTED YOU!!

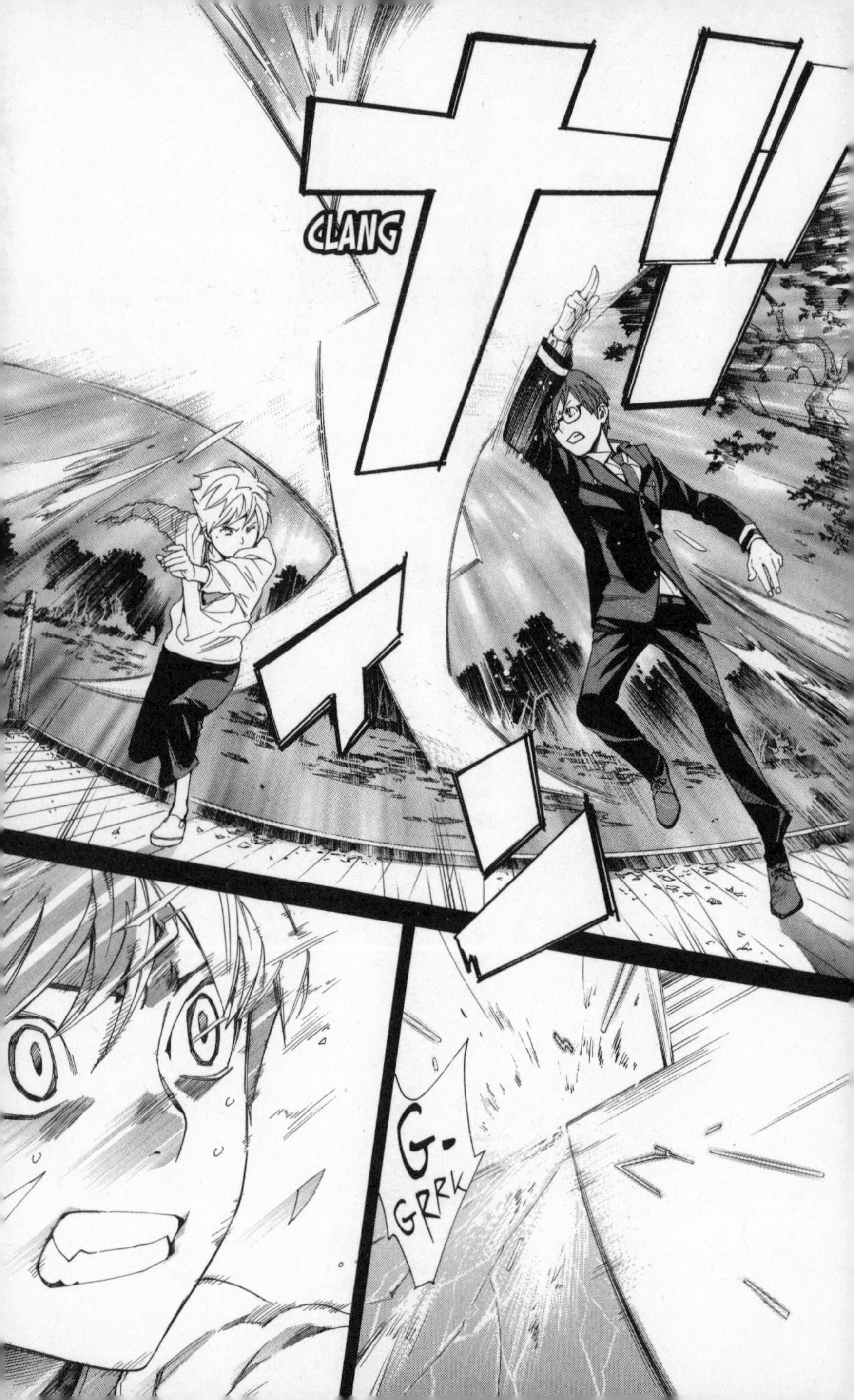
CLANG
G-
GRRK

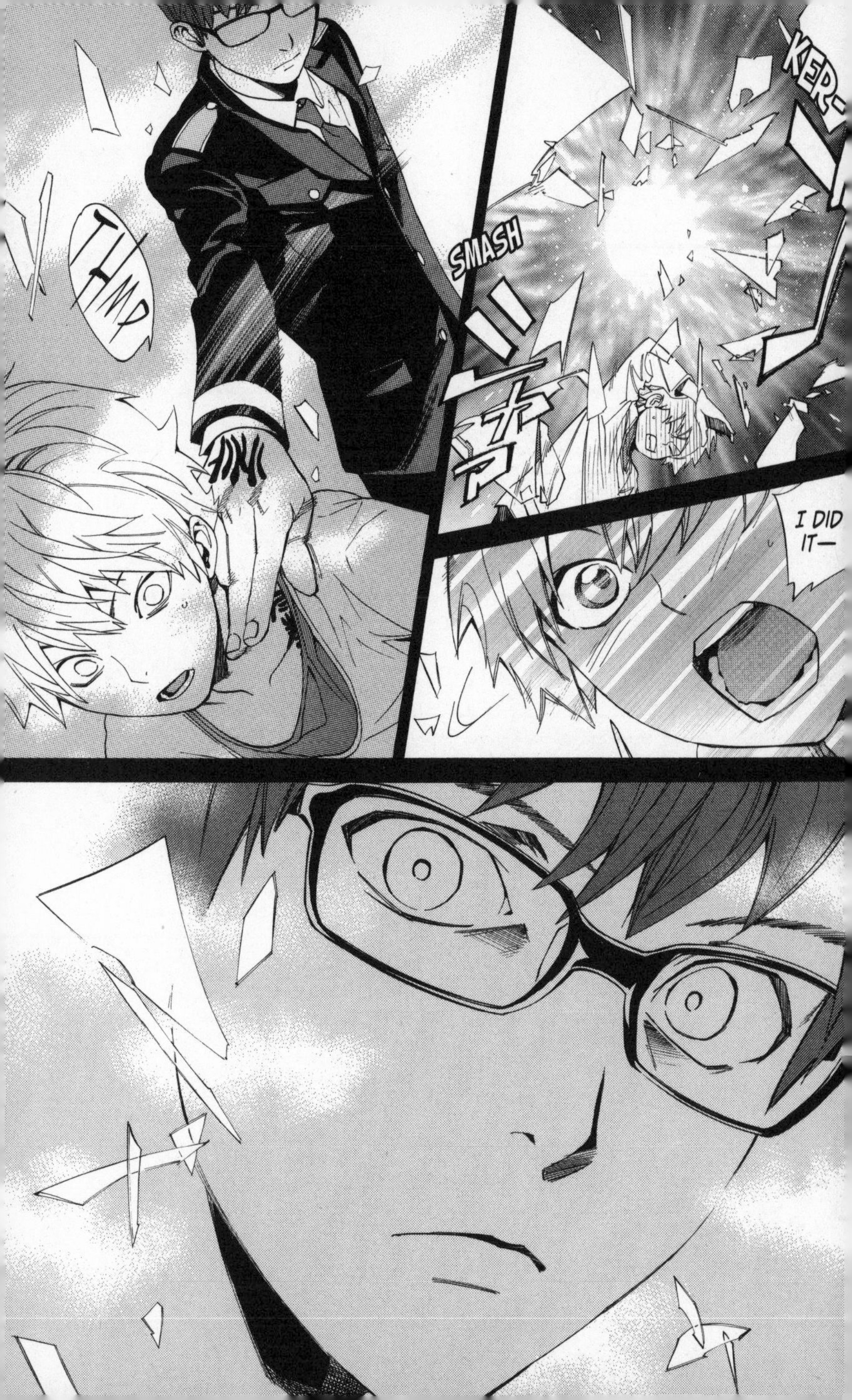
KER-
SMASH
I DID IT—
THMP

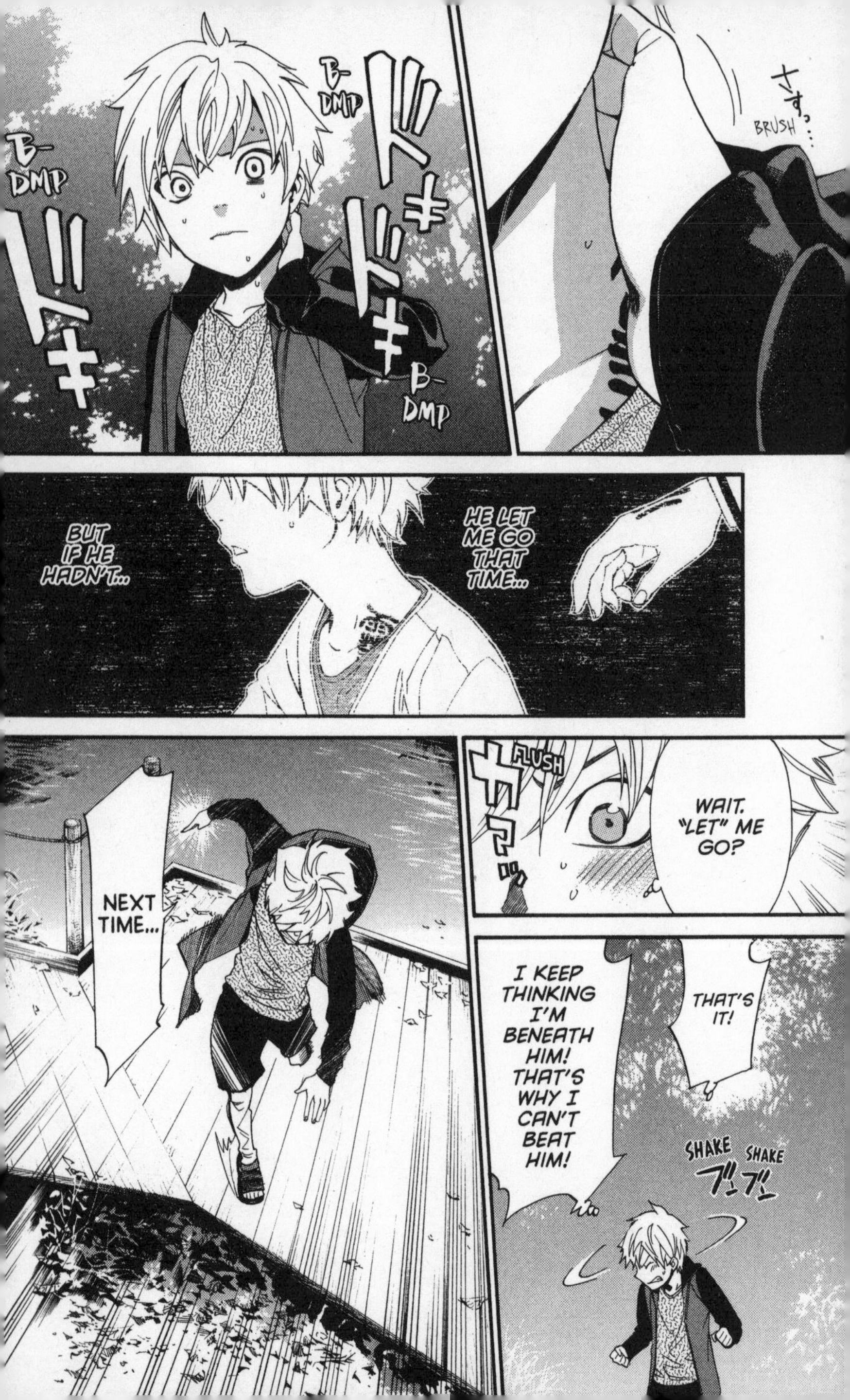
さすっ…
BRUSH…
B-DMP
B-DMP
ドキ
ドキ
ドキ
B-DMP
HE LET ME GO THAT TIME…
BUT IF HE HADN'T…
FLUSH
WAIT. "LET" ME GO?
THAT'S IT!
I KEEP THINKING I'M BENEATH HIM! THAT'S WHY I CAN'T BEAT HIM!
SHAKE SHAKE
NEXT TIME…

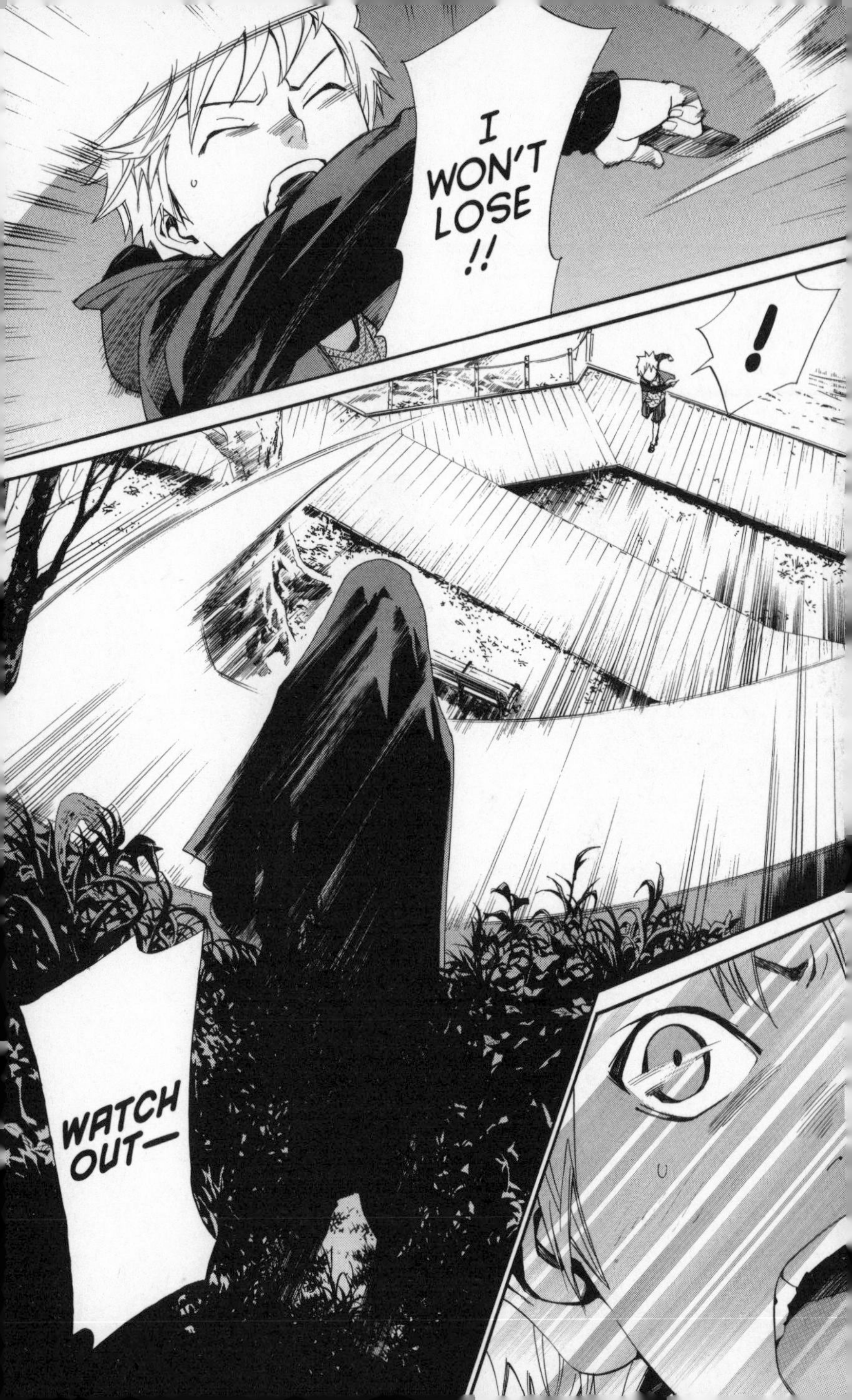
I WON'T LOSE !!
!
WATCH OUT—

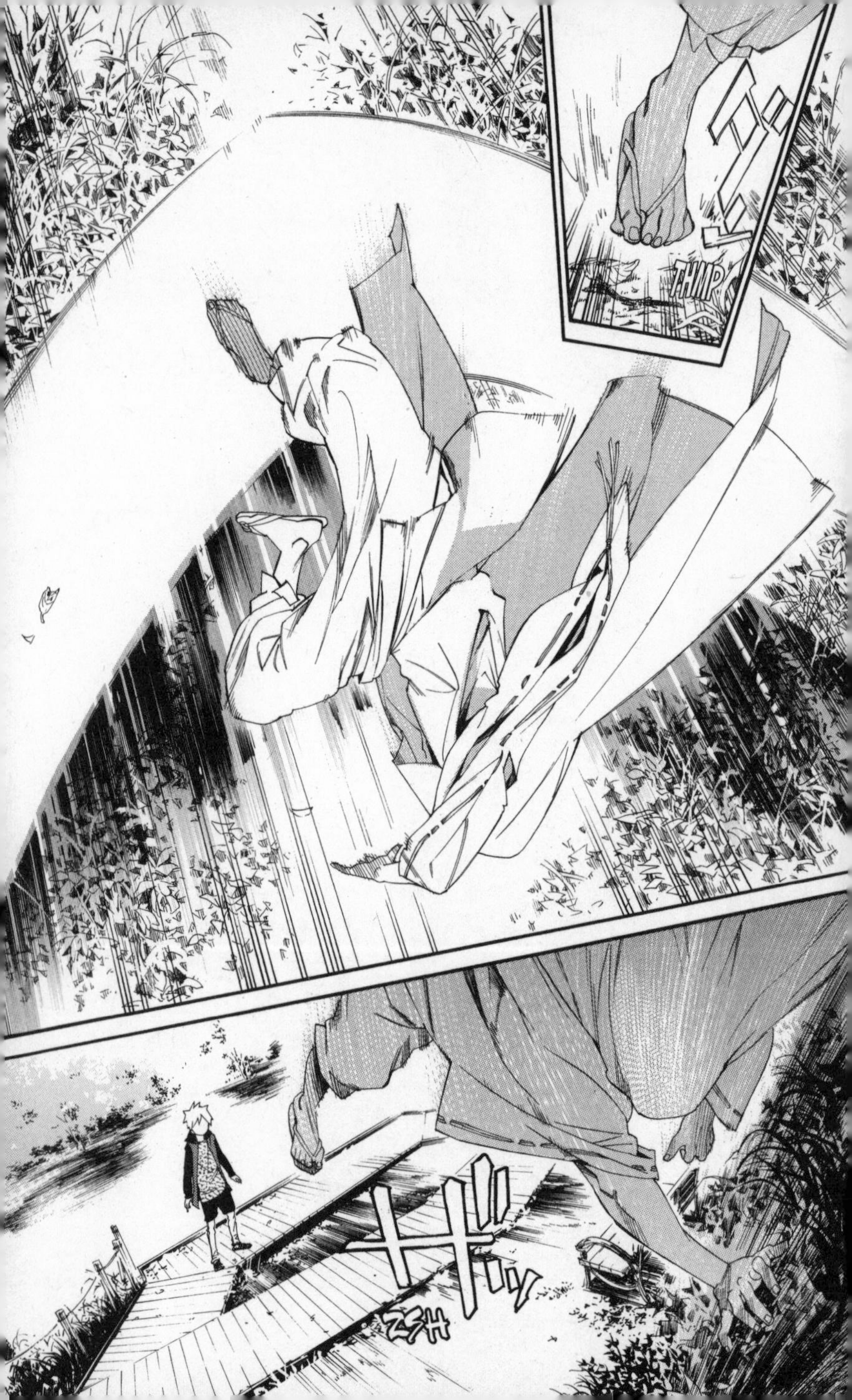
THIP
ZSH

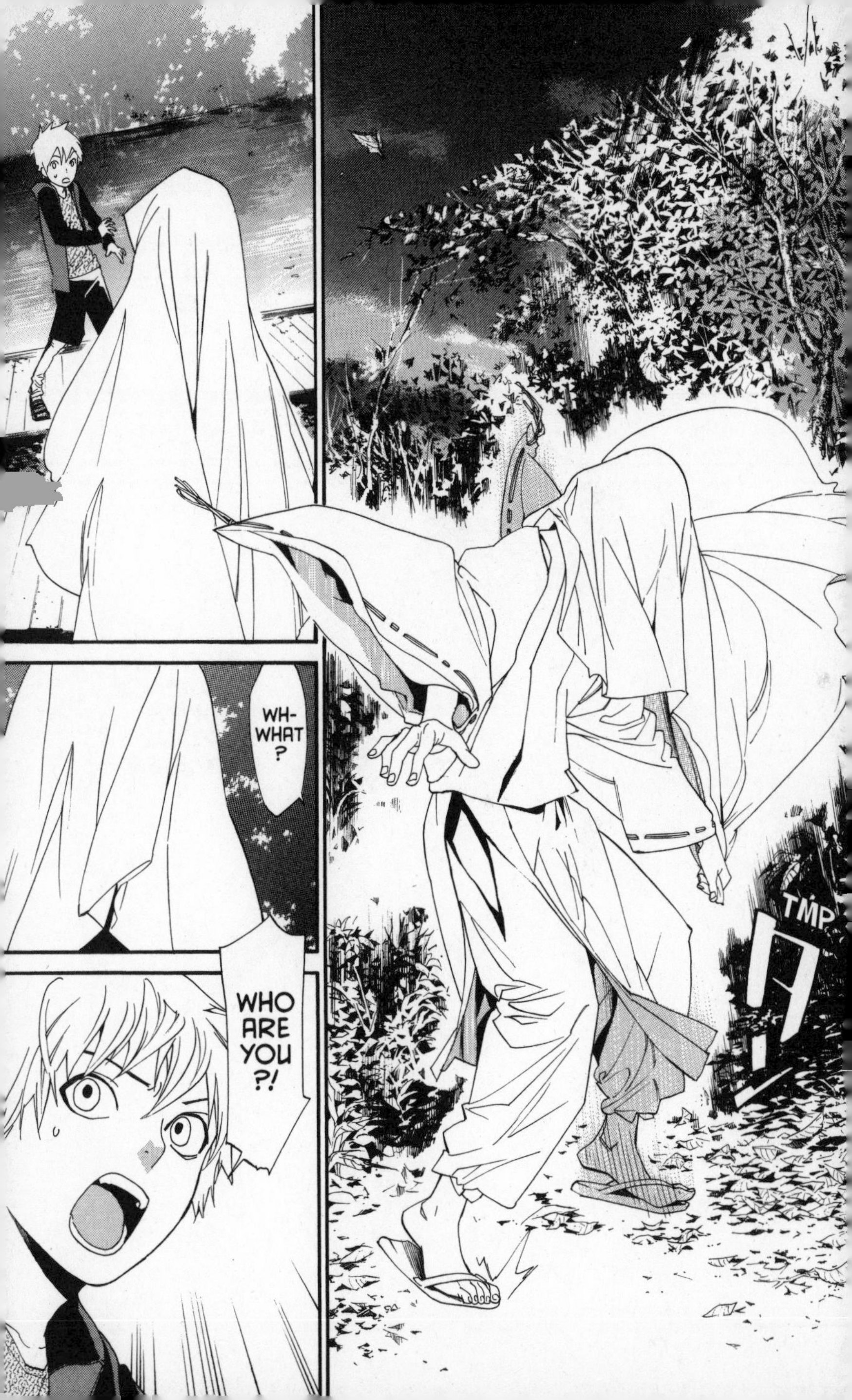
TMP
WH-WHAT?
WHO ARE YOU?!

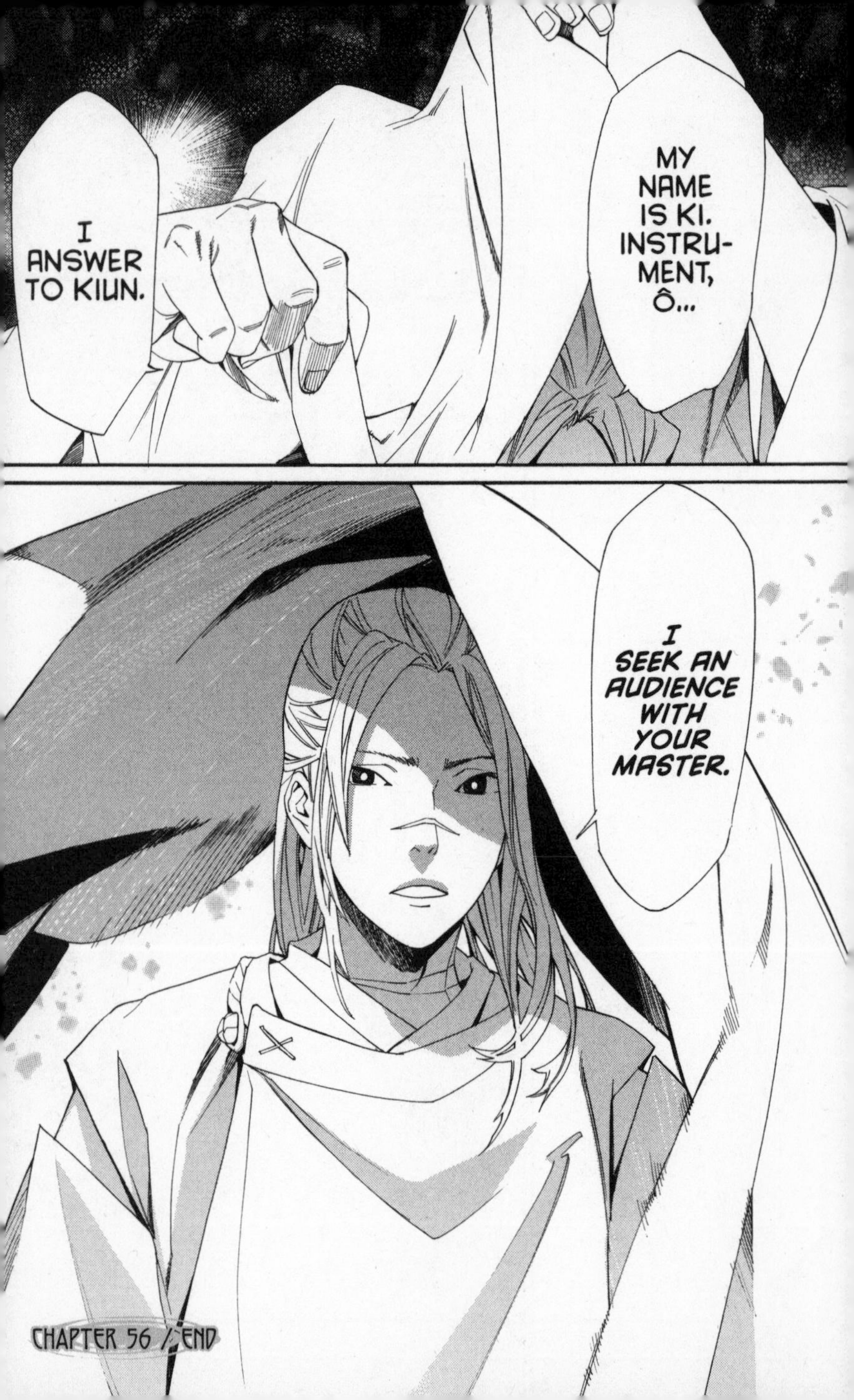
MY NAME IS KI. INSTRUMENT, Ô...
I ANSWER TO KIUN.
I SEEK AN AUDIENCE WITH YOUR MASTER.
CHAPTER 56 / END

野

甚

神

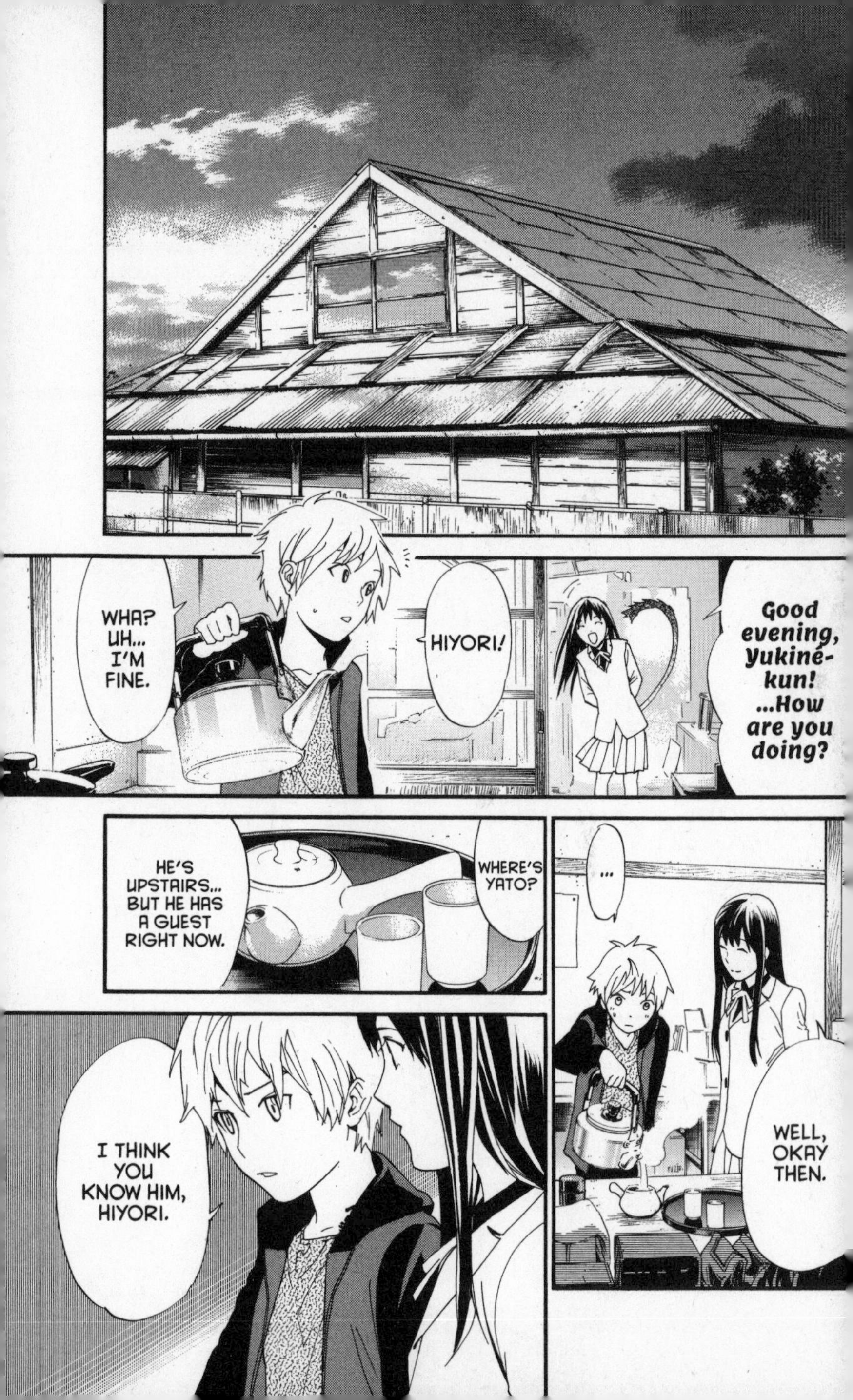

Good evening, Yukiné-kun! ...How are you doing?
HIYORI!
WHA? UH... I'M FINE.
...
WHERE'S YATO?
HE'S UPSTAIRS... BUT HE HAS A GUEST RIGHT NOW.
WELL, OKAY THEN.
I THINK YOU KNOW HIM, HIYORI.

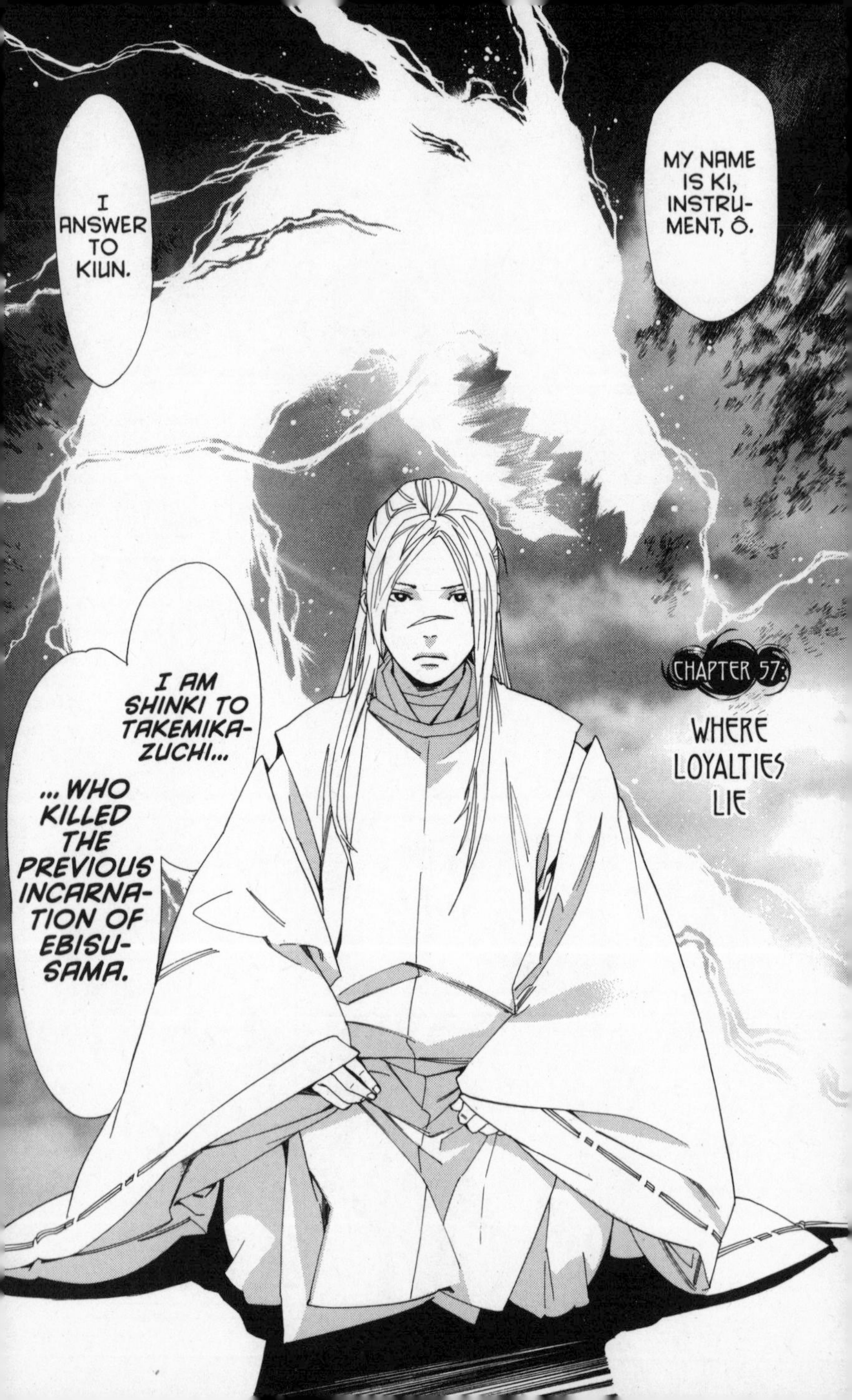
MY NAME IS KI, INSTRUMENT, Ô.
I ANSWER TO KIUN.
CHAPTER 57:
WHERE LOYALTIES LIE
I AM SHINKI TO TAKEMIKAZUCHI...
...WHO KILLED THE PREVIOUS INCARNATION OF EBISU-SAMA.

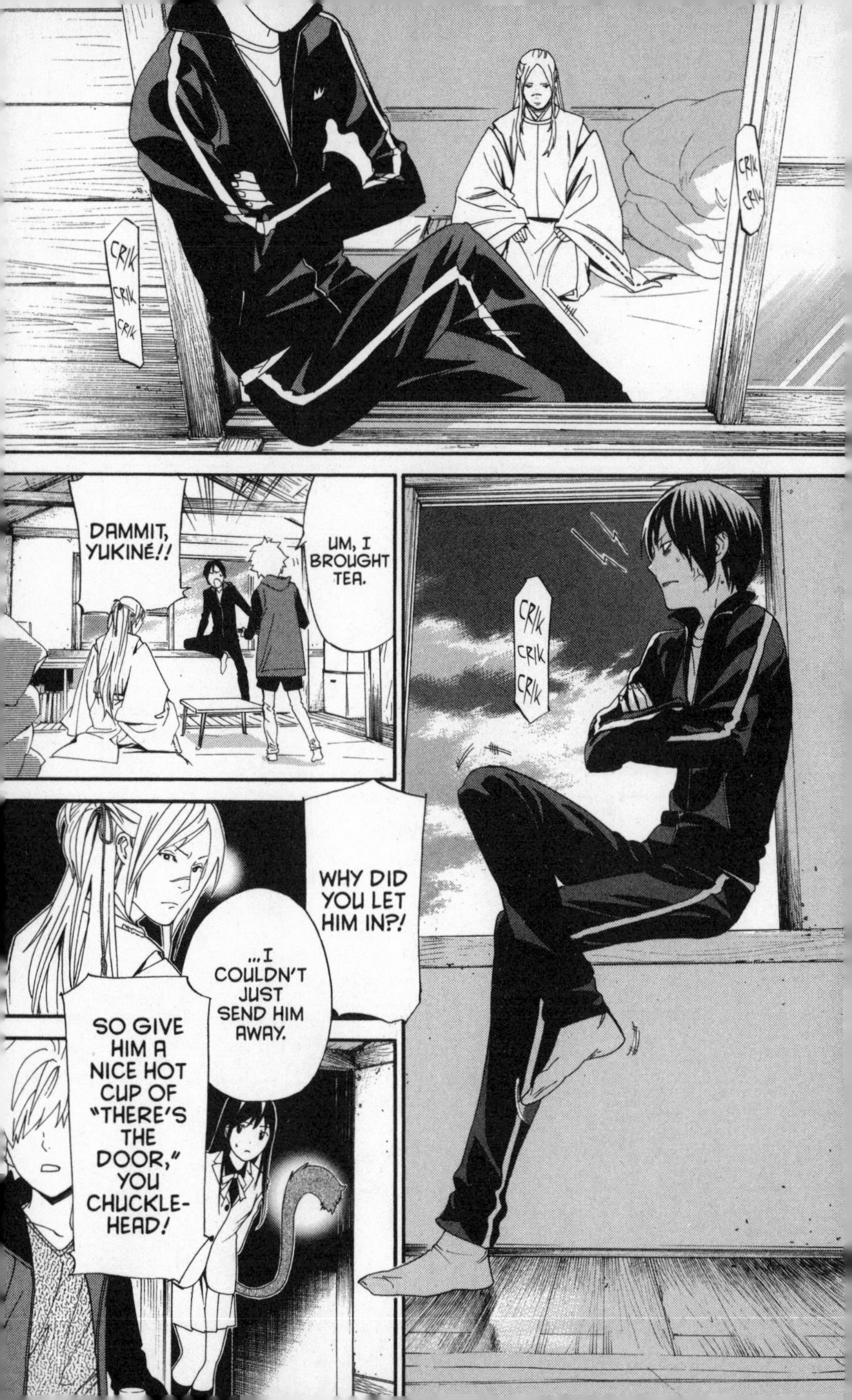
CRIK CRIK
CRIK CRIK CRIK
CRIK CRIK CRIK
UM, I BROUGHT TEA.
DAMMIT, YUKINÉ!!
WHY DID YOU LET HIM IN?!
...I COULDN'T JUST SEND HIM AWAY.
SO GIVE HIM A NICE HOT CUP OF "THERE'S THE DOOR," YOU CHUCKLE-HEAD!

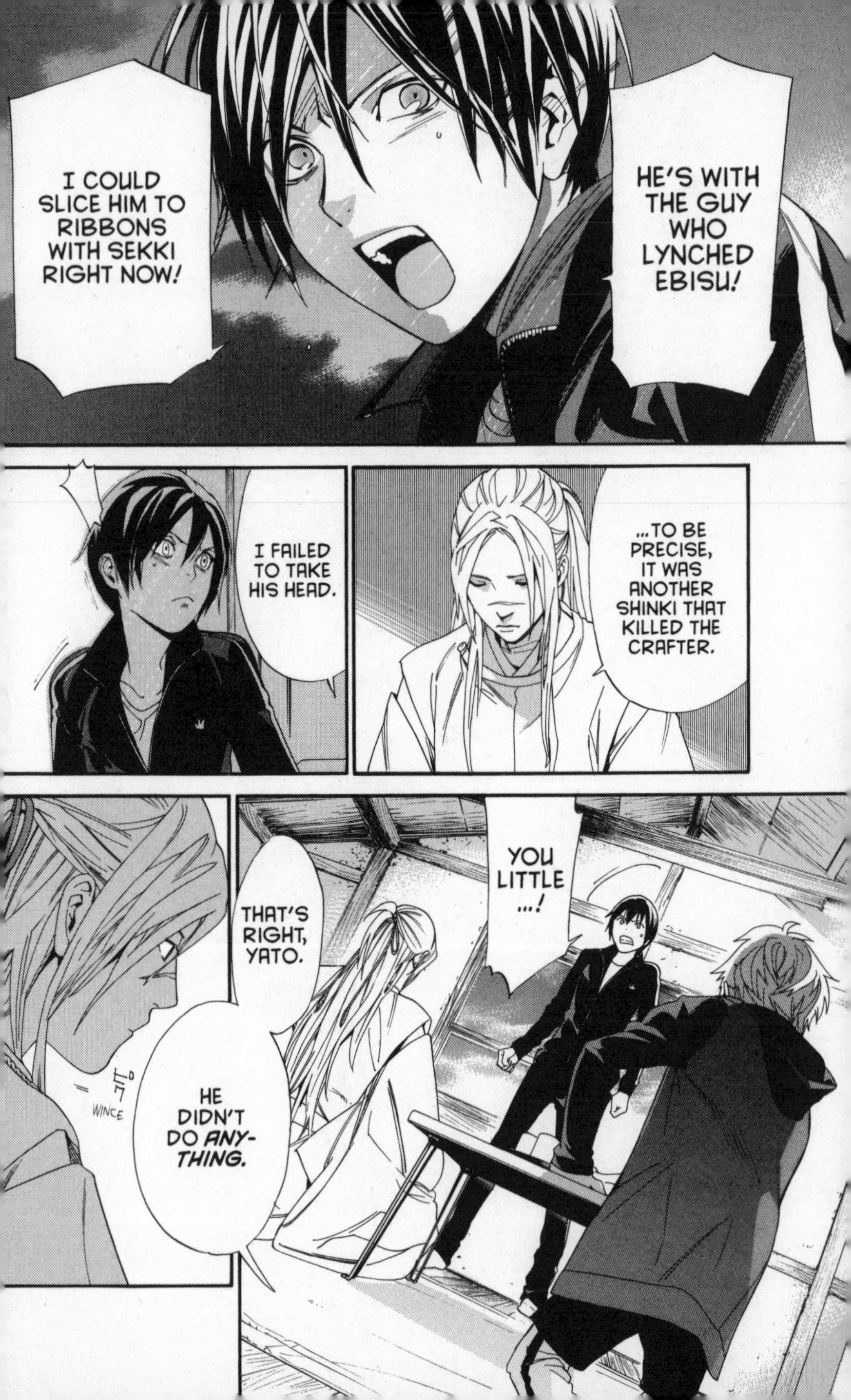
HE'S WITH THE GUY WHO LYNCHED EBISU!
I COULD SLICE HIM TO RIBBONS WITH SEKKI RIGHT NOW!
...TO BE PRECISE, IT WAS ANOTHER SHINKI THAT KILLED THE CRAFTER.
I FAILED TO TAKE HIS HEAD.
YOU LITTLE ...!
THAT'S RIGHT, YATO.
WINCE
HE DIDN'T DO *ANY-THING.*

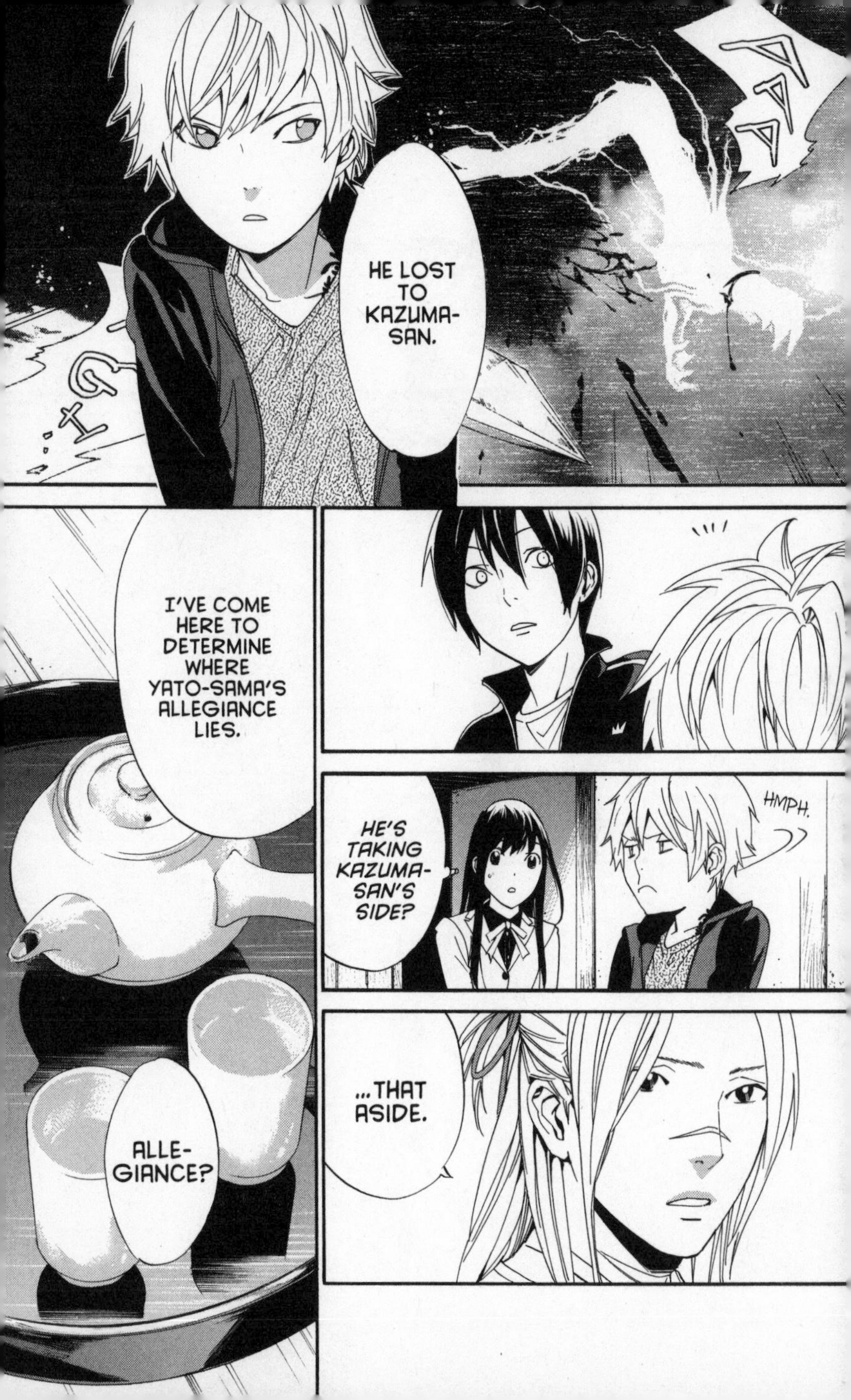
HE LOST TO KAZUMA-SAN.
HE'S TAKING KAZUMA-SAN'S SIDE?
HMPH.
...THAT ASIDE.
I'VE COME HERE TO DETERMINE WHERE YATO-SAMA'S ALLEGIANCE LIES.
ALLE-GIANCE?

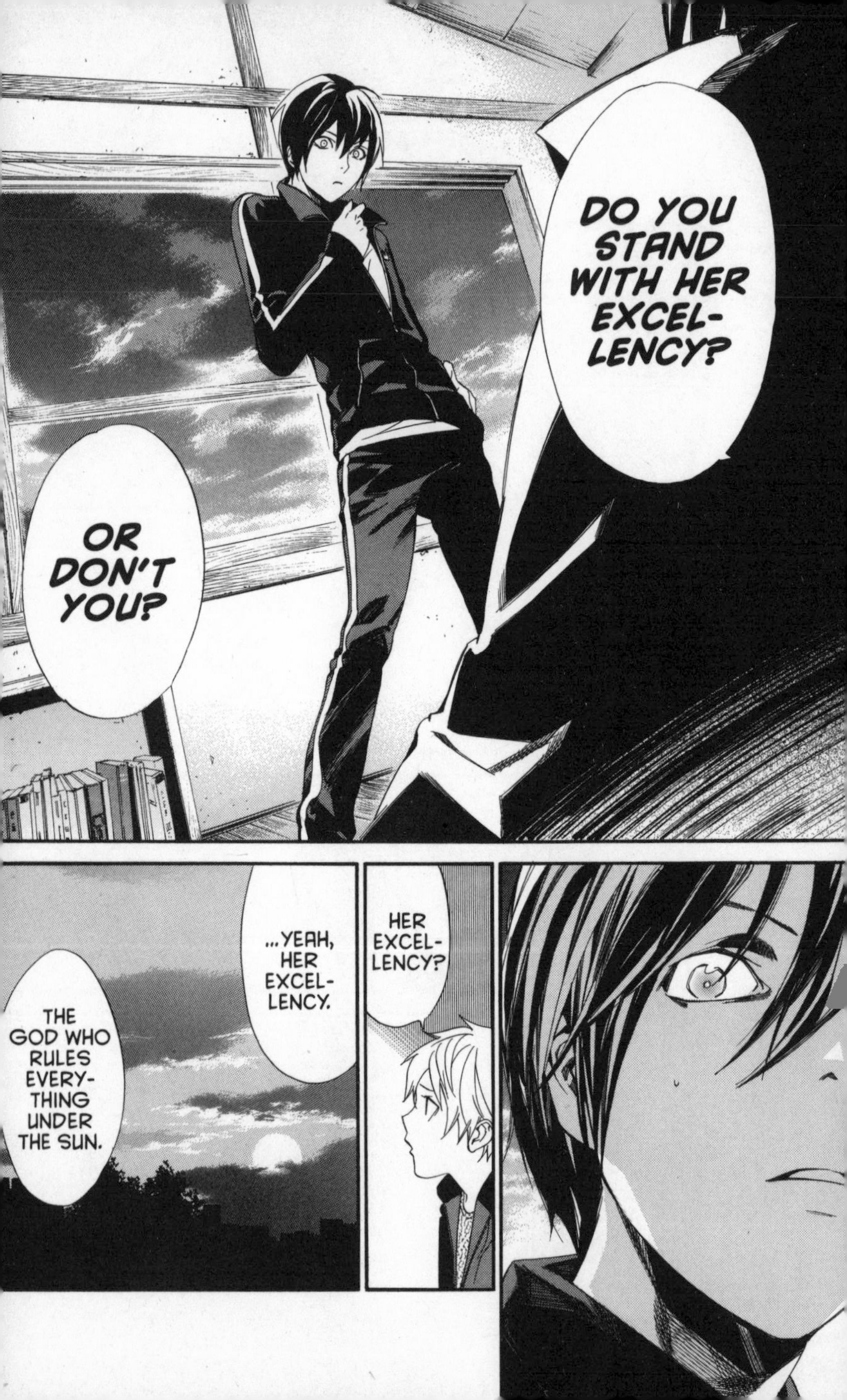
DO YOU STAND WITH HER EXCEL-LENCY?
OR DON'T YOU?
HER EXCEL-LENCY?
...YEAH, HER EXCEL-LENCY.
THE GOD WHO RULES EVERY-THING UNDER THE SUN.

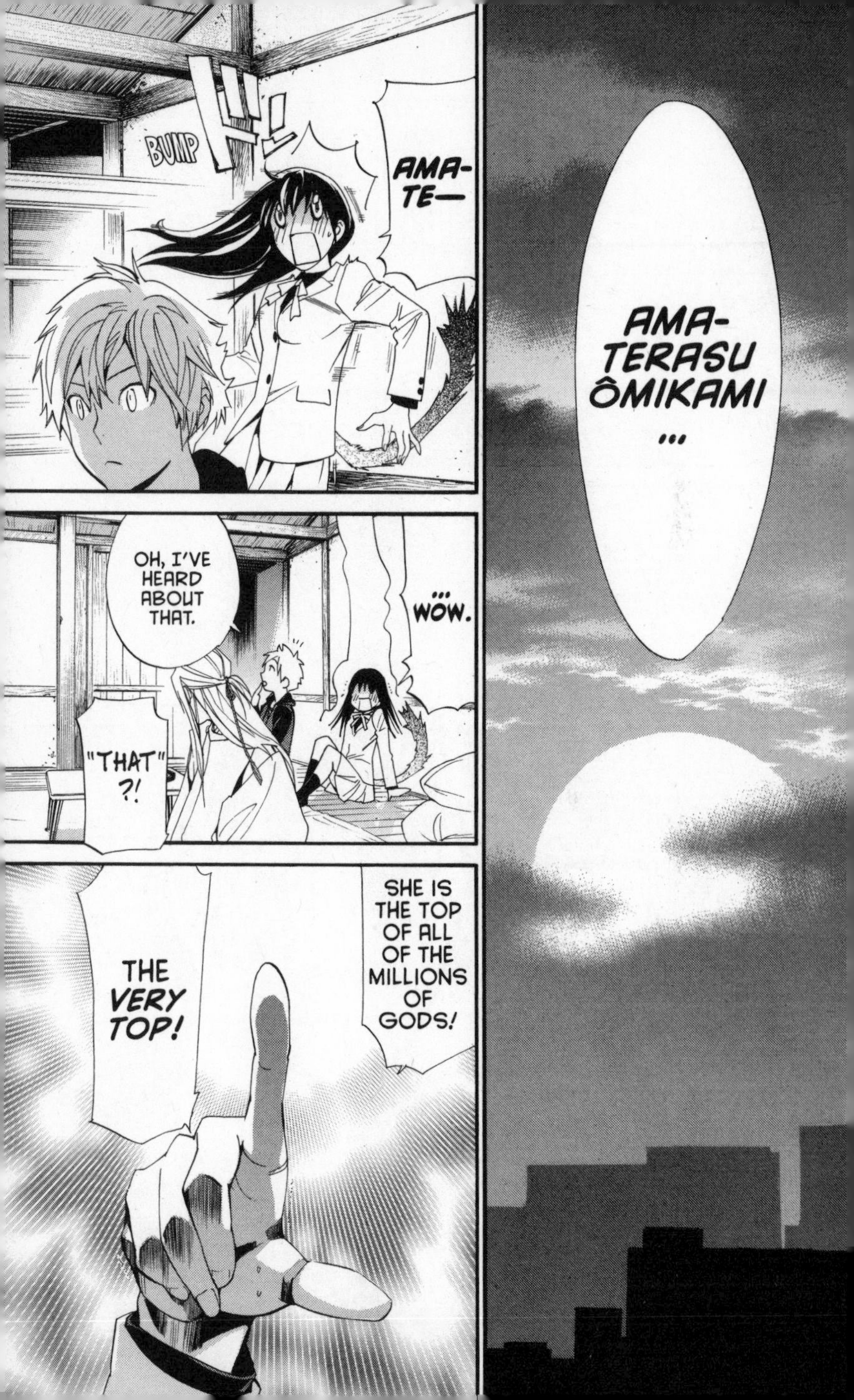
AMA-TERASU ÔMIKAMI ...
BUMP
AMA-TE—
... WOW.
OH, I'VE HEARD ABOUT THAT.
"THAT" ?!
SHE IS THE TOP OF ALL OF THE MILLIONS OF GODS!
THE VERY TOP!

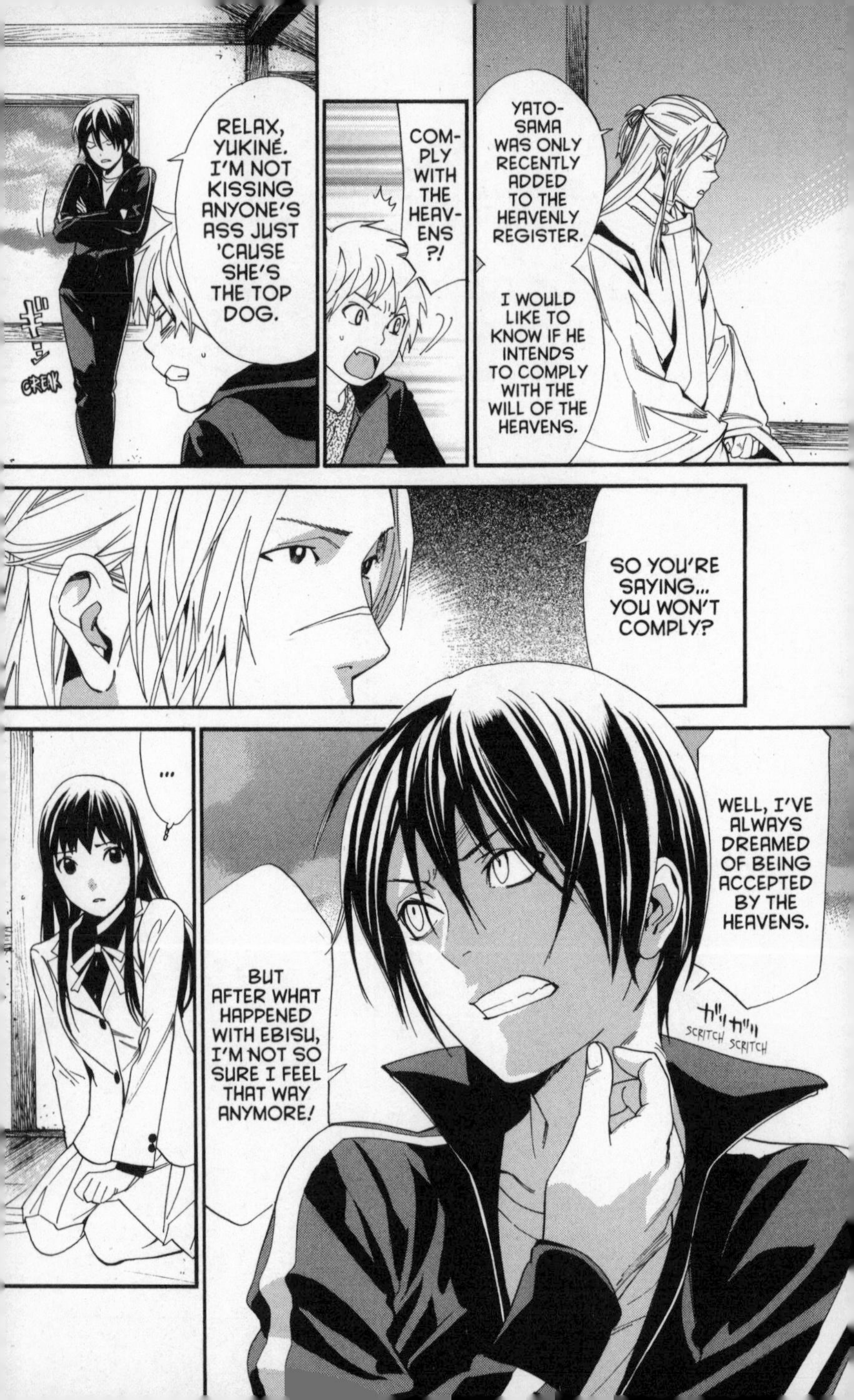
YATO-SAMA WAS ONLY RECENTLY ADDED TO THE HEAVENLY REGISTER.
I WOULD LIKE TO KNOW IF HE INTENDS TO COMPLY WITH THE WILL OF THE HEAVENS.
COMPLY WITH THE HEAVENS?!
RELAX, YUKINÉ. I'M NOT KISSING ANYONE'S ASS JUST 'CAUSE SHE'S THE TOP DOG.
CREAK
SO YOU'RE SAYING... YOU WON'T COMPLY?
WELL, I'VE ALWAYS DREAMED OF BEING ACCEPTED BY THE HEAVENS.
SCRITCH SCRITCH
BUT AFTER WHAT HAPPENED WITH EBISU, I'M NOT SO SURE I FEEL THAT WAY ANYMORE!
...

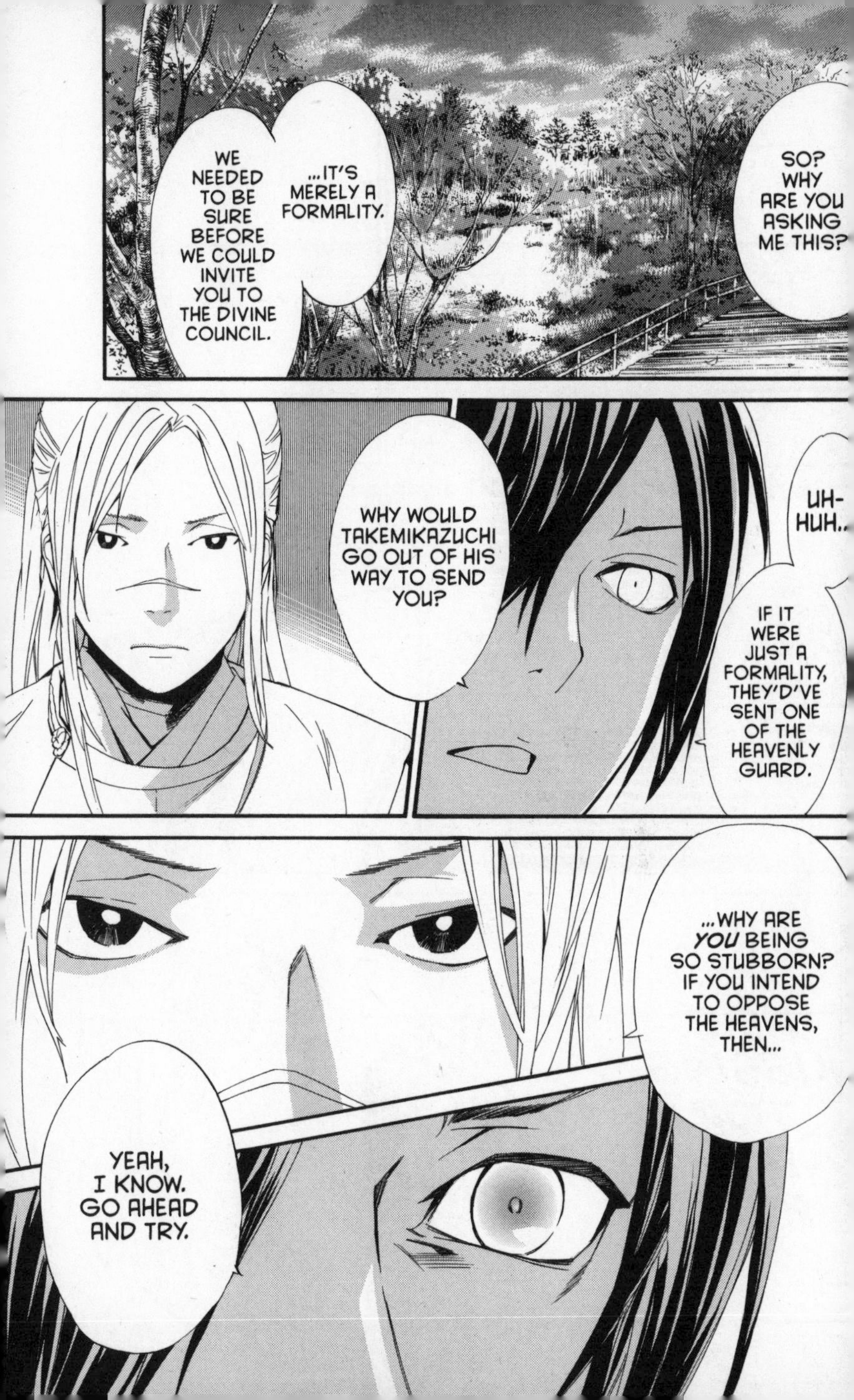
SO? WHY ARE YOU ASKING ME THIS?
...IT'S MERELY A FORMALITY.
WE NEEDED TO BE SURE BEFORE WE COULD INVITE YOU TO THE DIVINE COUNCIL.
UH-HUH...
IF IT WERE JUST A FORMALITY, THEY'D'VE SENT ONE OF THE HEAVENLY GUARD.
WHY WOULD TAKEMIKAZUCHI GO OUT OF HIS WAY TO SEND YOU?
...WHY ARE *YOU* BEING SO STUBBORN? IF YOU INTEND TO OPPOSE THE HEAVENS, THEN...
YEAH, I KNOW. GO AHEAD AND TRY.

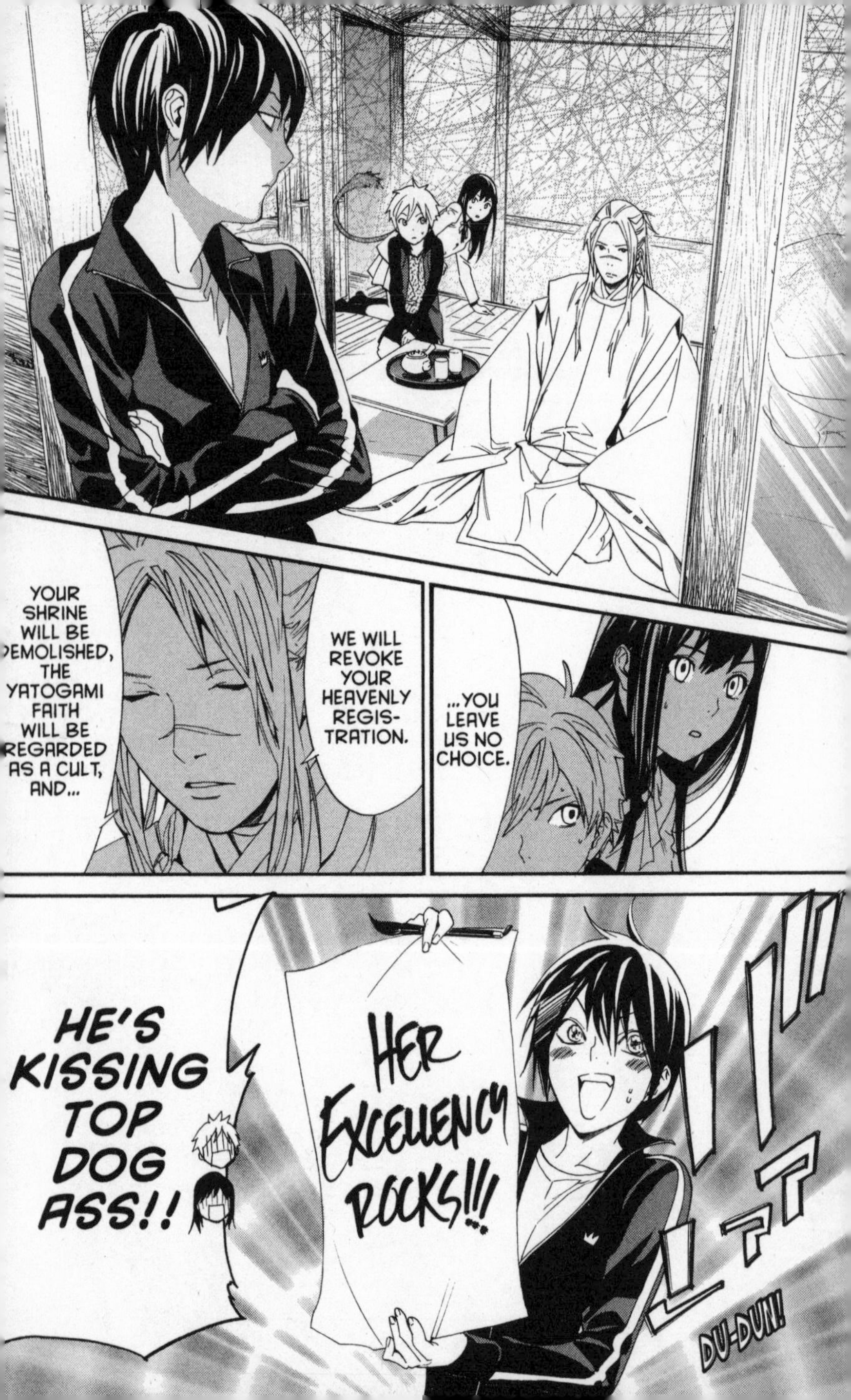

...YOU LEAVE US NO CHOICE.
WE WILL REVOKE YOUR HEAVENLY REGIS-TRATION.
YOUR SHRINE WILL BE DEMOLISHED, THE YATOGAMI FAITH WILL BE REGARDED AS A CULT, AND...
DU-DUN!
HER EXCELLENCY ROCKS!!!
HE'S KISSING TOP DOG ASS!!

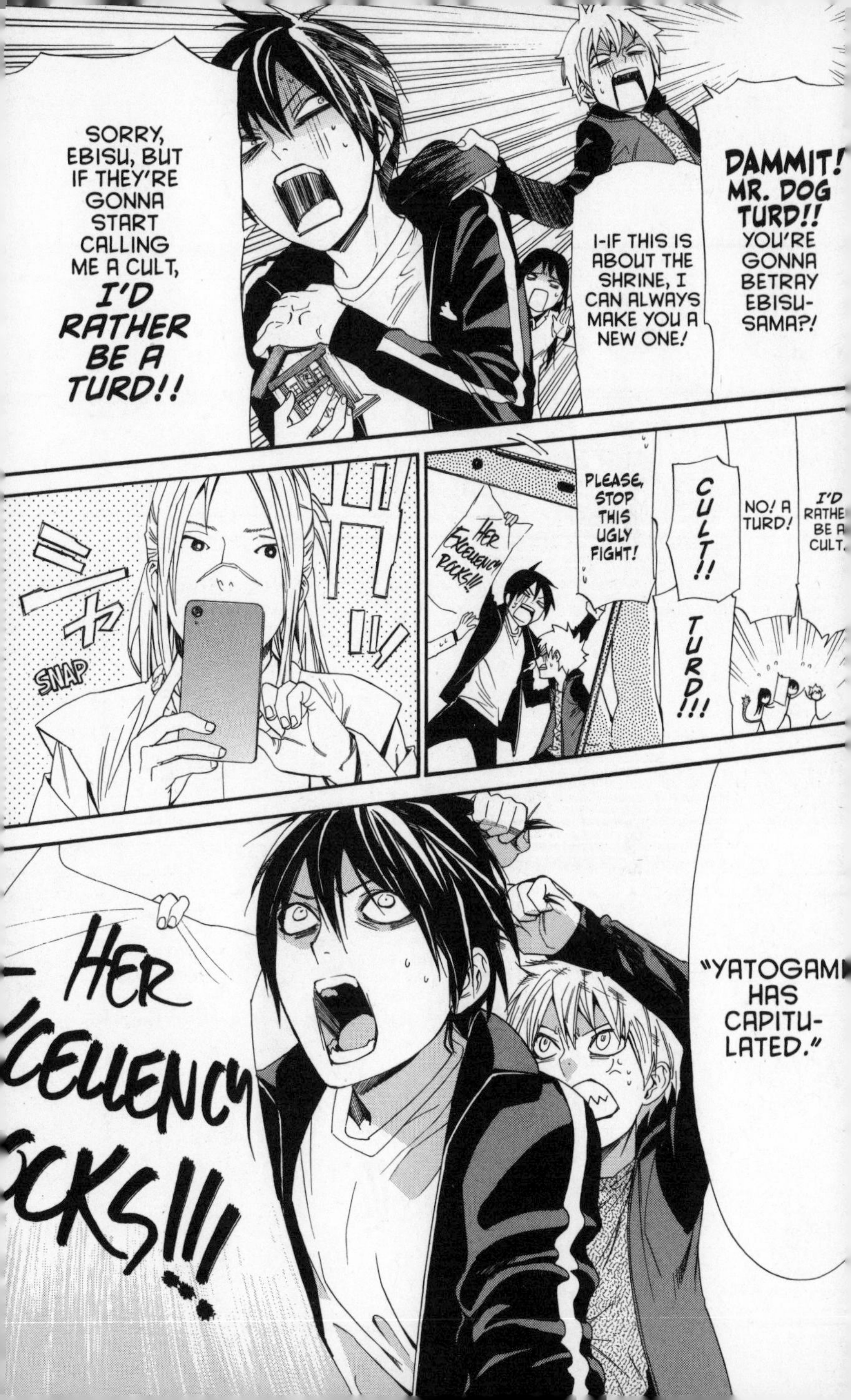
DAMMIT! MR. DOG TURD!! YOU'RE GONNA BETRAY EBISU-SAMA?!
I-IF THIS IS ABOUT THE SHRINE, I CAN ALWAYS MAKE YOU A NEW ONE!
SORRY, EBISU, BUT IF THEY'RE GONNA START CALLING ME A CULT, I'D RATHER BE A TURD!!
I'D RATHE BE A CULT.
NO! A TURD!
CULT!!
TURD!!!
PLEASE, STOP THIS UGLY FIGHT!
HER EXCELLENCY ROCKS!!!
SNAP
"YATOGAMI HAS CAPITULATED."
HER
CELLENCY
CKS!!!

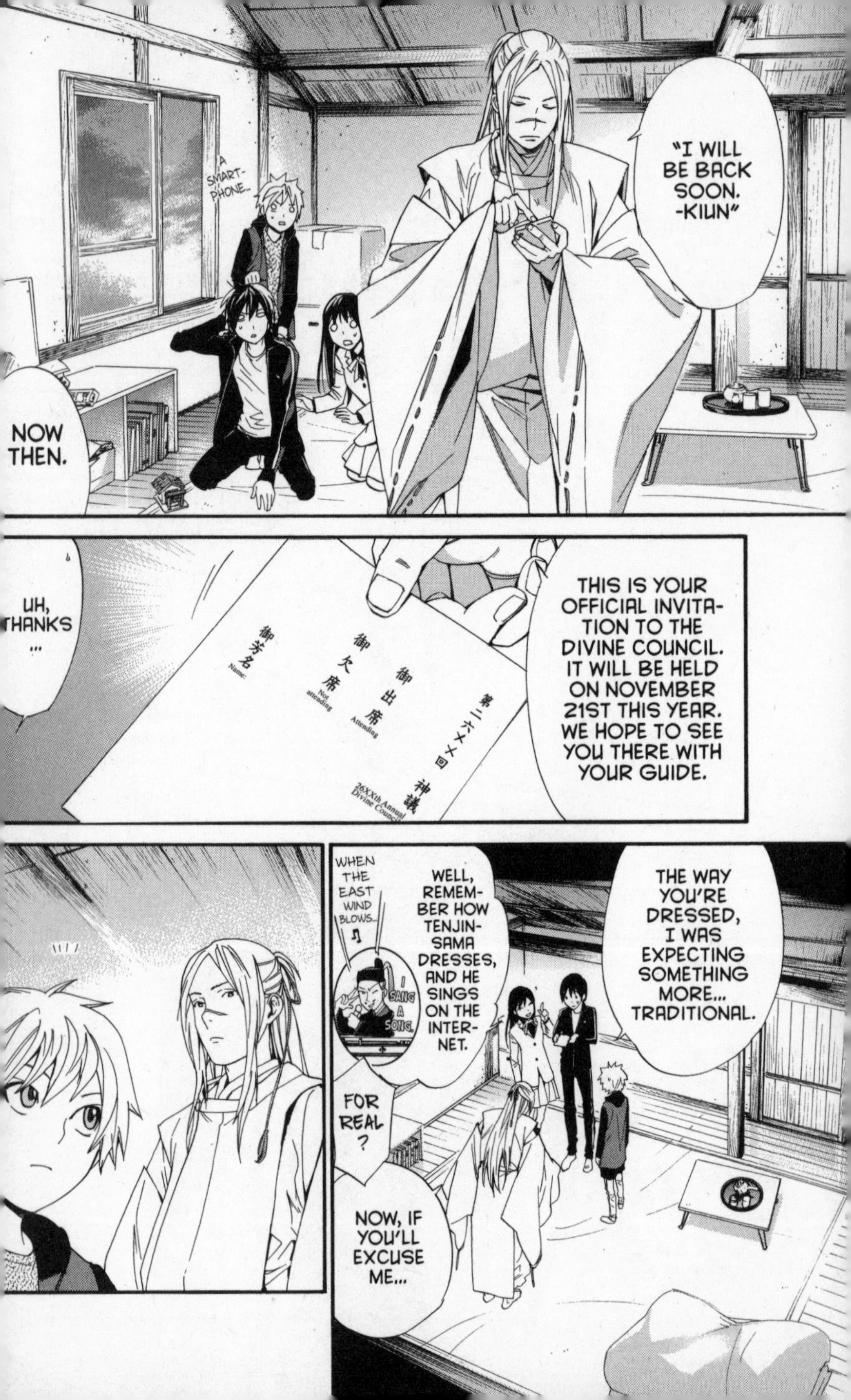
"I WILL BE BACK SOON. -KIUN"
A SMARTPHONE...
NOW THEN.
THIS IS YOUR OFFICIAL INVITATION TO THE DIVINE COUNCIL. IT WILL BE HELD ON NOVEMBER 21ST THIS YEAR. WE HOPE TO SEE YOU THERE WITH YOUR GUIDE.
第二六××回 神議
26XXth Annual Divine Council
御出席
Attending
御欠席
Not attending
御芳名
Name:
UH, THANKS...
THE WAY YOU'RE DRESSED, I WAS EXPECTING SOMETHING MORE... TRADITIONAL.
WELL, REMEMBER HOW TENJIN-SAMA DRESSES, AND HE SINGS ON THE INTERNET.
WHEN THE EAST WIND BLOWS... ♫
I SANG A SONG.
FOR REAL?
NOW, IF YOU'LL EXCUSE ME...

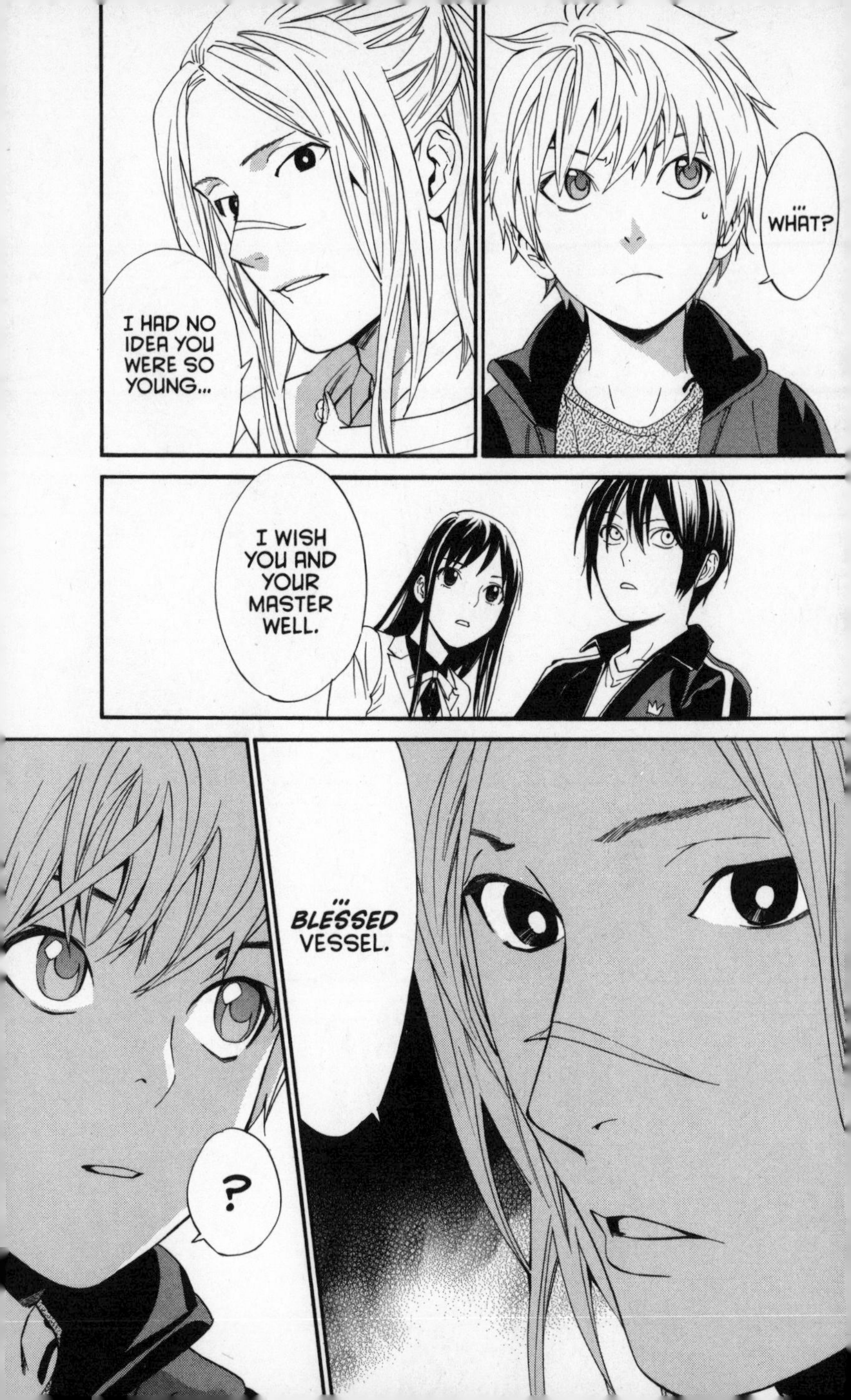

...WHAT?
I HAD NO IDEA YOU WERE SO YOUNG...
I WISH YOU AND YOUR MASTER WELL.
...BLESSED VESSEL.
?

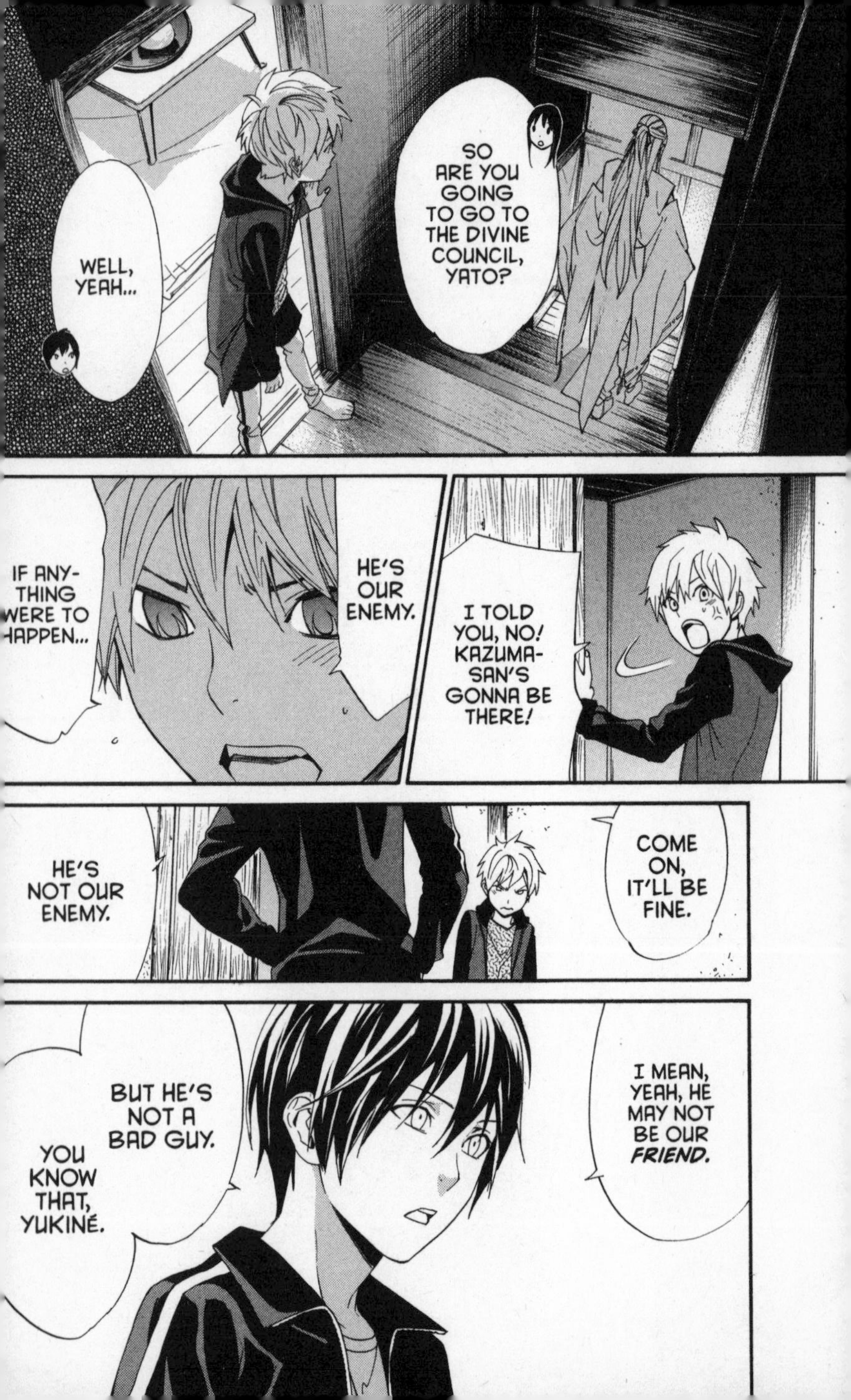
SO ARE YOU GOING TO GO TO THE DIVINE COUNCIL, YATO?
WELL, YEAH...
I TOLD YOU, NO! KAZUMA-SAN'S GONNA BE THERE!
HE'S OUR ENEMY.
IF ANY-THING WERE TO HAPPEN...
COME ON, IT'LL BE FINE.
HE'S NOT OUR ENEMY.
I MEAN, YEAH, HE MAY NOT BE OUR FRIEND.
BUT HE'S NOT A BAD GUY.
YOU KNOW THAT, YUKINÉ.

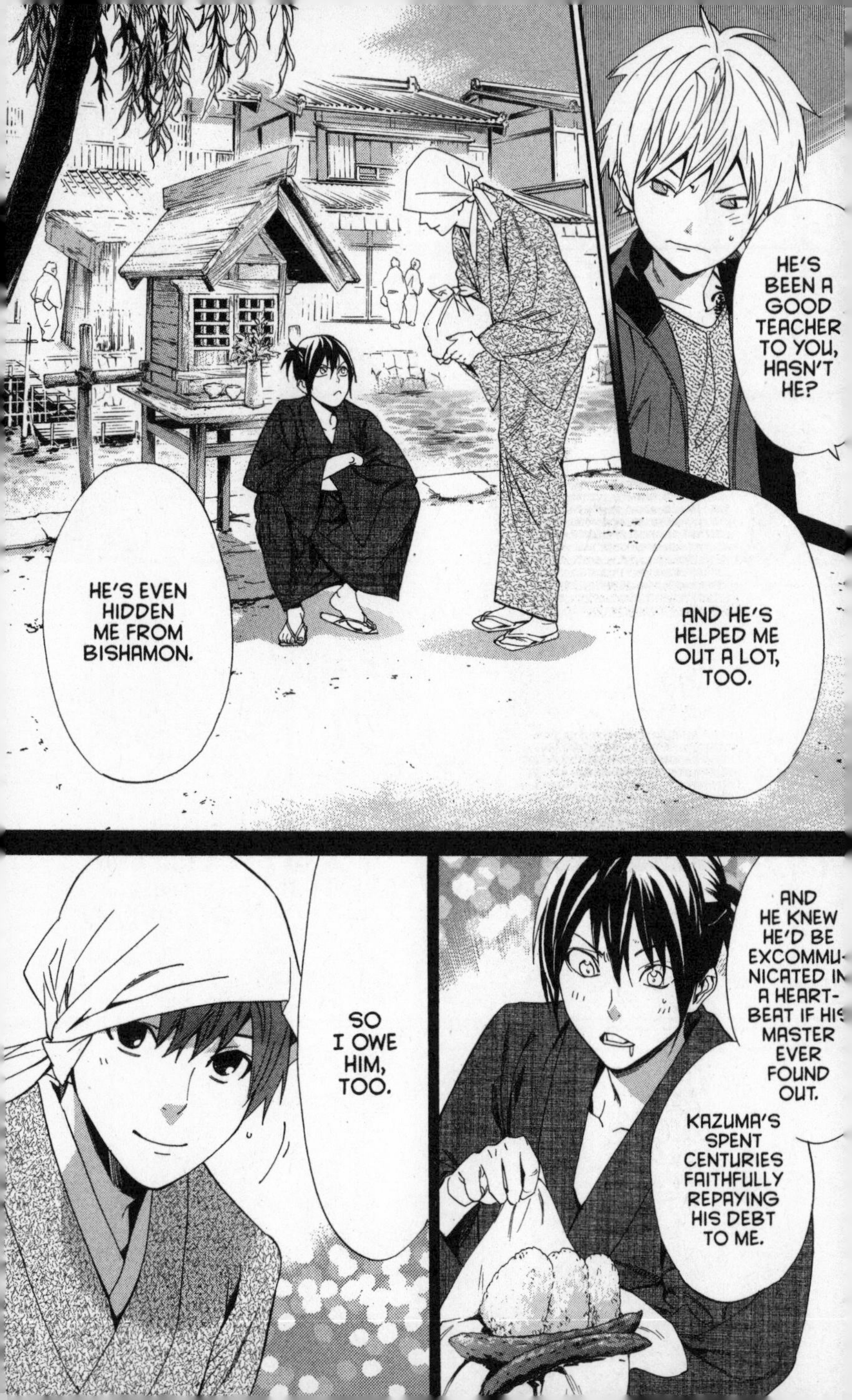
HE'S BEEN A GOOD TEACHER TO YOU, HASN'T HE?
AND HE'S HELPED ME OUT A LOT, TOO.
HE'S EVEN HIDDEN ME FROM BISHAMON.
AND HE KNEW HE'D BE EXCOMMUNICATED IN A HEARTBEAT IF HIS MASTER EVER FOUND OUT.
KAZUMA'S SPENT CENTURIES FAITHFULLY REPAYING HIS DEBT TO ME.
SO I OWE HIM, TOO.

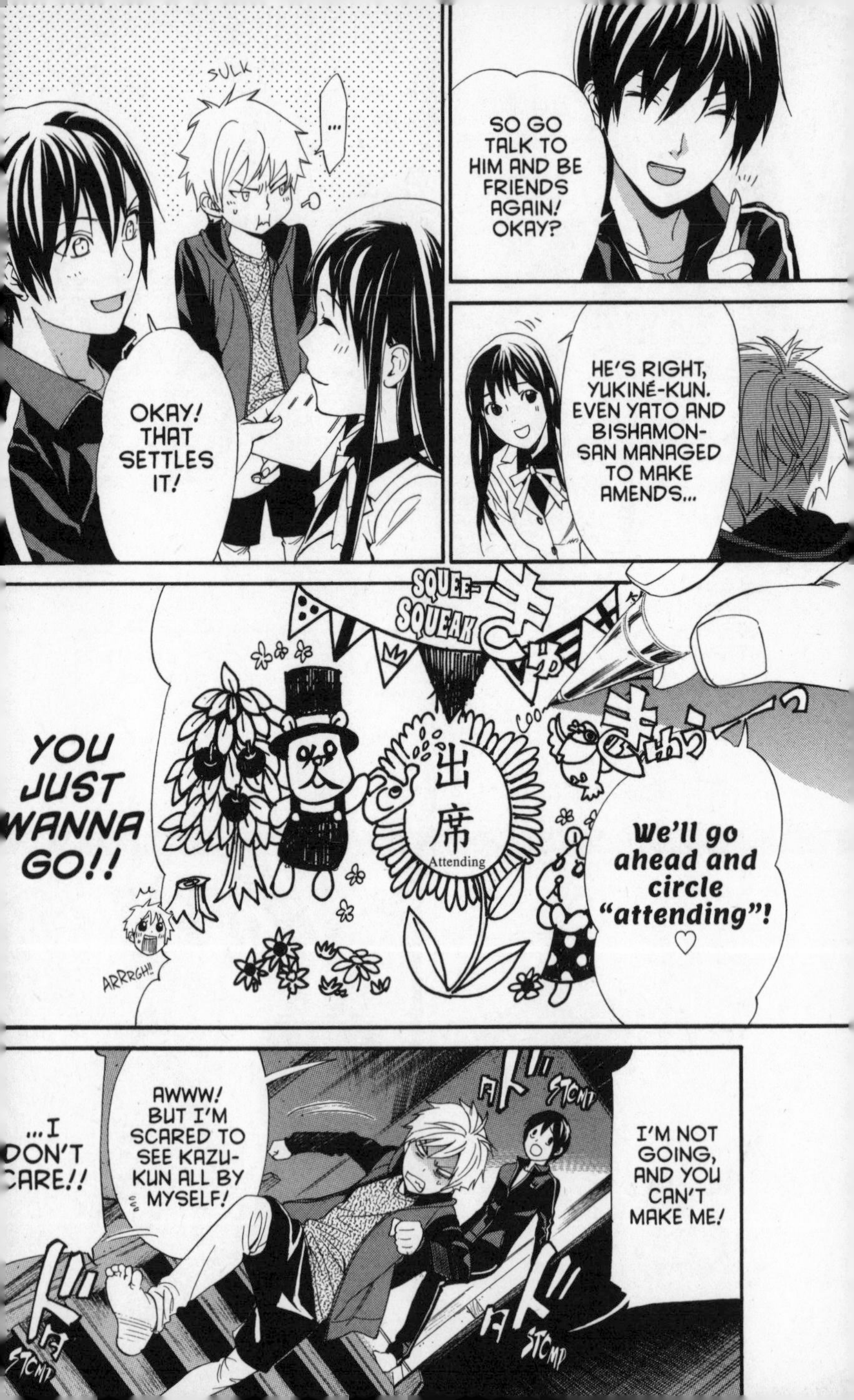
SO GO TALK TO HIM AND BE FRIENDS AGAIN! OKAY?
HE'S RIGHT, YUKINÉ-KUN. EVEN YATO AND BISHAMON-SAN MANAGED TO MAKE AMENDS...
SULK
...
OKAY! THAT SETTLES IT!
SQUEE-SQUEAK
きゅ
きゅうーっ
We'll go ahead and circle "attending"! ♡
出席
Attending
YOU JUST WANNA GO!!
ARRRGH!!
I'M NOT GOING, AND YOU CAN'T MAKE ME!
STOMP
AWWW! BUT I'M SCARED TO SEE KAZU-KUN ALL BY MYSELF!
...I DON'T CARE!!
STOMP
STOMP

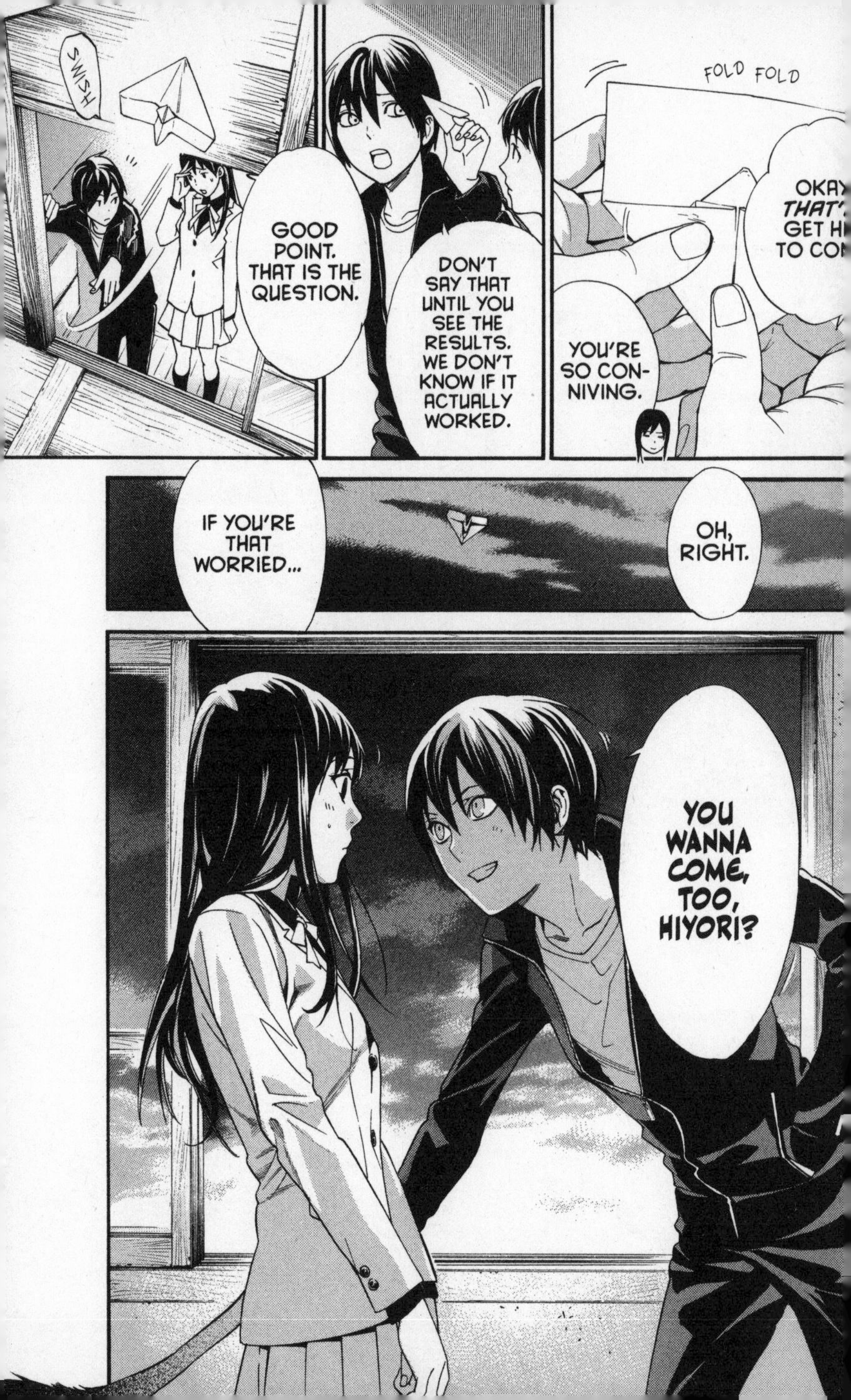
FOLD FOLD
OKAY THAT' GET H TO CO
YOU'RE SO CON-NIVING.
DON'T SAY THAT UNTIL YOU SEE THE RESULTS. WE DON'T KNOW IF IT ACTUALLY WORKED.
GOOD POINT. THAT IS THE QUESTION.
SWISH
OH, RIGHT.
IF YOU'RE THAT WORRIED...
YOU WANNA COME, TOO, HIYORI?

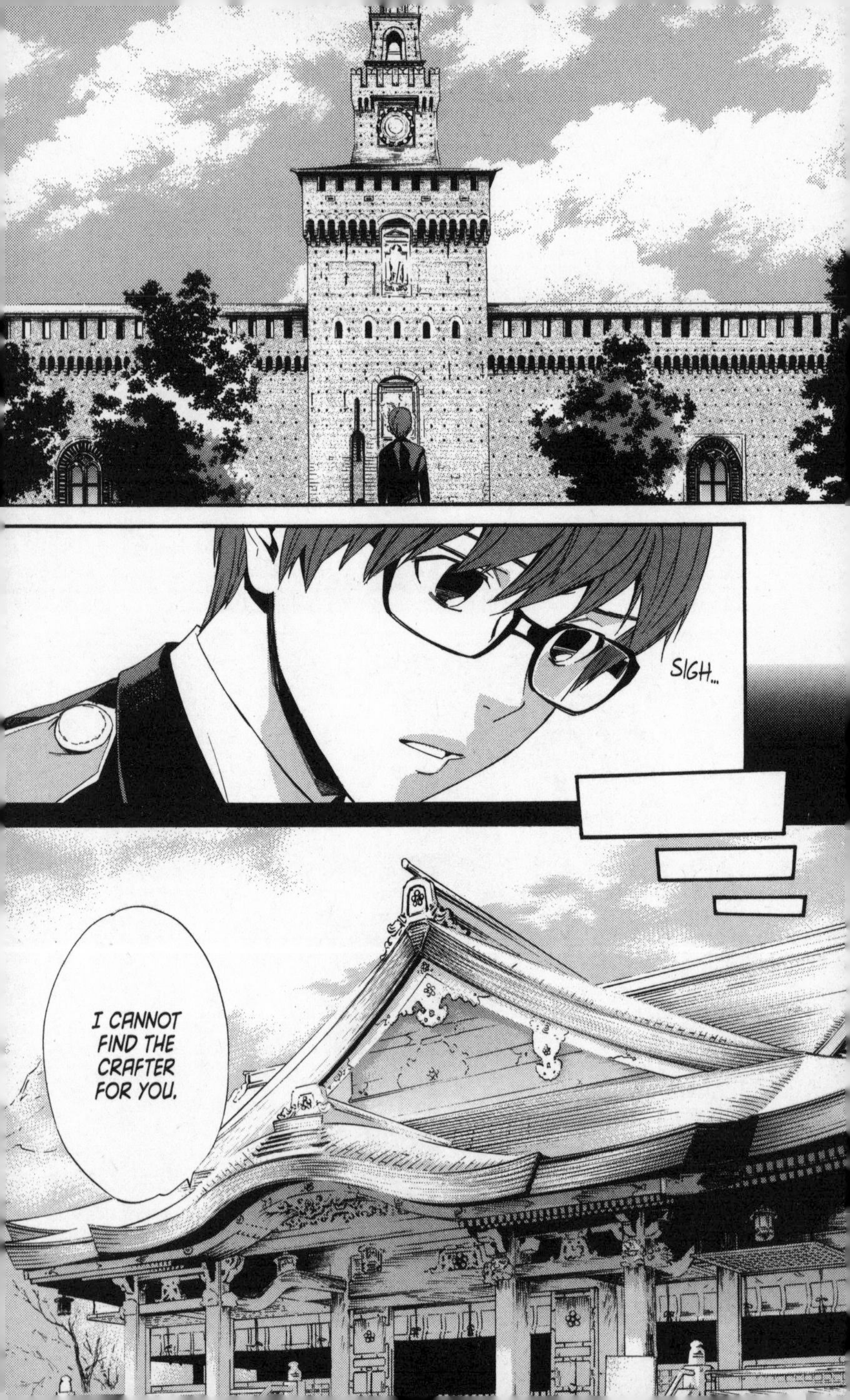
SIGH...
I CANNOT FIND THE CRAFTER FOR YOU.

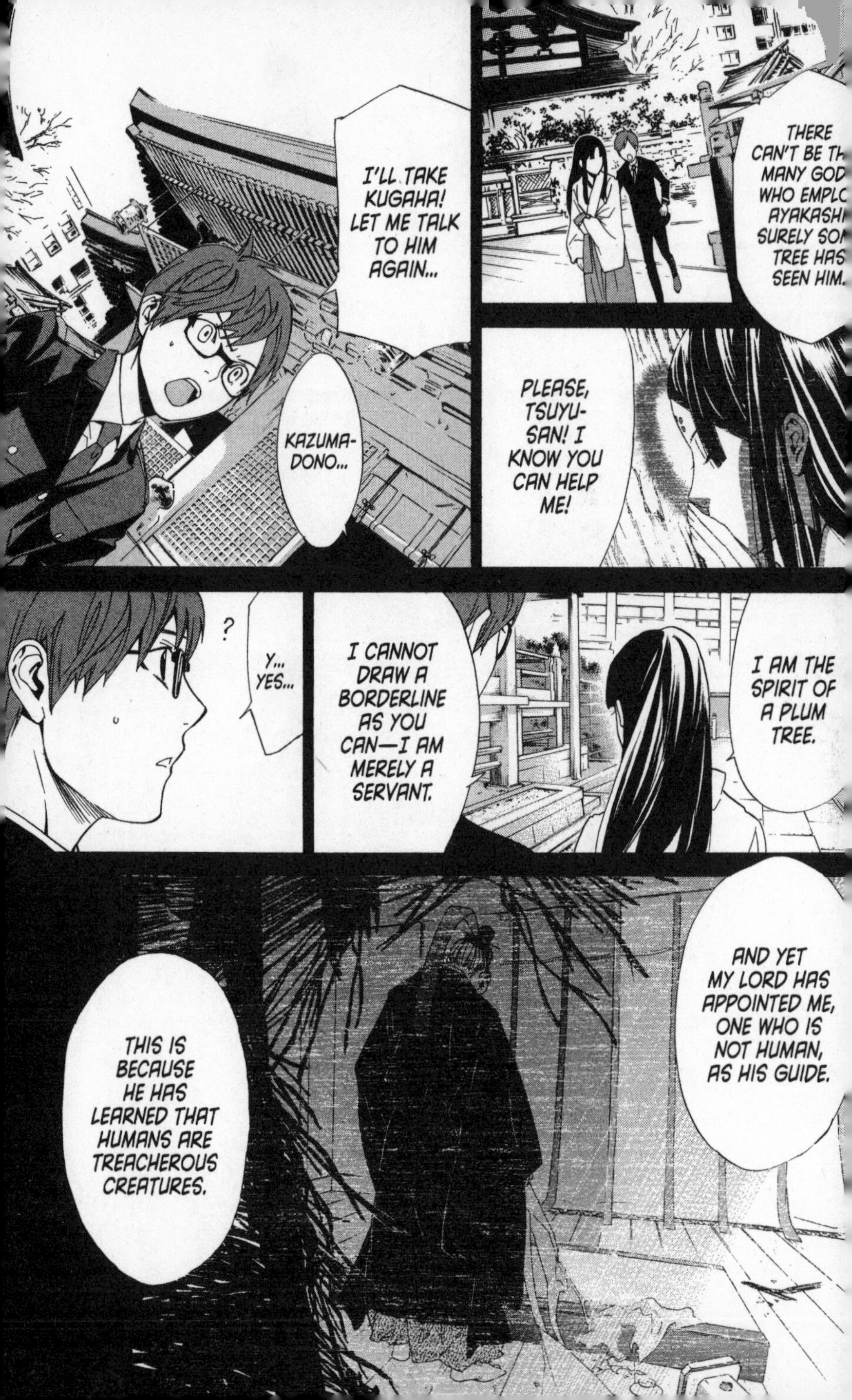
THERE CAN'T BE TH MANY GOD WHO EMPLO AYAKASHI SURELY SO TREE HAS SEEN HIM.
PLEASE, TSUYU-SAN! I KNOW YOU CAN HELP ME!
I'LL TAKE KUGAHA! LET ME TALK TO HIM AGAIN...
KAZUMA-DONO...
I AM THE SPIRIT OF A PLUM TREE.
I CANNOT DRAW A BORDERLINE AS YOU CAN—I AM MERELY A SERVANT.
?
Y... YES...
AND YET MY LORD HAS APPOINTED ME, ONE WHO IS NOT HUMAN, AS HIS GUIDE.
THIS IS BECAUSE HE HAS LEARNED THAT HUMANS ARE TREACHEROUS CREATURES.

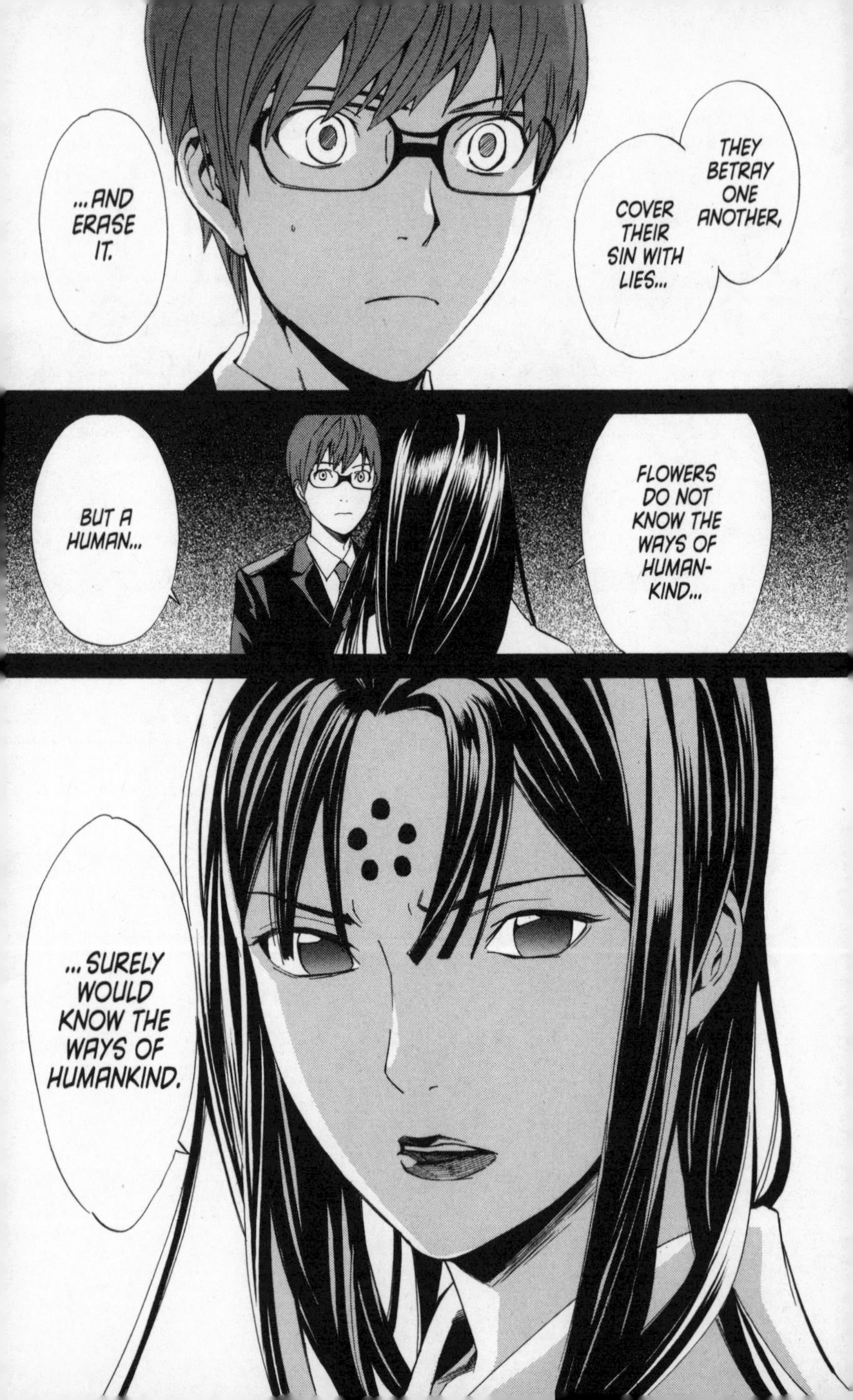
THEY BETRAY ONE ANOTHER, COVER THEIR SIN WITH LIES...
...AND ERASE IT.
FLOWERS DO NOT KNOW THE WAYS OF HUMAN-KIND...
BUT A HUMAN...
...SURELY WOULD KNOW THE WAYS OF HUMANKIND.

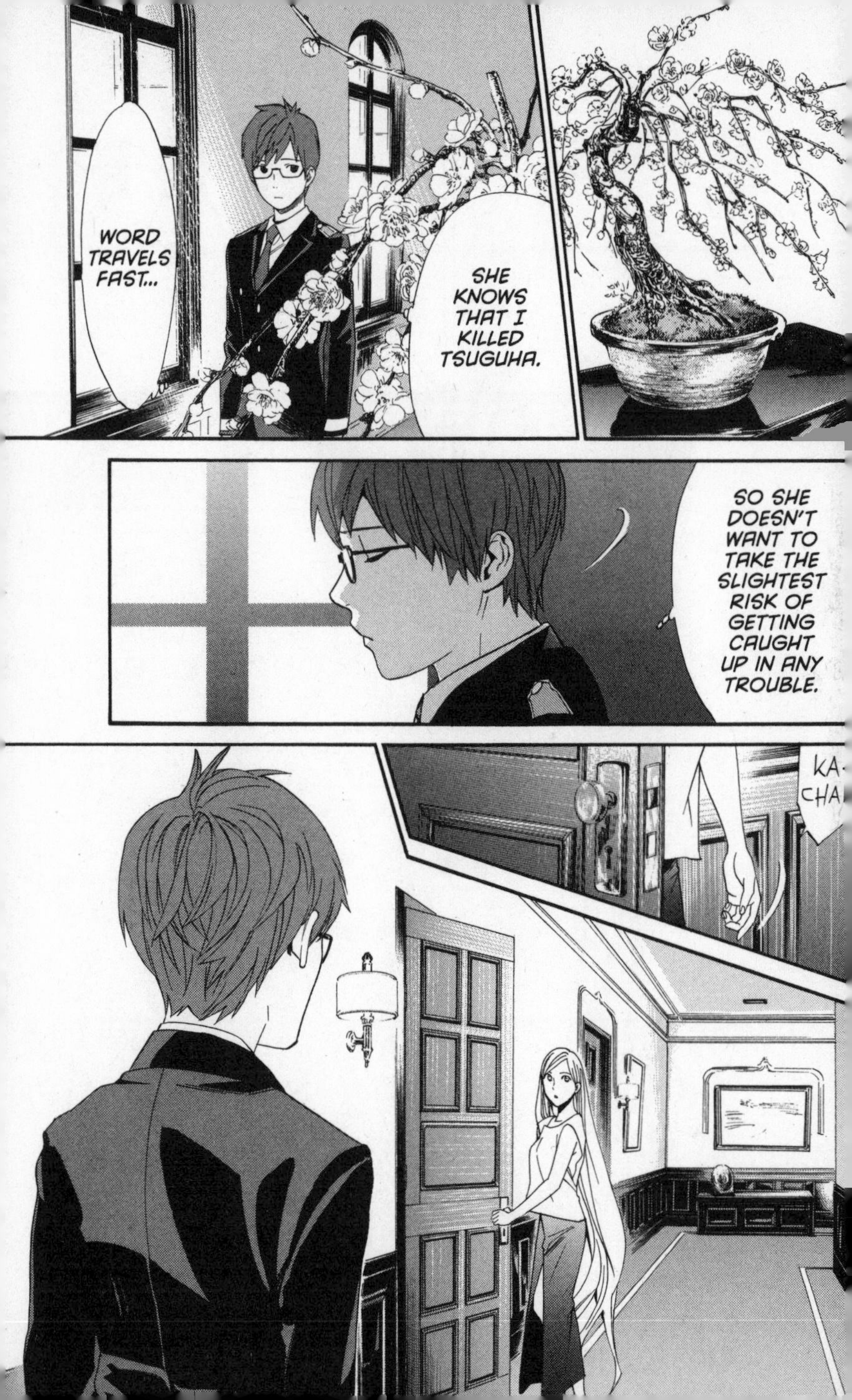
SHE KNOWS THAT I KILLED TSUGUHA.
WORD TRAVELS FAST...
SO SHE DOESN'T WANT TO TAKE THE SLIGHTEST RISK OF GETTING CAUGHT UP IN ANY TROUBLE.
KA-CHA

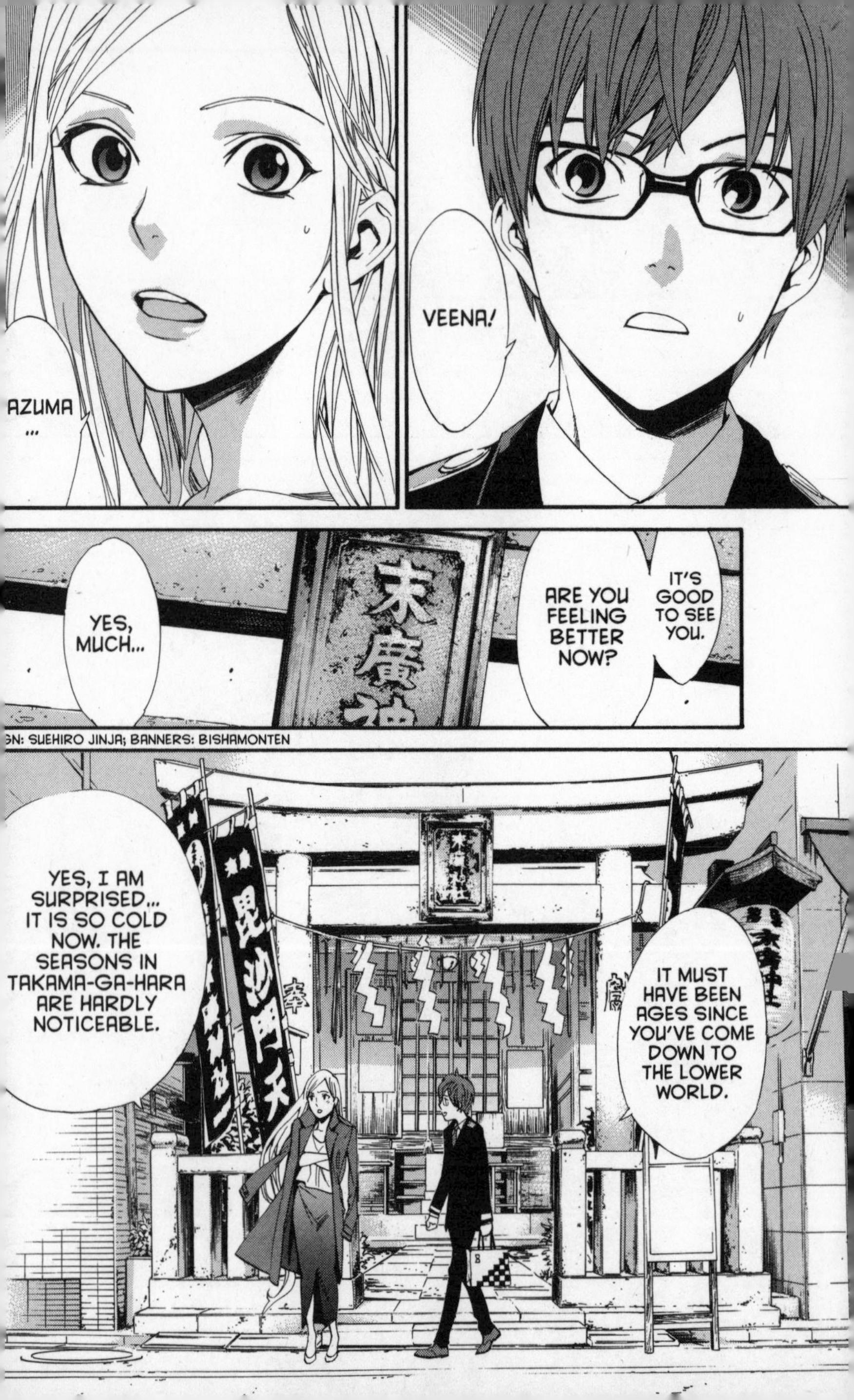
VEENA!
AZUMA ...
IT'S GOOD TO SEE YOU.
ARE YOU FEELING BETTER NOW?
YES, MUCH...
GN: SUEHIRO JINJA; BANNERS: BISHAMONTEN
IT MUST HAVE BEEN AGES SINCE YOU'VE COME DOWN TO THE LOWER WORLD.
YES, I AM SURPRISED... IT IS SO COLD NOW. THE SEASONS IN TAKAMA-GA-HARA ARE HARDLY NOTICEABLE.

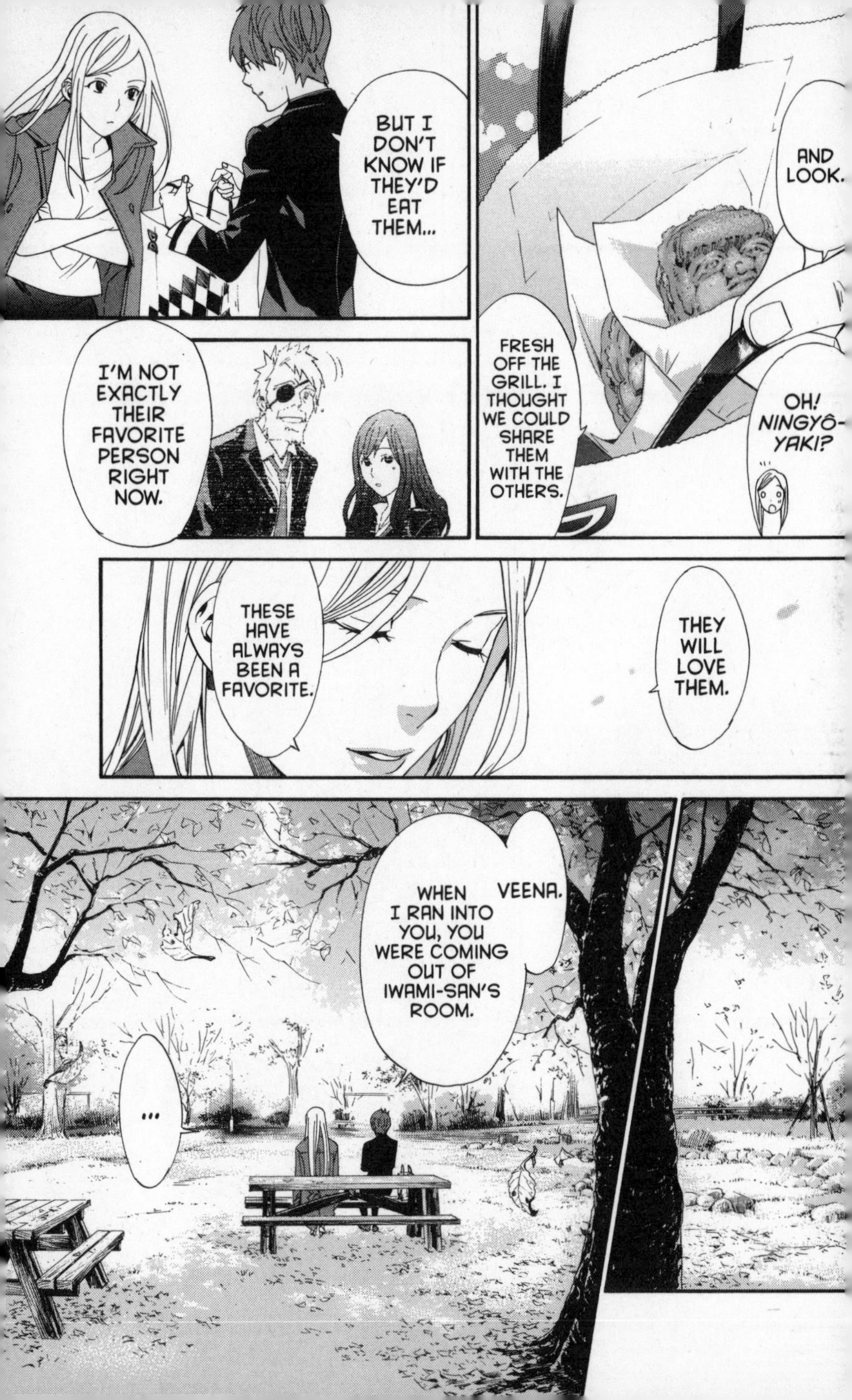
AND LOOK.
OH! NINGYÔ-YAKI?
FRESH OFF THE GRILL. I THOUGHT WE COULD SHARE THEM WITH THE OTHERS.
BUT I DON'T KNOW IF THEY'D EAT THEM...
I'M NOT EXACTLY THEIR FAVORITE PERSON RIGHT NOW.
THEY WILL LOVE THEM.
THESE HAVE ALWAYS BEEN A FAVORITE.
VEENA.
WHEN I RAN INTO YOU, YOU WERE COMING OUT OF IWAMI-SAN'S ROOM.
...

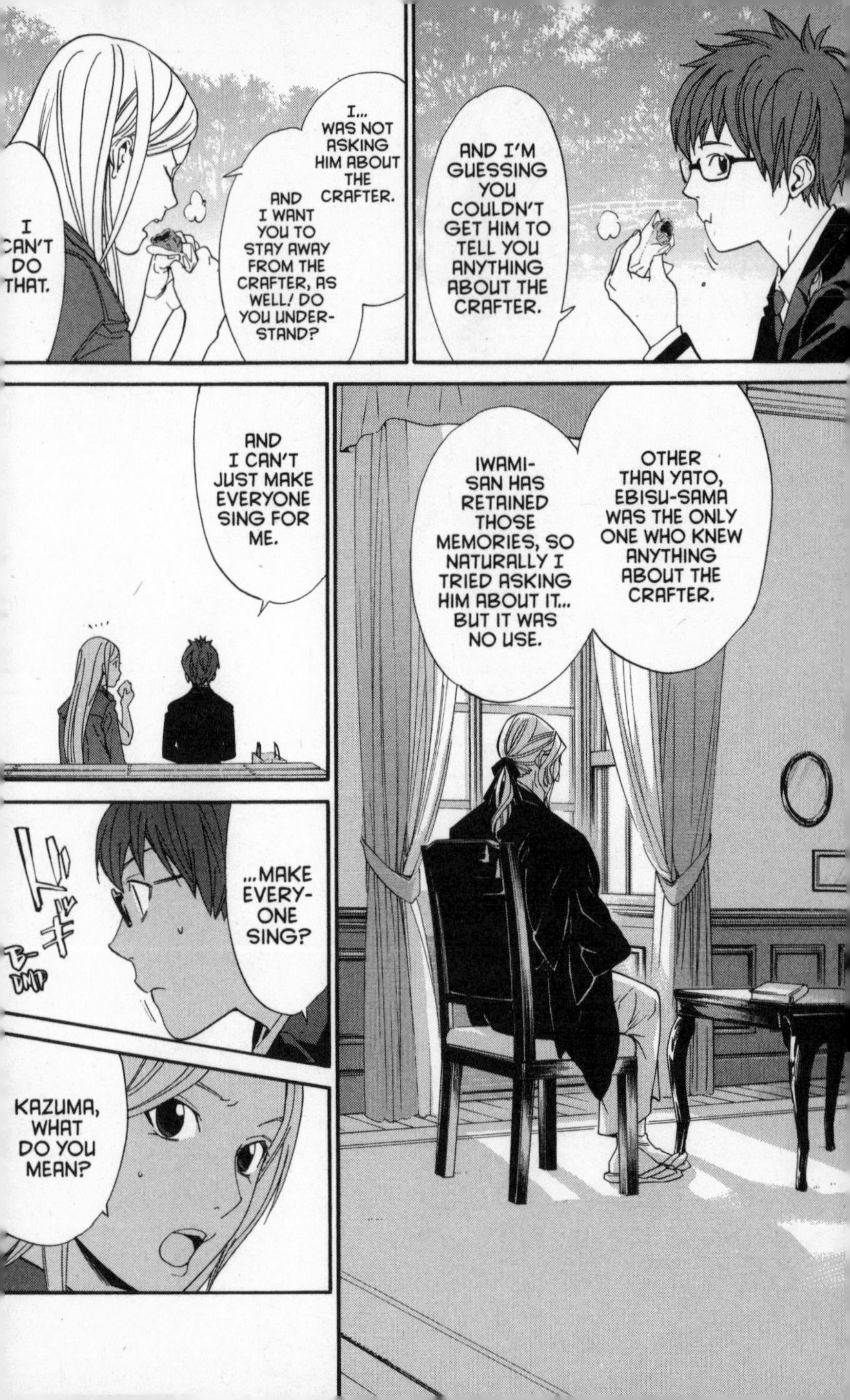

AND I'M GUESSING YOU COULDN'T GET HIM TO TELL YOU ANYTHING ABOUT THE CRAFTER.
I... WAS NOT ASKING HIM ABOUT THE CRAFTER.
AND I WANT YOU TO STAY AWAY FROM THE CRAFTER, AS WELL! DO YOU UNDERSTAND?
I CAN'T DO THAT.
OTHER THAN YATO, EBISU-SAMA WAS THE ONLY ONE WHO KNEW ANYTHING ABOUT THE CRAFTER.
IWAMI-SAN HAS RETAINED THOSE MEMORIES, SO NATURALLY I TRIED ASKING HIM ABOUT IT... BUT IT WAS NO USE.
AND I CAN'T JUST MAKE EVERYONE SING FOR ME.
...MAKE EVERYONE SING?
B-DMP
KAZUMA, WHAT DO YOU MEAN?

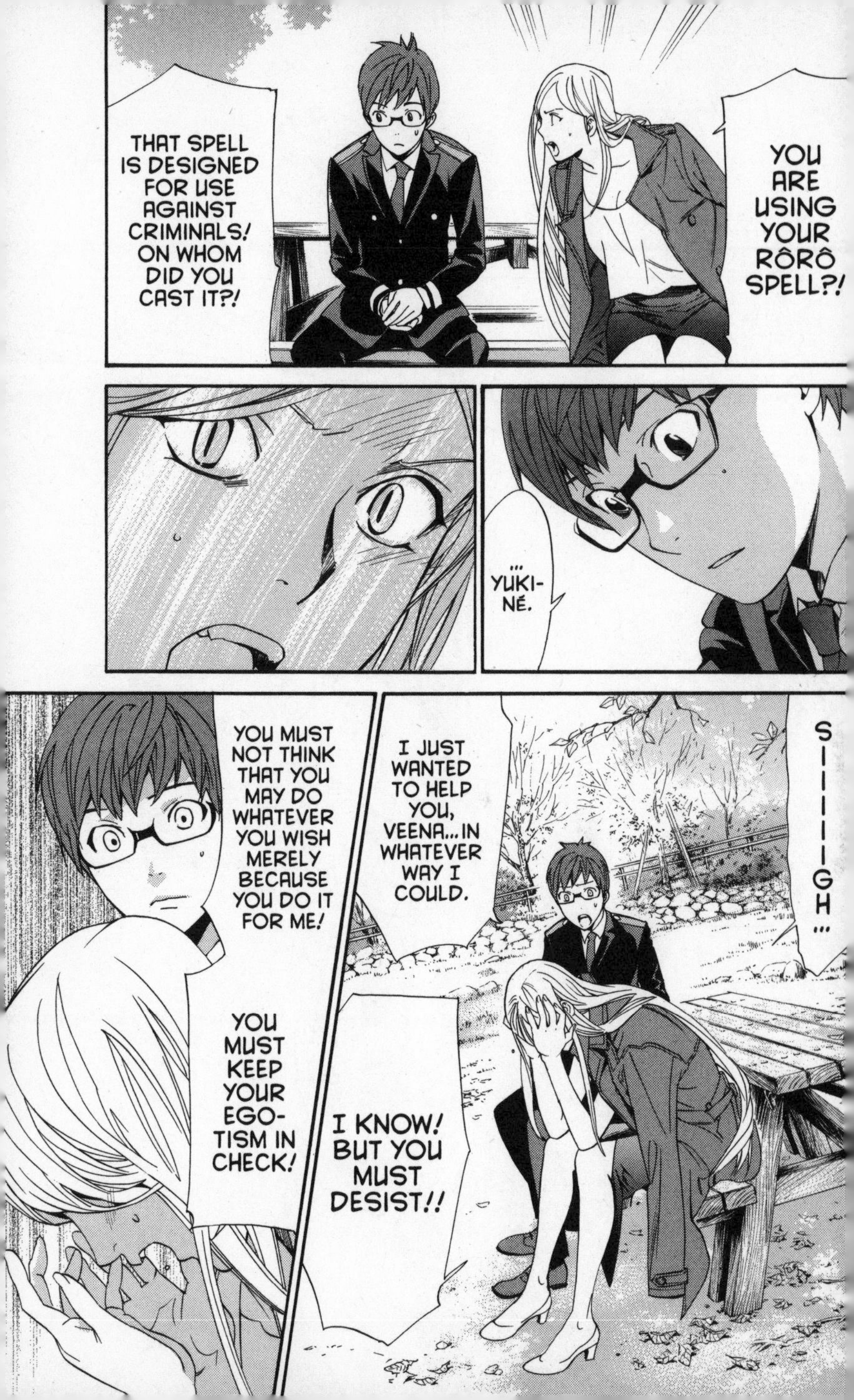

YOU ARE USING YOUR RÔRÔ SPELL?!
THAT SPELL IS DESIGNED FOR USE AGAINST CRIMINALS! ON WHOM DID YOU CAST IT?!
... YUKINÉ.
S-I-I-I-I-GH...
I JUST WANTED TO HELP YOU, VEENA...IN WHATEVER WAY I COULD.
I KNOW! BUT YOU MUST DESIST!!
YOU MUST NOT THINK THAT YOU MAY DO WHATEVER YOU WISH MERELY BECAUSE YOU DO IT FOR ME!
YOU MUST KEEP YOUR EGO-TISM IN CHECK!

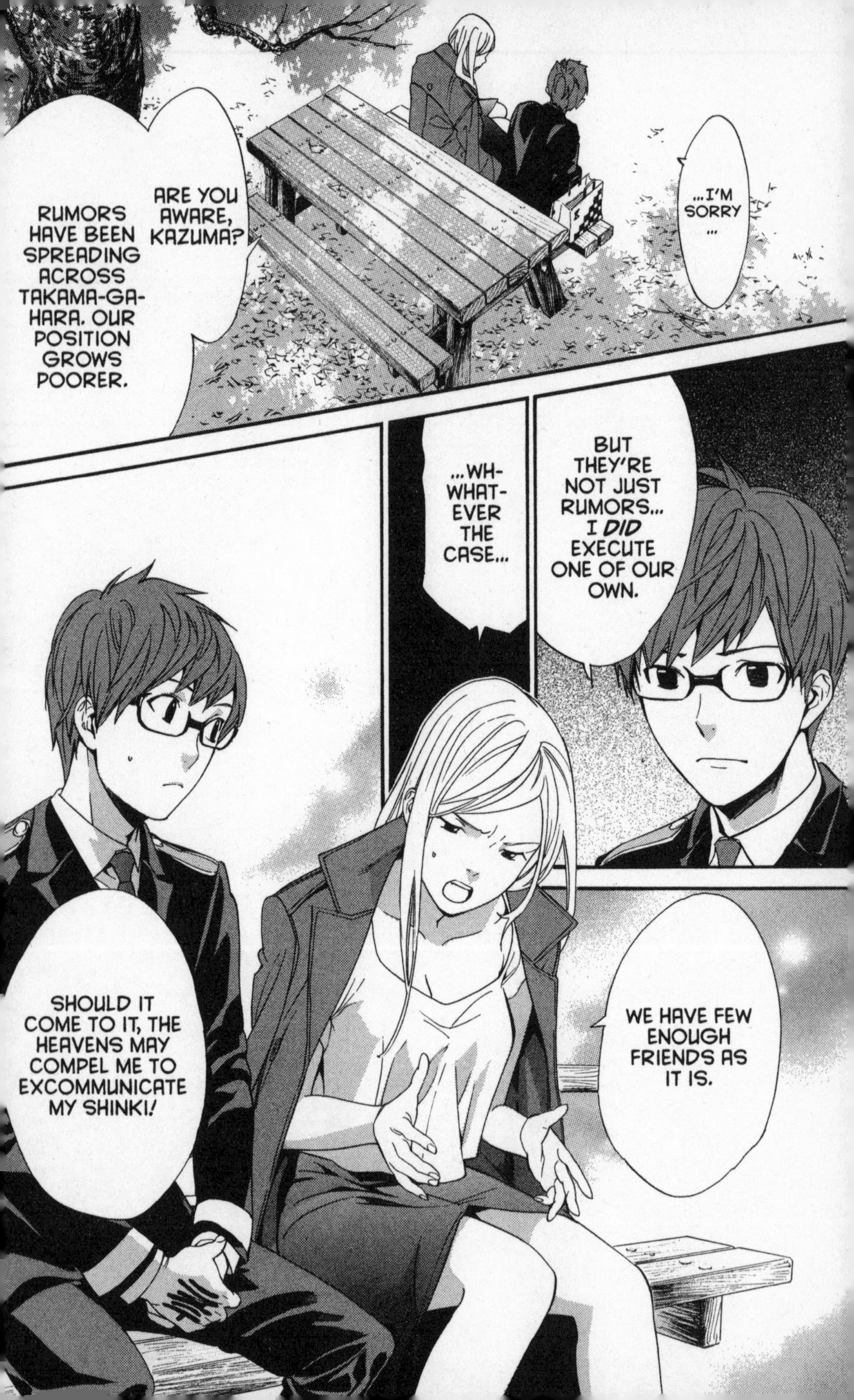
ARE YOU AWARE, KAZUMA?
RUMORS HAVE BEEN SPREADING ACROSS TAKAMA-GA-HARA. OUR POSITION GROWS POORER.
...I'M SORRY ...
BUT THEY'RE NOT JUST RUMORS... I *DID* EXECUTE ONE OF OUR OWN.
...WH-WHATEVER THE CASE...
WE HAVE FEW ENOUGH FRIENDS AS IT IS.
SHOULD IT COME TO IT, THE HEAVENS MAY COMPEL ME TO EXCOMMUNICATE MY SHINKI!

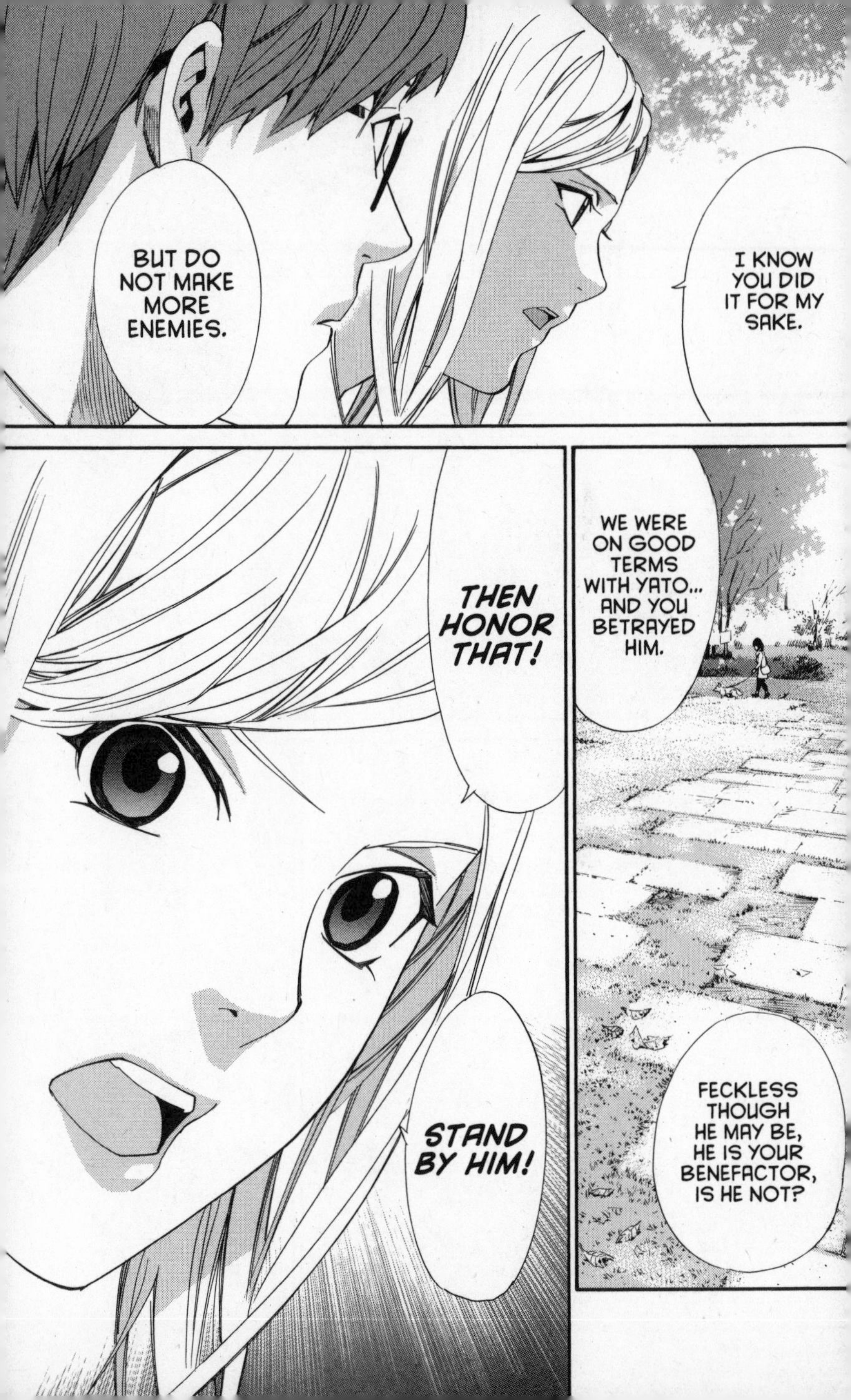
I KNOW YOU DID IT FOR MY SAKE.
BUT DO NOT MAKE MORE ENEMIES.
WE WERE ON GOOD TERMS WITH YATO... AND YOU BETRAYED HIM.
FECKLESS THOUGH HE MAY BE, HE IS YOUR BENEFACTOR, IS HE NOT?
THEN HONOR THAT!
STAND BY HIM!

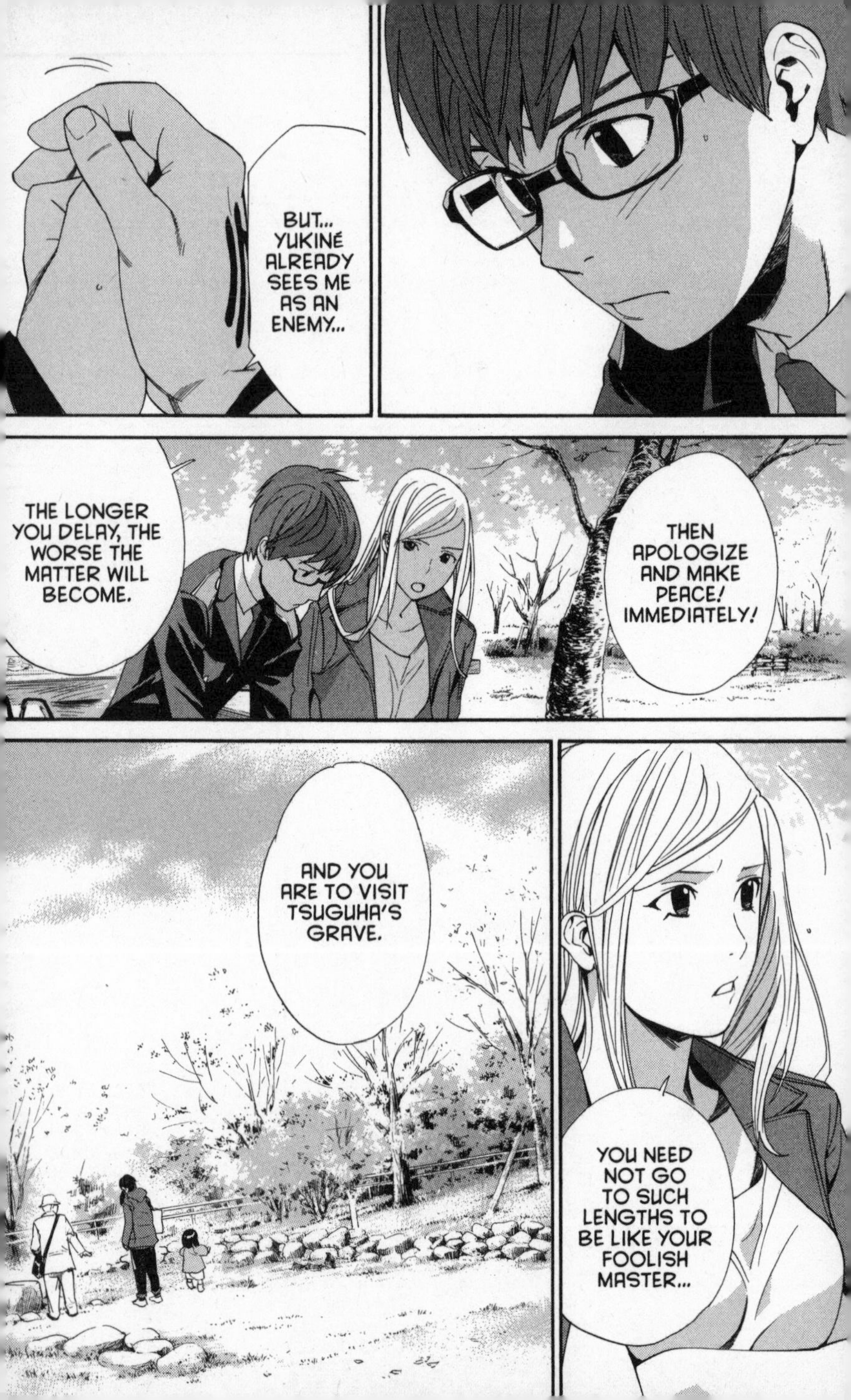
BUT... YUKINÉ ALREADY SEES ME AS AN ENEMY...
THEN APOLOGIZE AND MAKE PEACE! IMMEDIATELY!
THE LONGER YOU DELAY, THE WORSE THE MATTER WILL BECOME.
YOU NEED NOT GO TO SUCH LENGTHS TO BE LIKE YOUR FOOLISH MASTER...
AND YOU ARE TO VISIT TSUGUHA'S GRAVE.

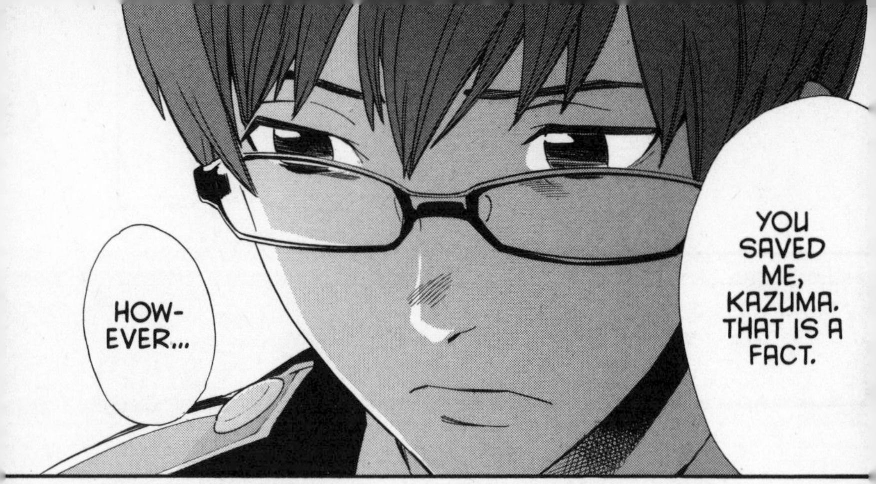
YOU SAVED ME, KAZUMA. THAT IS A FACT.
HOW-EVER...

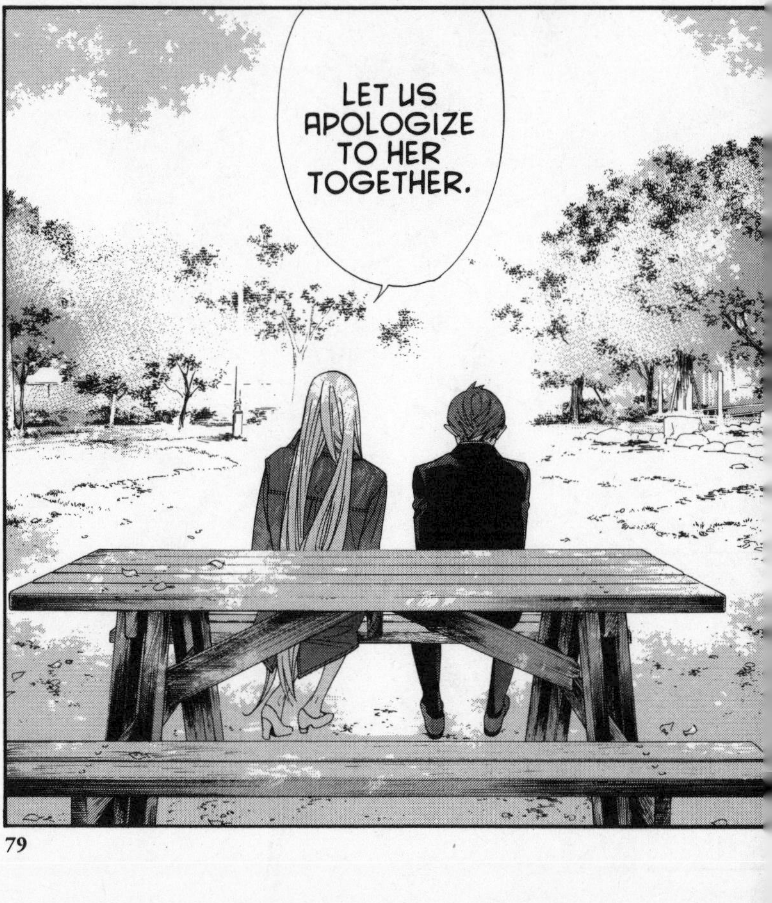
LET US APOLOGIZE TO HER TOGETHER.

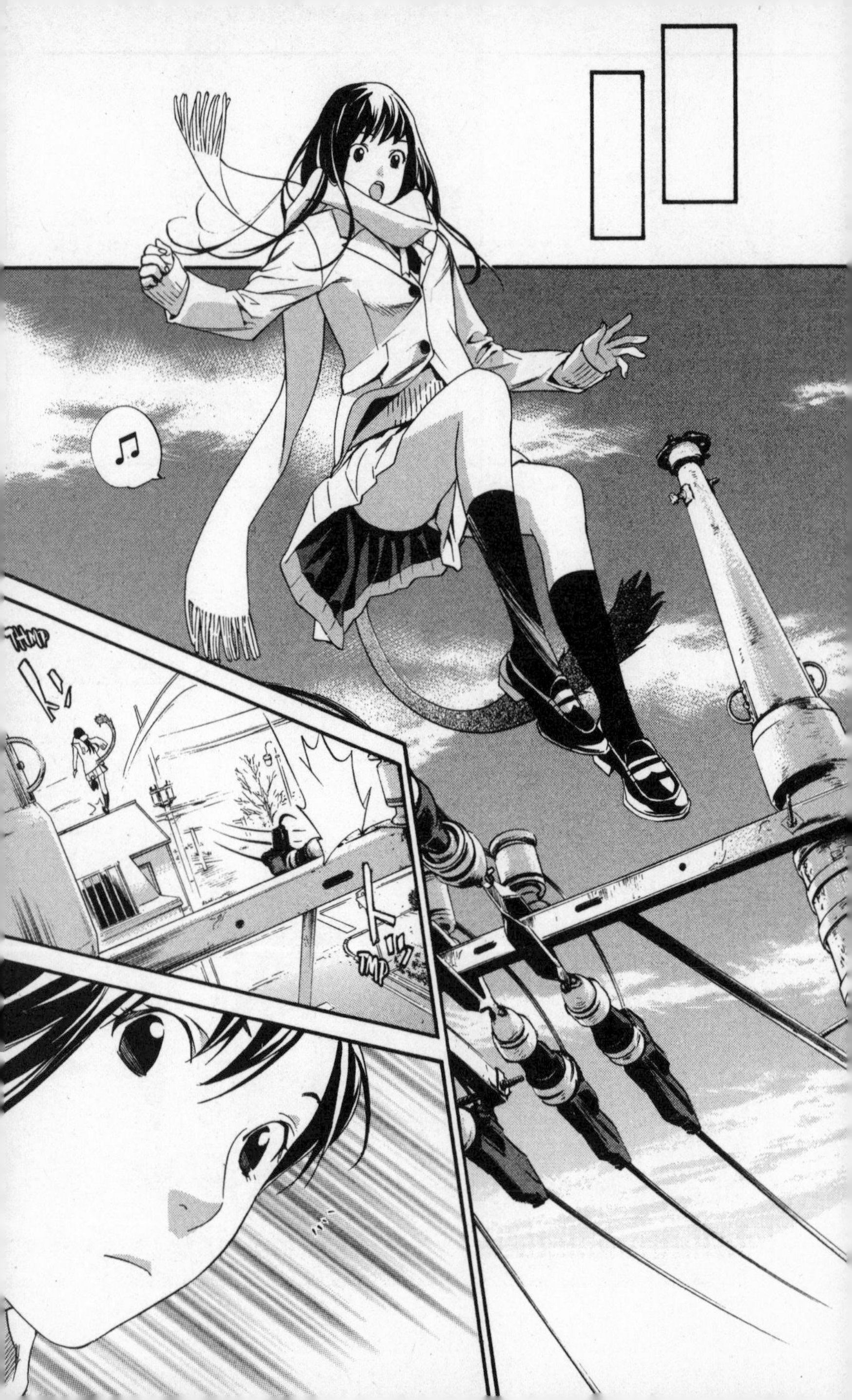
♫
THMP
TMP

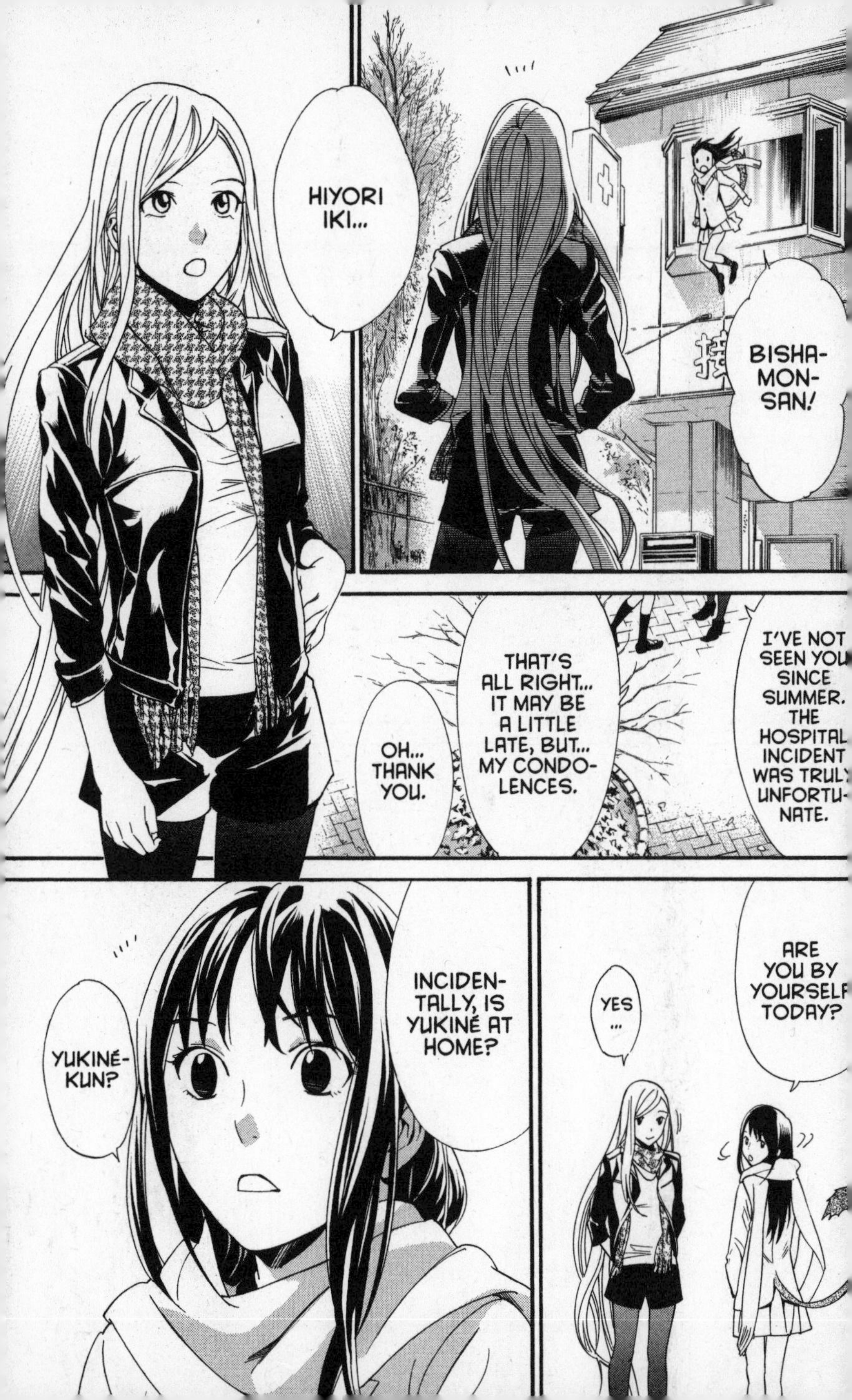
BISHA-MON-SAN!
I'VE NOT SEEN YOU SINCE SUMMER. THE HOSPITAL INCIDENT WAS TRULY UNFORTU-NATE.
THAT'S ALL RIGHT... IT MAY BE A LITTLE LATE, BUT... MY CONDO-LENCES.
OH... THANK YOU.
HIYORI IKI...
ARE YOU BY YOURSELF TODAY?
YES ...
INCIDEN-TALLY, IS YUKINÉ AT HOME?
YUKINÉ-KUN?

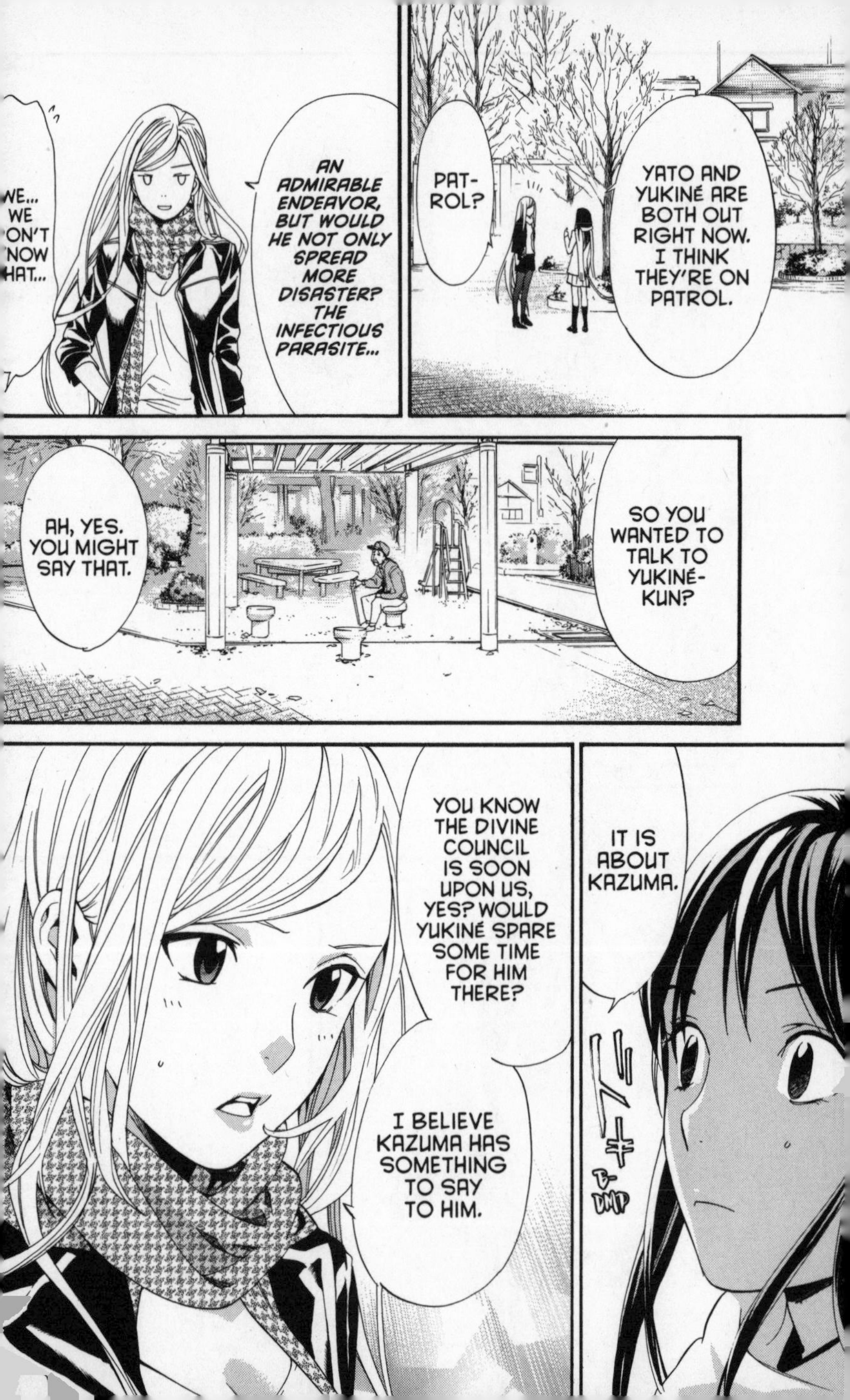
YATO AND YUKINÉ ARE BOTH OUT RIGHT NOW. I THINK THEY'RE ON PATROL.
PAT-ROL?
AN ADMIRABLE ENDEAVOR, BUT WOULD HE NOT ONLY SPREAD MORE DISASTER? THE INFECTIOUS PARASITE...
WE... WE ON'T NOW HAT...
SO YOU WANTED TO TALK TO YUKINÉ-KUN?
AH, YES. YOU MIGHT SAY THAT.
IT IS ABOUT KAZUMA.
B-DMP
YOU KNOW THE DIVINE COUNCIL IS SOON UPON US, YES? WOULD YUKINÉ SPARE SOME TIME FOR HIM THERE?
I BELIEVE KAZUMA HAS SOMETHING TO SAY TO HIM.

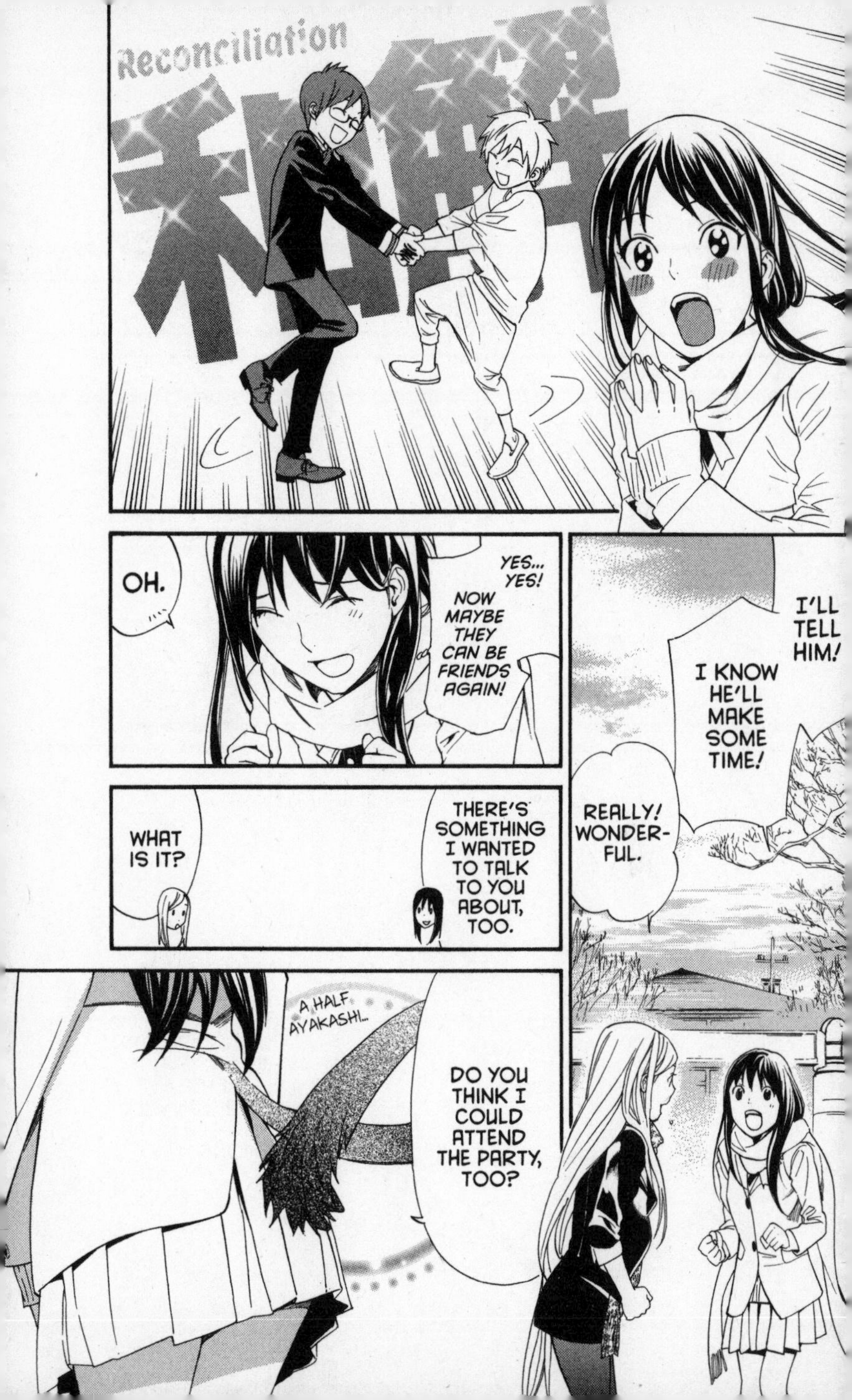
Reconciliation
和解
I'LL TELL HIM!
I KNOW HE'LL MAKE SOME TIME!
REALLY! WONDERFUL.
YES... YES!
NOW MAYBE THEY CAN BE FRIENDS AGAIN!
OH.
THERE'S SOMETHING I WANTED TO TALK TO YOU ABOUT, TOO.
WHAT IS IT?
DO YOU THINK I COULD ATTEND THE PARTY, TOO?
A HALF AYAKASHI...

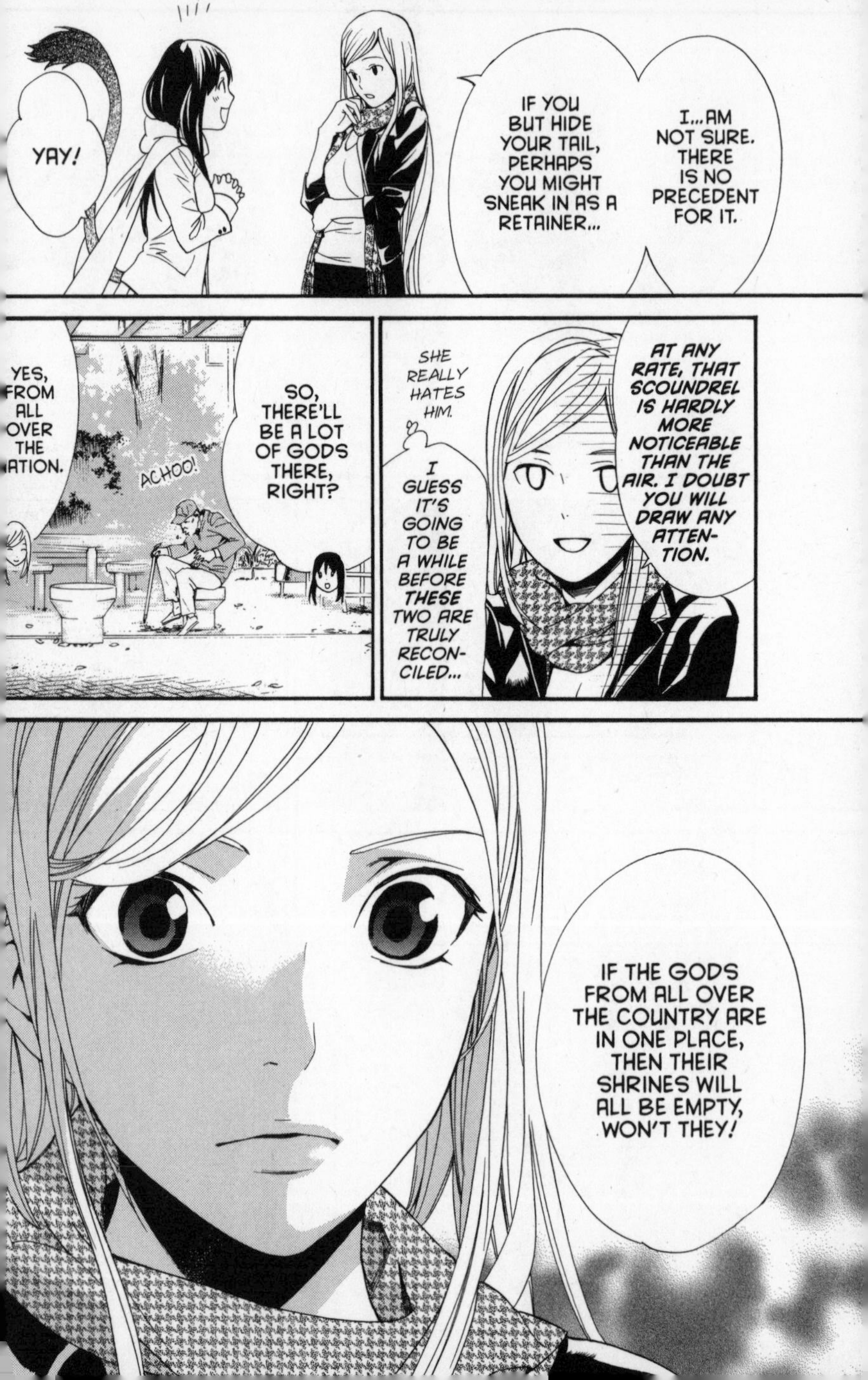
I...AM NOT SURE. THERE IS NO PRECEDENT FOR IT.
IF YOU BUT HIDE YOUR TAIL, PERHAPS YOU MIGHT SNEAK IN AS A RETAINER...
YAY!
AT ANY RATE, THAT SCOUNDREL IS HARDLY MORE NOTICEABLE THAN THE AIR. I DOUBT YOU WILL DRAW ANY ATTENTION.
SHE REALLY HATES HIM.
I GUESS IT'S GOING TO BE A WHILE BEFORE THESE TWO ARE TRULY RECONCILED...
SO, THERE'LL BE A LOT OF GODS THERE, RIGHT?
ACHOO!
YES, FROM ALL OVER THE ATION.
IF THE GODS FROM ALL OVER THE COUNTRY ARE IN ONE PLACE, THEN THEIR SHRINES WILL ALL BE EMPTY, WON'T THEY!

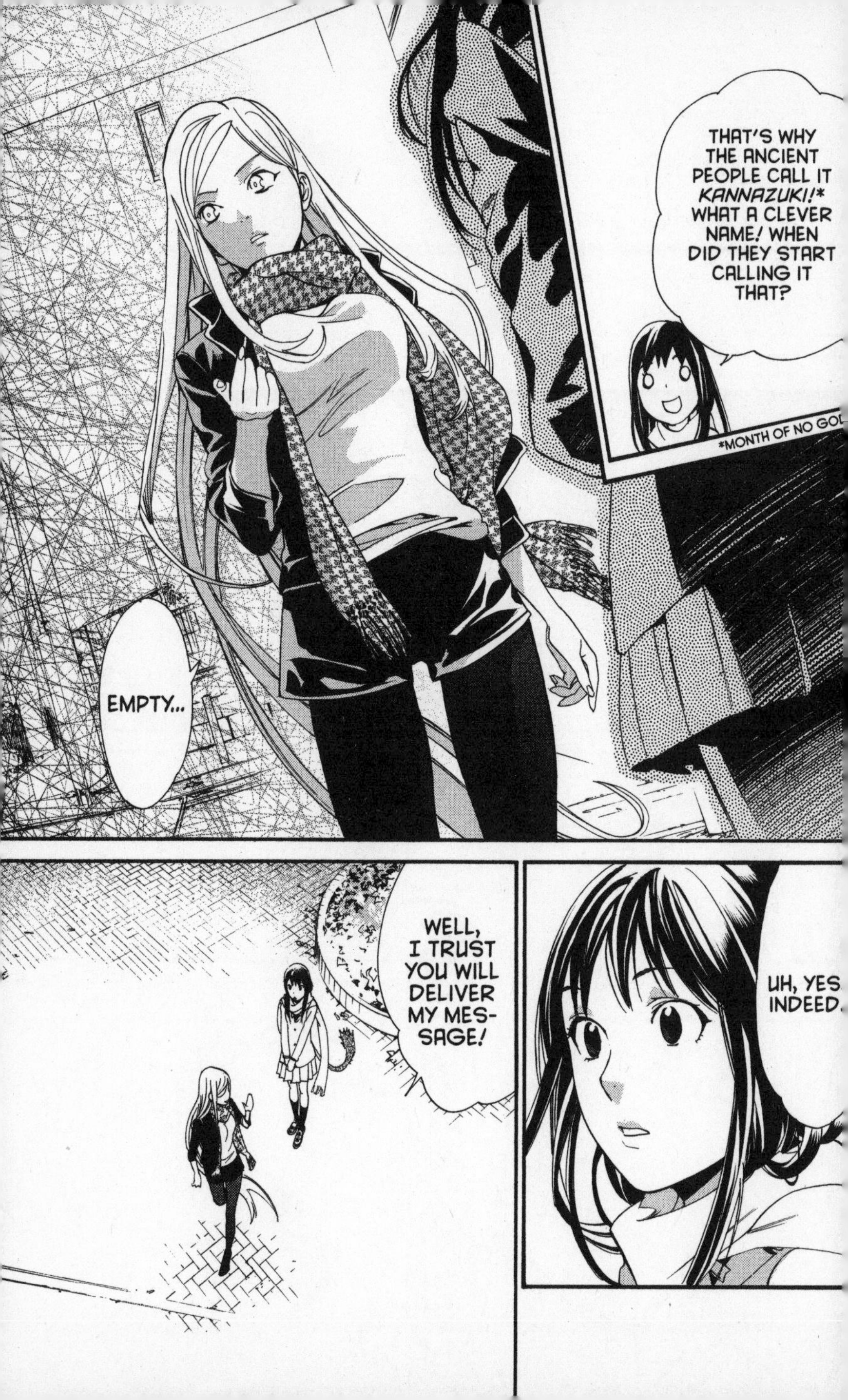
THAT'S WHY THE ANCIENT PEOPLE CALL IT *KANNAZUKI!** WHAT A CLEVER NAME! WHEN DID THEY START CALLING IT THAT?
*MONTH OF NO GOD
EMPTY...
UH, YES INDEED.
WELL, I TRUST YOU WILL DELIVER MY MES-SAGE!

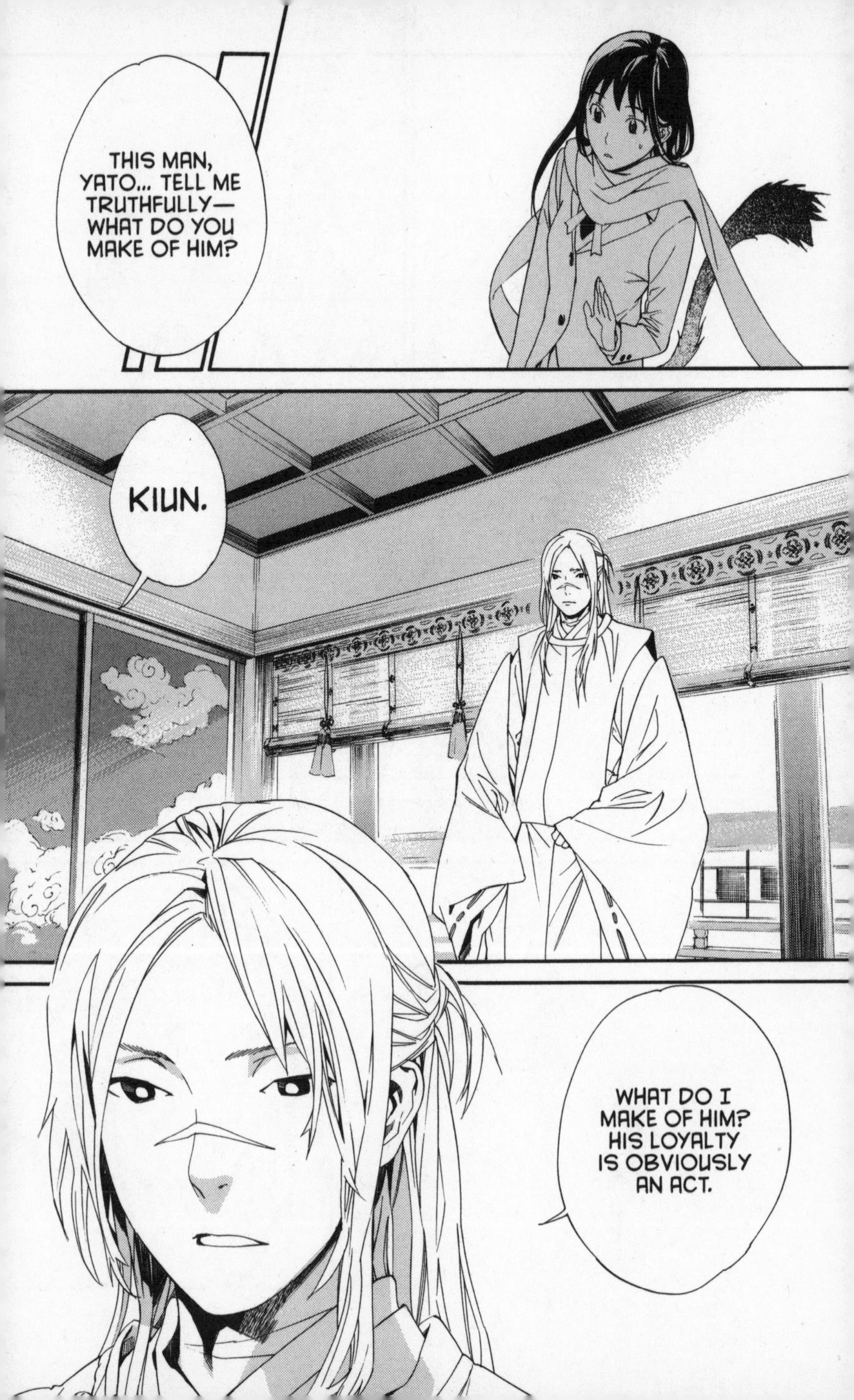
THIS MAN, YATO... TELL ME TRUTHFULLY— WHAT DO YOU MAKE OF HIM?
KIUN.
WHAT DO I MAKE OF HIM? HIS LOYALTY IS OBVIOUSLY AN ACT.

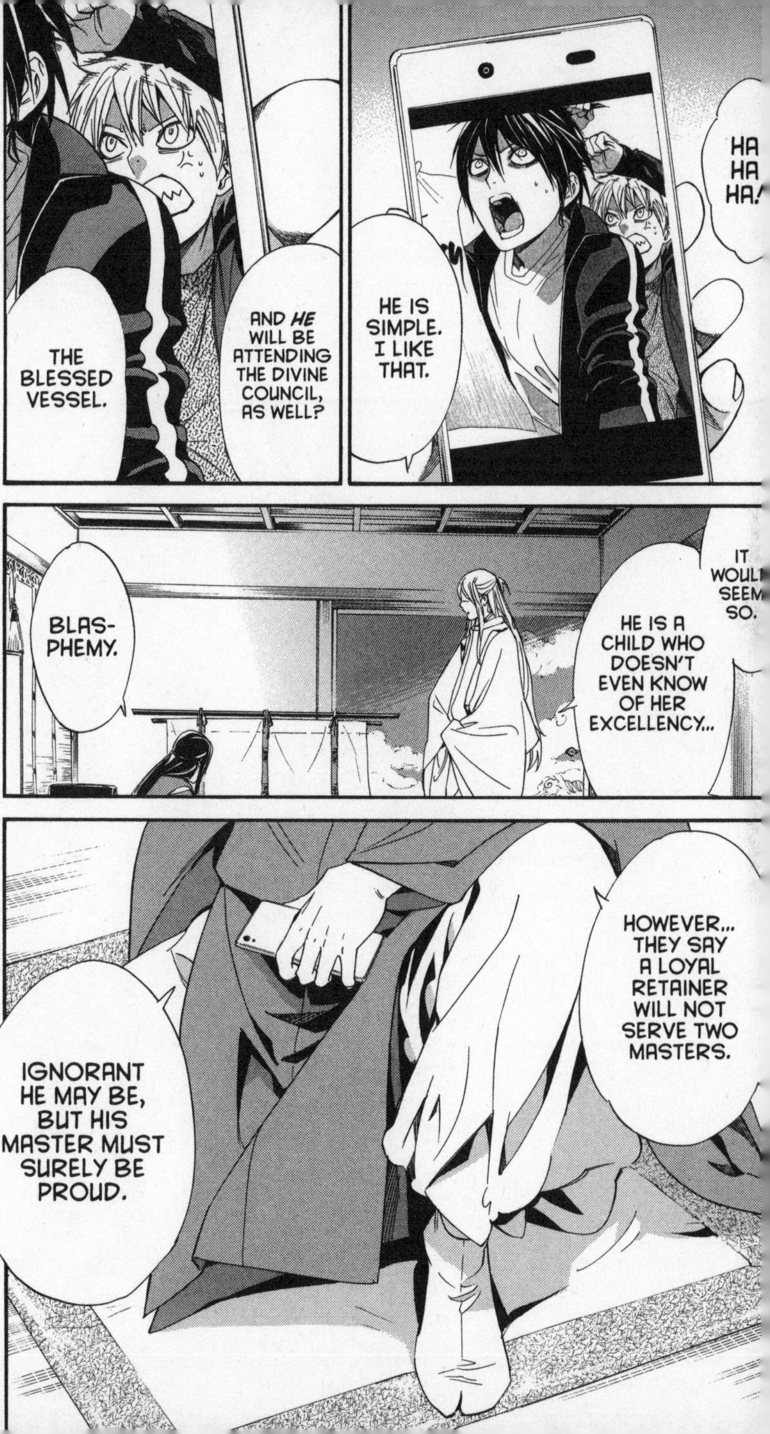
HA HA HA!
HE IS SIMPLE. I LIKE THAT.
AND *HE* WILL BE ATTENDING THE DIVINE COUNCIL, AS WELL?
THE BLESSED VESSEL.
IT WOUL SEEM SO.
HE IS A CHILD WHO DOESN'T EVEN KNOW OF HER EXCELLENCY...
BLAS-PHEMY.
HOWEVER... THEY SAY A LOYAL RETAINER WILL NOT SERVE TWO MASTERS.
IGNORANT HE MAY BE, BUT HIS MASTER MUST SURELY BE PROUD.

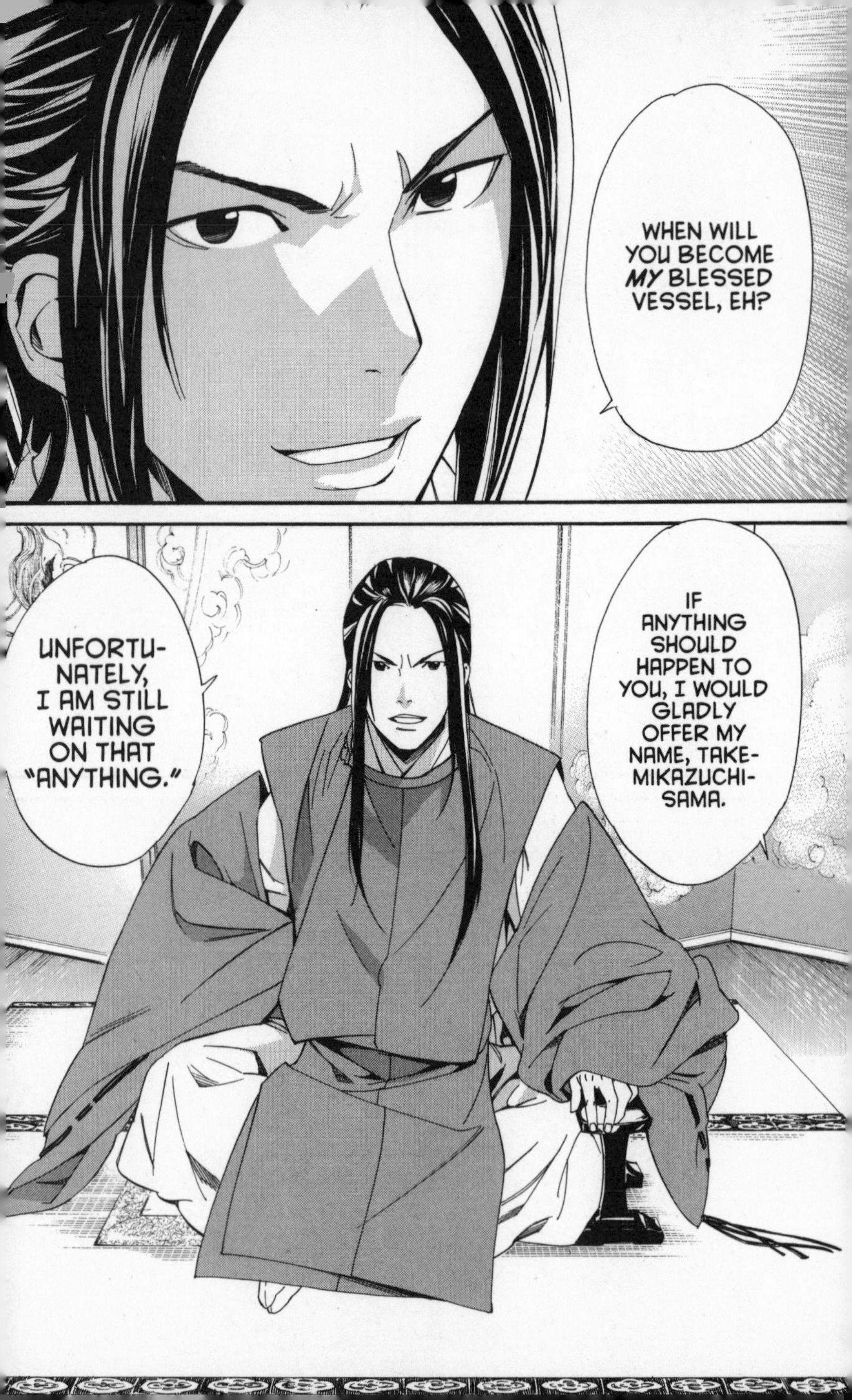
WHEN WILL YOU BECOME *MY* BLESSED VESSEL, EH?
IF ANYTHING SHOULD HAPPEN TO YOU, I WOULD GLADLY OFFER MY NAME, TAKE-MIKAZUCHI-SAMA.
UNFORTU-NATELY, I AM STILL WAITING ON THAT "ANYTHING."

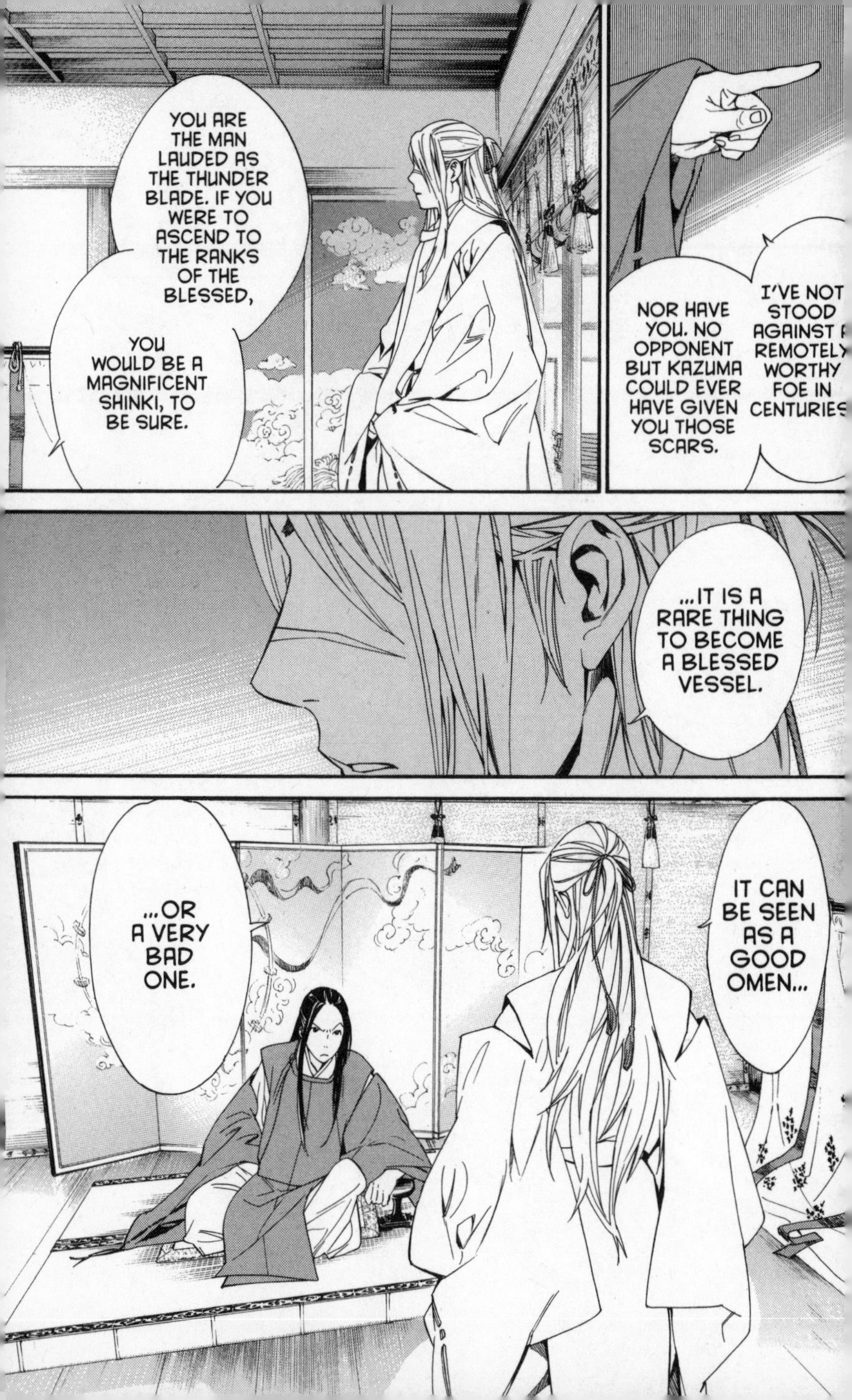
I'VE NOT STOOD AGAINST REMOTELY WORTHY FOE IN CENTURIES
NOR HAVE YOU. NO OPPONENT BUT KAZUMA COULD EVER HAVE GIVEN YOU THOSE SCARS.
YOU ARE THE MAN LAUDED AS THE THUNDER BLADE. IF YOU WERE TO ASCEND TO THE RANKS OF THE BLESSED,
YOU WOULD BE A MAGNIFICENT SHINKI, TO BE SURE.
...IT IS A RARE THING TO BECOME A BLESSED VESSEL.
IT CAN BE SEEN AS A GOOD OMEN...
...OR A VERY BAD ONE.

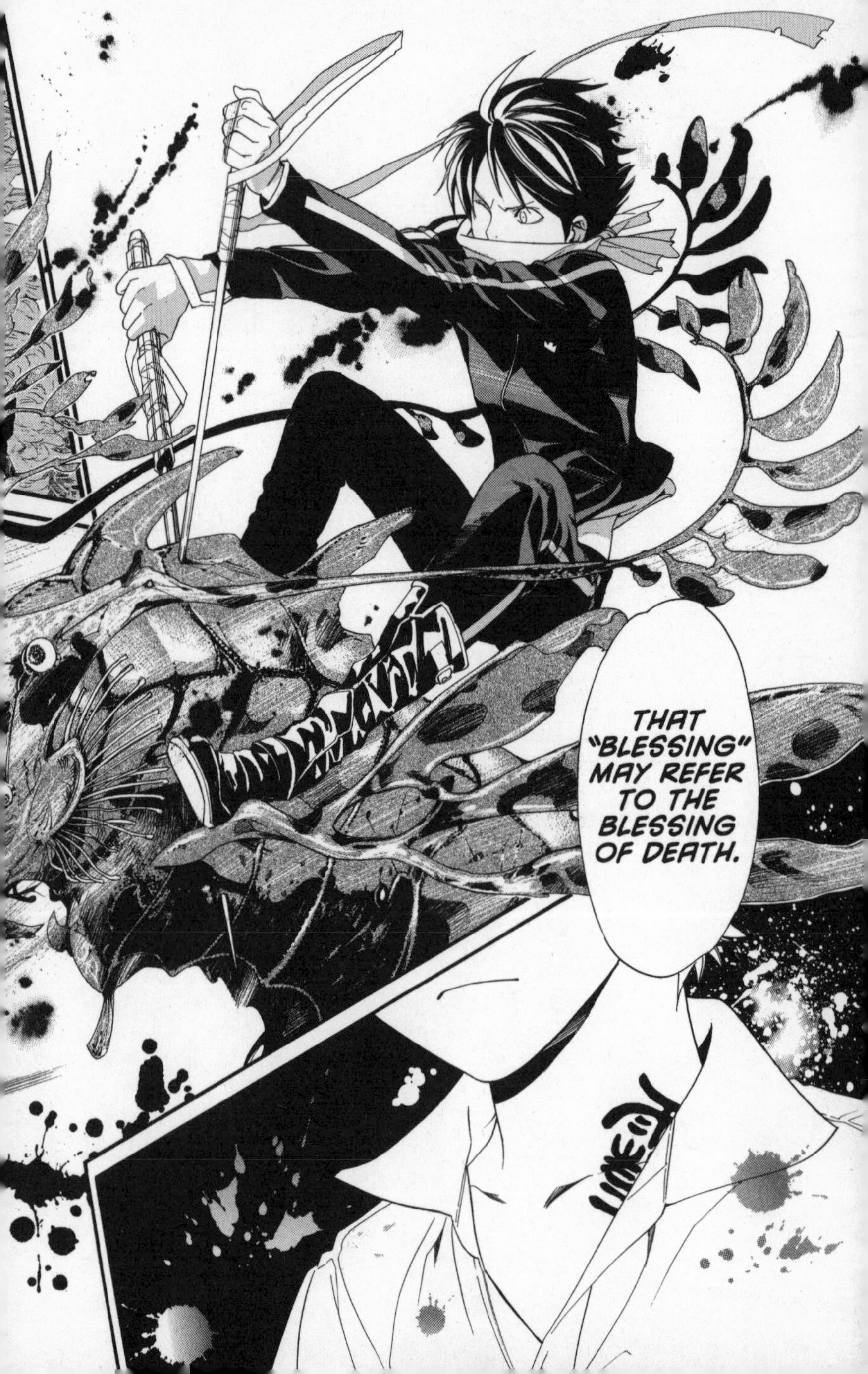
THAT "BLESSING" MAY REFER TO THE BLESSING OF DEATH.

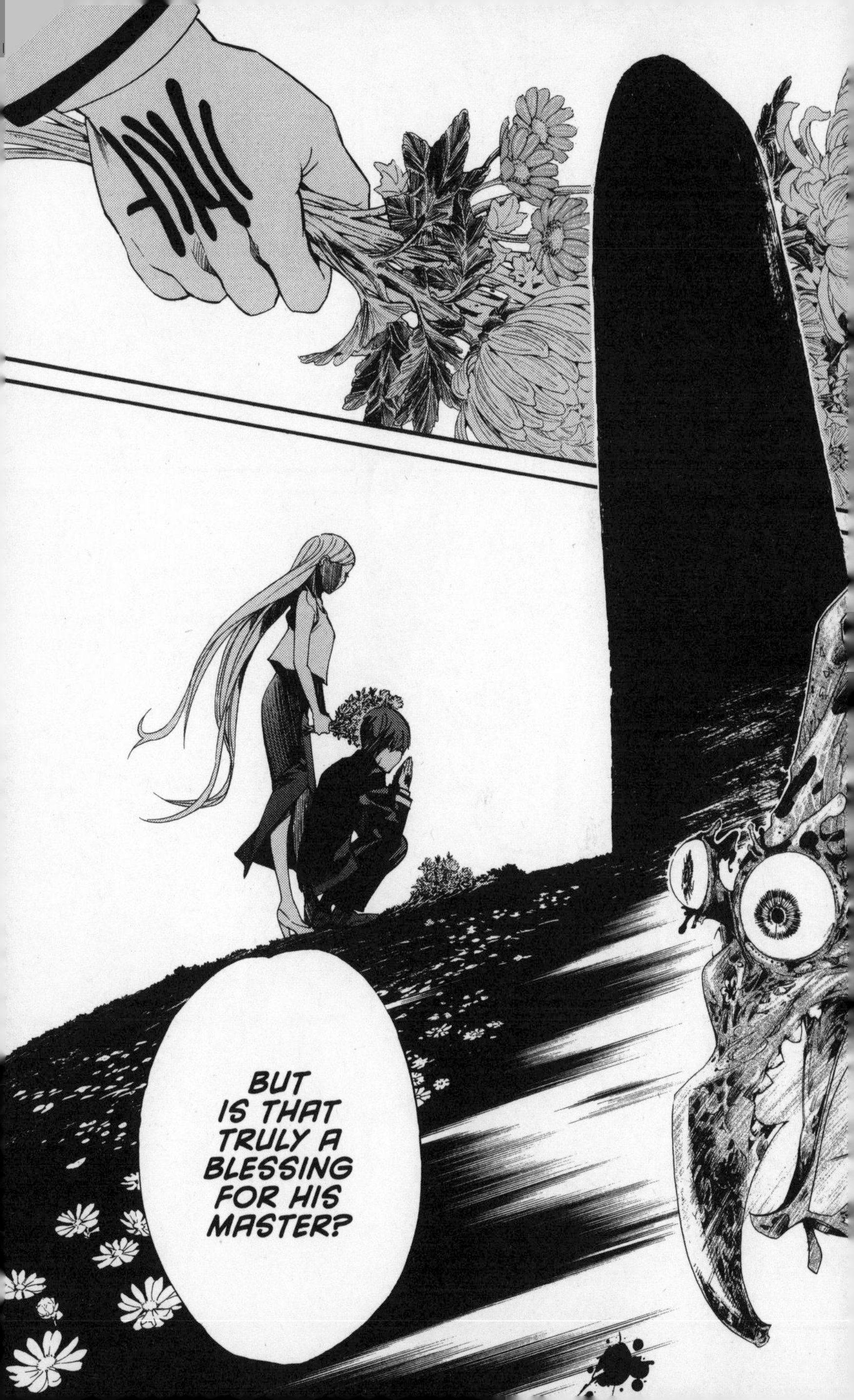
BUT IS THAT TRULY A BLESSING FOR HIS MASTER?

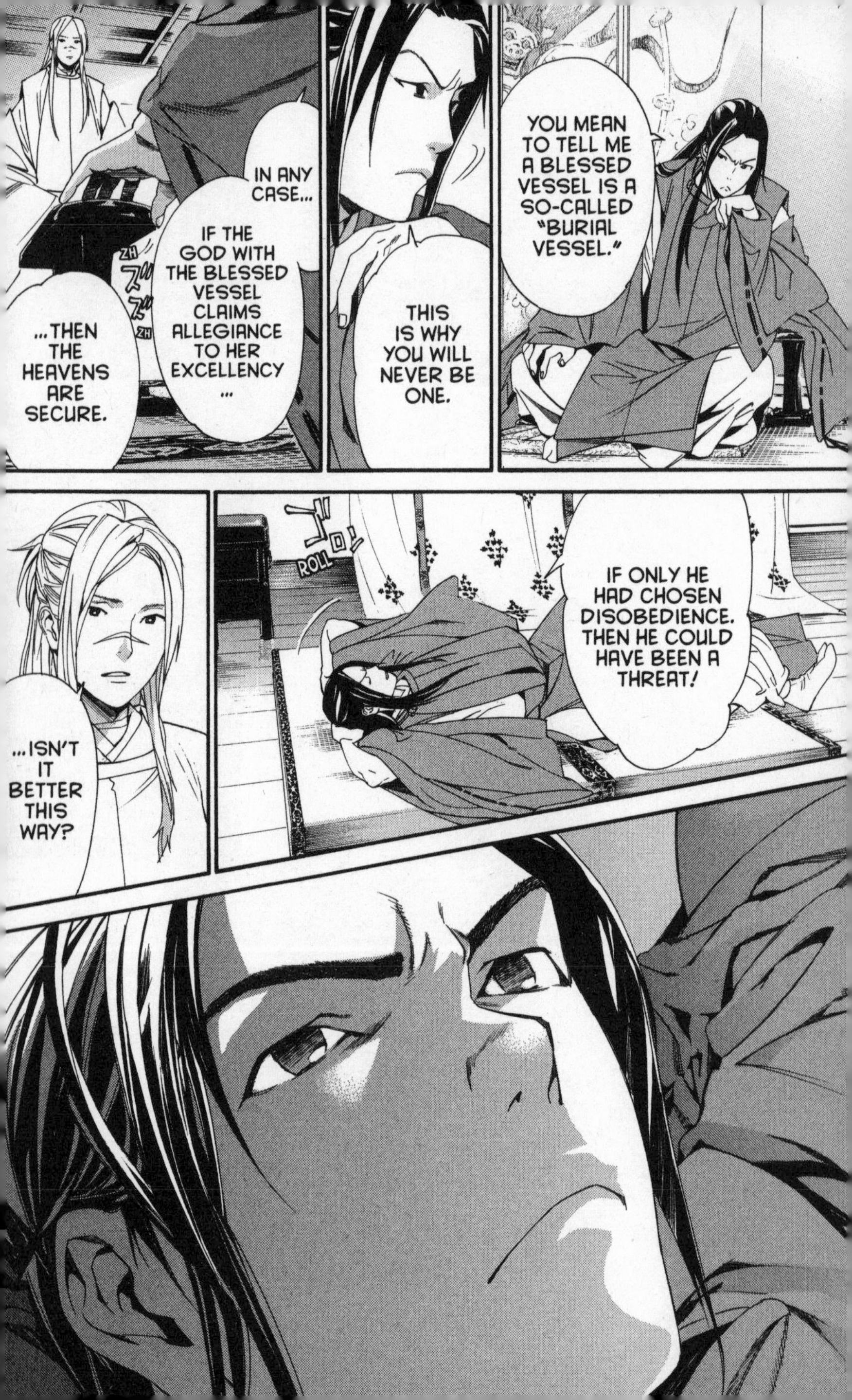
YOU MEAN TO TELL ME A BLESSED VESSEL IS A SO-CALLED "BURIAL VESSEL."
THIS IS WHY YOU WILL NEVER BE ONE.
IN ANY CASE...
IF THE GOD WITH THE BLESSED VESSEL CLAIMS ALLEGIANCE TO HER EXCELLENCY ...
ZH ズズ ZH
...THEN THE HEAVENS ARE SECURE.
ゴロッ ROLL
IF ONLY HE HAD CHOSEN DISOBEDIENCE. THEN HE COULD HAVE BEEN A THREAT!
...ISN'T IT BETTER THIS WAY?

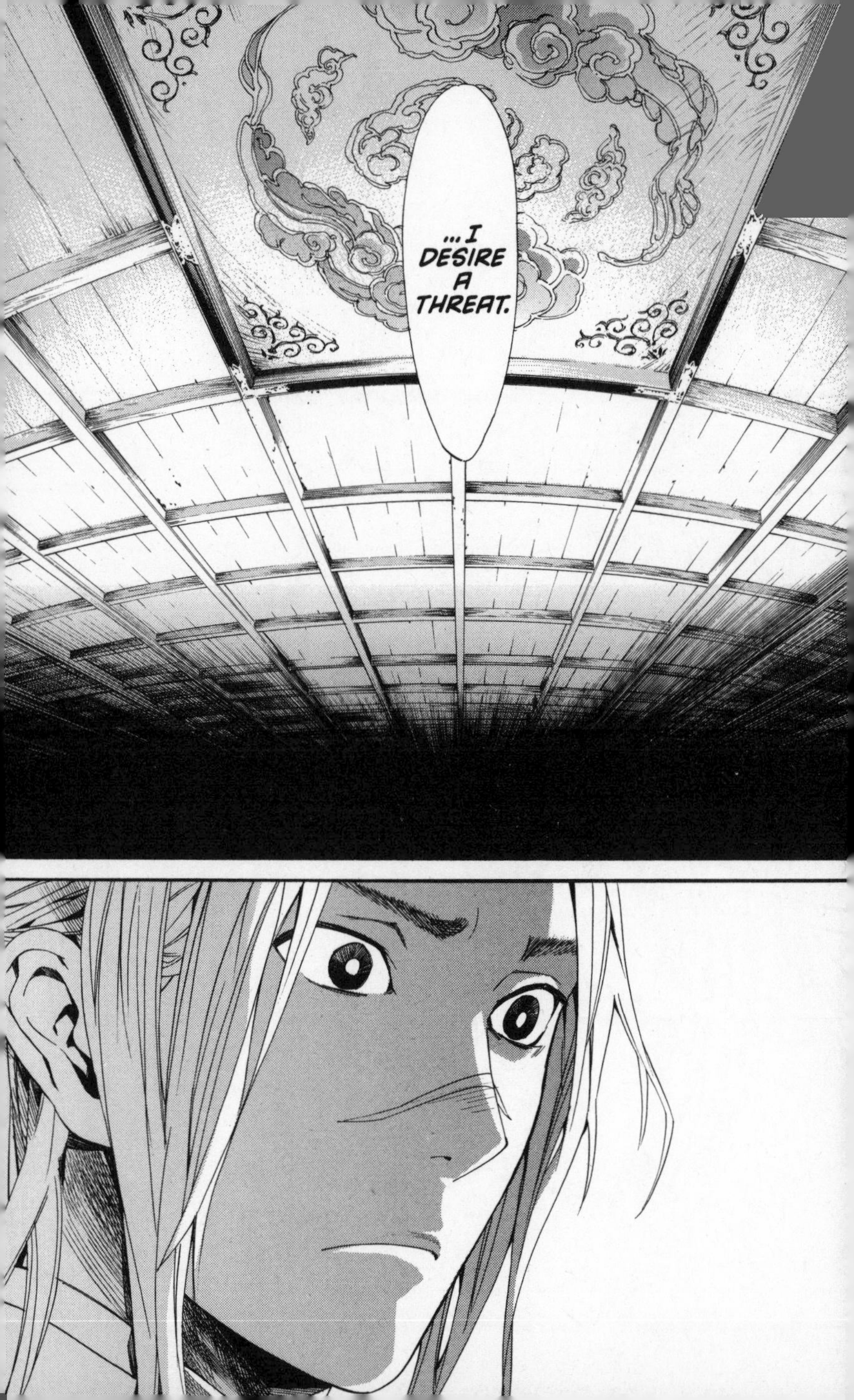
...I DESIRE A THREAT.

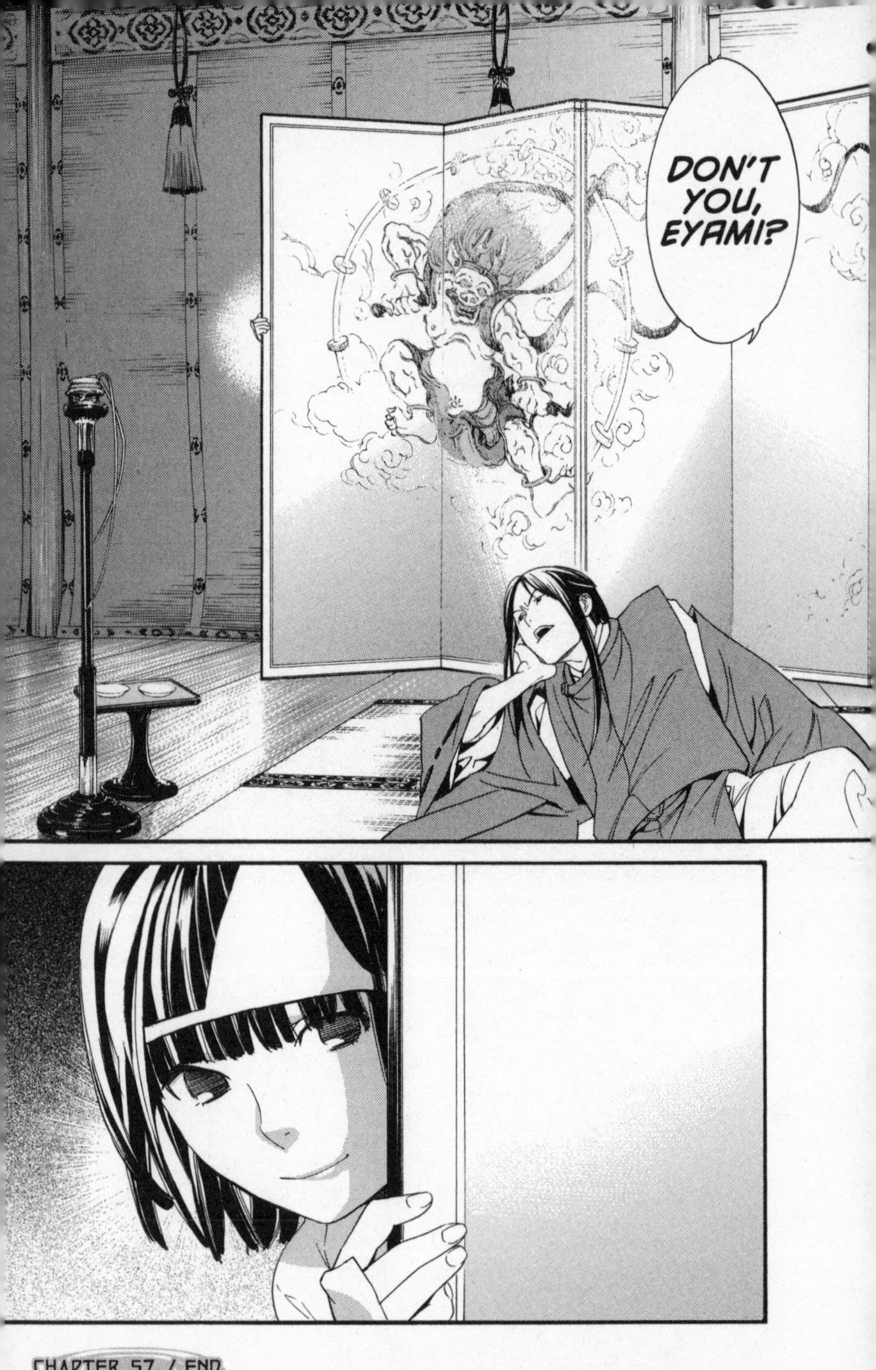
DON'T YOU, EYAMI?

CHAPTER 57 / END

野

良

神

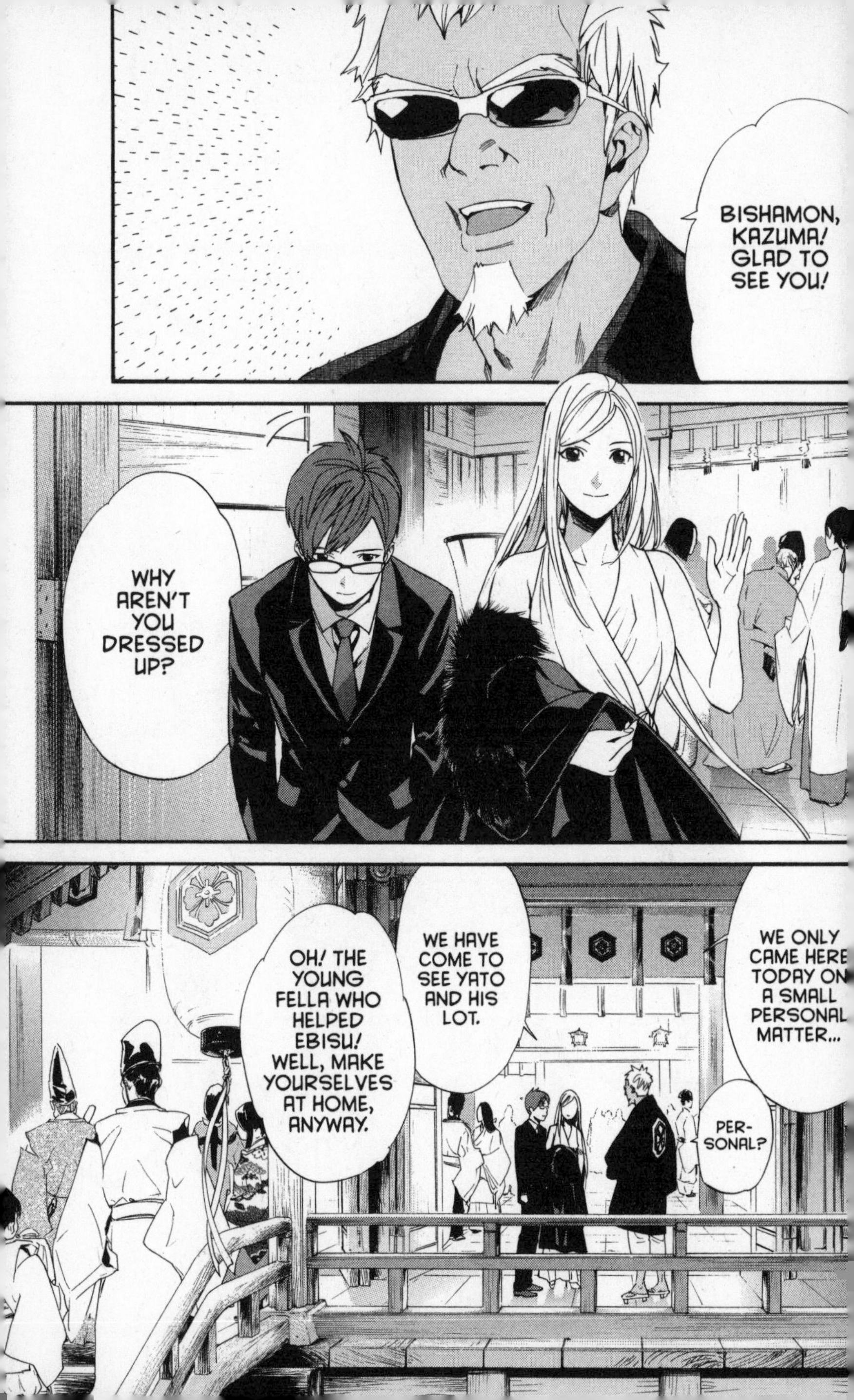
BISHAMON, KAZUMA! GLAD TO SEE YOU!
WHY AREN'T YOU DRESSED UP?
WE ONLY CAME HERE TODAY ON A SMALL PERSONAL MATTER...
PER-SONAL?
WE HAVE COME TO SEE YATO AND HIS LOT.
OH! THE YOUNG FELLA WHO HELPED EBISU! WELL, MAKE YOURSELVES AT HOME, ANYWAY.

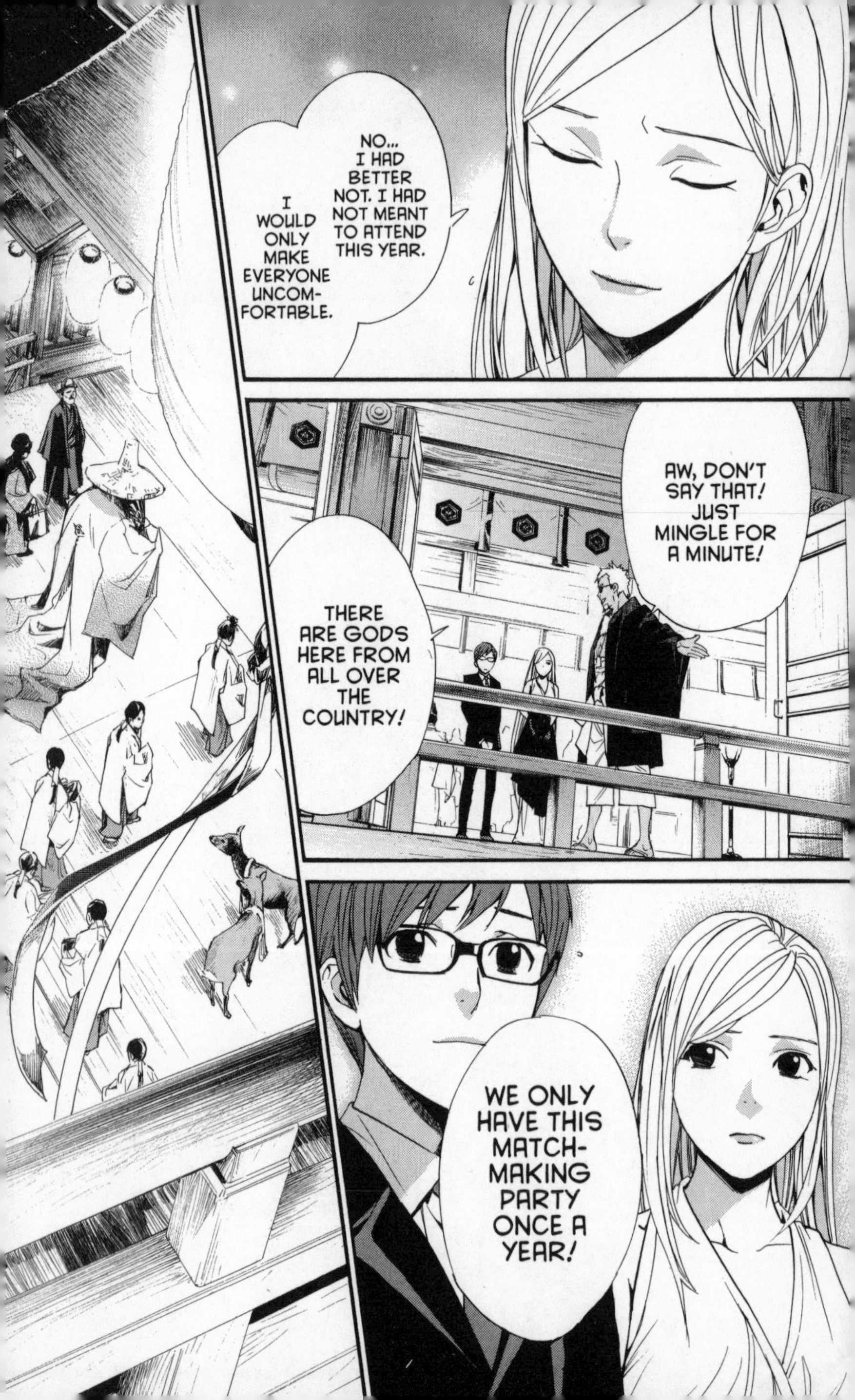
NO... I HAD BETTER NOT. I HAD NOT MEANT TO ATTEND THIS YEAR.
I WOULD ONLY MAKE EVERYONE UNCOMFORTABLE.
AW, DON'T SAY THAT! JUST MINGLE FOR A MINUTE!
THERE ARE GODS HERE FROM ALL OVER THE COUNTRY!
WE ONLY HAVE THIS MATCH-MAKING PARTY ONCE A YEAR!

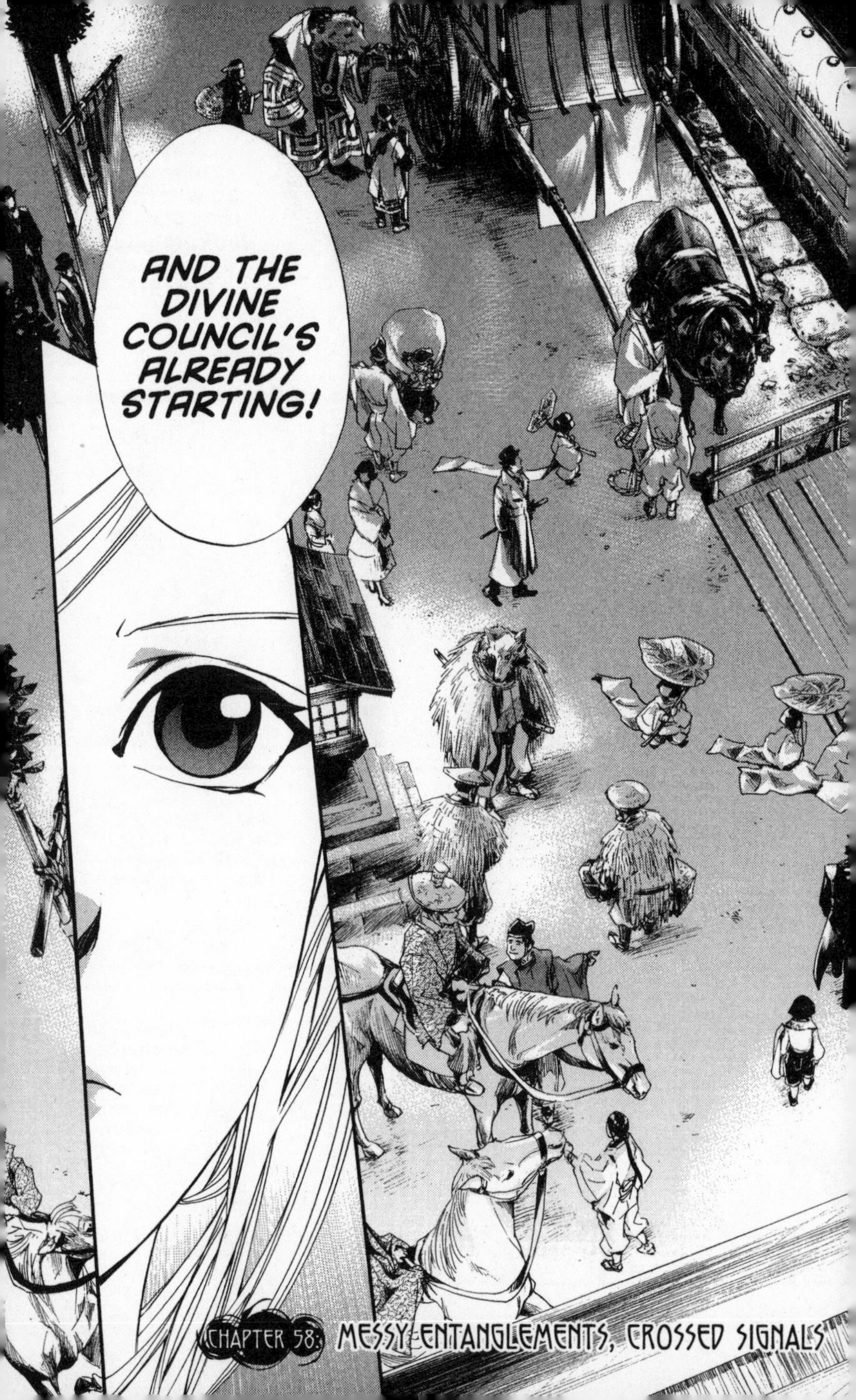
AND THE DIVINE COUNCIL'S ALREADY STARTING!
CHAPTER 58: MESSY ENTANGLEMENTS, CROSSED SIGNALS

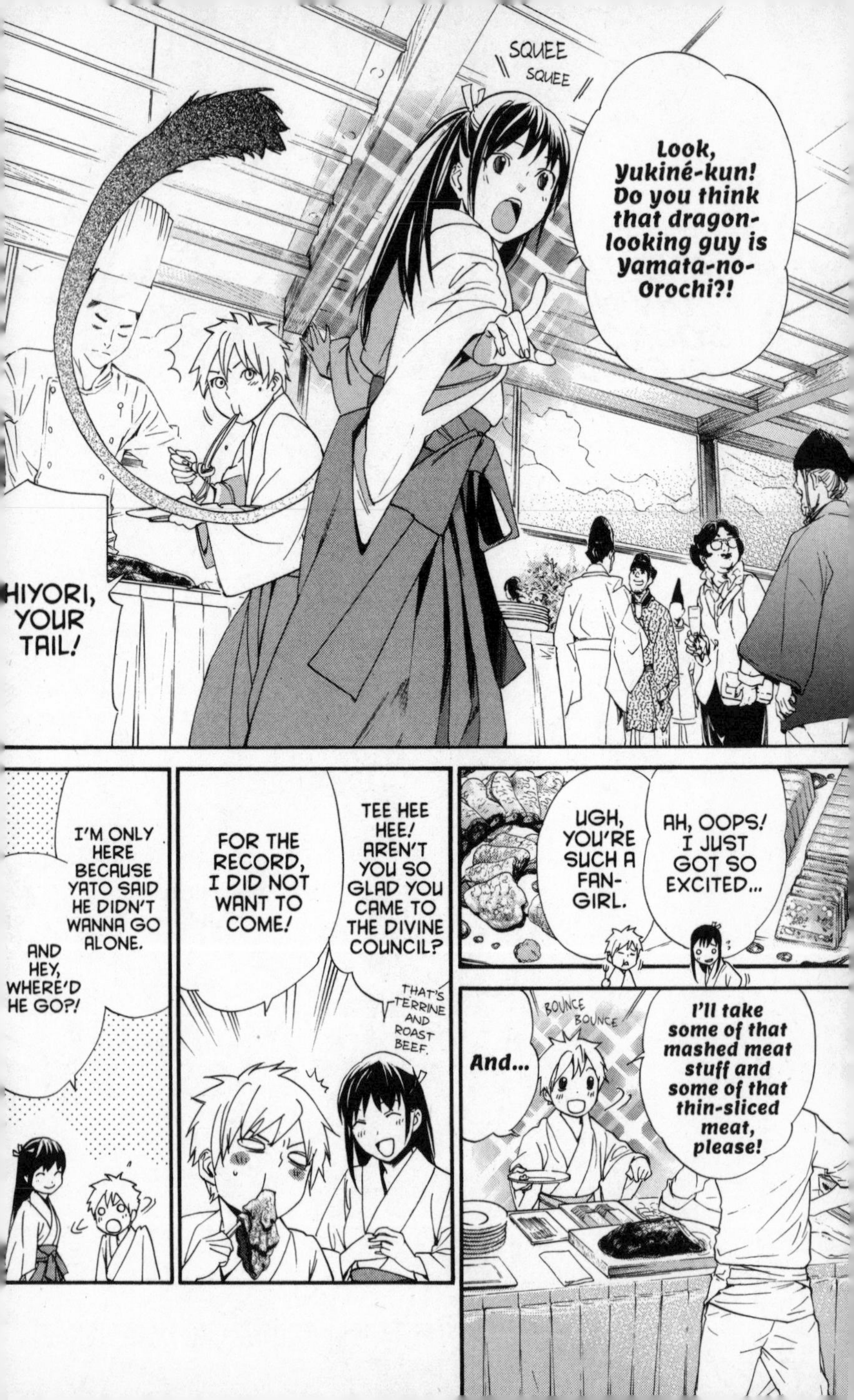
SQUEE SQUEE
Look, Yukiné-kun! Do you think that dragon-looking guy is Yamata-no-Orochi?!
HIYORI, YOUR TAIL!
AH, OOPS! I JUST GOT SO EXCITED...
UGH, YOU'RE SUCH A FAN-GIRL.
I'll take some of that mashed meat stuff and some of that thin-sliced meat, please!
BOUNCE BOUNCE
And...
TEE HEE HEE! AREN'T YOU SO GLAD YOU CAME TO THE DIVINE COUNCIL?
FOR THE RECORD, I DID NOT WANT TO COME!
THAT'S TERRINE AND ROAST BEEF.
I'M ONLY HERE BECAUSE YATO SAID HE DIDN'T WANNA GO ALONE.
AND HEY, WHERE'D HE GO?!

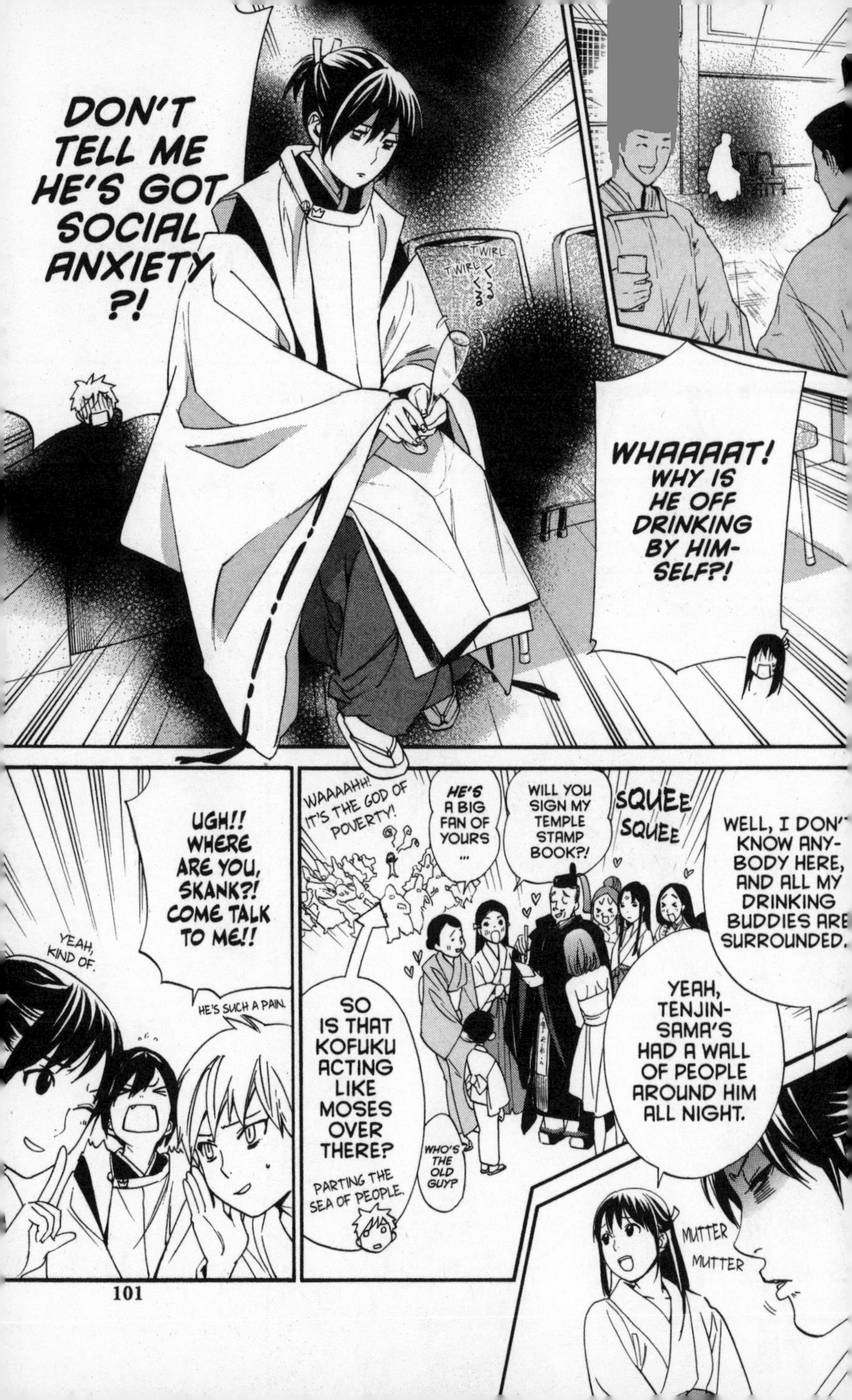
WHAAAAT! WHY IS HE OFF DRINKING BY HIM-SELF?!
DON'T TELL ME HE'S GOT SOCIAL ANXIETY ?!
TWIRL TWIRL
WELL, I DON'T KNOW ANY-BODY HERE, AND ALL MY DRINKING BUDDIES ARE SURROUNDED.
SQUEE SQUEE
WILL YOU SIGN MY TEMPLE STAMP BOOK?!
HE'S A BIG FAN OF YOURS ...
WAAAAHH! IT'S THE GOD OF POVERTY!
YEAH, TENJIN-SAMA'S HAD A WALL OF PEOPLE AROUND HIM ALL NIGHT.
SO IS THAT KOFUKU ACTING LIKE MOSES OVER THERE?
WHO'S THE OLD GUY?
PARTING THE SEA OF PEOPLE.
MUTTER MUTTER
UGH!! WHERE ARE YOU, SKANK?! COME TALK TO ME!!
YEAH, KIND OF.
HE'S SUCH A PAIN.

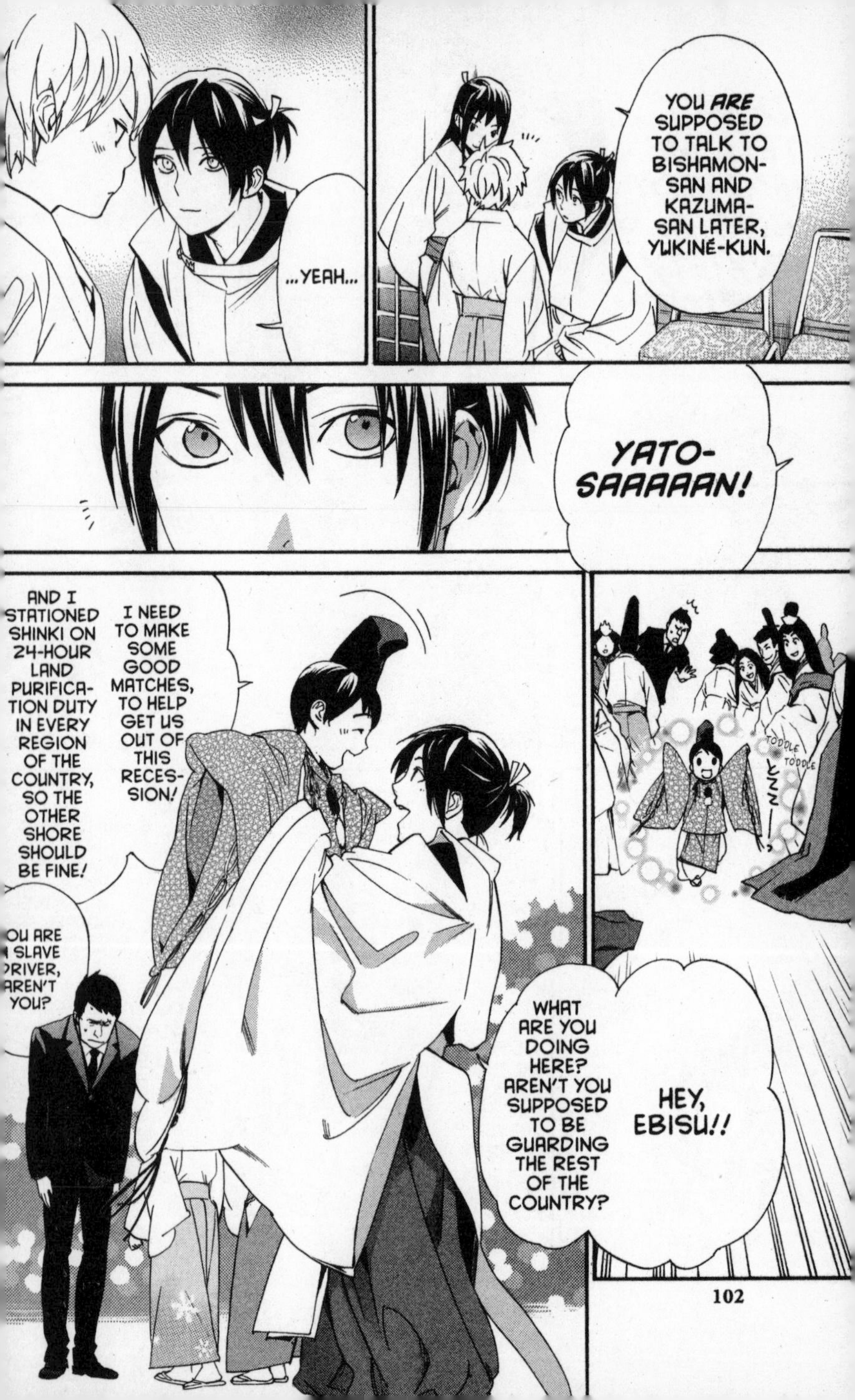

YOU ARE SUPPOSED TO TALK TO BISHAMON-SAN AND KAZUMA-SAN LATER, YUKINÉ-KUN.
...YEAH...
YATO-SAAAAAN!
TODDLE TODDLE
HEY, EBISU!!
WHAT ARE YOU DOING HERE? AREN'T YOU SUPPOSED TO BE GUARDING THE REST OF THE COUNTRY?
I NEED TO MAKE SOME GOOD MATCHES, TO HELP GET US OUT OF THIS RECESSION!
AND I STATIONED SHINKI ON 24-HOUR LAND PURIFICATION DUTY IN EVERY REGION OF THE COUNTRY, SO THE OTHER SHORE SHOULD BE FINE!
OU ARE A SLAVE DRIVER, AREN'T YOU?

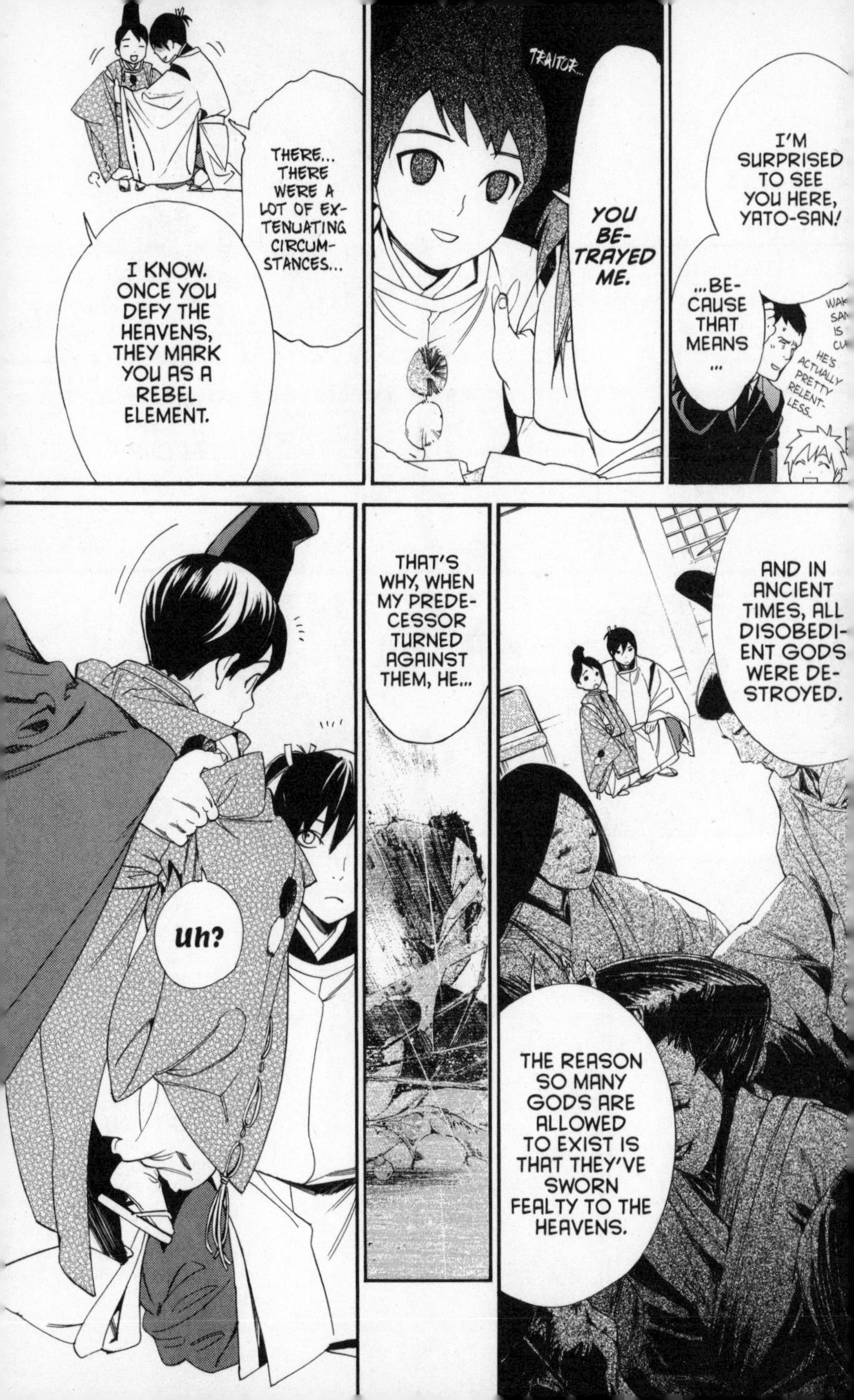
I'M SURPRISED TO SEE YOU HERE, YATO-SAN!
...BECAUSE THAT MEANS ...
HE'S ACTUALLY PRETTY RELENTLESS...
TRAITOR...
YOU BETRAYED ME.
THERE... THERE WERE A LOT OF EXTENUATING CIRCUMSTANCES...
I KNOW. ONCE YOU DEFY THE HEAVENS, THEY MARK YOU AS A REBEL ELEMENT.
AND IN ANCIENT TIMES, ALL DISOBEDIENT GODS WERE DESTROYED.
THE REASON SO MANY GODS ARE ALLOWED TO EXIST IS THAT THEY'VE SWORN FEALTY TO THE HEAVENS.
THAT'S WHY, WHEN MY PREDECESSOR TURNED AGAINST THEM, HE...
Uh?

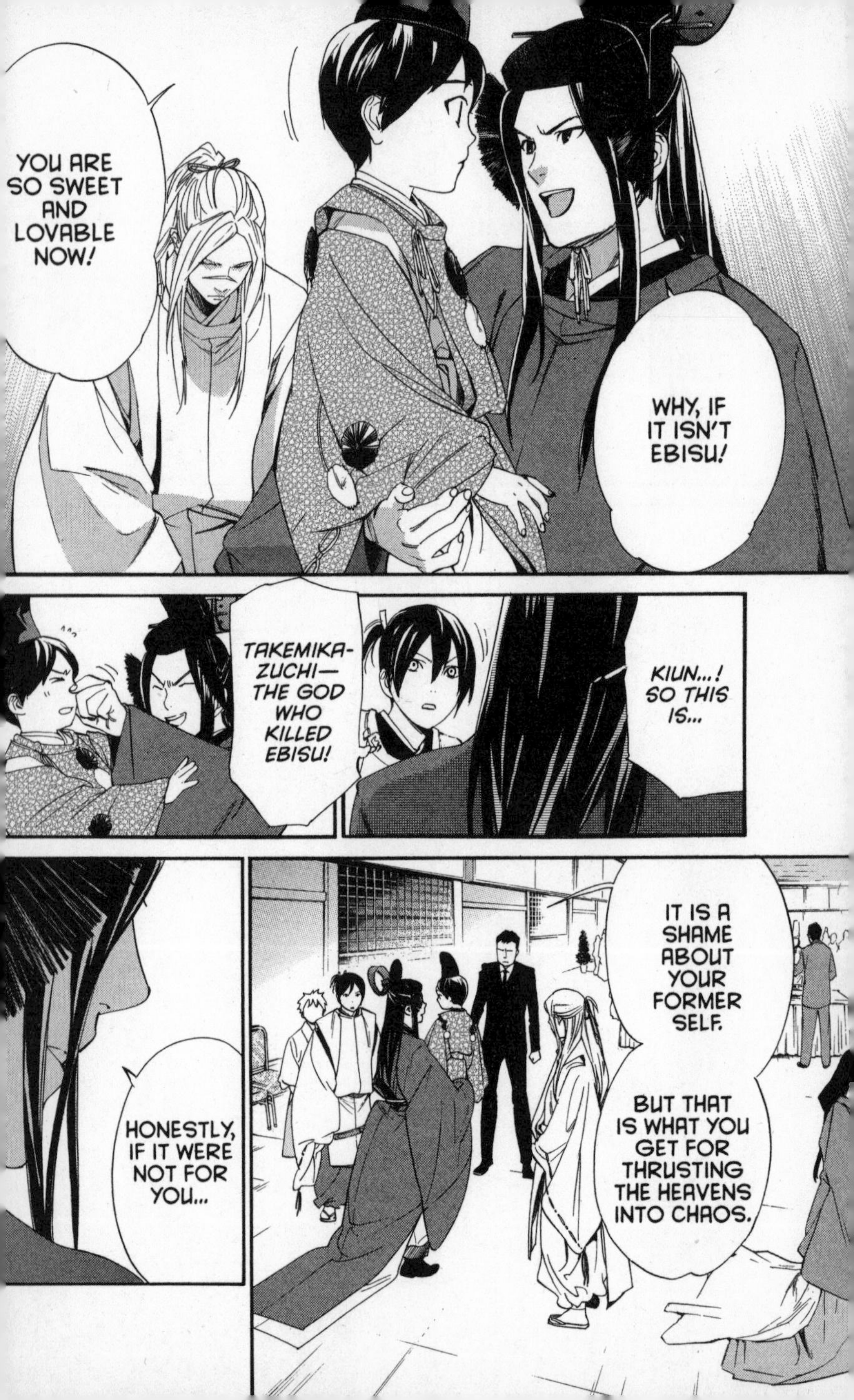
WHY, IF IT ISN'T EBISU!
YOU ARE SO SWEET AND LOVABLE NOW!
KIUN...! SO THIS IS...
TAKEMIKA-ZUCHI— THE GOD WHO KILLED EBISU!
IT IS A SHAME ABOUT YOUR FORMER SELF.
BUT THAT IS WHAT YOU GET FOR THRUSTING THE HEAVENS INTO CHAOS.
HONESTLY, IF IT WERE NOT FOR YOU...

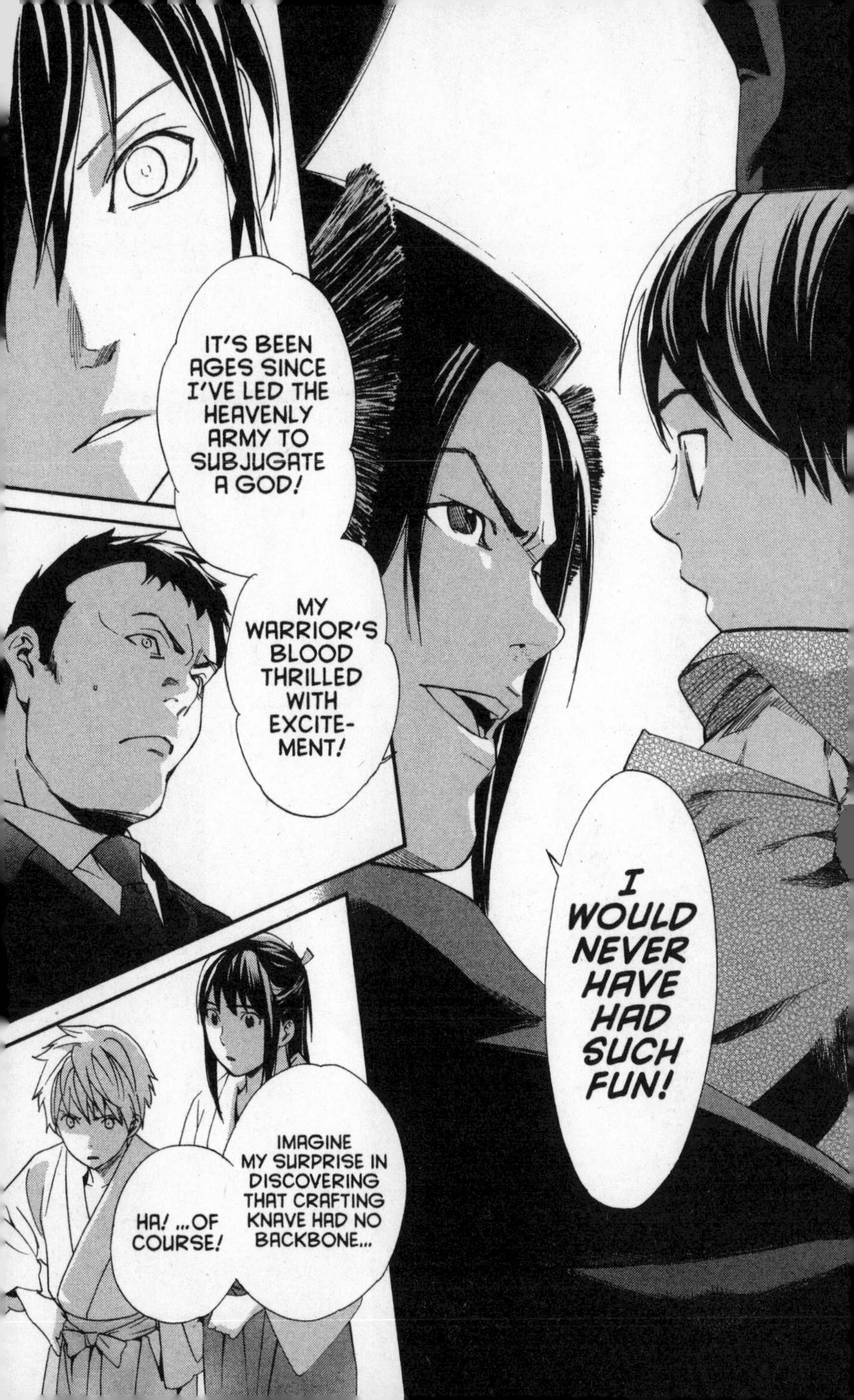
IT'S BEEN AGES SINCE I'VE LED THE HEAVENLY ARMY TO SUBJUGATE A GOD!
MY WARRIOR'S BLOOD THRILLED WITH EXCITE-MENT!
I WOULD NEVER HAVE HAD SUCH FUN!
IMAGINE MY SURPRISE IN DISCOVERING THAT CRAFTING KNAVE HAD NO BACKBONE...
HA! ...OF COURSE!

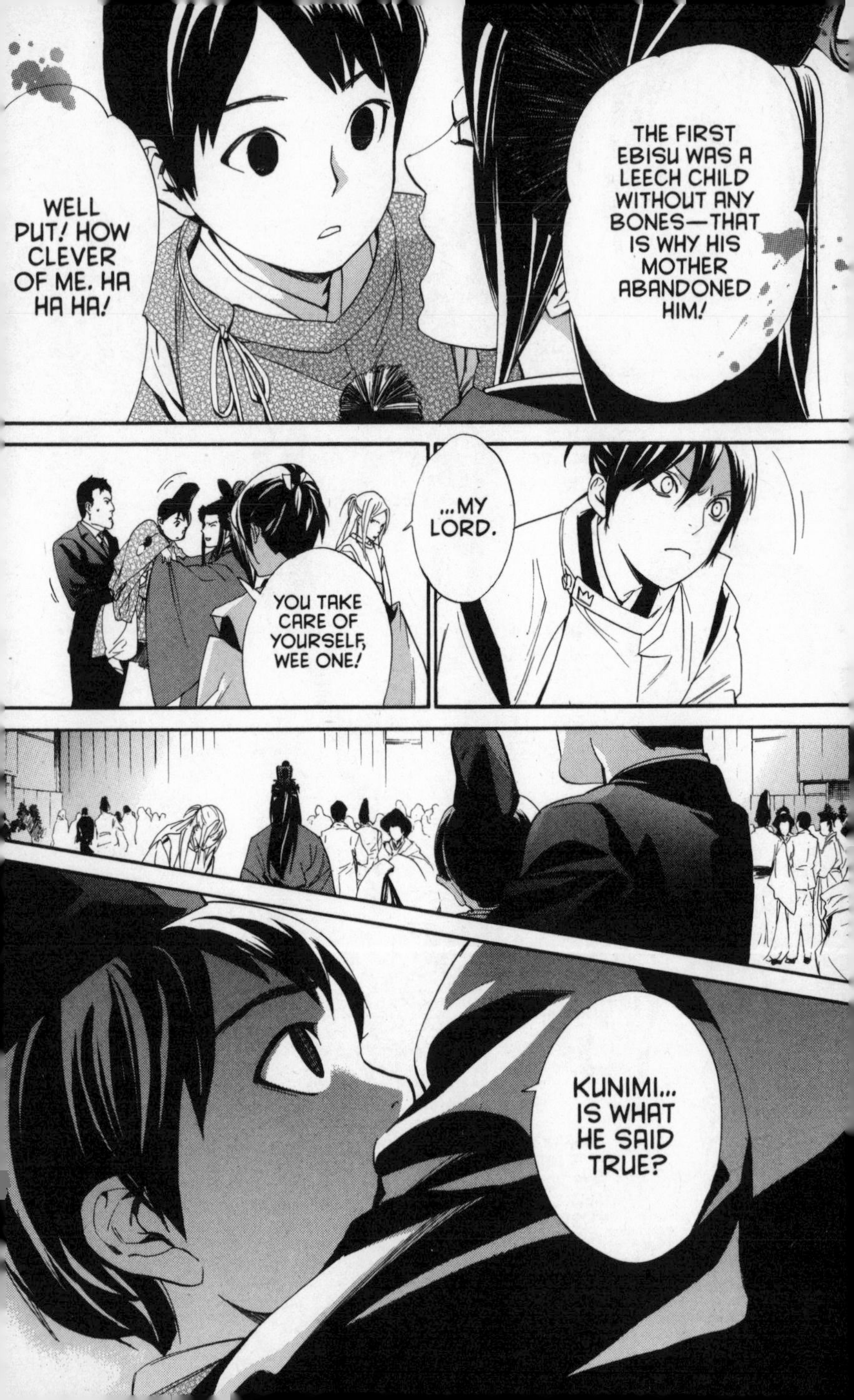
THE FIRST EBISU WAS A LEECH CHILD WITHOUT ANY BONES—THAT IS WHY HIS MOTHER ABANDONED HIM!
WELL PUT! HOW CLEVER OF ME. HA HA HA!
...MY LORD.
YOU TAKE CARE OF YOURSELF, WEE ONE!
KUNIMI... IS WHAT HE SAID TRUE?

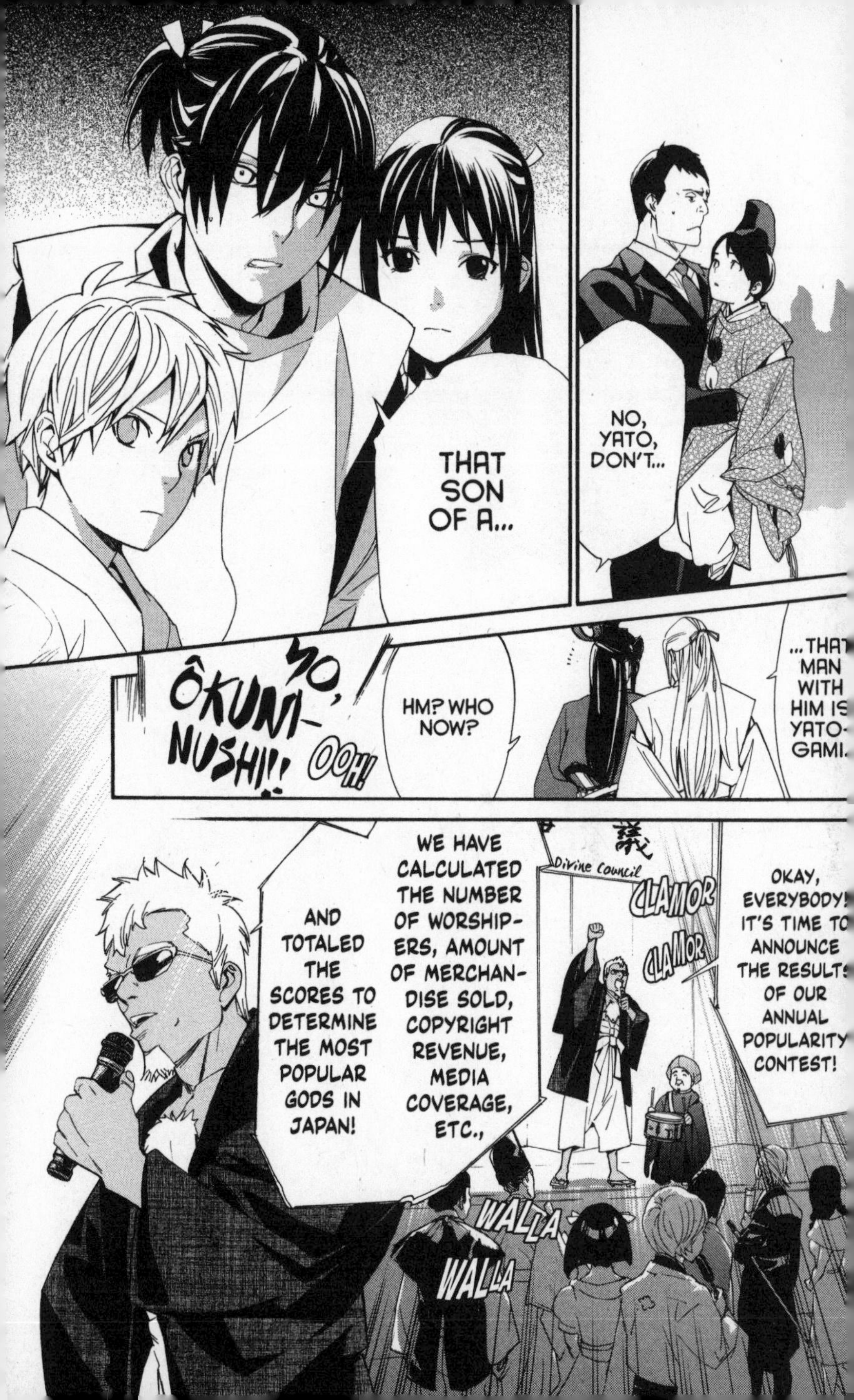
NO, YATO, DON'T...
THAT SON OF A...
...THAT MAN WITH HIM IS YATO-GAMI.
HM? WHO NOW?
OOH!
SO, ÔKUNI-NUSHI!!
OKAY, EVERYBODY! IT'S TIME TO ANNOUNCE THE RESULTS OF OUR ANNUAL POPULARITY CONTEST!
CLAMOR
CLAMOR
Divine Council
WE HAVE CALCULATED THE NUMBER OF WORSHIP-ERS, AMOUNT OF MERCHAN-DISE SOLD, COPYRIGHT REVENUE, MEDIA COVERAGE, ETC.,
AND TOTALED THE SCORES TO DETERMINE THE MOST POPULAR GODS IN JAPAN!
WALLA
WALLA

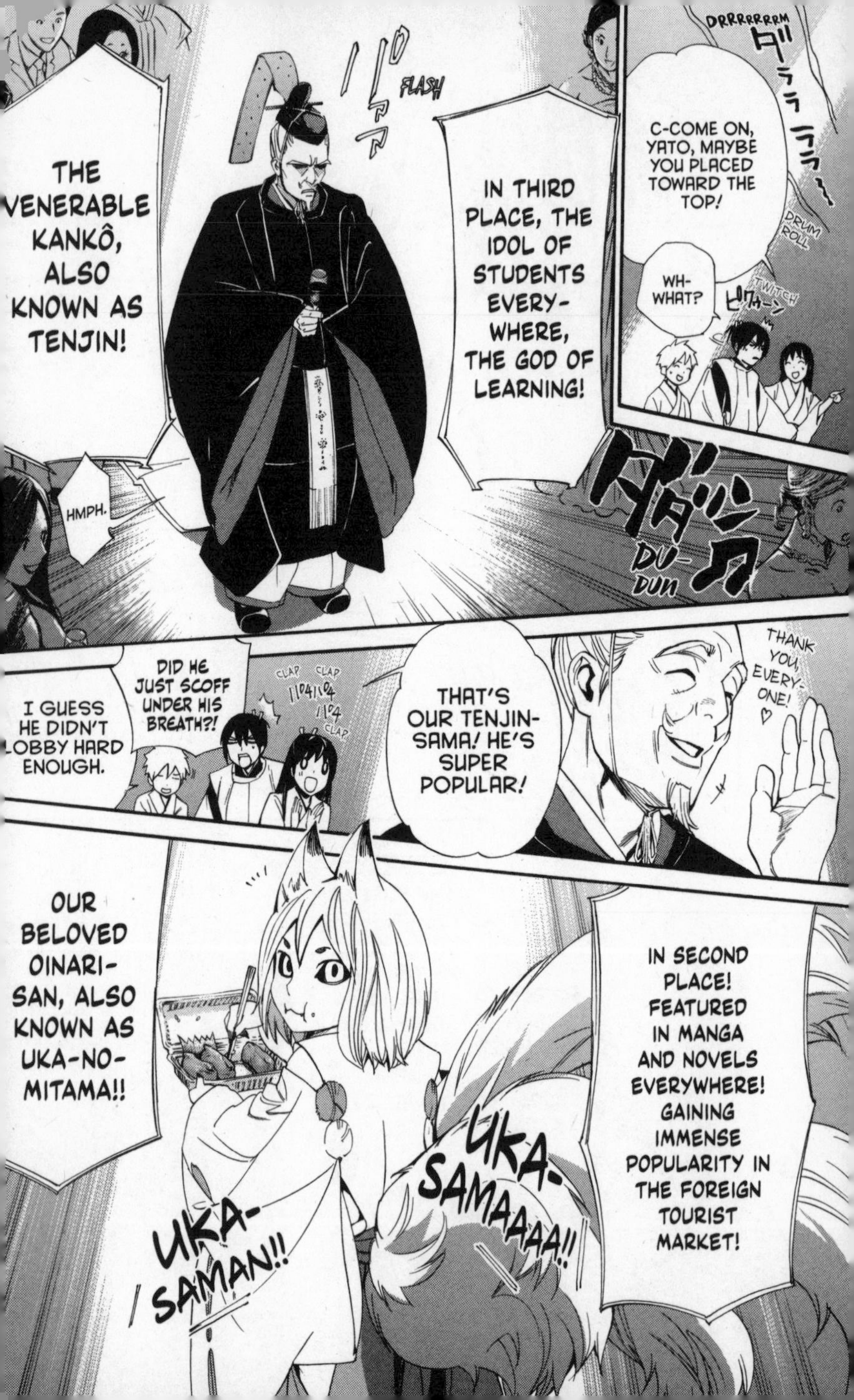
DRRRRRRRM
C-COME ON, YATO, MAYBE YOU PLACED TOWARD THE TOP!
DRUM ROLL
WH-WHAT?
TWITCH
FLASH
IN THIRD PLACE, THE IDOL OF STUDENTS EVERYWHERE, THE GOD OF LEARNING!
THE VENERABLE KANKÔ, ALSO KNOWN AS TENJIN!
HMPH.
DU-DUN
THANK YOU, EVERYONE!
THAT'S OUR TENJIN-SAMA! HE'S SUPER POPULAR!
CLAP CLAP CLAP
DID HE JUST SCOFF UNDER HIS BREATH?!
I GUESS HE DIDN'T LOBBY HARD ENOUGH.
IN SECOND PLACE! FEATURED IN MANGA AND NOVELS EVERYWHERE! GAINING IMMENSE POPULARITY IN THE FOREIGN TOURIST MARKET!
OUR BELOVED OINARI-SAN, ALSO KNOWN AS UKA-NO-MITAMA!!
UKA-SAMAAAAA!!
UKA-SAMAN!!

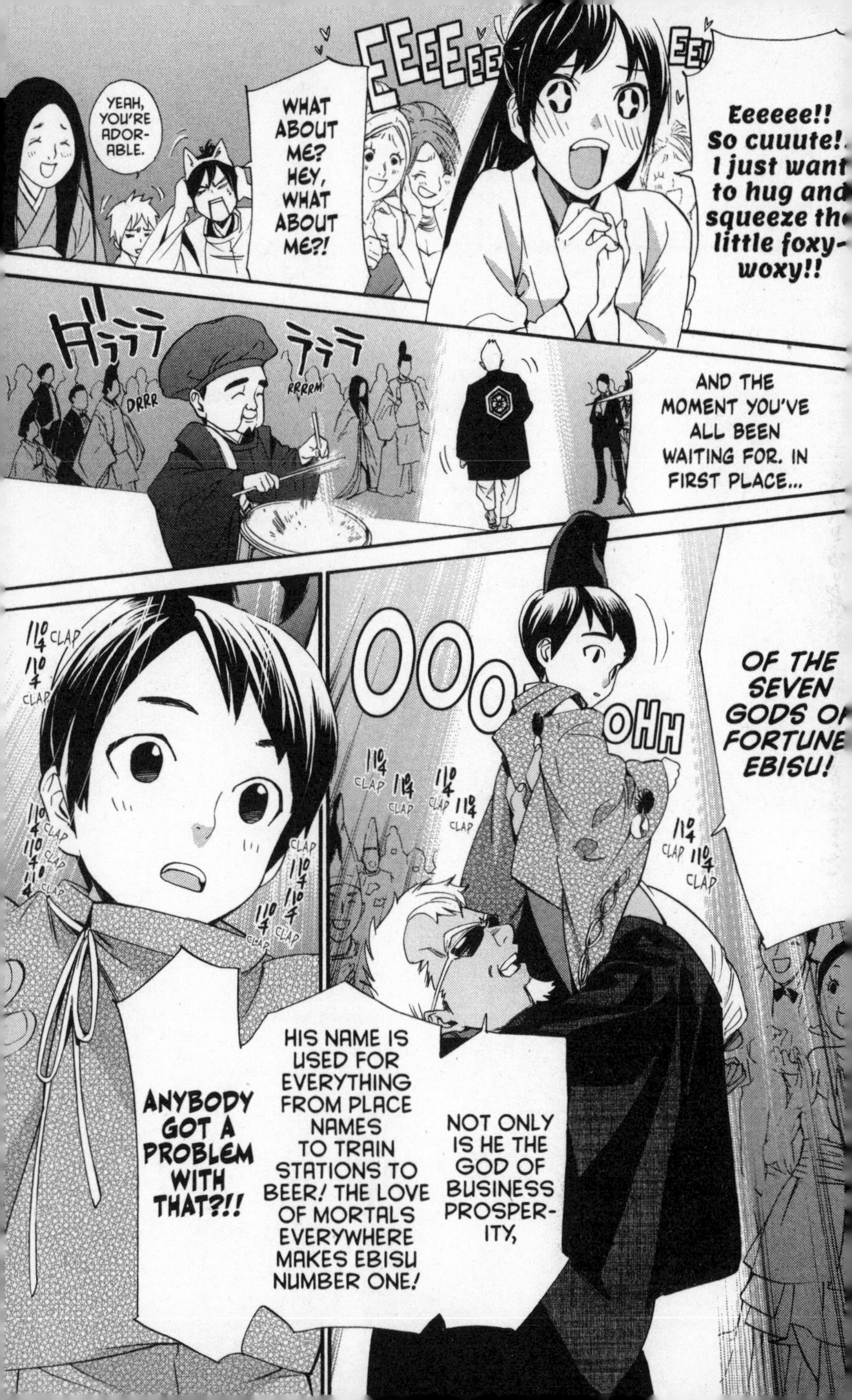
EEEEEEE EE!
Eeeeee!! So cuuute!! I just want to hug and squeeze the little foxy-woxy!!
WHAT ABOUT ME? HEY, WHAT ABOUT ME?!
YEAH, YOU'RE ADORABLE.
AND THE MOMENT YOU'VE ALL BEEN WAITING FOR. IN FIRST PLACE...
RRRRM
DRRR
OF THE SEVEN GODS OF FORTUNE EBISU!
OOOOHH
CLAP CLAP CLAP CLAP CLAP CLAP
NOT ONLY IS HE THE GOD OF BUSINESS PROSPERITY,
HIS NAME IS USED FOR EVERYTHING FROM PLACE NAMES TO TRAIN STATIONS TO BEER! THE LOVE OF MORTALS EVERYWHERE MAKES EBISU NUMBER ONE!
CLAP CLAP CLAP CLAP CLAP CLAP CLAP CLAP
ANYBODY GOT A PROBLEM WITH THAT?!!

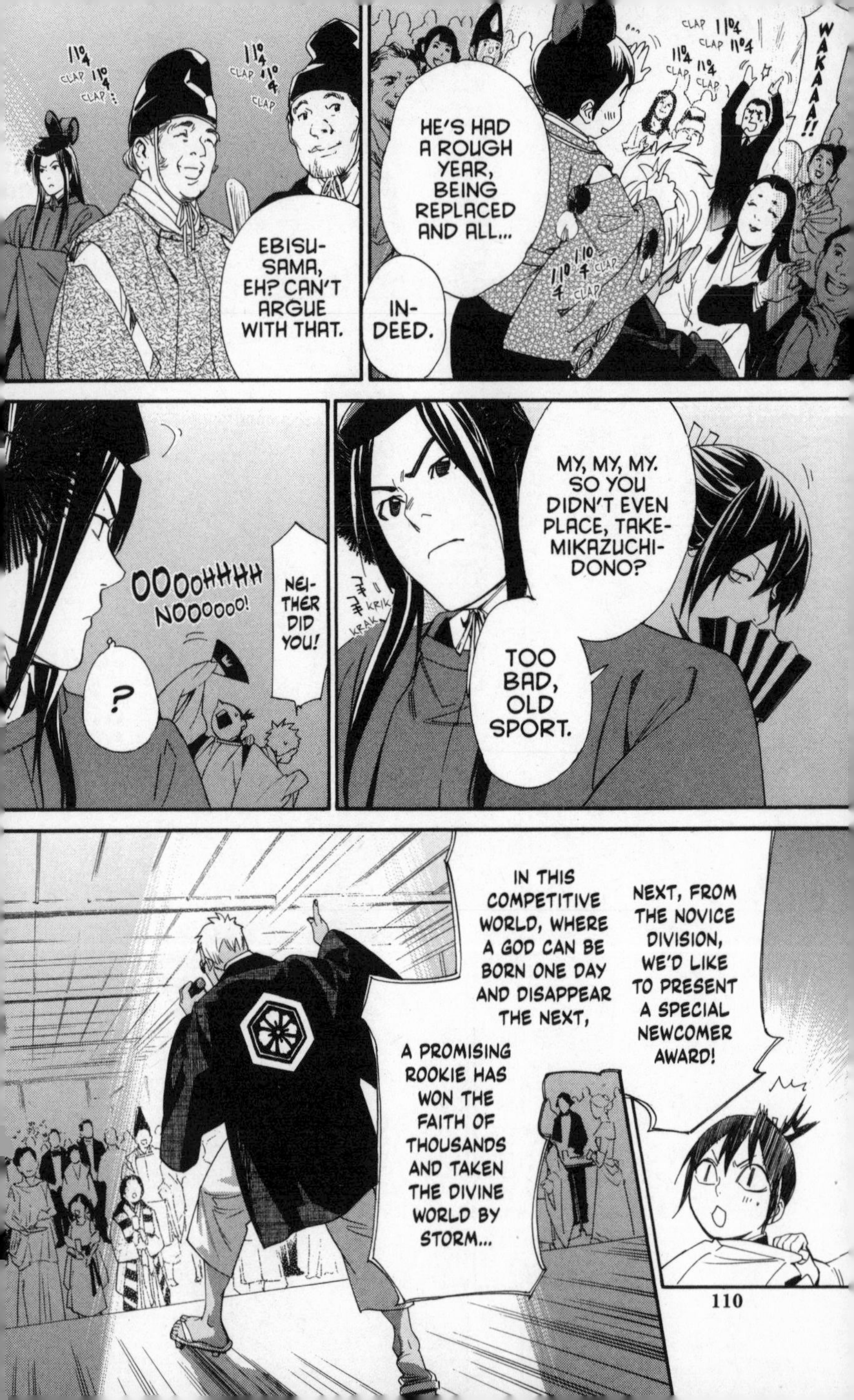
WAKAAAA!!
CLAP CLAP
CLAP CLAP
HE'S HAD A ROUGH YEAR, BEING REPLACED AND ALL...
IN-DEED.
CLAP CLAP
EBISU-SAMA, EH? CAN'T ARGUE WITH THAT.
CLAP CLAP
CLAP CLAP
MY, MY, MY. SO YOU DIDN'T EVEN PLACE, TAKE-MIKAZUCHI-DONO?
TOO BAD, OLD SPORT.
NEI-THER DID YOU!
KRIK KRAK
OOOoHHHH NOOOooo!
?
NEXT, FROM THE NOVICE DIVISION, WE'D LIKE TO PRESENT A SPECIAL NEWCOMER AWARD!
IN THIS COMPETITIVE WORLD, WHERE A GOD CAN BE BORN ONE DAY AND DISAPPEAR THE NEXT,
A PROMISING ROOKIE HAS WON THE FAITH OF THOUSANDS AND TAKEN THE DIVINE WORLD BY STORM...

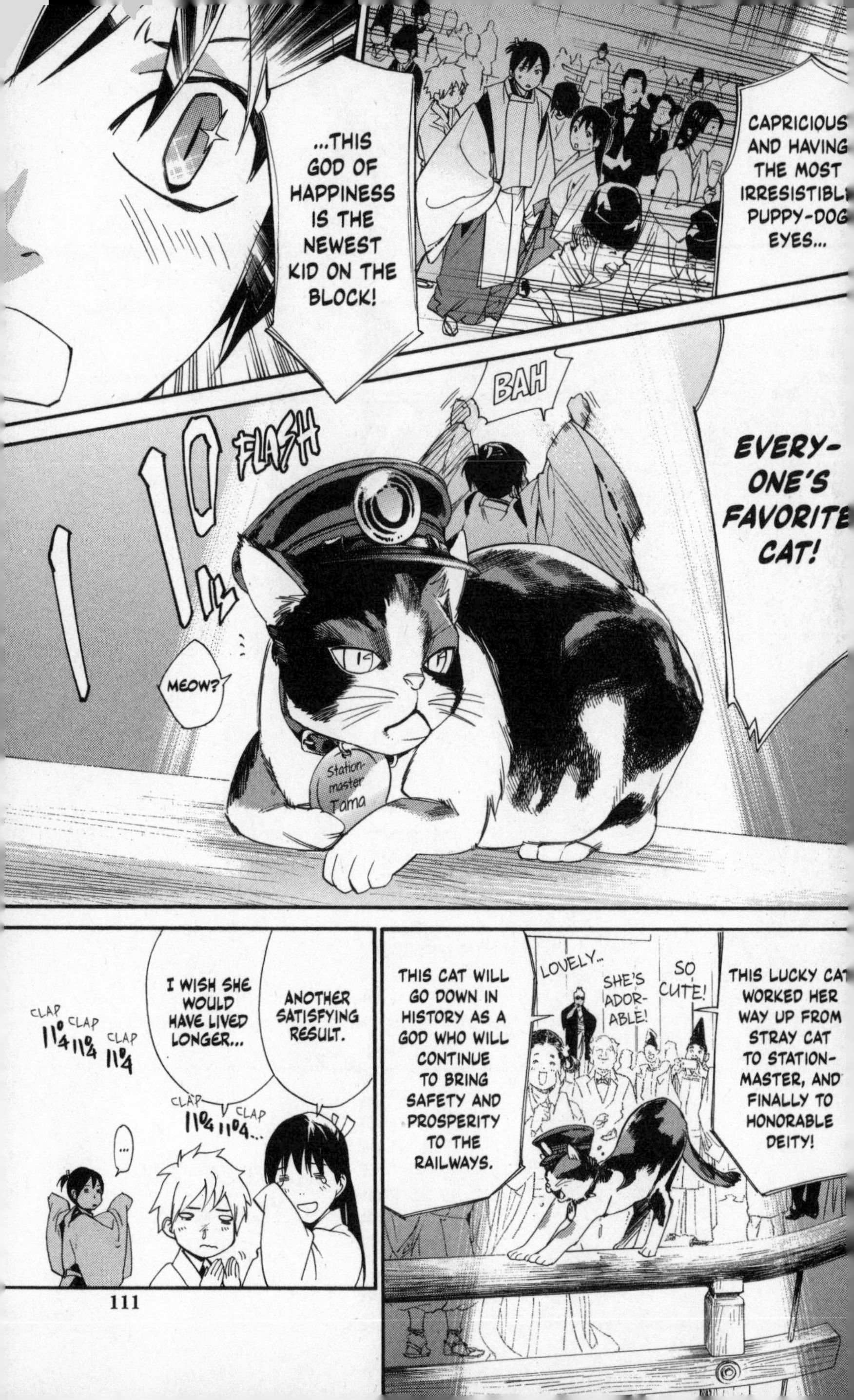

CAPRICIOUS AND HAVING THE MOST IRRESISTIBLE PUPPY-DOG EYES...
...THIS GOD OF HAPPINESS IS THE NEWEST KID ON THE BLOCK!
BAH
FLASH
EVERY-ONE'S FAVORITE CAT!
MEOW?
Station-master Tama
THIS LUCKY CAT WORKED HER WAY UP FROM STRAY CAT TO STATION-MASTER, AND FINALLY TO HONORABLE DEITY!
SO CUTE!
SHE'S ADOR-ABLE!
LOVELY...
THIS CAT WILL GO DOWN IN HISTORY AS A GOD WHO WILL CONTINUE TO BRING SAFETY AND PROSPERITY TO THE RAILWAYS.
ANOTHER SATISFYING RESULT.
I WISH SHE WOULD HAVE LIVED LONGER...
CLAP CLAP
...
CLAP CLAP CLAP

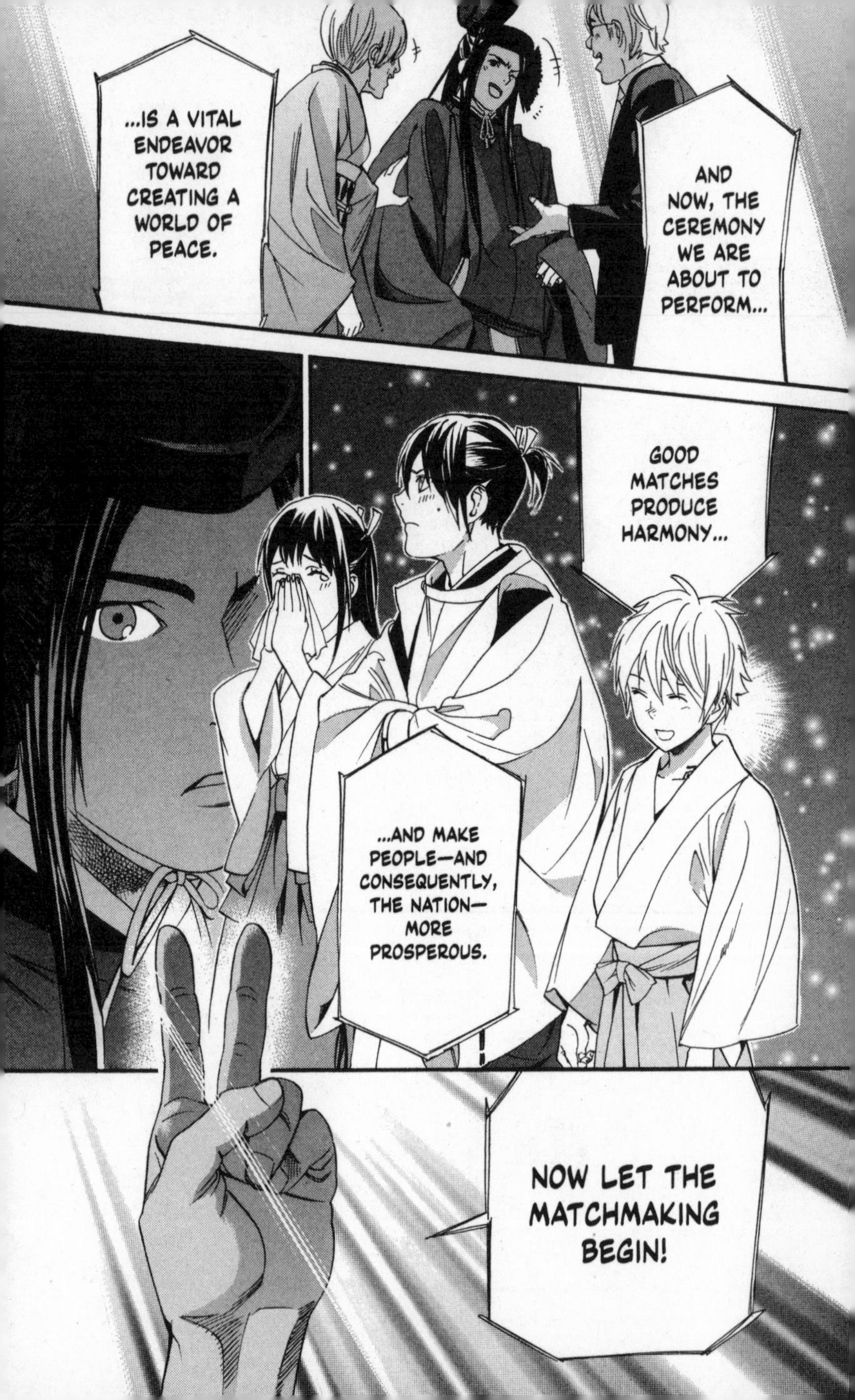
AND NOW, THE CEREMONY WE ARE ABOUT TO PERFORM...
...IS A VITAL ENDEAVOR TOWARD CREATING A WORLD OF PEACE.
GOOD MATCHES PRODUCE HARMONY...
...AND MAKE PEOPLE—AND CONSEQUENTLY, THE NATION—MORE PROSPEROUS.
NOW LET THE MATCHMAKING BEGIN!

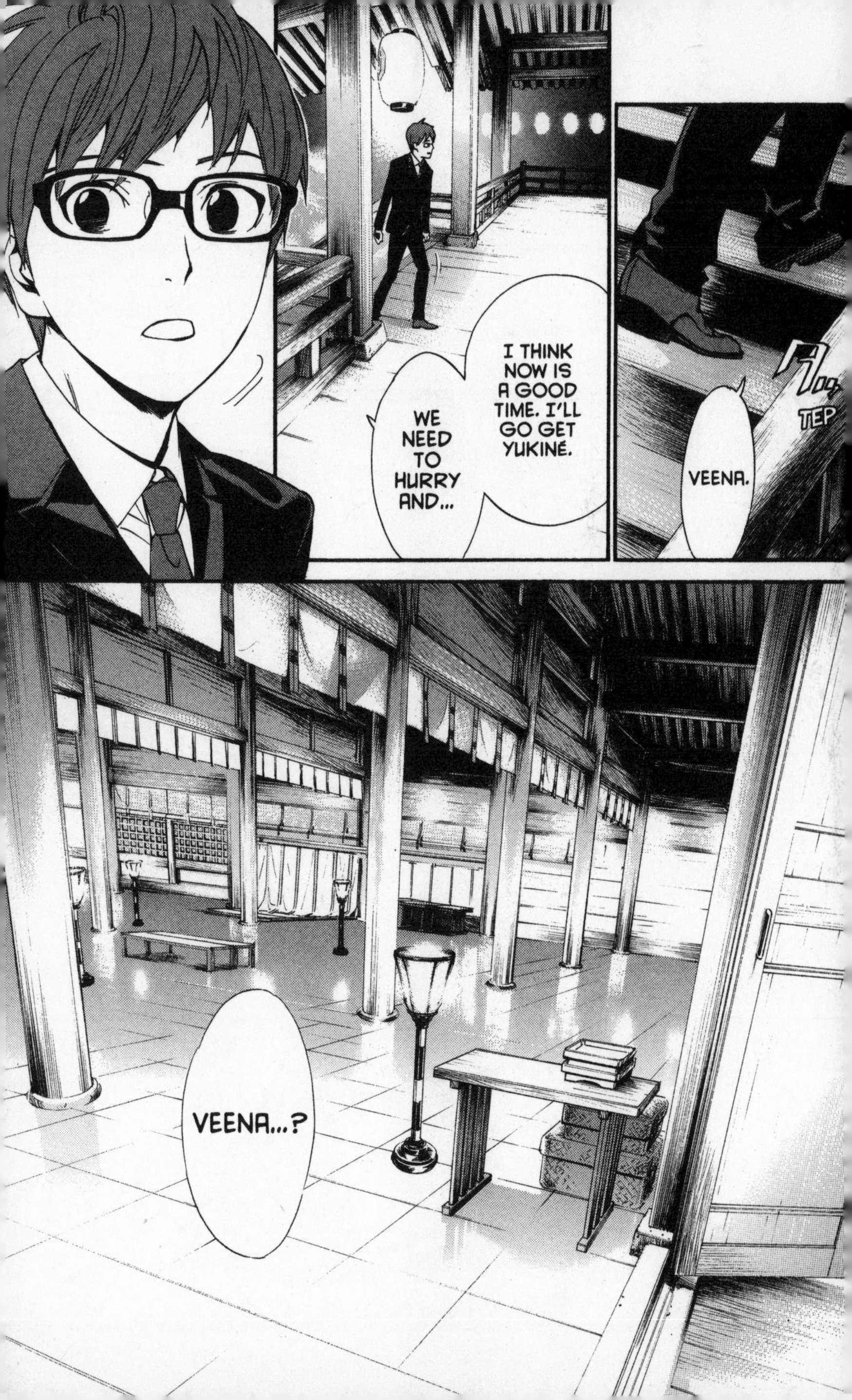
TEP
VEENA.
I THINK NOW IS A GOOD TIME. I'LL GO GET YUKINE.
WE NEED TO HURRY AND...
VEENA...?

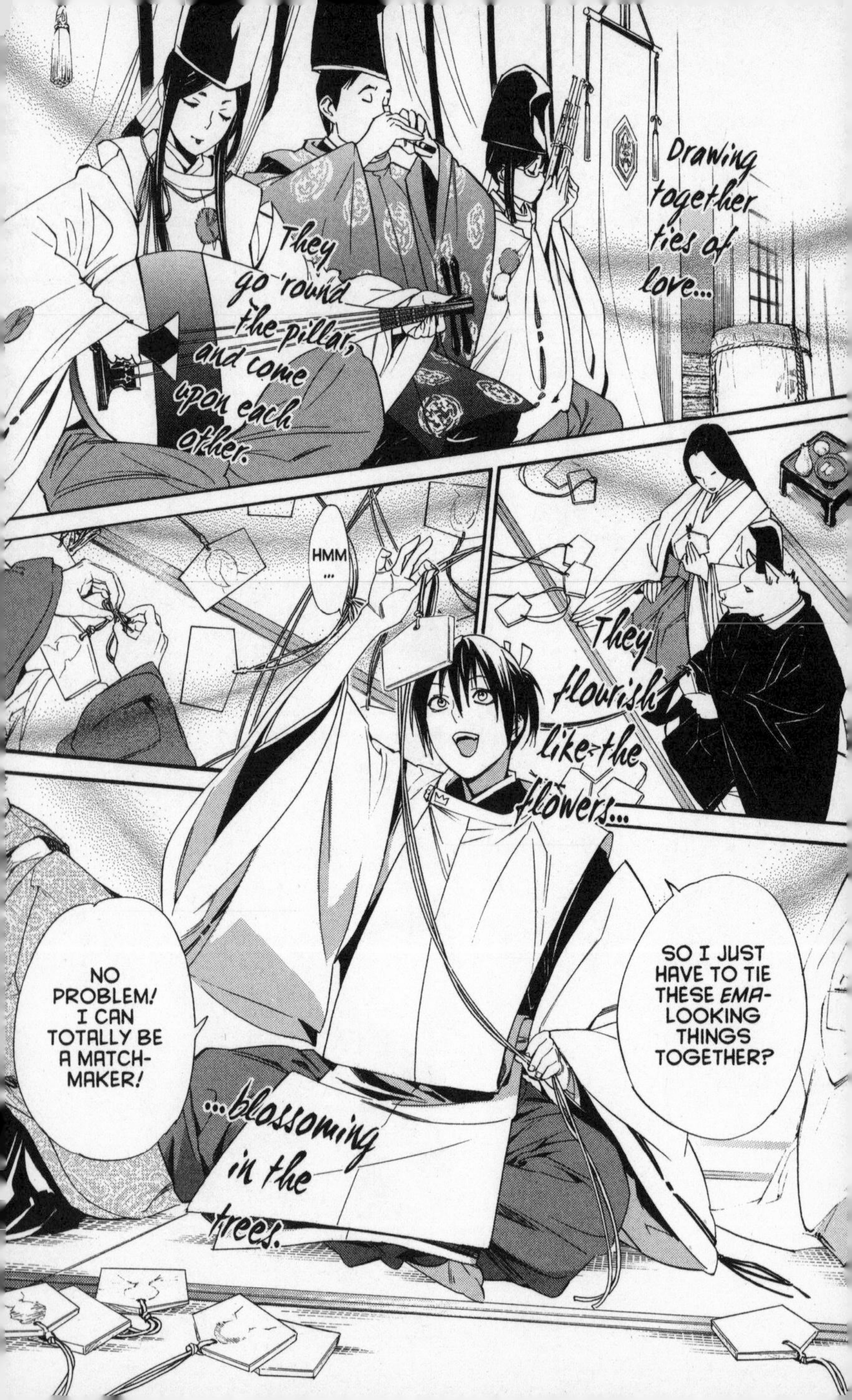
Drawing together ties of love...
They go 'round the pillar, and come upon each other.
They flourish like the flowers...
HMM...
SO I JUST HAVE TO TIE THESE *EMA*-LOOKING THINGS TOGETHER?
NO PROBLEM! I CAN TOTALLY BE A MATCH-MAKER!
...blossoming in the trees.

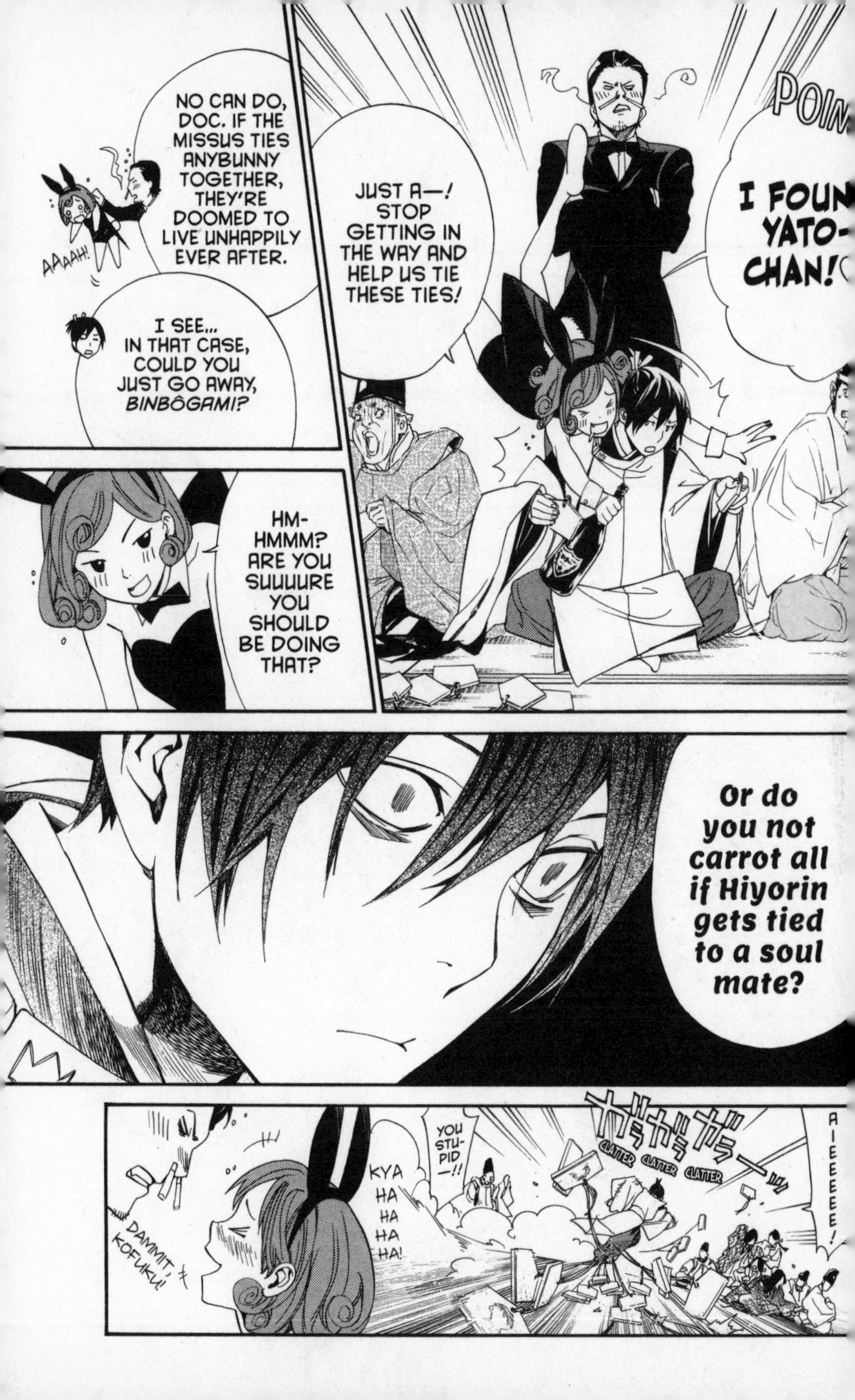
POIN
I FOUN YATO-CHAN!
JUST A—! STOP GETTING IN THE WAY AND HELP US TIE THESE TIES!
NO CAN DO, DOC. IF THE MISSUS TIES ANYBUNNY TOGETHER, THEY'RE DOOMED TO LIVE UNHAPPILY EVER AFTER.
AAAAH!
I SEE... IN THAT CASE, COULD YOU JUST GO AWAY, BINBÔGAMI?
HM-HMMM? ARE YOU SUUUURE YOU SHOULD BE DOING THAT?
Or do you not carrot all if Hiyorin gets tied to a soul mate?
AIEEEEEE!
CLATTER CLATTER CLATTER
YOU STUPID—!!
KYA HA HA HA HA!
DAMMIT, KOFUKU!

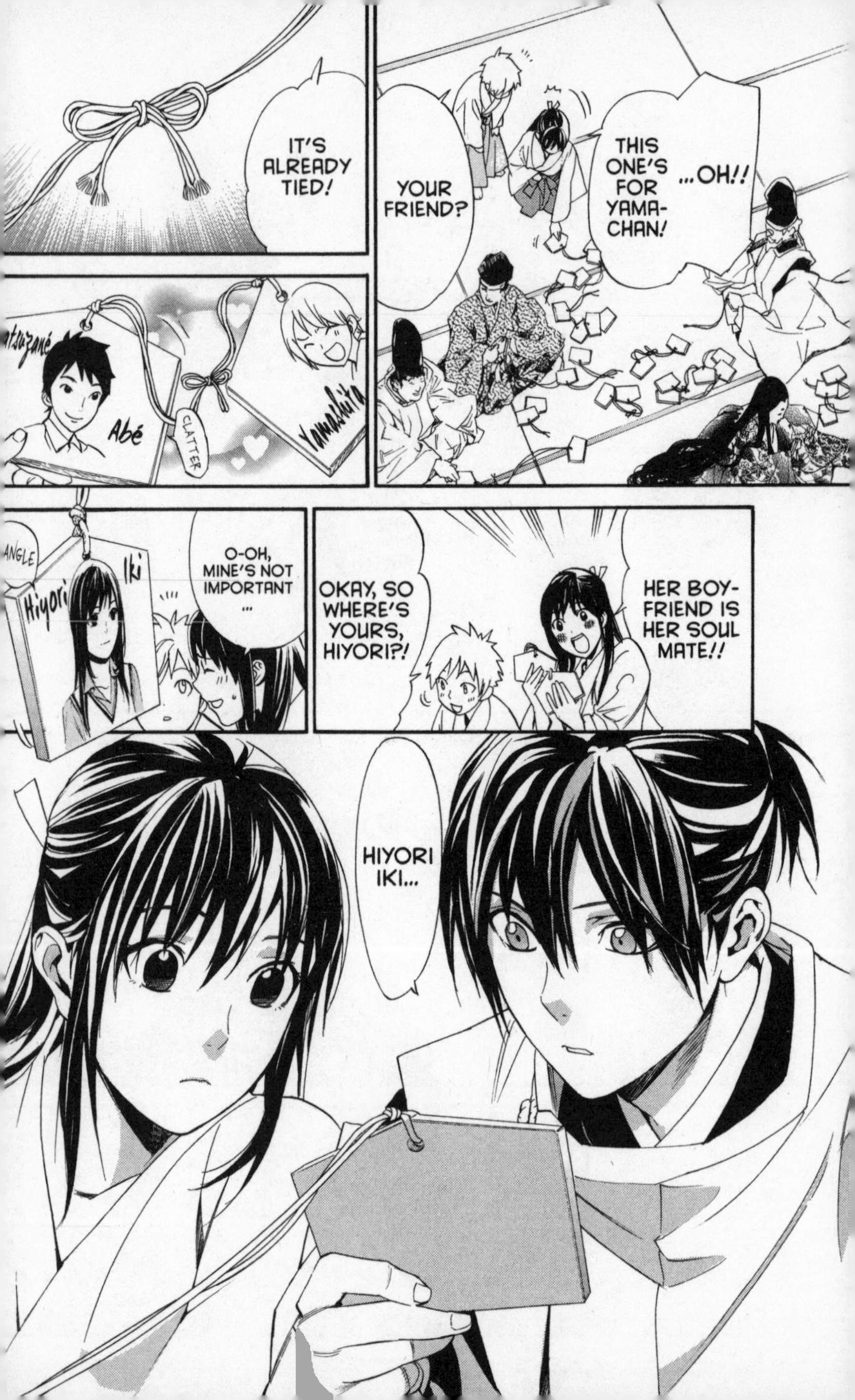
THIS ONE'S FOR YAMA-CHAN!
...OH!!
YOUR FRIEND?
IT'S ALREADY TIED!
Yamashita
CLATTER
Abé
HER BOY-FRIEND IS HER SOUL MATE!!
OKAY, SO WHERE'S YOURS, HIYORI?!
O-OH, MINE'S NOT IMPORTANT ...
Iki
Hiyori
HIYORI IKI...

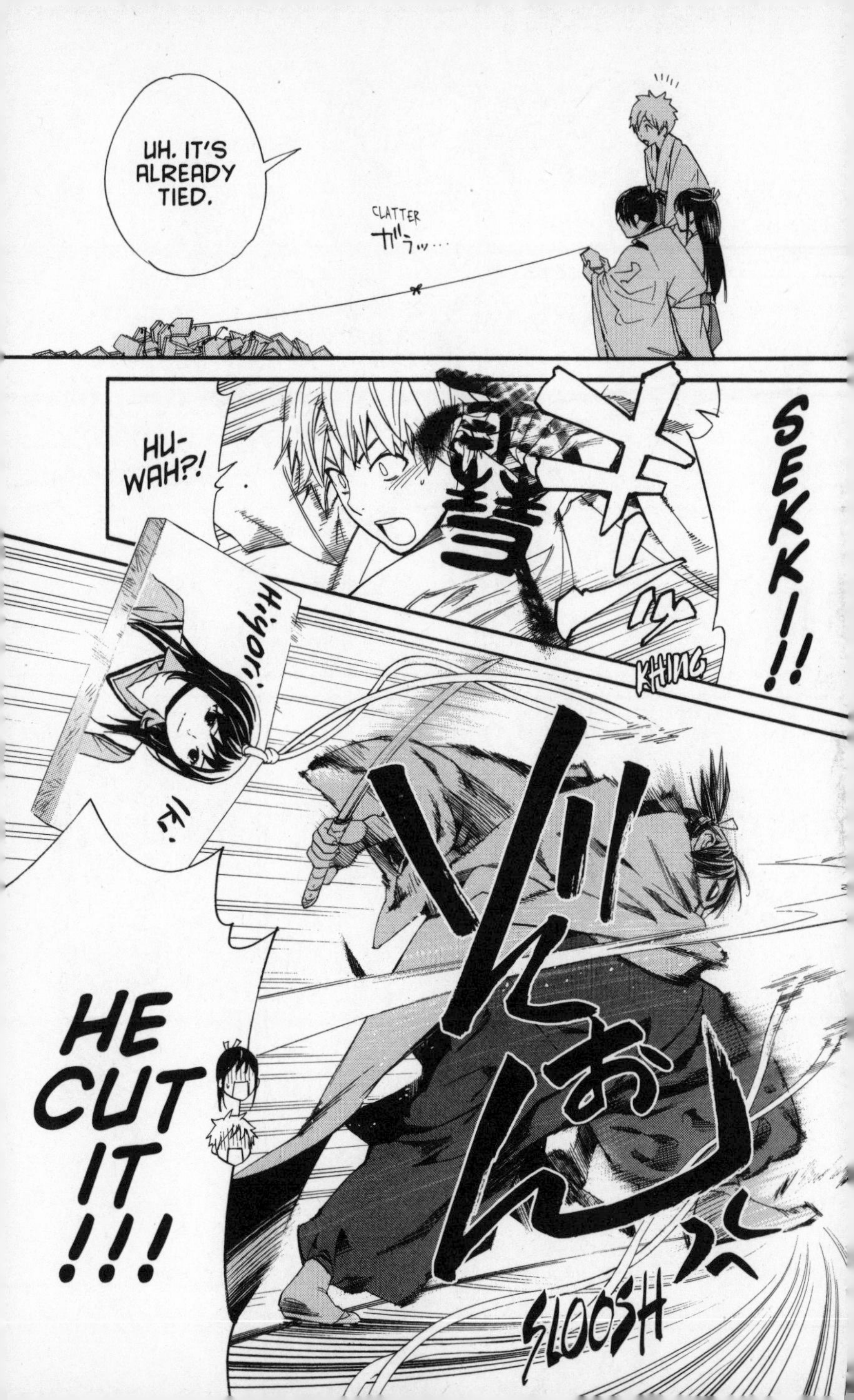
UH. IT'S ALREADY TIED.
CLATTER
ガラッ…
HU-WAH?!
SEKKI!!
KHING
Hiyori!
HE CUT IT!!!
SLOOSH

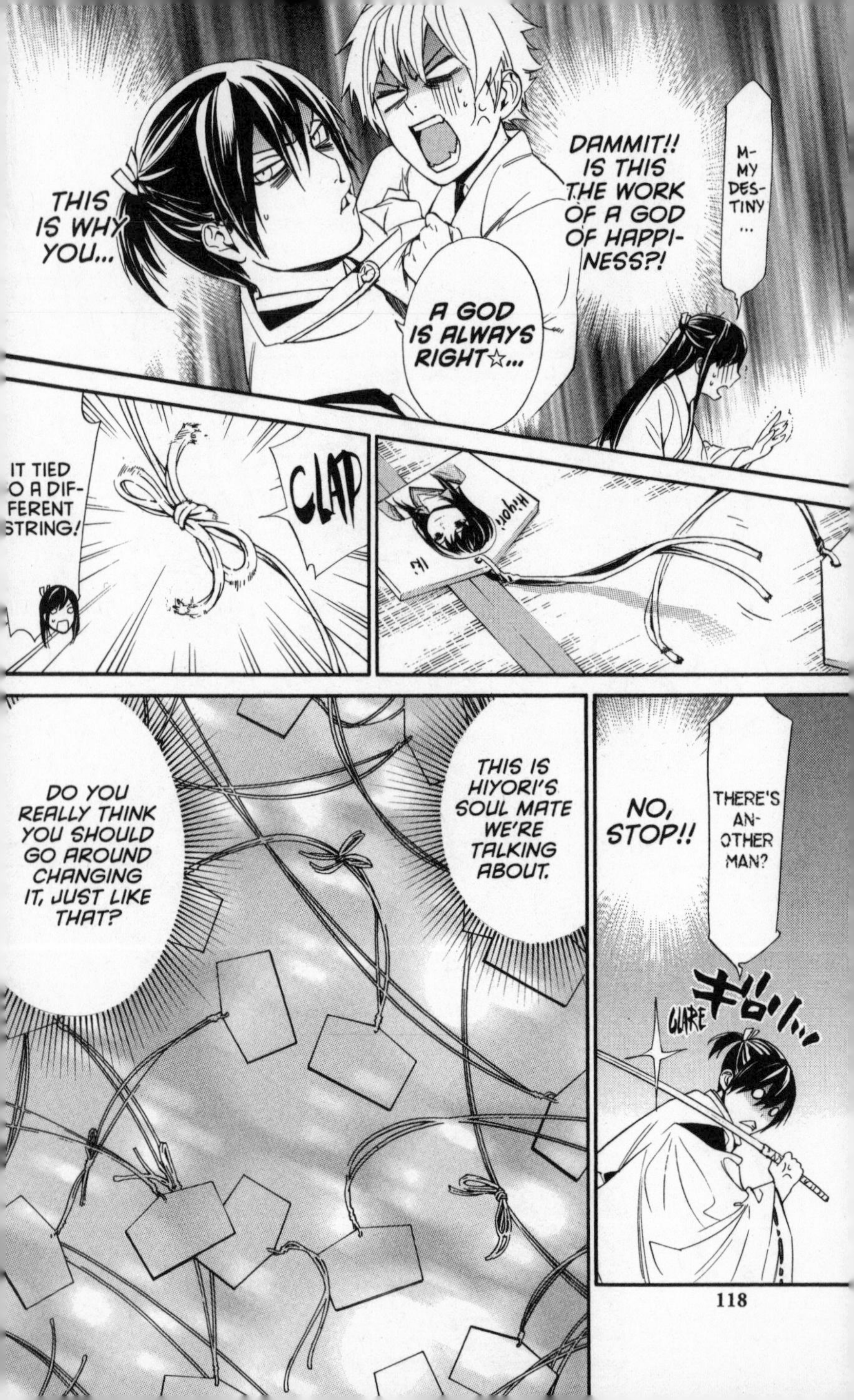

M-MY DESTINY...
DAMMIT!! IS THIS THE WORK OF A GOD OF HAPPINESS?!
A GOD IS ALWAYS RIGHT☆...
THIS IS WHY YOU...
Hiyori
CLAP
IT TIED O A DIF-FERENT STRING!
THERE'S ANOTHER MAN?
NO, STOP!!
GLARE
THIS IS HIYORI'S SOUL MATE WE'RE TALKING ABOUT.
DO YOU REALLY THINK YOU SHOULD GO AROUND CHANGING IT, JUST LIKE THAT?

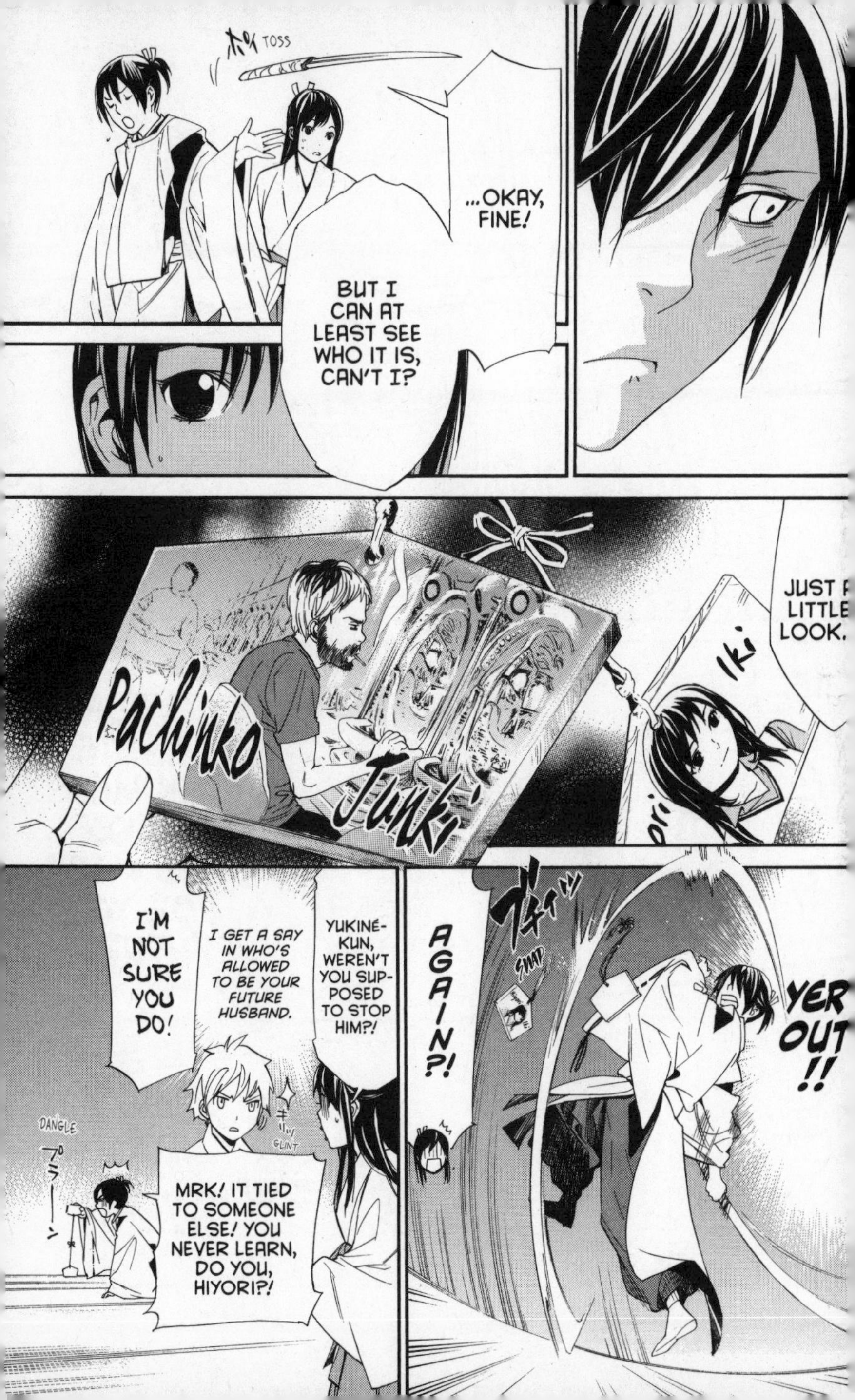
TOSS
...OKAY, FINE!
BUT I CAN AT LEAST SEE WHO IT IS, CAN'T I?
JUST A LITTLE LOOK.
Iki
Pachinko
Junki
SNAP
YER OUT!!
AGAIN?!
YUKINÉ-KUN, WEREN'T YOU SUPPOSED TO STOP HIM?!
I GET A SAY IN WHO'S ALLOWED TO BE YOUR FUTURE HUSBAND.
I'M NOT SURE YOU DO!
GLINT
DANGLE
MRK! IT TIED TO SOMEONE ELSE! YOU NEVER LEARN, DO YOU, HIYORI?!

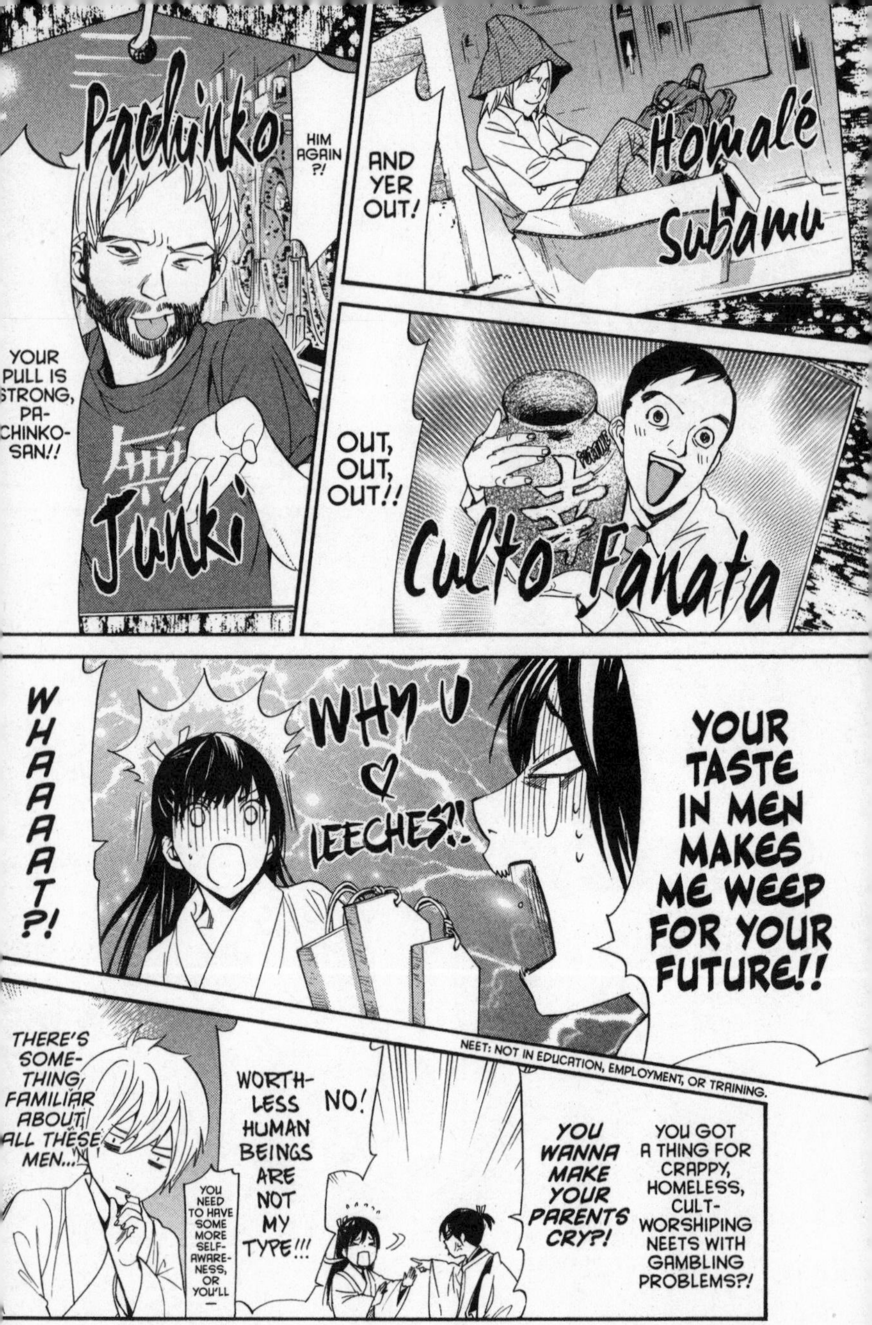
AND YER OUT!
Homalé Subamu
OUT, OUT, OUT!!
Culto Fanata
HIM AGAIN?!
Pachinko Junki
YOUR PULL IS STRONG, PA-CHINKO-SAN!!
YOUR TASTE IN MEN MAKES ME WEEP FOR YOUR FUTURE!!
WHY U ♥ LEECHES?!
WHAAAAAAT?!
NEET: NOT IN EDUCATION, EMPLOYMENT, OR TRAINING.
YOU GOT A THING FOR CRAPPY, HOMELESS, CULT-WORSHIPING NEETS WITH GAMBLING PROBLEMS?!
YOU WANNA MAKE YOUR PARENTS CRY?!
NO!
WORTH-LESS HUMAN BEINGS ARE NOT MY TYPE!!!
YOU NEED TO HAVE SOME MORE SELF-AWARE-NESS, OR YOU'LL —
THERE'S SOME-THING FAMILIAR ABOUT ALL THESE MEN...

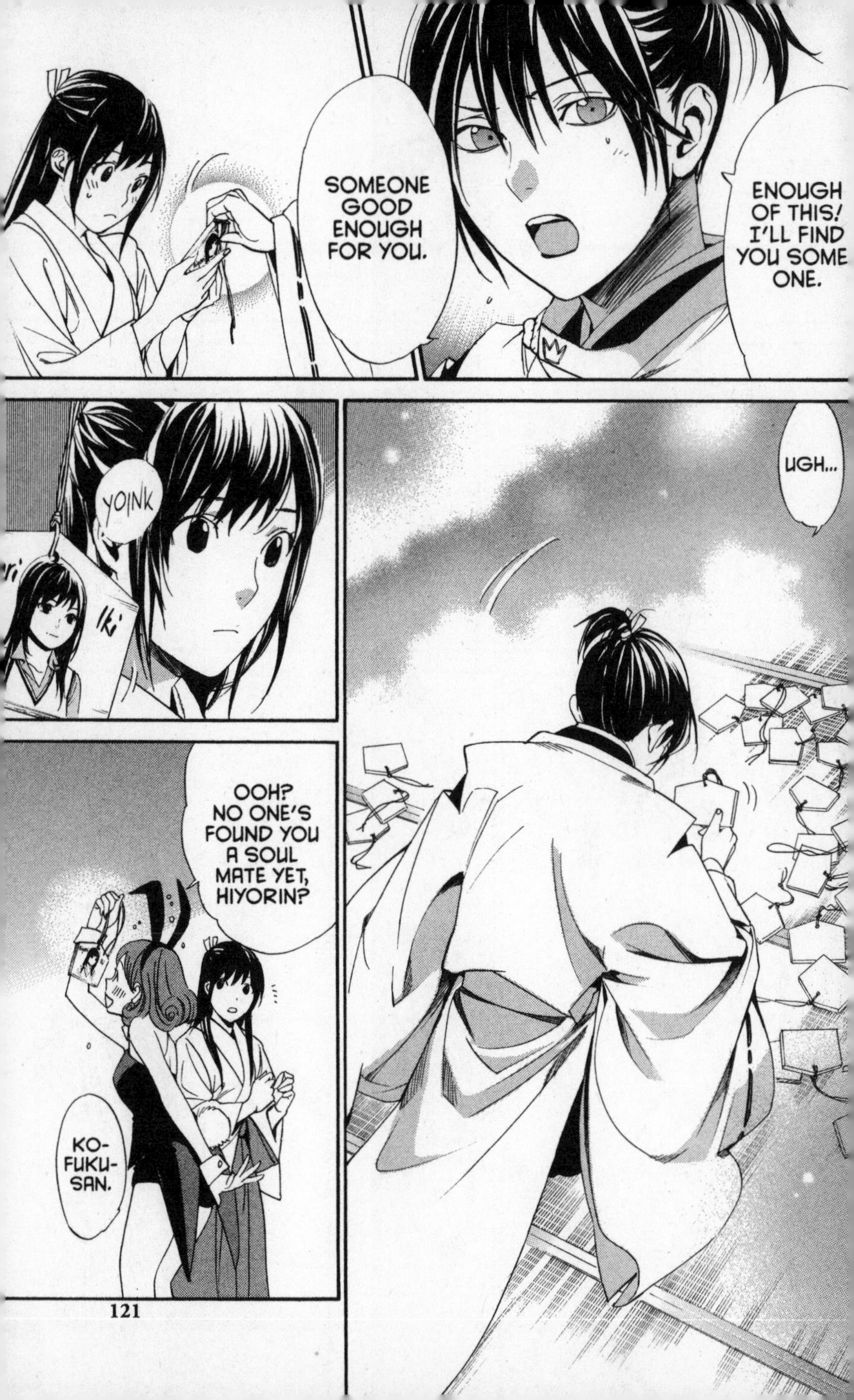
ENOUGH OF THIS! I'LL FIND YOU SOME ONE.
SOMEONE GOOD ENOUGH FOR YOU.
UGH...
YOINK
OOH? NO ONE'S FOUND YOU A SOUL MATE YET, HIYORIN?
KO-FUKU-SAN.

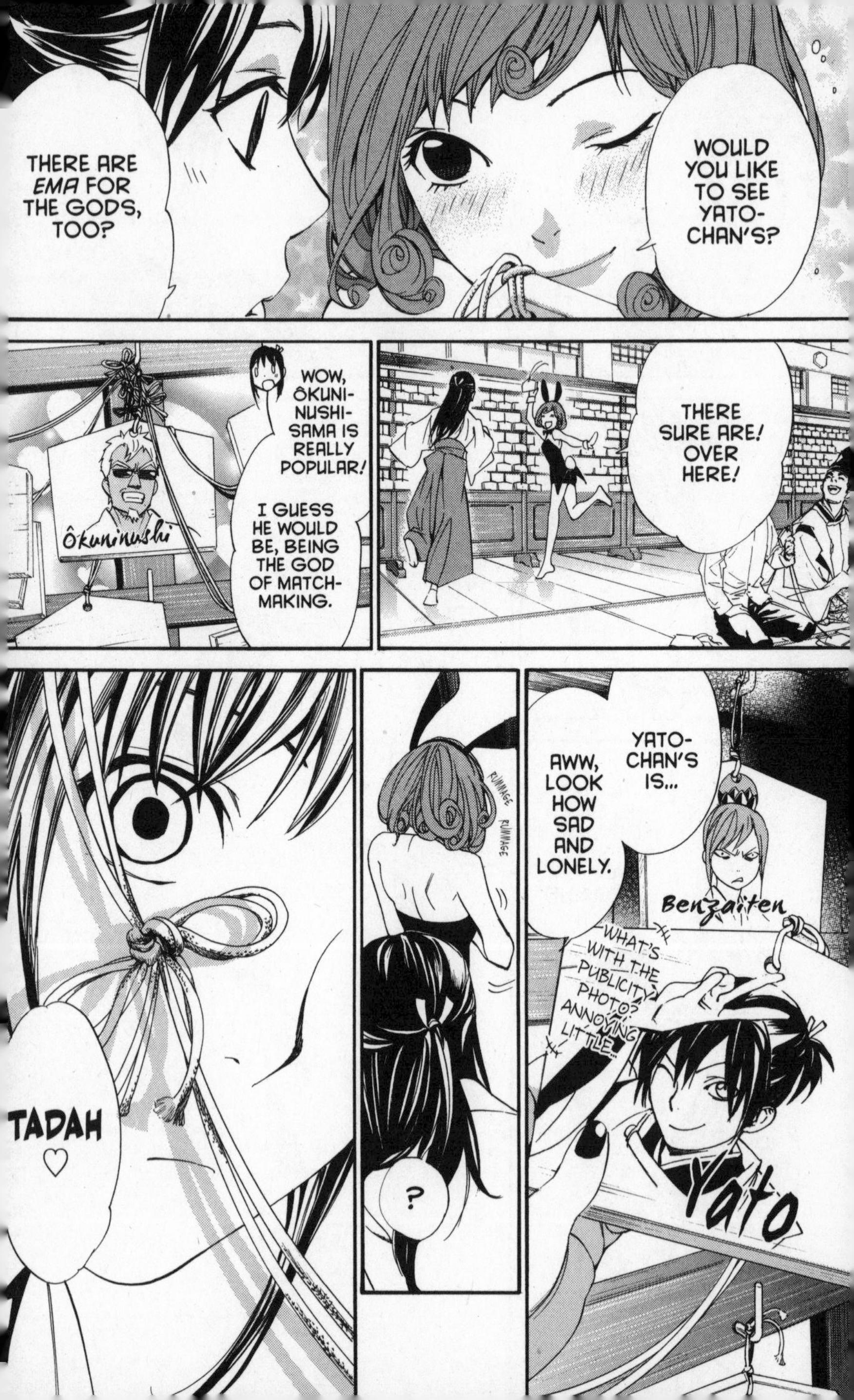
WOULD YOU LIKE TO SEE YATO-CHAN'S?
THERE ARE *EMA* FOR THE GODS, TOO?
THERE SURE ARE! OVER HERE!
WOW, ÔKUNINUSHI-SAMA IS REALLY POPULAR!
I GUESS HE WOULD BE, BEING THE GOD OF MATCH-MAKING.
Ôkuninushi
YATO-CHAN'S IS...
AWW, LOOK HOW SAD AND LONELY.
Benzaiten
WHAT'S WITH THE PUBLICITY PHOTO? ANNOYING LITTLE...
Yato
RUMMAGE
RUMMAGE
?
TADAH ♡

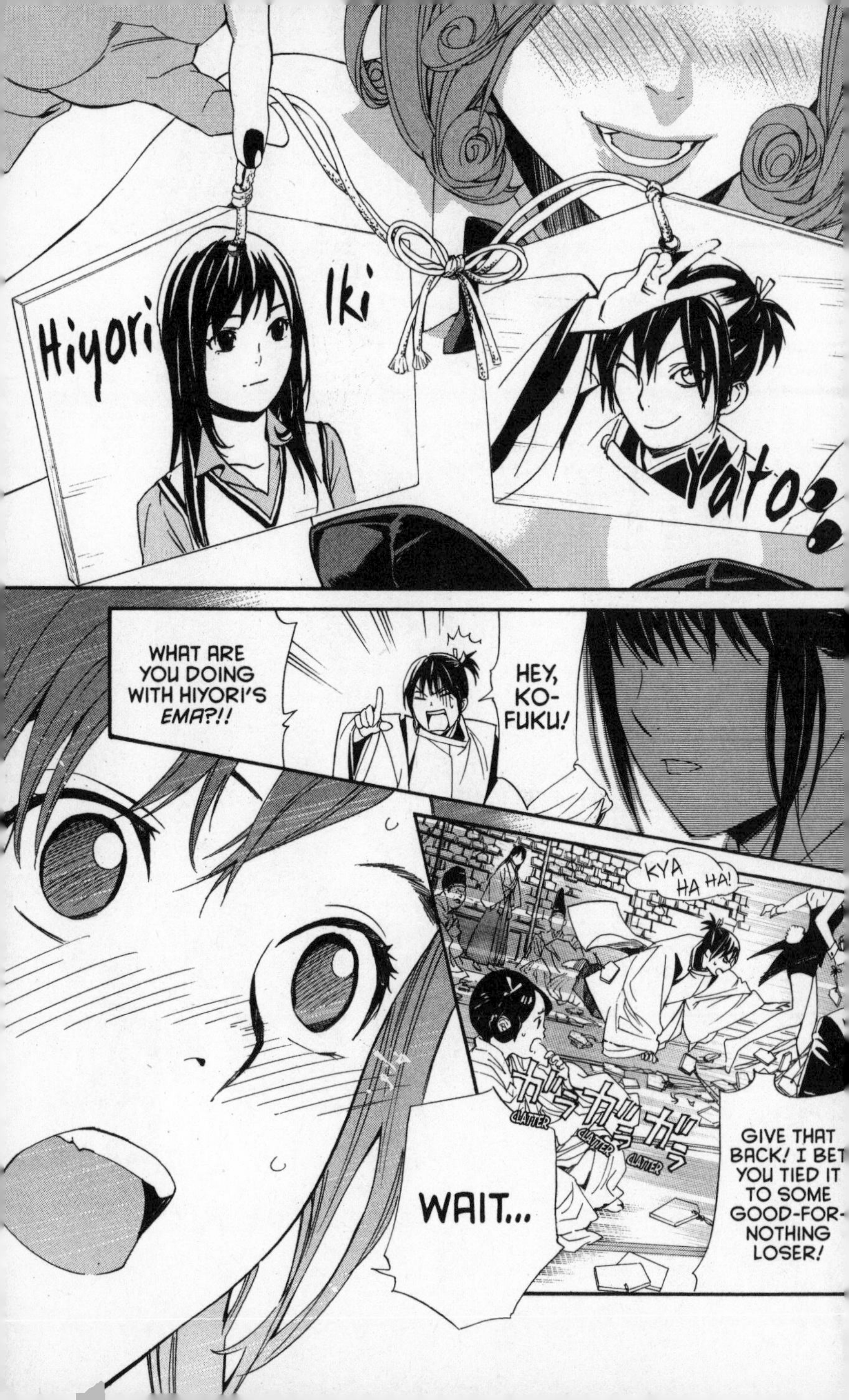

Hiyori Iki
Yato
HEY, KO-FUKU!
WHAT ARE YOU DOING WITH HIYORI'S EMA?!!
KYA HA HA!
GIVE THAT BACK! I BET YOU TIED IT TO SOME GOOD-FOR-NOTHING LOSER!
CLATTER
CLATTER
CLATTER
WAIT...

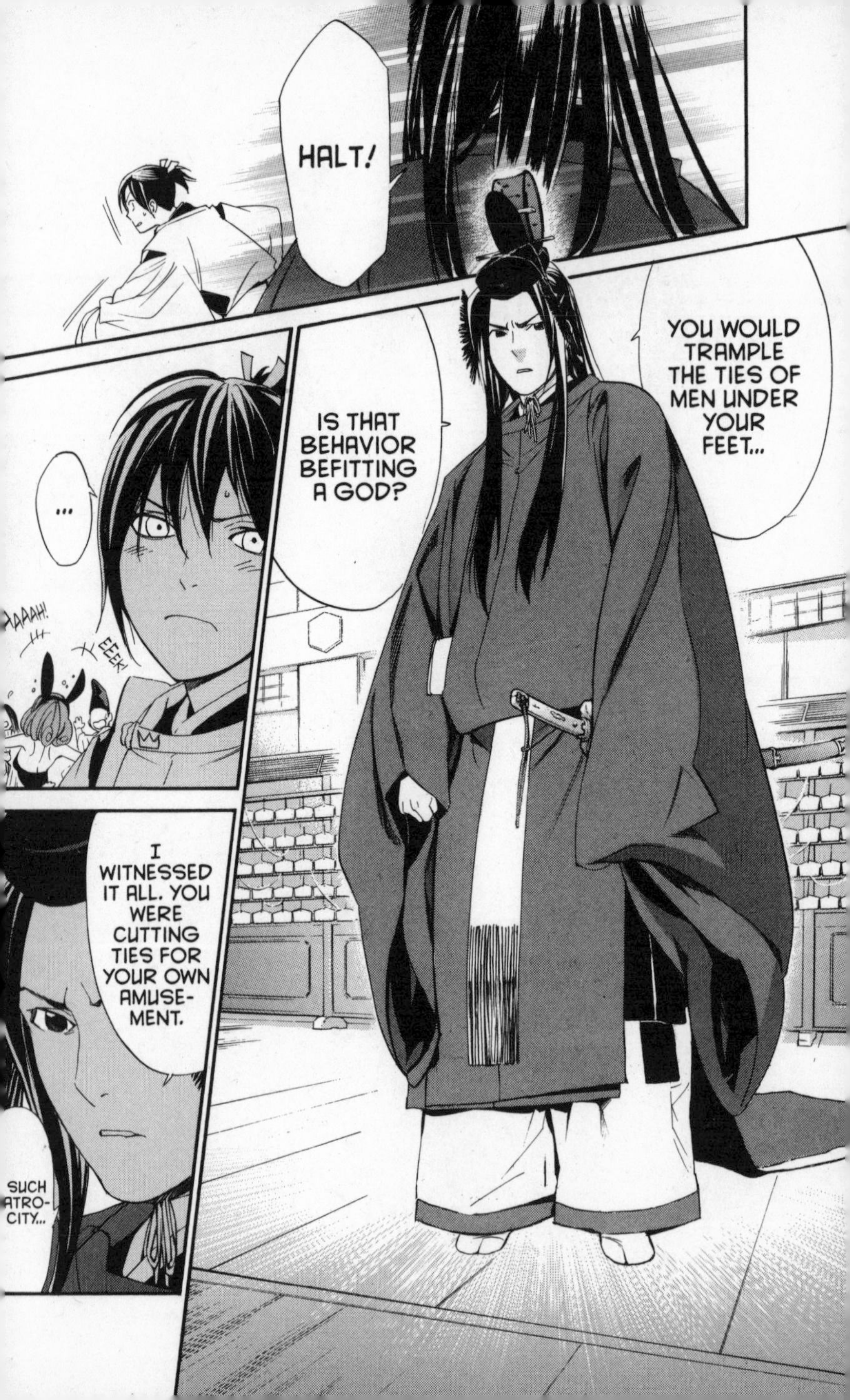
HALT!
YOU WOULD TRAMPLE THE TIES OF MEN UNDER YOUR FEET...
IS THAT BEHAVIOR BEFITTING A GOD?
...
EEEK!
AAAAH!
I WITNESSED IT ALL. YOU WERE CUTTING TIES FOR YOUR OWN AMUSE-MENT.
SUCH ATRO-CITY...

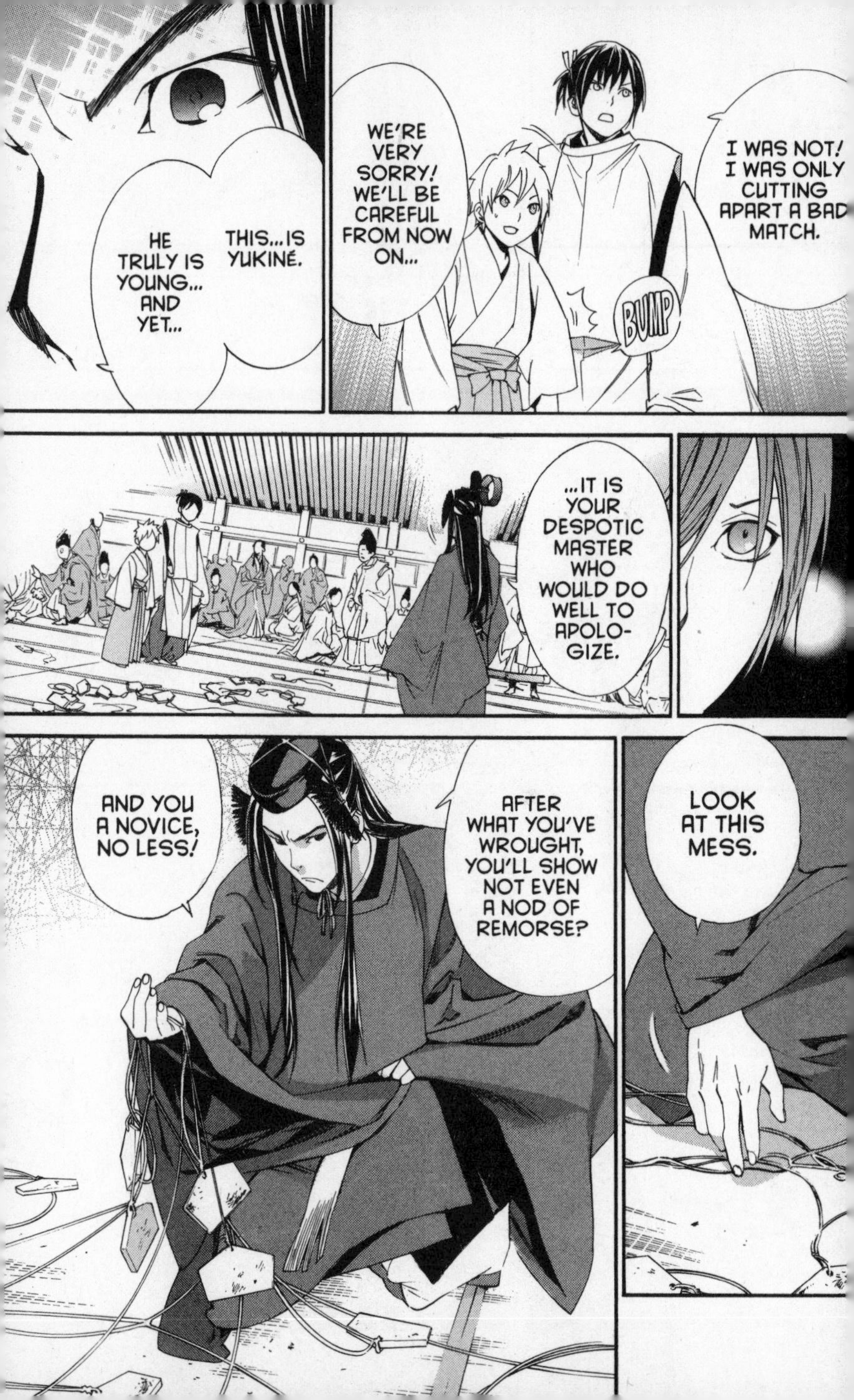
I WAS NOT! I WAS ONLY CUTTING APART A BAD MATCH.
BUMP
WE'RE VERY SORRY! WE'LL BE CAREFUL FROM NOW ON...
THIS...IS YUKINÉ.
HE TRULY IS YOUNG... AND YET...
...IT IS YOUR DESPOTIC MASTER WHO WOULD DO WELL TO APOLOGIZE.
LOOK AT THIS MESS.
AFTER WHAT YOU'VE WROUGHT, YOU'LL SHOW NOT EVEN A NOD OF REMORSE?
AND YOU A NOVICE, NO LESS!

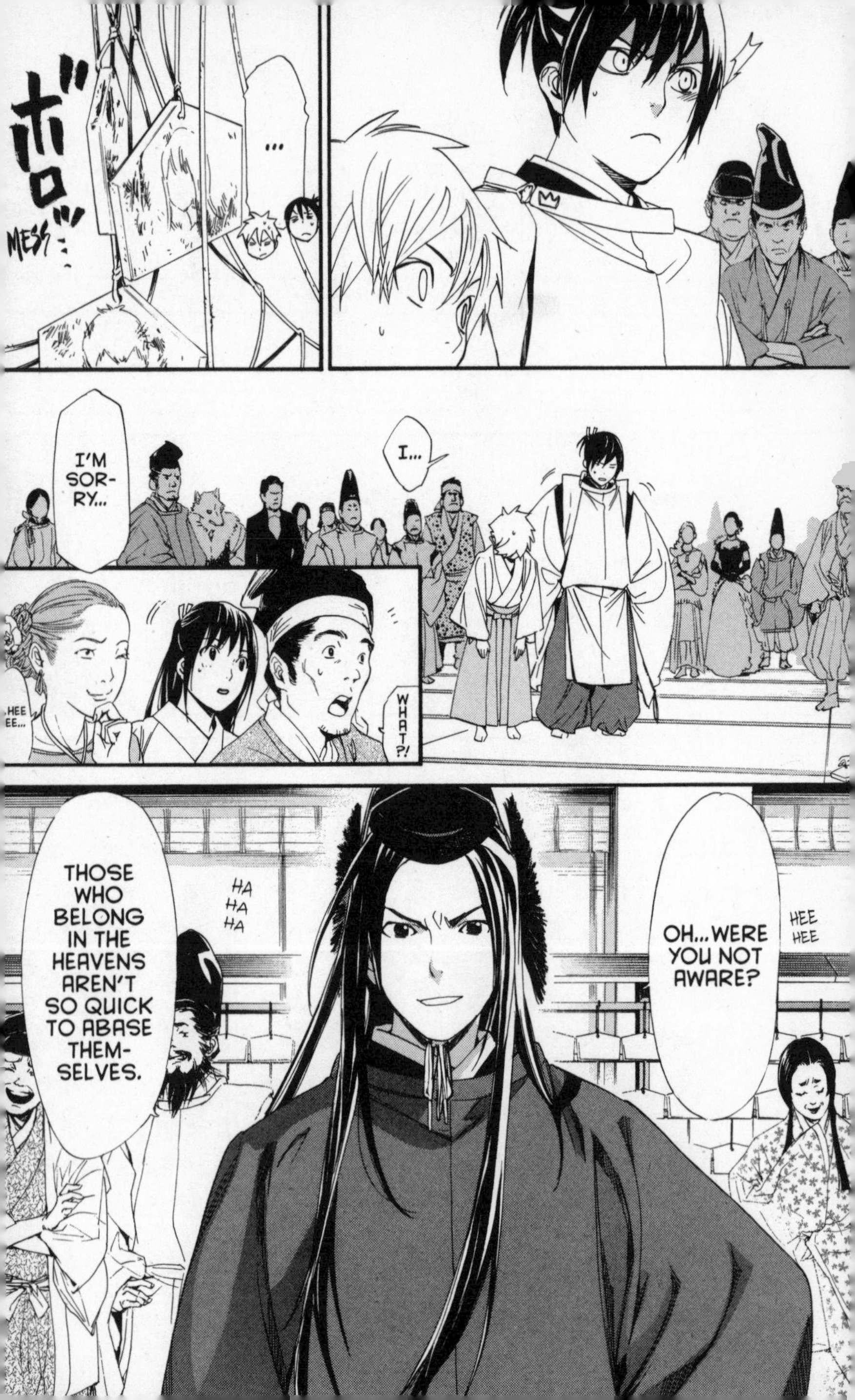
...
ボロッ
MESS
I...
I'M SORRY...
WHAT?!
HEE HEE...
OH... WERE YOU NOT AWARE?
HEE HEE
HA HA HA
THOSE WHO BELONG IN THE HEAVENS AREN'T SO QUICK TO ABASE THEMSELVES.

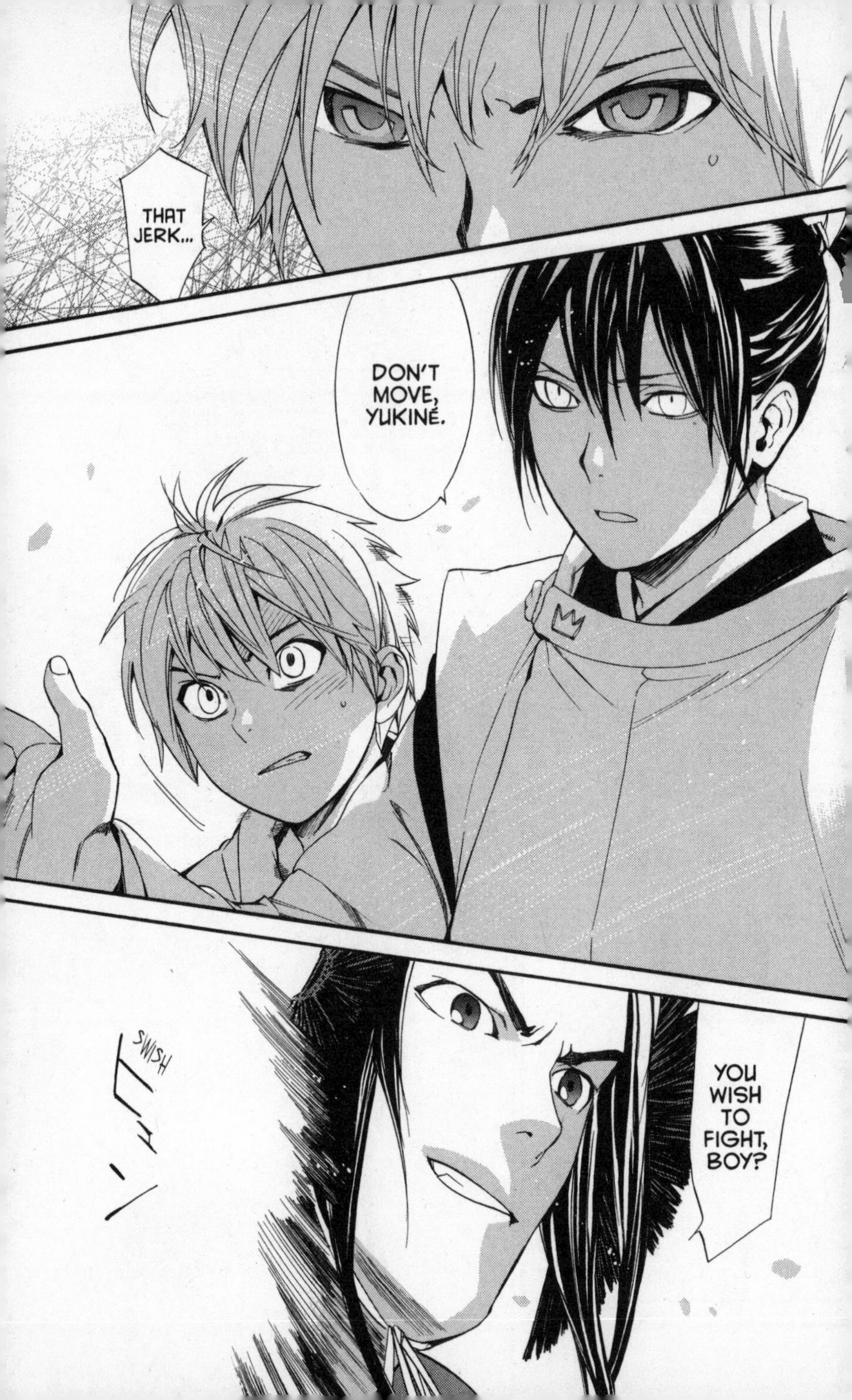
THAT JERK...
DON'T MOVE, YUKINÉ.
YOU WISH TO FIGHT, BOY?
SWISH

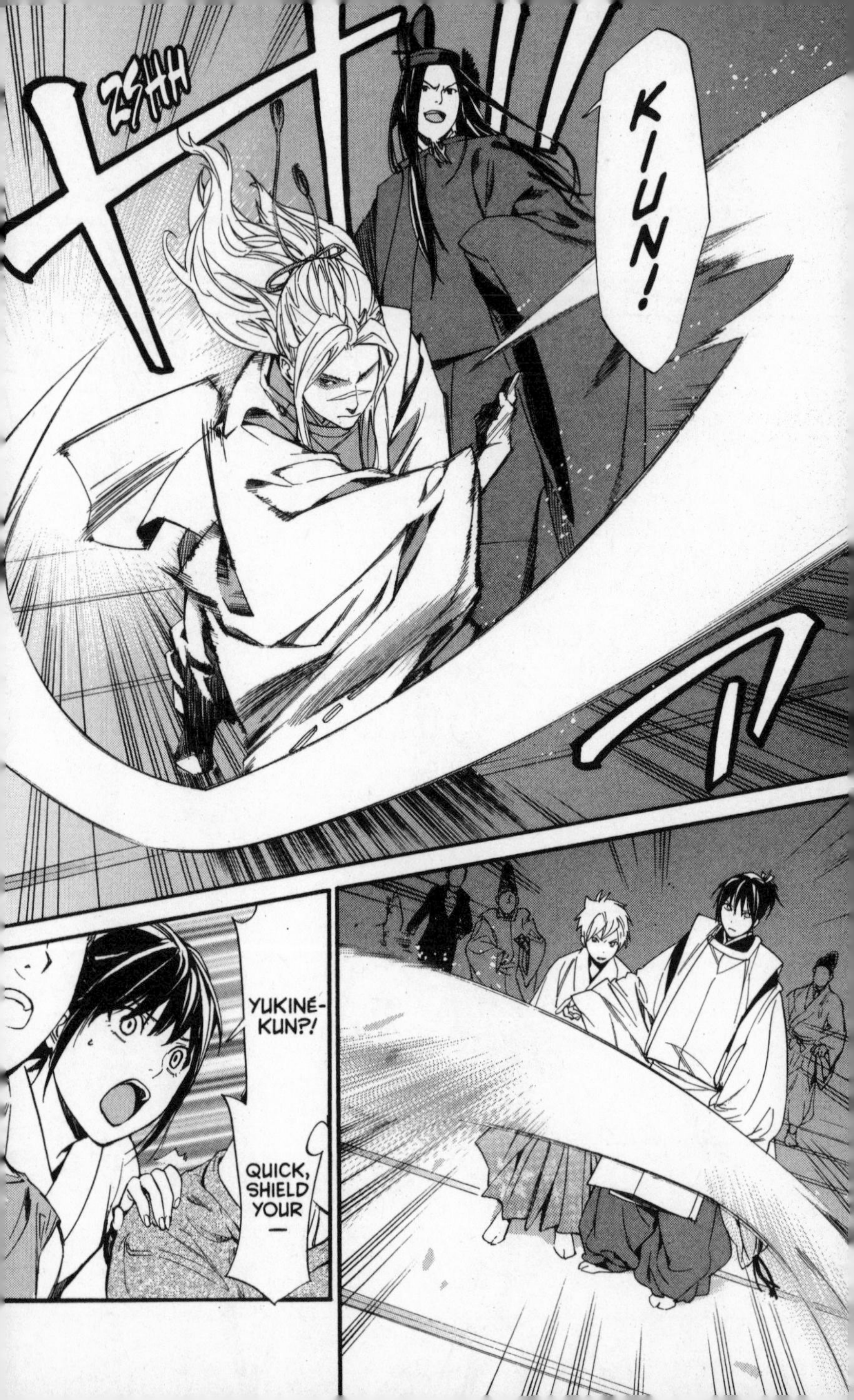
KIUN!
ZSHH
YUKINÉ-KUN?!
QUICK, SHIELD YOUR —

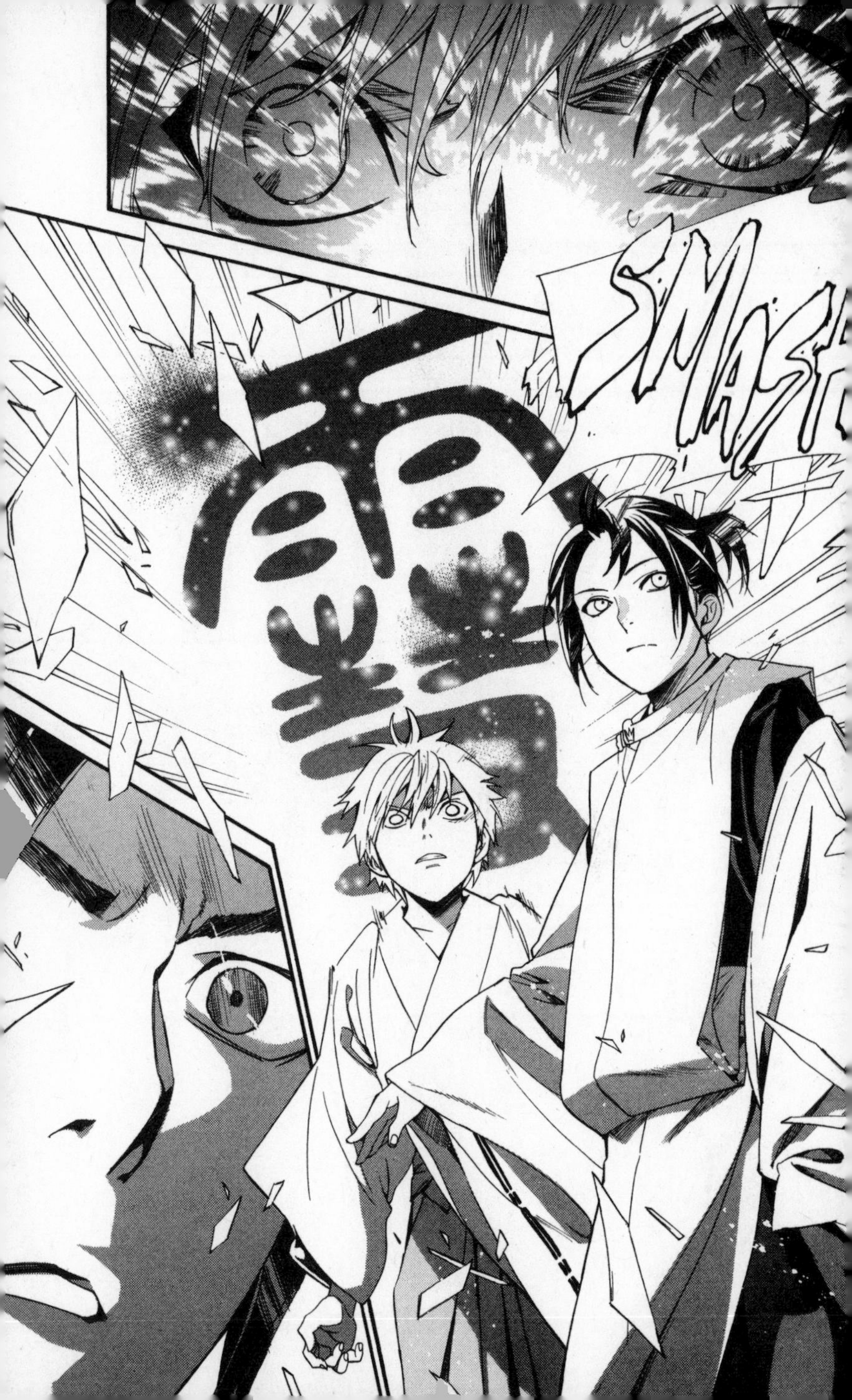
SMASH

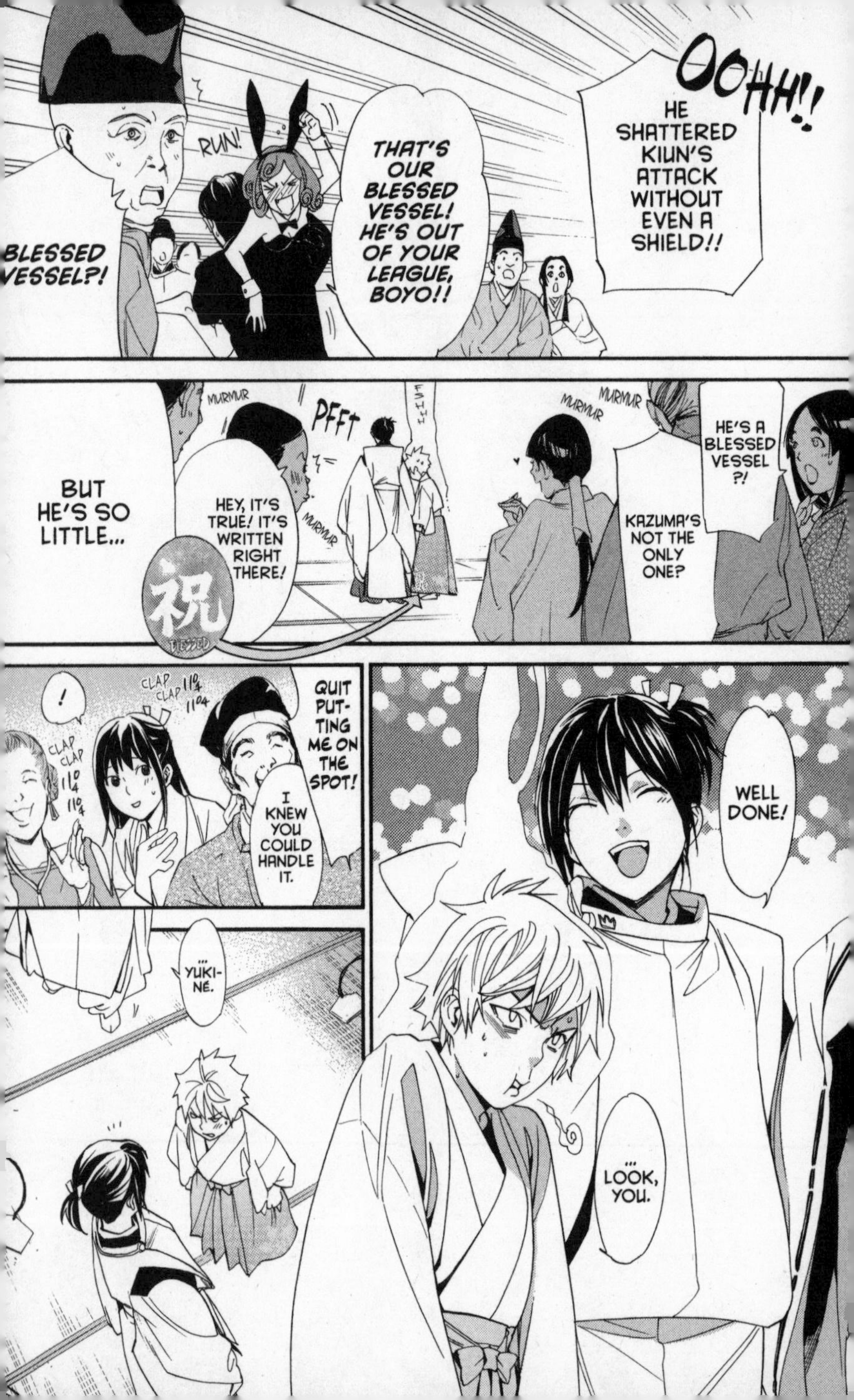
OOHH!!
HE SHATTERED KIUN'S ATTACK WITHOUT EVEN A SHIELD!!
THAT'S OUR BLESSED VESSEL! HE'S OUT OF YOUR LEAGUE, BOYO!!
RUN!
BLESSED VESSEL?!
HE'S A BLESSED VESSEL ?!
KAZUMA'S NOT THE ONLY ONE?
MURMUR
MURMUR
FSHHH
PFFT
MURMUR
MURMUR
HEY, IT'S TRUE! IT'S WRITTEN RIGHT THERE!
BUT HE'S SO LITTLE...
祝
BLESSED
WELL DONE!
...LOOK, YOU.
QUIT PUTTING ME ON THE SPOT!
I KNEW YOU COULD HANDLE IT.
CLAP CLAP
CLAP CLAP
!
...YUKINE.

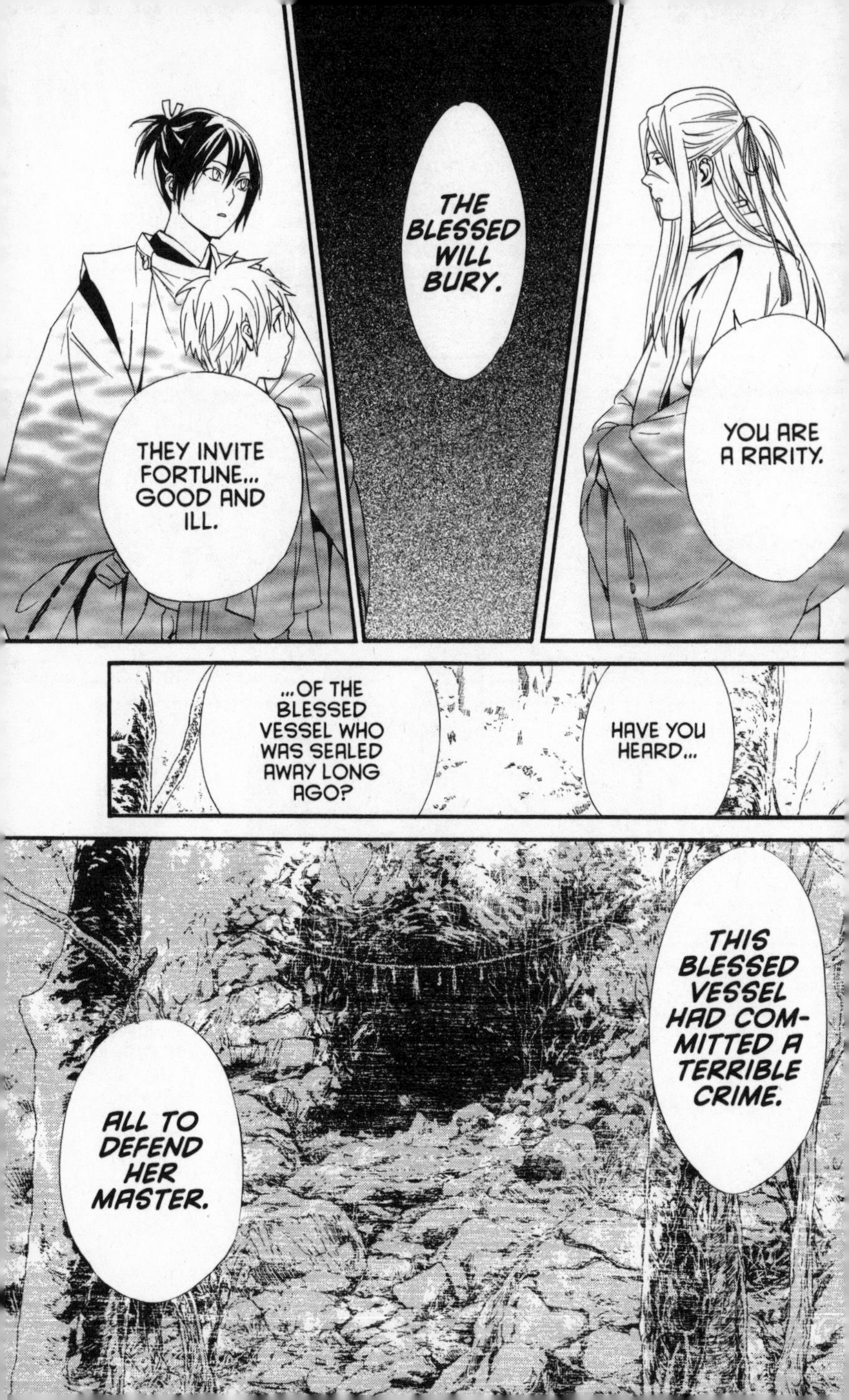
YOU ARE A RARITY.
THE BLESSED WILL BURY.
THEY INVITE FORTUNE... GOOD AND ILL.
HAVE YOU HEARD...
...OF THE BLESSED VESSEL WHO WAS SEALED AWAY LONG AGO?
THIS BLESSED VESSEL HAD COM-MITTED A TERRIBLE CRIME.
ALL TO DEFEND HER MASTER.

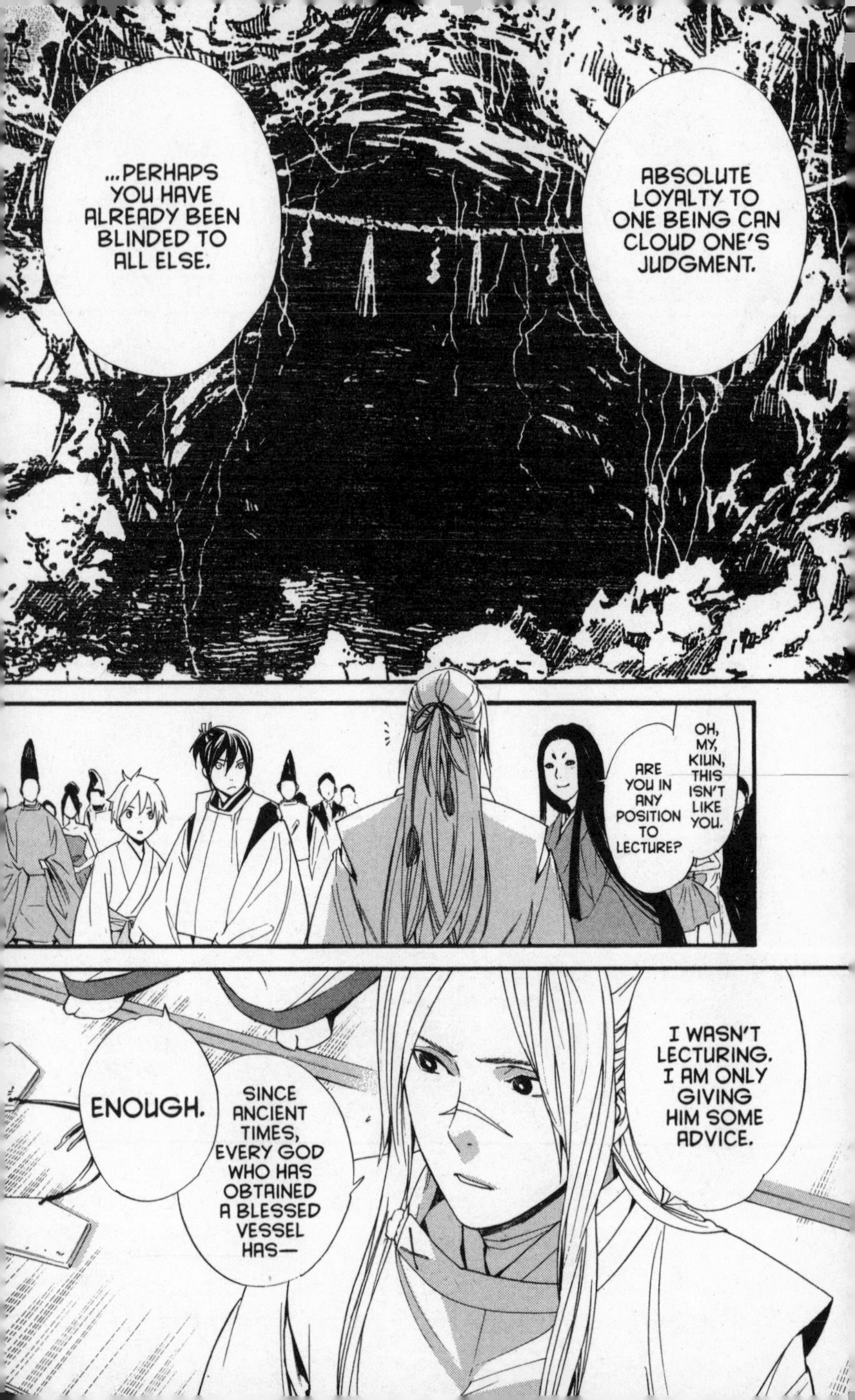
ABSOLUTE LOYALTY TO ONE BEING CAN CLOUD ONE'S JUDGMENT.
...PERHAPS YOU HAVE ALREADY BEEN BLINDED TO ALL ELSE.
OH, MY, KIUN, THIS ISN'T LIKE YOU.
ARE YOU IN ANY POSITION TO LECTURE?
I WASN'T LECTURING. I AM ONLY GIVING HIM SOME ADVICE.
SINCE ANCIENT TIMES, EVERY GOD WHO HAS OBTAINED A BLESSED VESSEL HAS—
ENOUGH.

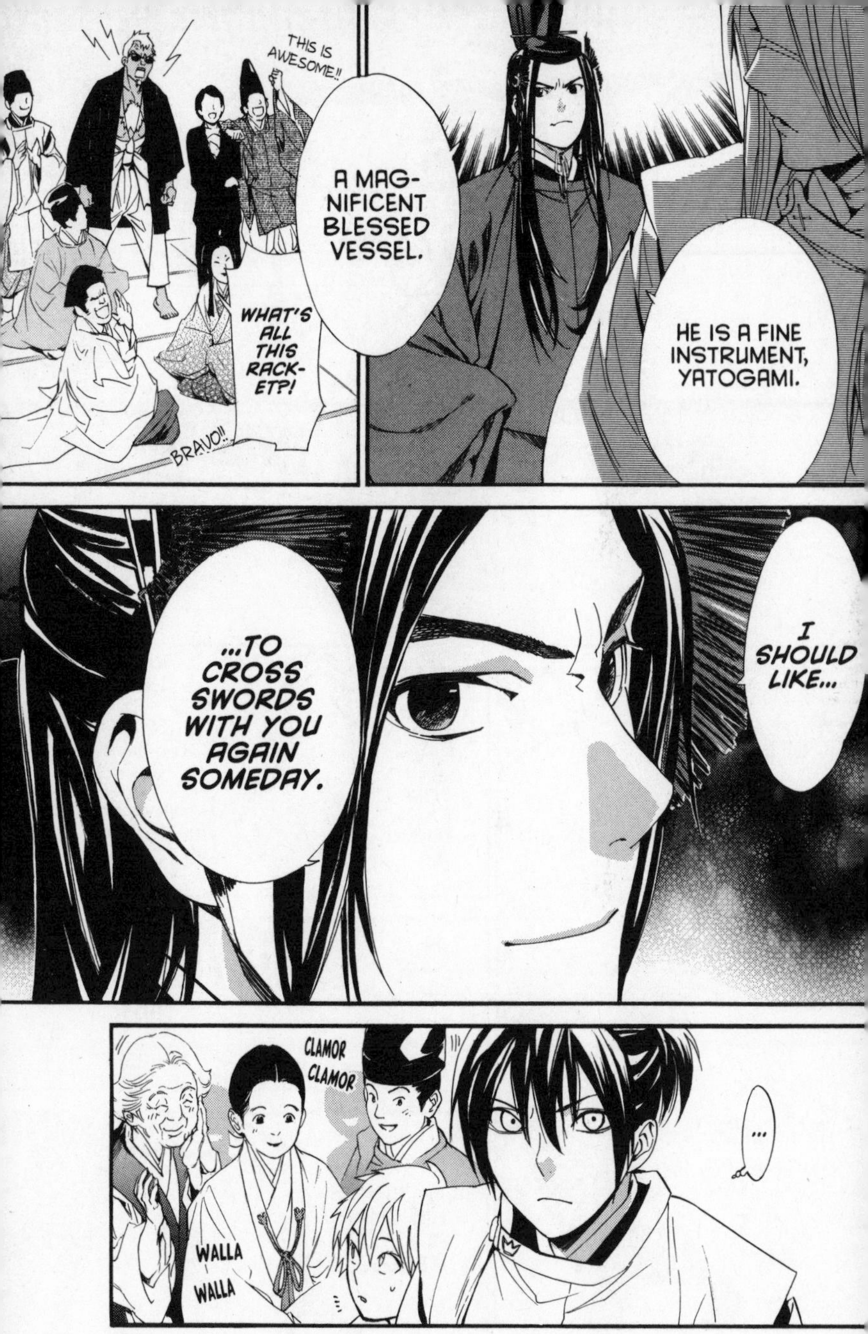
HE IS A FINE INSTRUMENT, YATOGAMI.
A MAG-NIFICENT BLESSED VESSEL.
THIS IS AWESOME!!
WHAT'S ALL THIS RACK-ET?!
BRAVO!!
I SHOULD LIKE...
...TO CROSS SWORDS WITH YOU AGAIN SOMEDAY.
...
CLAMOR CLAMOR
WALLA WALLA

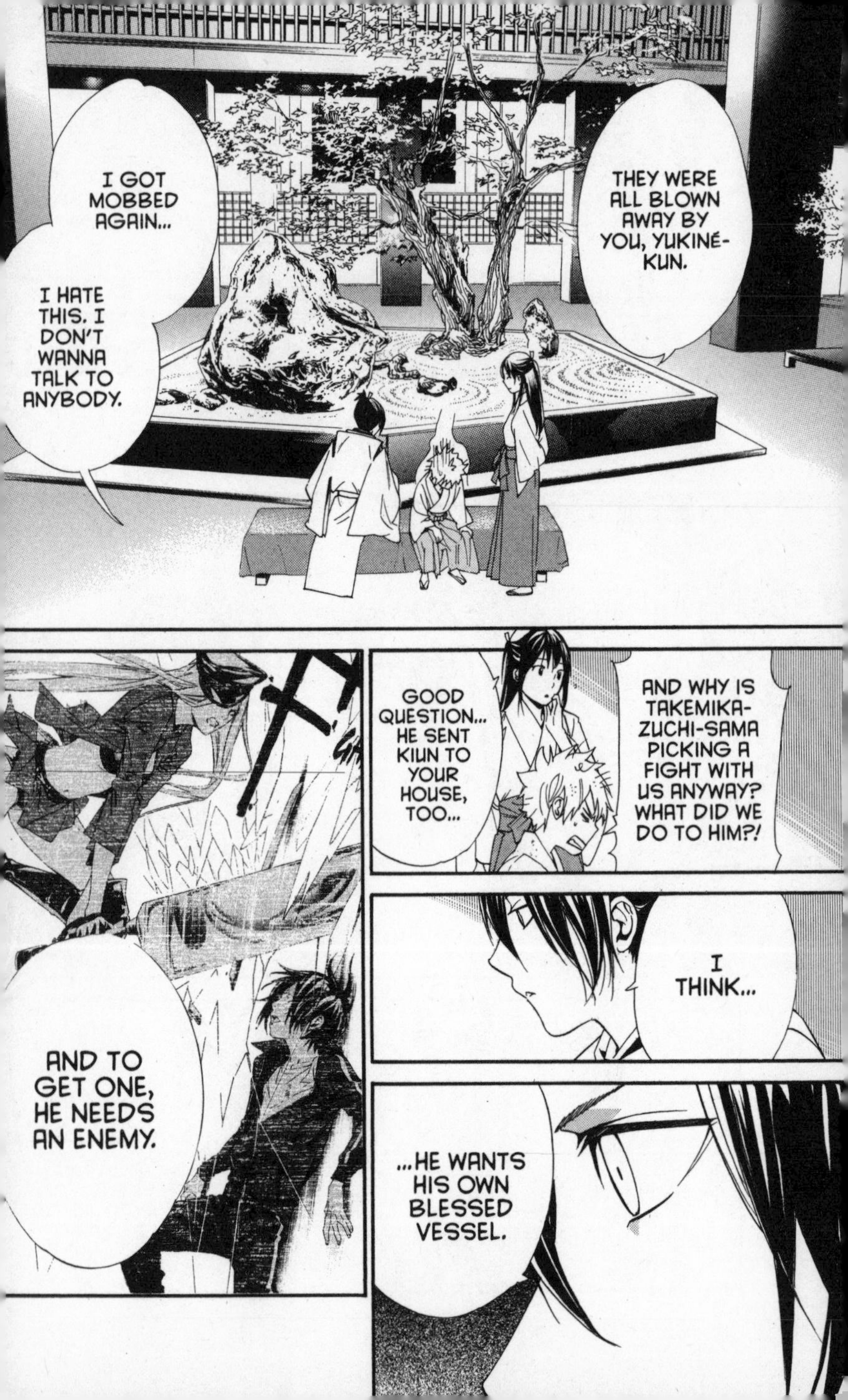
THEY WERE ALL BLOWN AWAY BY YOU, YUKINÉ-KUN.
I GOT MOBBED AGAIN...
I HATE THIS. I DON'T WANNA TALK TO ANYBODY.
AND WHY IS TAKEMIKA-ZUCHI-SAMA PICKING A FIGHT WITH US ANYWAY? WHAT DID WE DO TO HIM?!
GOOD QUESTION... HE SENT KIUN TO YOUR HOUSE, TOO...
I THINK...
...HE WANTS HIS OWN BLESSED VESSEL.
AND TO GET ONE, HE NEEDS AN ENEMY.

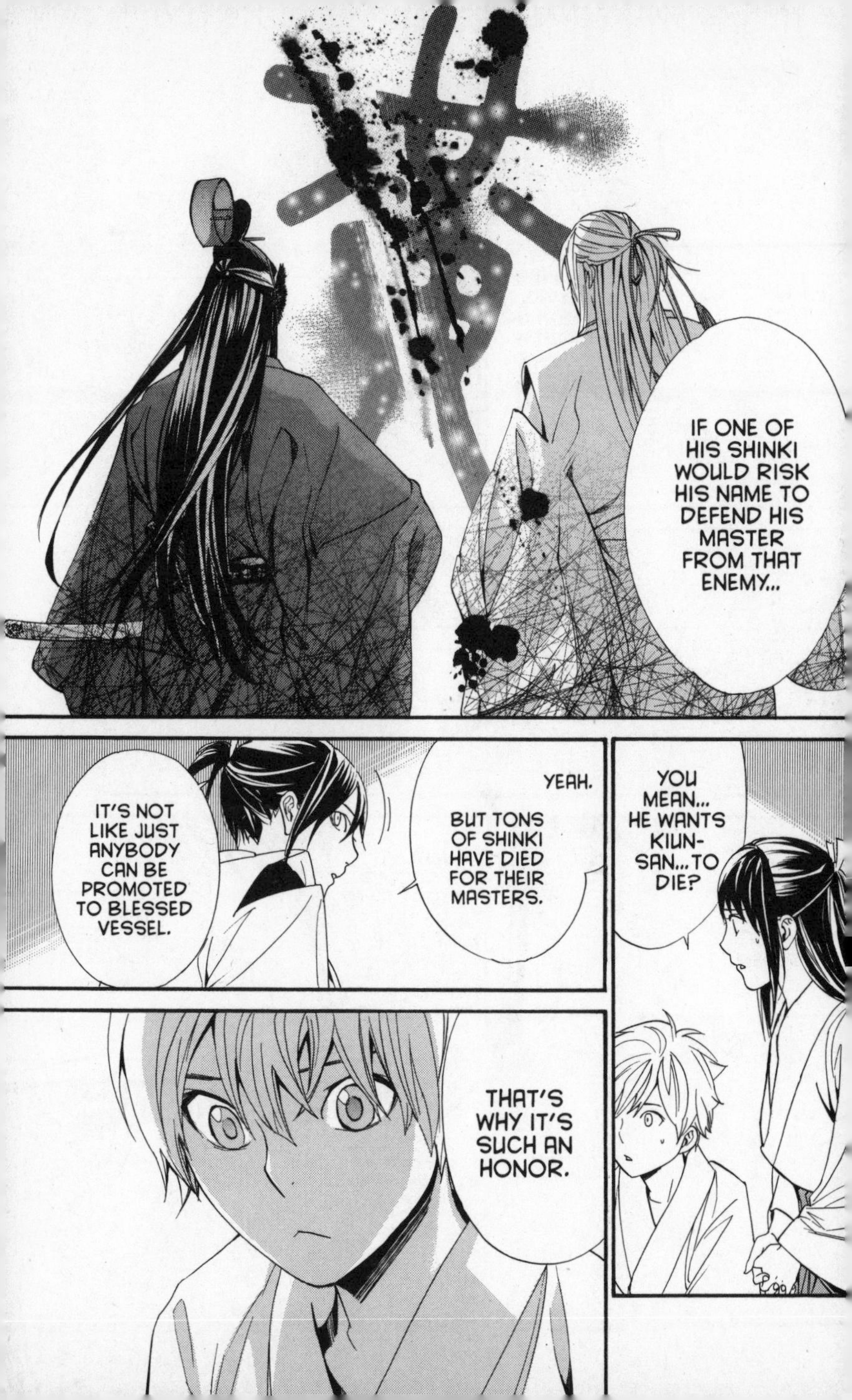
IF ONE OF HIS SHINKI WOULD RISK HIS NAME TO DEFEND HIS MASTER FROM THAT ENEMY...
YOU MEAN... HE WANTS KIUN-SAN...TO DIE?
YEAH.
BUT TONS OF SHINKI HAVE DIED FOR THEIR MASTERS.
IT'S NOT LIKE JUST ANYBODY CAN BE PROMOTED TO BLESSED VESSEL.
THAT'S WHY IT'S SUCH AN HONOR.

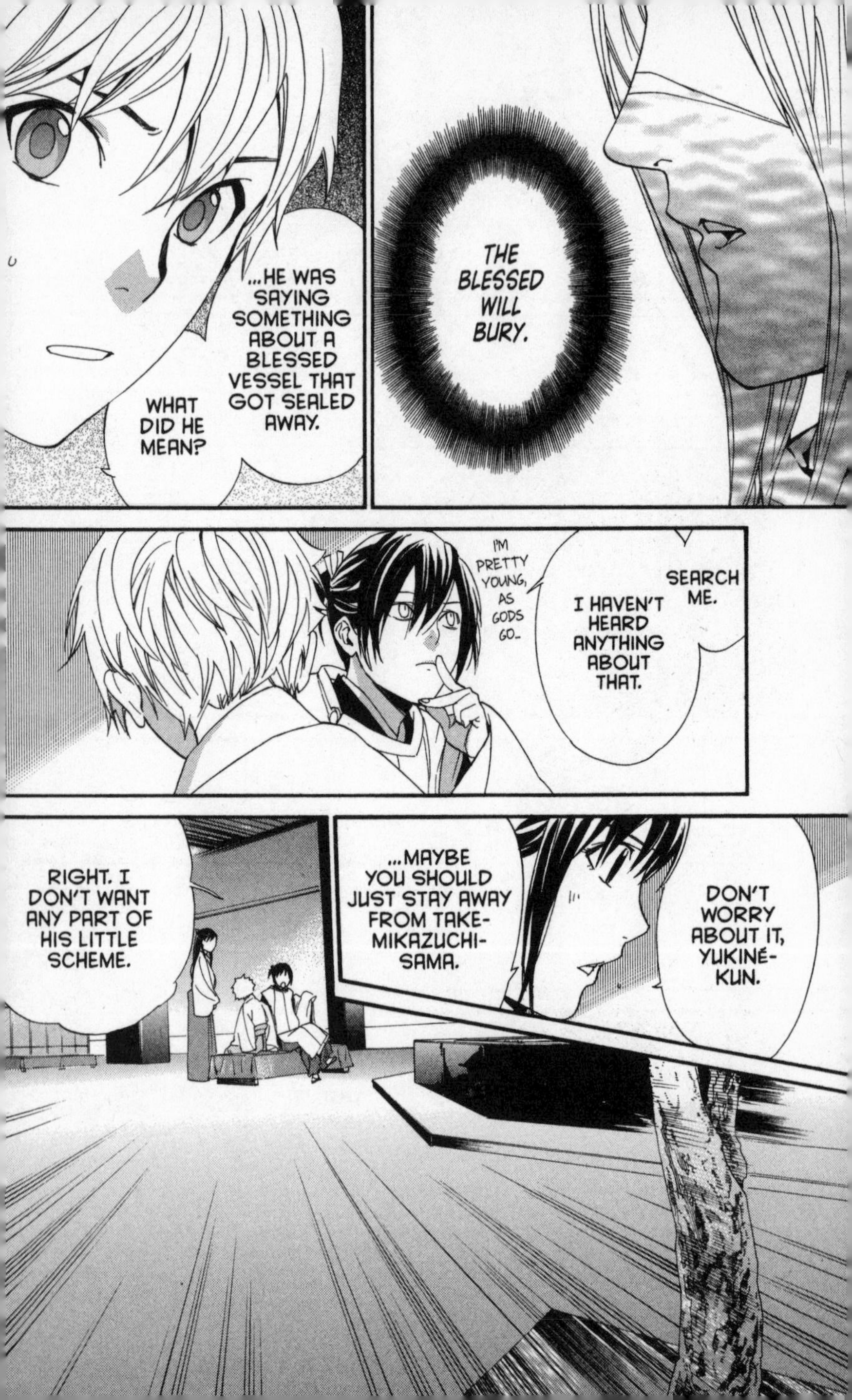
THE BLESSED WILL BURY.
...HE WAS SAYING SOMETHING ABOUT A BLESSED VESSEL THAT GOT SEALED AWAY.
WHAT DID HE MEAN?
SEARCH ME.
I HAVEN'T HEARD ANYTHING ABOUT THAT.
I'M PRETTY YOUNG, AS GODS GO...
DON'T WORRY ABOUT IT, YUKINÉ-KUN.
...MAYBE YOU SHOULD JUST STAY AWAY FROM TAKE-MIKAZUCHI-SAMA.
RIGHT. I DON'T WANT ANY PART OF HIS LITTLE SCHEME.

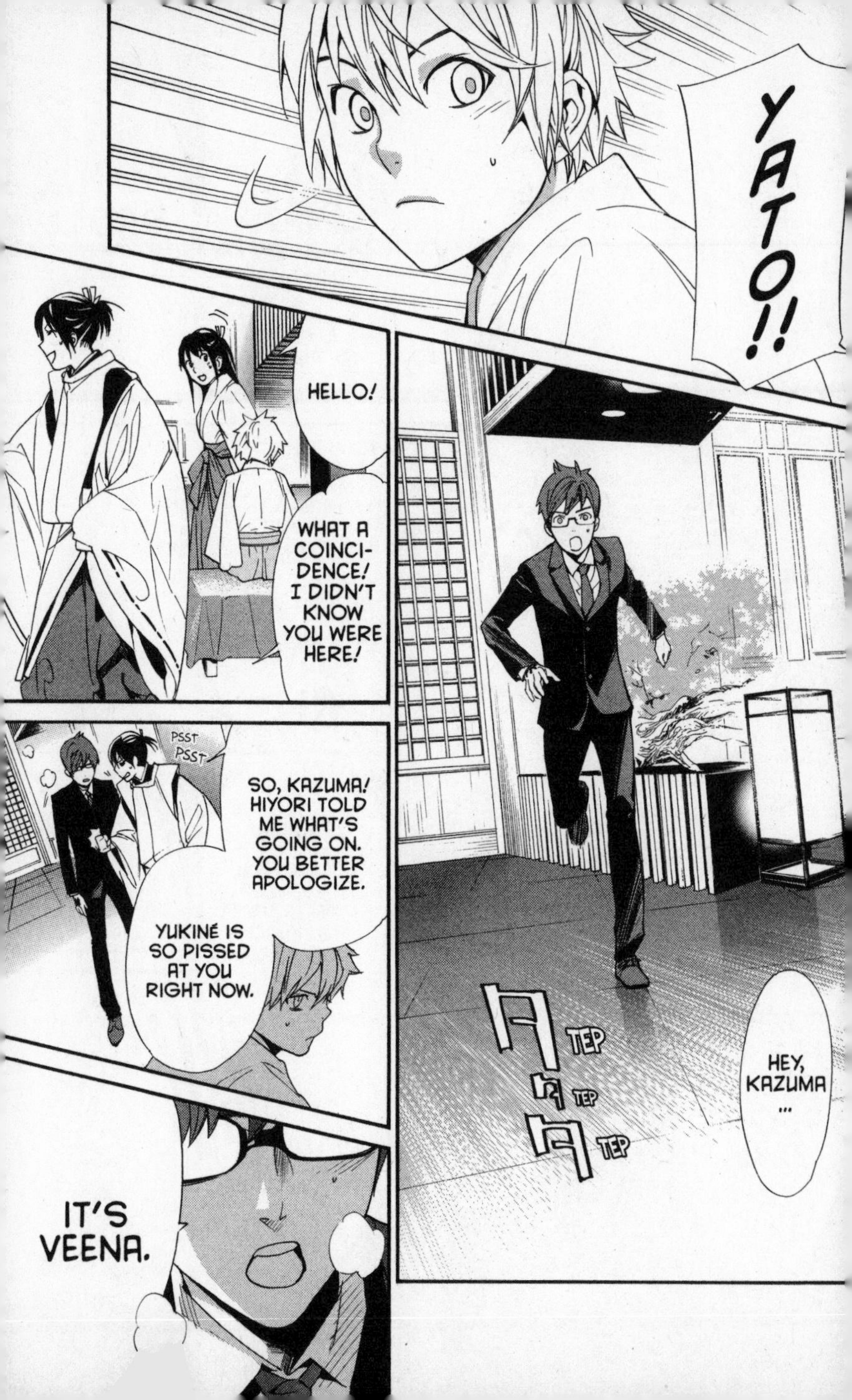
YATO!!
HEY, KAZUMA ...
TEP TEP TEP
HELLO!
WHAT A COINCIDENCE! I DIDN'T KNOW YOU WERE HERE!
PSST PSST
SO, KAZUMA! HIYORI TOLD ME WHAT'S GOING ON. YOU BETTER APOLOGIZE.
YUKINÉ IS SO PISSED AT YOU RIGHT NOW.
IT'S VEENA.

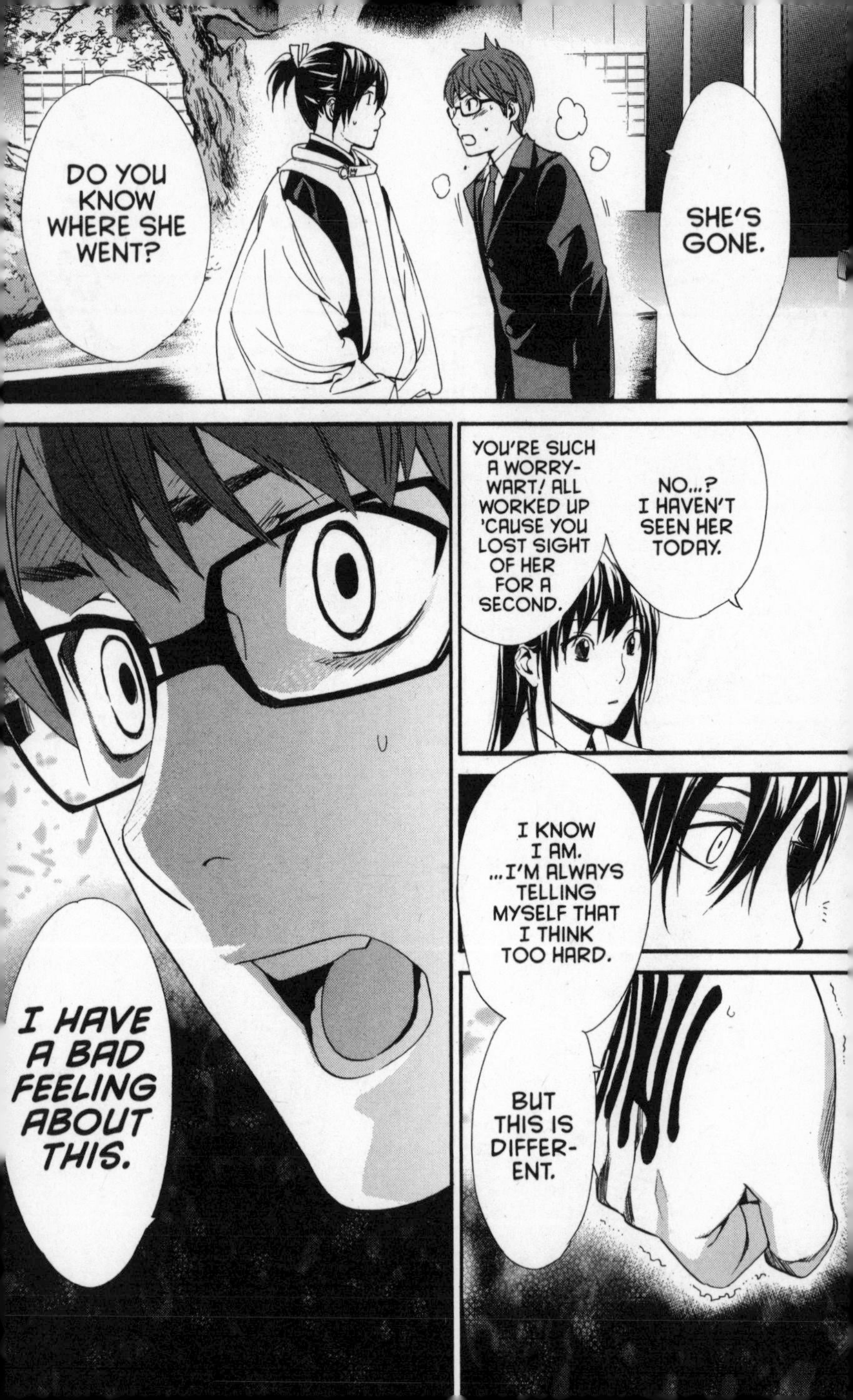
SHE'S GONE.
DO YOU KNOW WHERE SHE WENT?
NO...? I HAVEN'T SEEN HER TODAY.
YOU'RE SUCH A WORRY-WART! ALL WORKED UP 'CAUSE YOU LOST SIGHT OF HER FOR A SECOND.
I KNOW I AM. ...I'M ALWAYS TELLING MYSELF THAT I THINK TOO HARD.
BUT THIS IS DIFFER-ENT.
I HAVE A BAD FEELING ABOUT THIS.

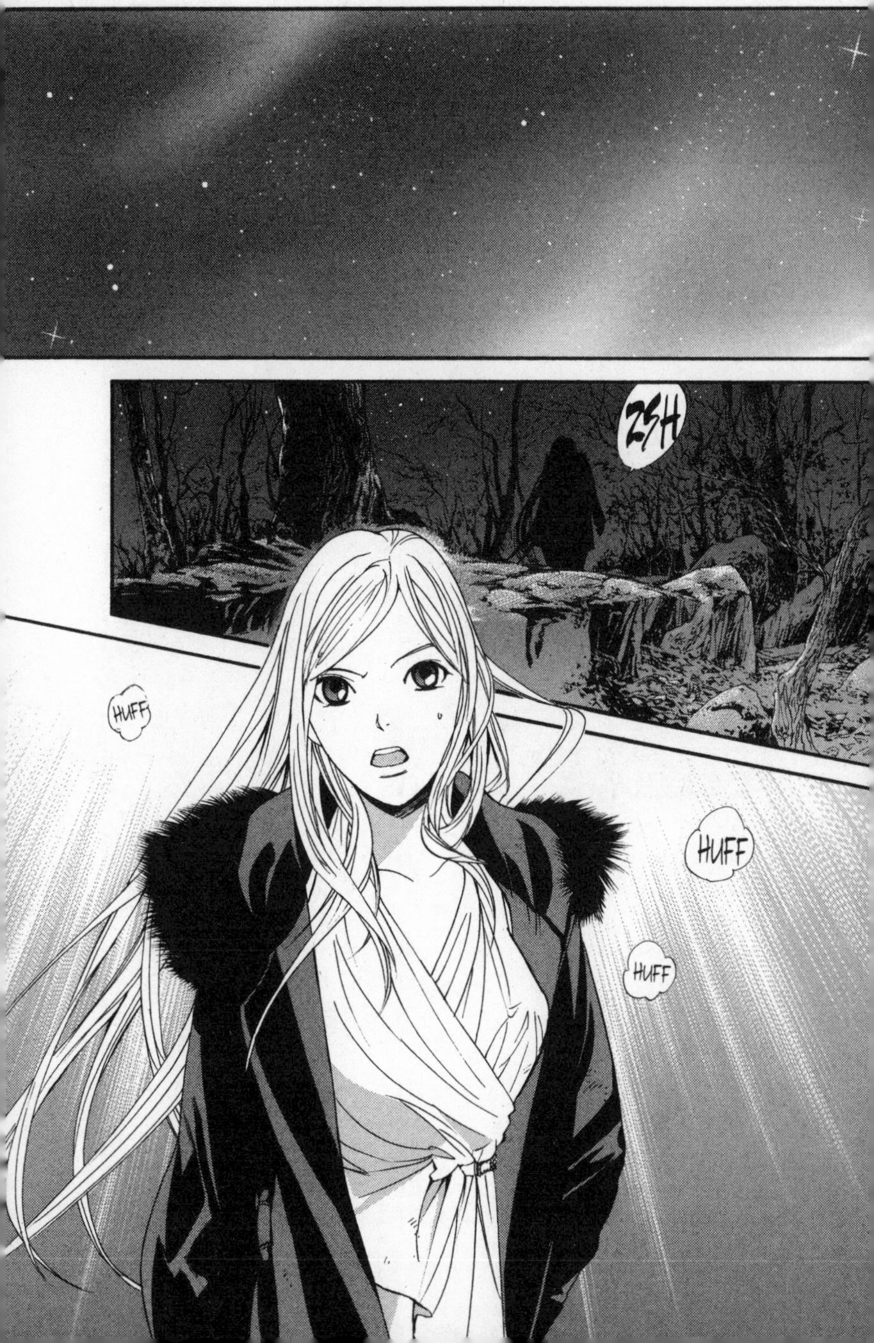
ZSH
HUFF
HUFF
HUFF

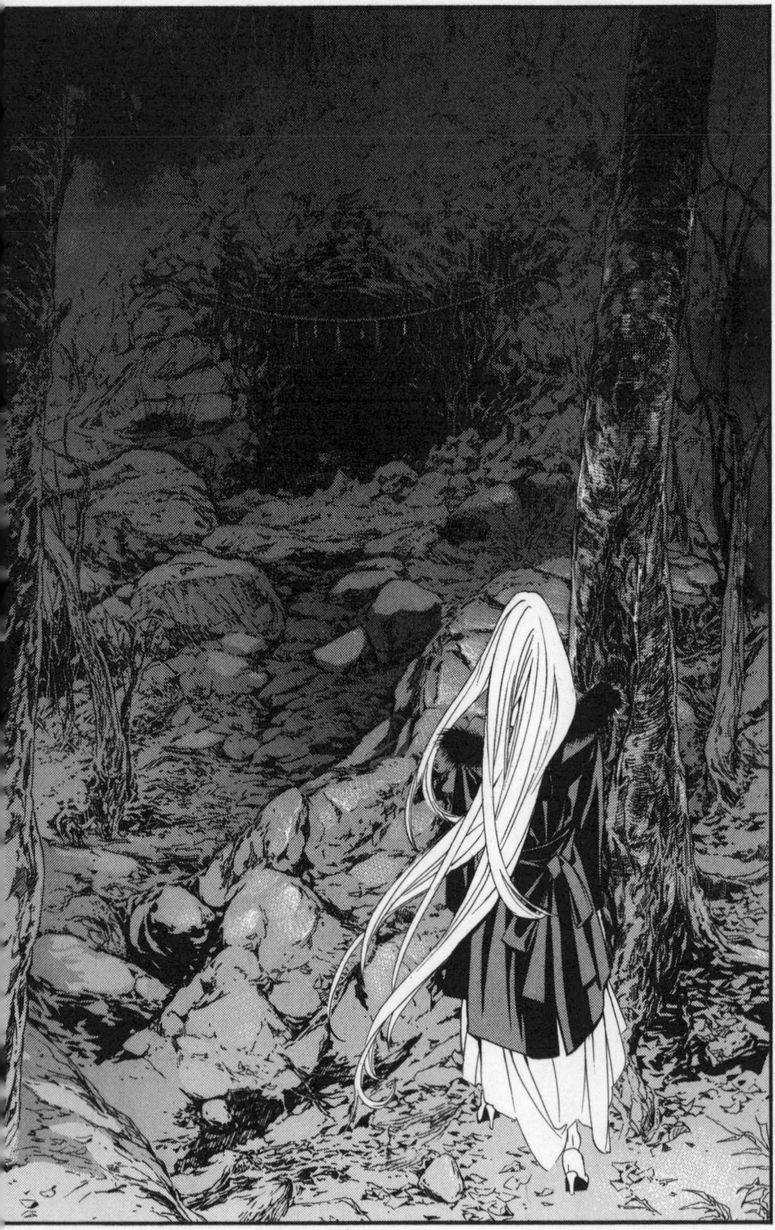

CHAPTER 58 / END

野

史

神

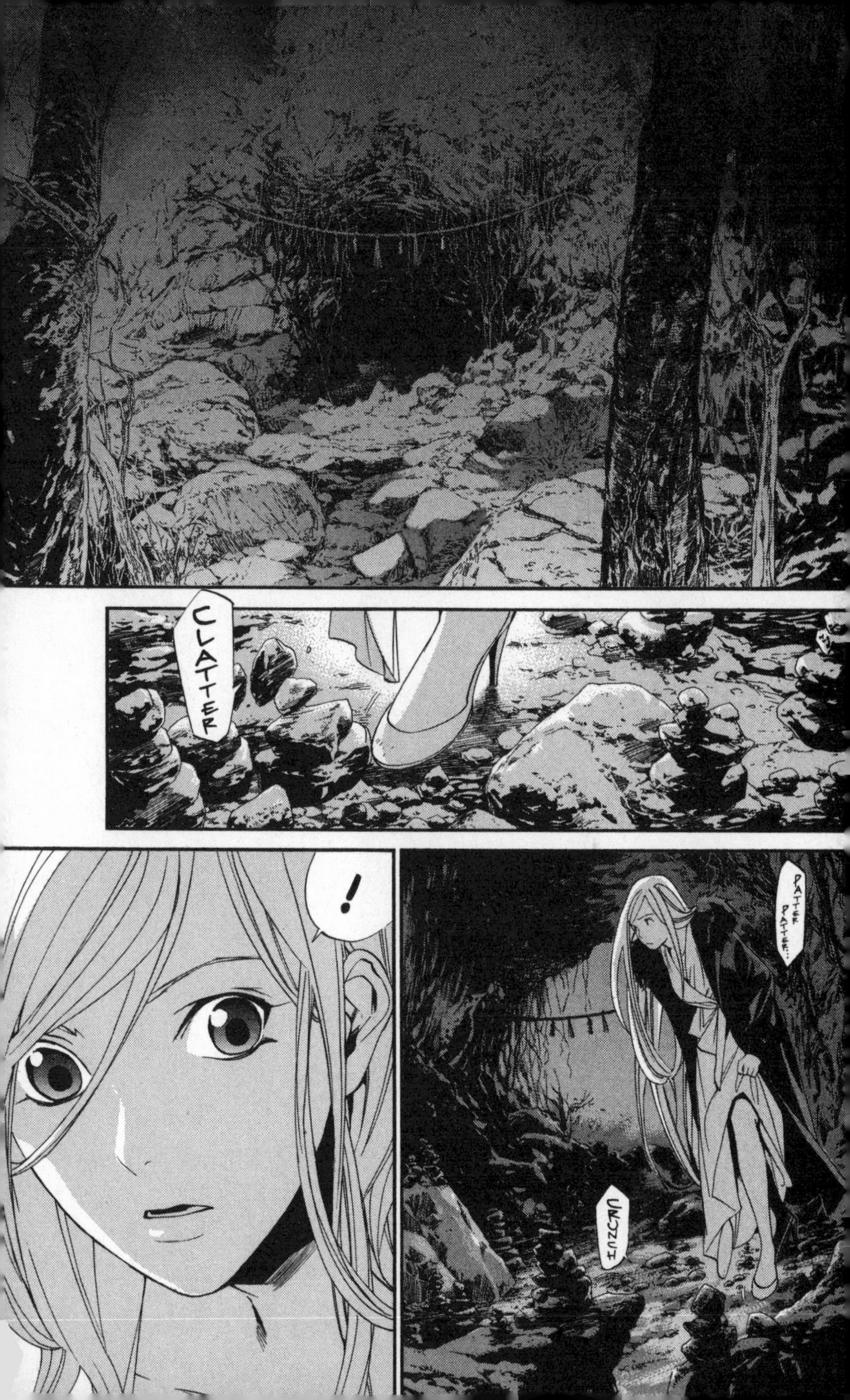
CLATTER
PATTER PATTER...
CRUNCH
!

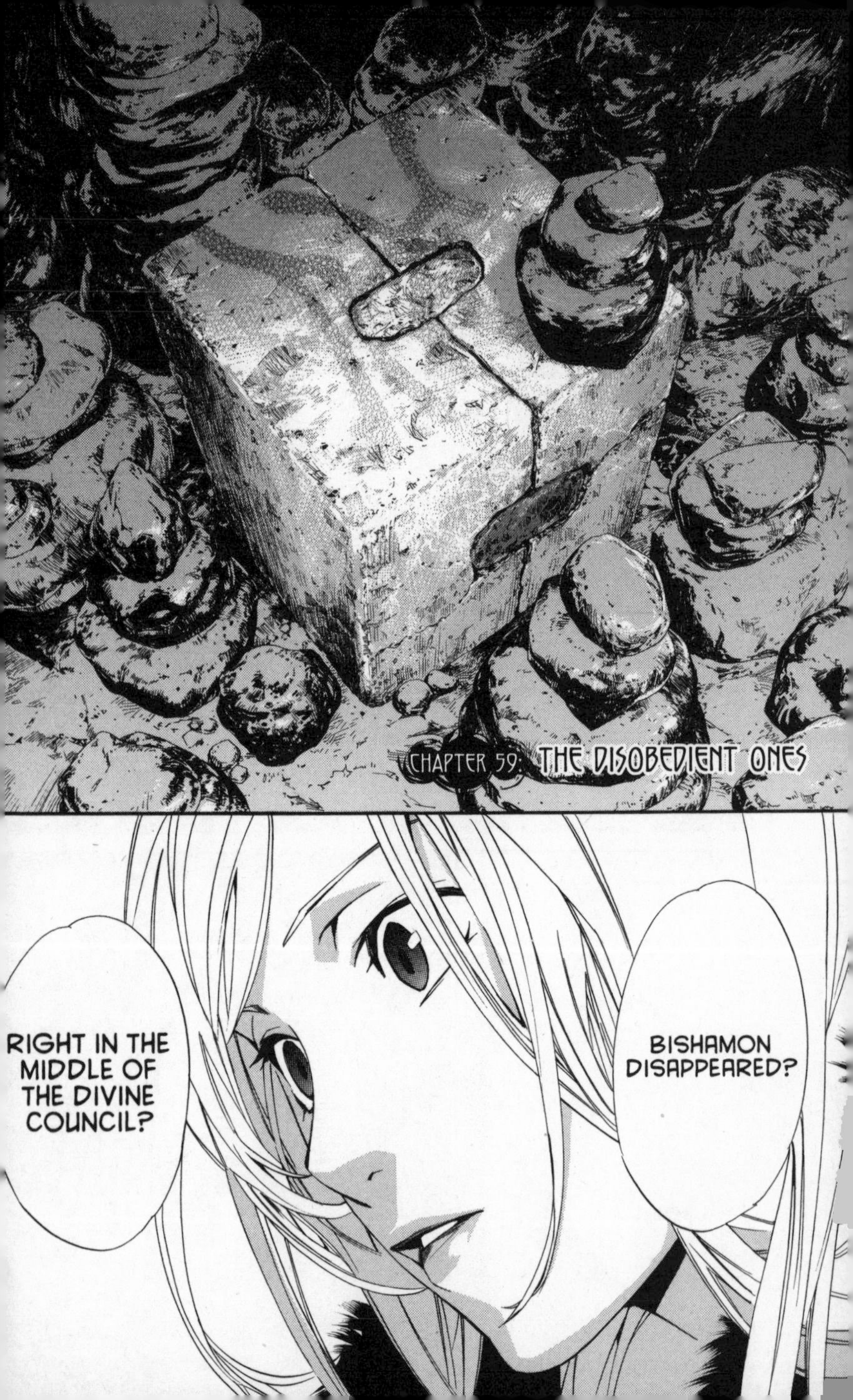
CHAPTER 59: THE DISOBEDIENT ONES
BISHAMON DISAPPEARED?
RIGHT IN THE MIDDLE OF THE DIVINE COUNCIL?

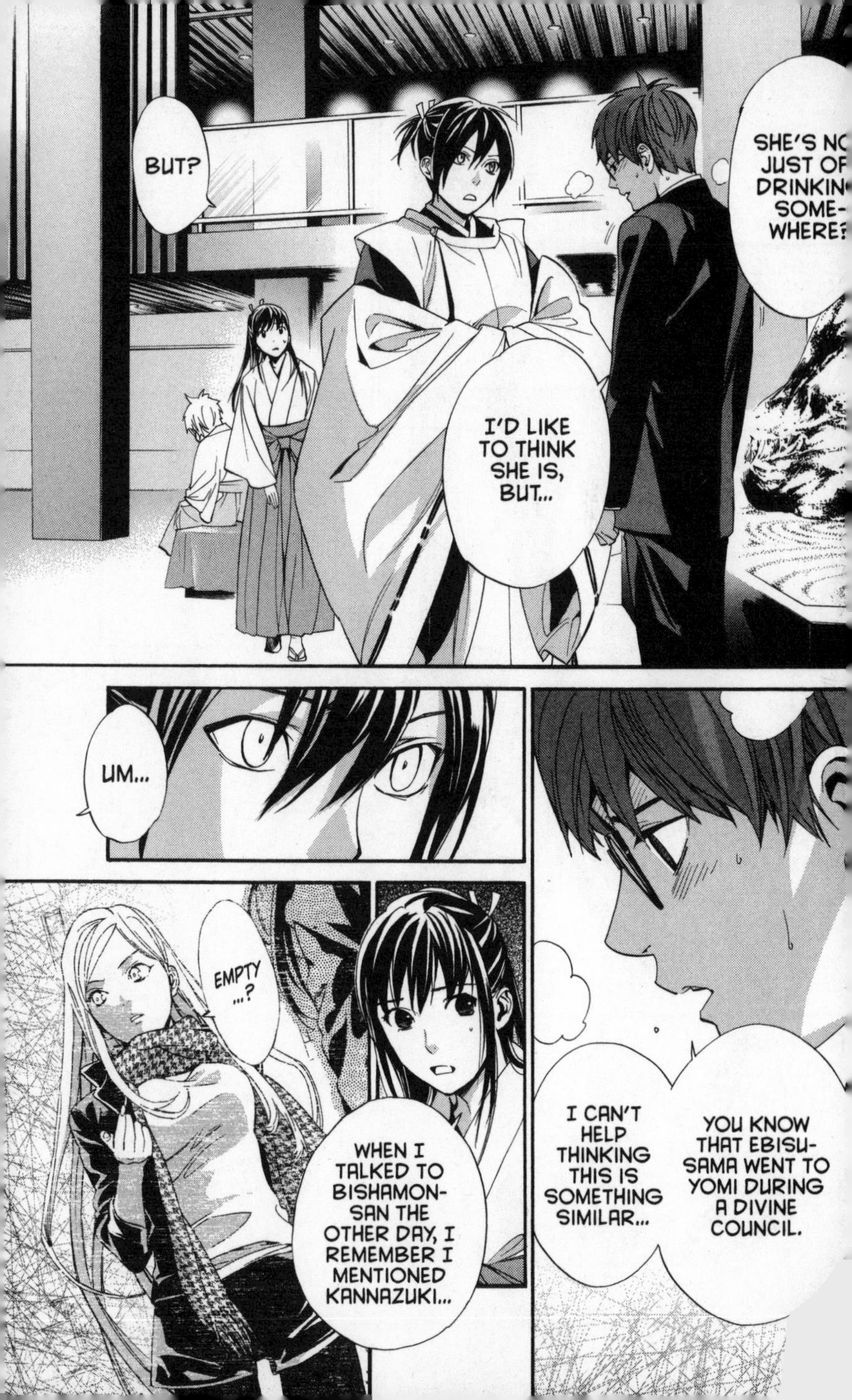
SHE'S N JUST O DRINKIN SOME-WHERE?
I'D LIKE TO THINK SHE IS, BUT...
BUT?
YOU KNOW THAT EBISU-SAMA WENT TO YOMI DURING A DIVINE COUNCIL.
I CAN'T HELP THINKING THIS IS SOMETHING SIMILAR...
UM...
WHEN I TALKED TO BISHAMON-SAN THE OTHER DAY, I REMEMBER I MENTIONED KANNAZUKI...
EMPTY ...?

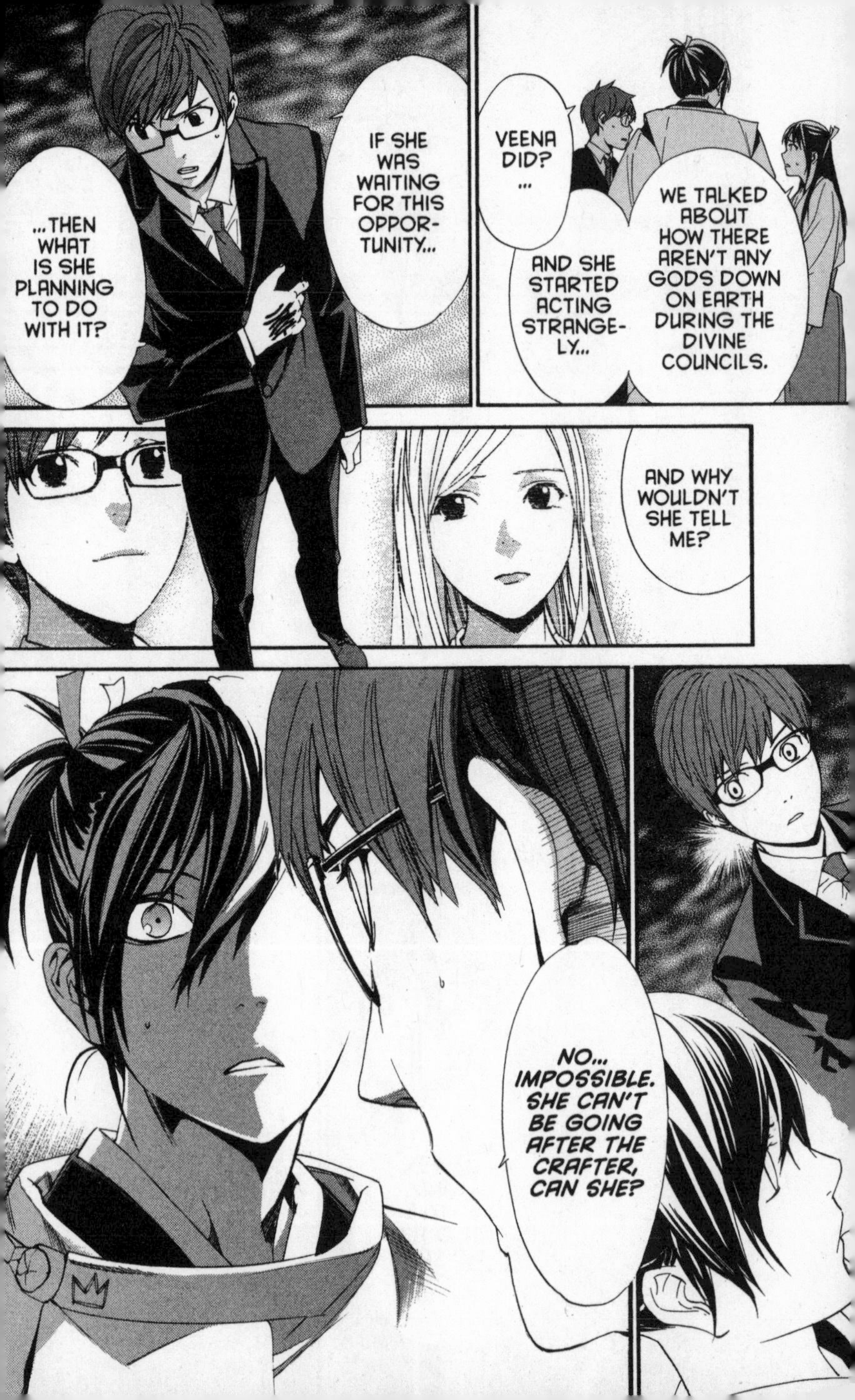
VEENA DID? ...
WE TALKED ABOUT HOW THERE AREN'T ANY GODS DOWN ON EARTH DURING THE DIVINE COUNCILS.
AND SHE STARTED ACTING STRANGE-LY...
IF SHE WAS WAITING FOR THIS OPPOR-TUNITY...
...THEN WHAT IS SHE PLANNING TO DO WITH IT?
AND WHY WOULDN'T SHE TELL ME?
NO... IMPOSSIBLE. SHE CAN'T BE GOING AFTER THE CRAFTER, CAN SHE?

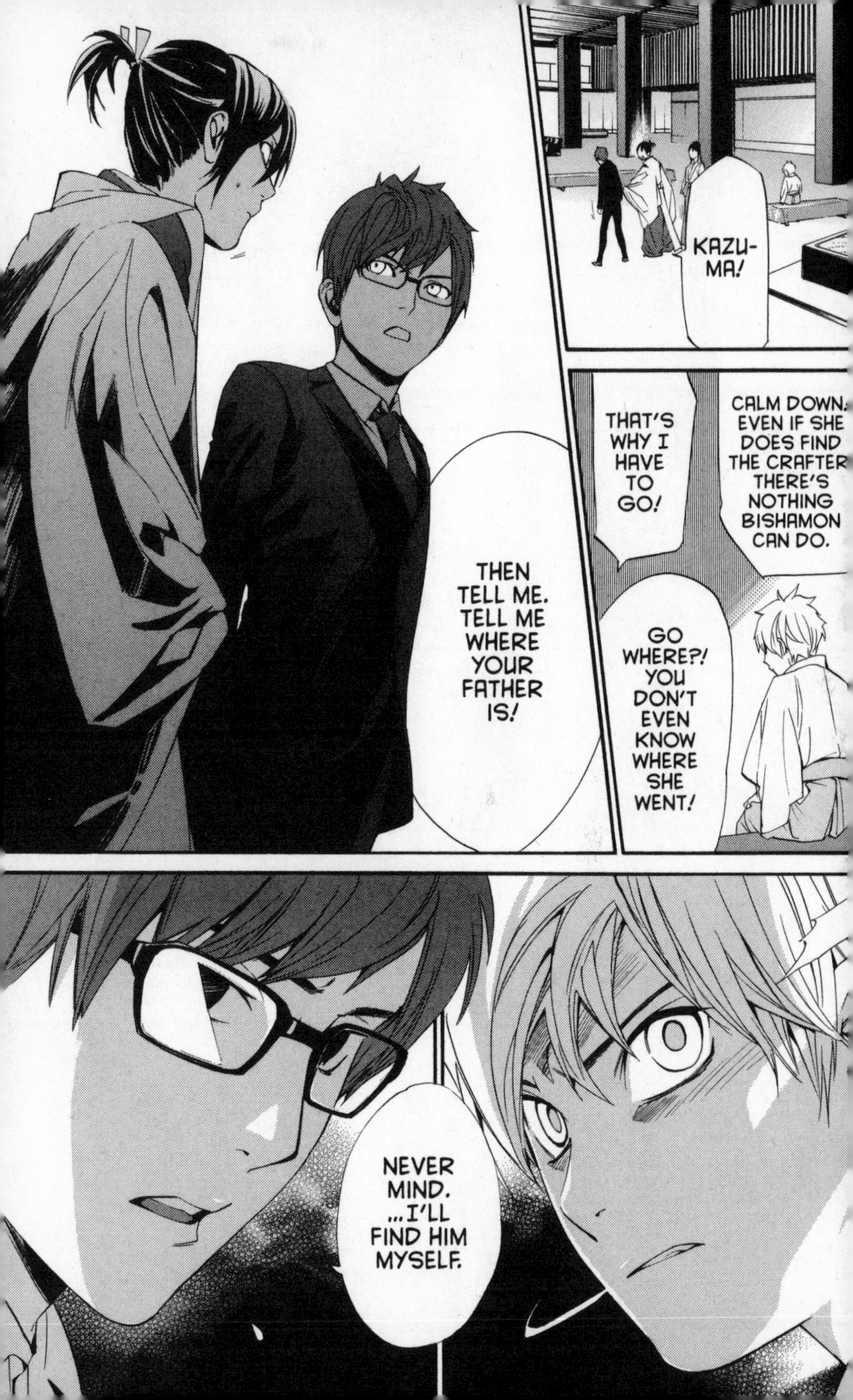
KAZU-MA!
CALM DOWN. EVEN IF SHE DOES FIND THE CRAFTER THERE'S NOTHING BISHAMON CAN DO.
THAT'S WHY I HAVE TO GO!
GO WHERE?! YOU DON'T EVEN KNOW WHERE SHE WENT!
THEN TELL ME. TELL ME WHERE YOUR FATHER IS!
NEVER MIND. ...I'LL FIND HIM MYSELF.

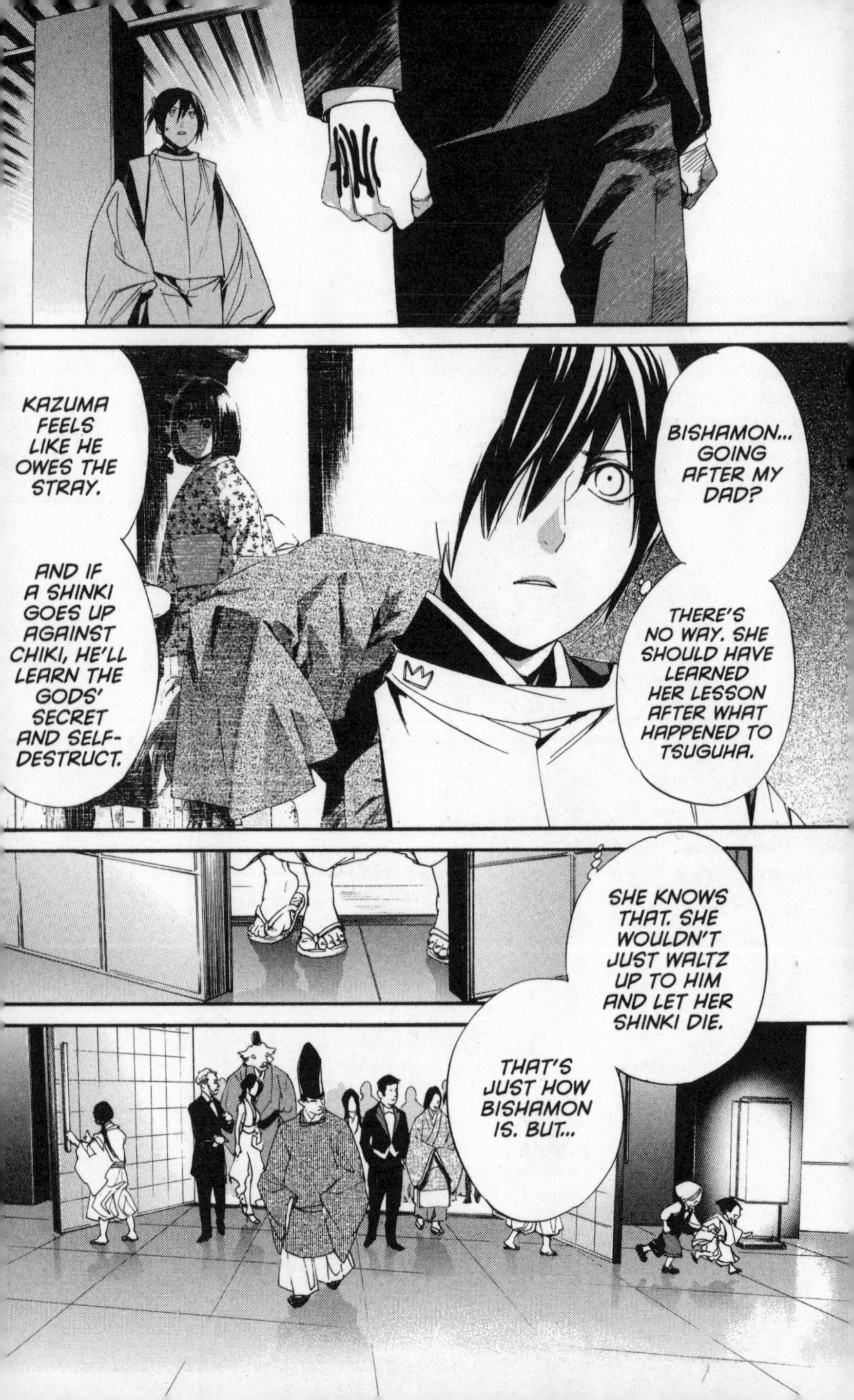
BISHAMON... GOING AFTER MY DAD?
THERE'S NO WAY. SHE SHOULD HAVE LEARNED HER LESSON AFTER WHAT HAPPENED TO TSUGUHA.
KAZUMA FEELS LIKE HE OWES THE STRAY.
AND IF A SHINKI GOES UP AGAINST CHIKI, HE'LL LEARN THE GODS' SECRET AND SELF-DESTRUCT.
SHE KNOWS THAT. SHE WOULDN'T JUST WALTZ UP TO HIM AND LET HER SHINKI DIE.
THAT'S JUST HOW BISHAMON IS. BUT...

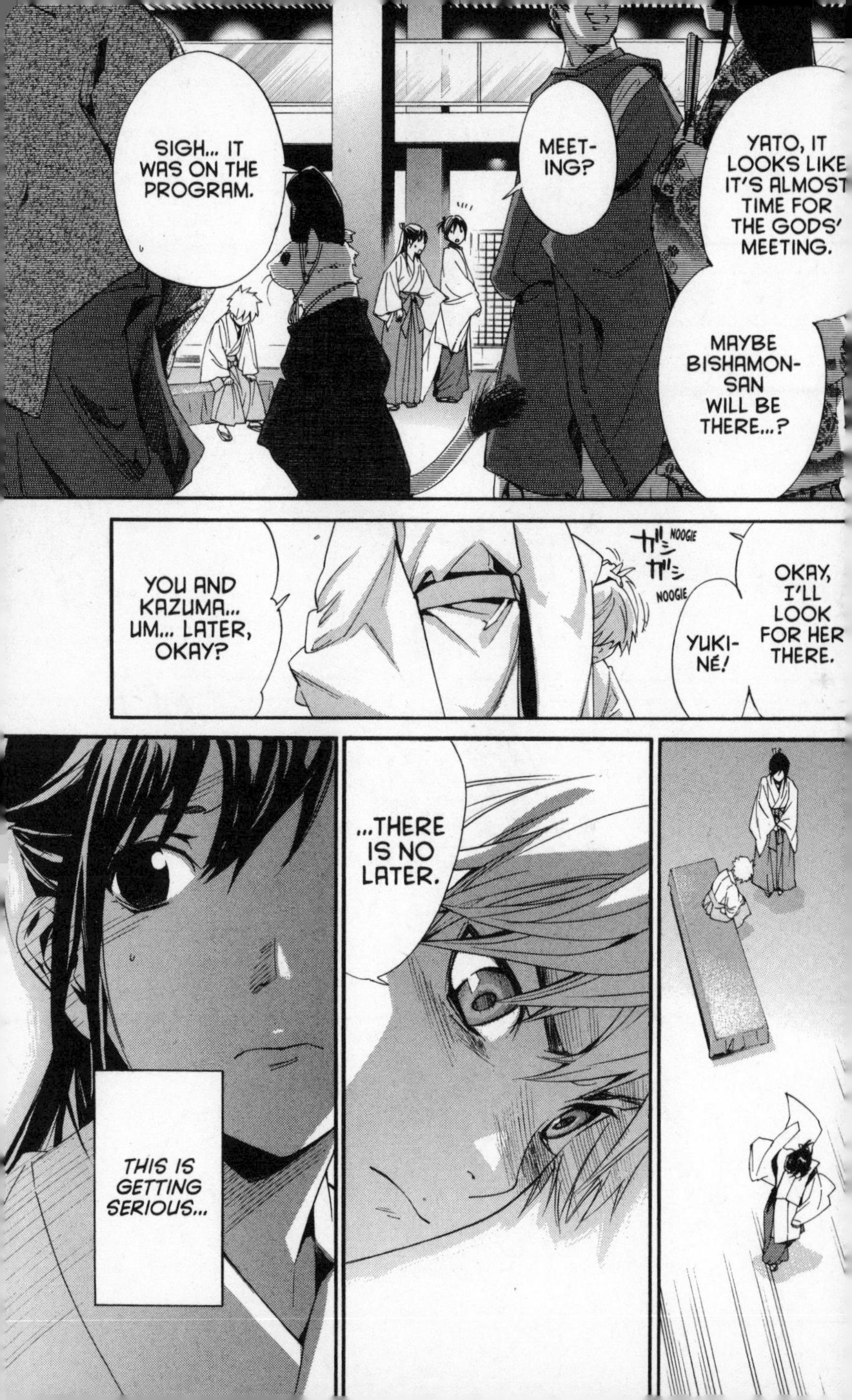
YATO, IT LOOKS LIKE IT'S ALMOST TIME FOR THE GODS' MEETING.
MAYBE BISHAMON-SAN WILL BE THERE...?
MEET-ING?
SIGH... IT WAS ON THE PROGRAM.
OKAY, I'LL LOOK FOR HER THERE.
ガシ NOOGIE
ガシ NOOGIE
YUKI-NÉ!
YOU AND KAZUMA... UM... LATER, OKAY?
...THERE IS NO LATER.
THIS IS GETTING SERIOUS...

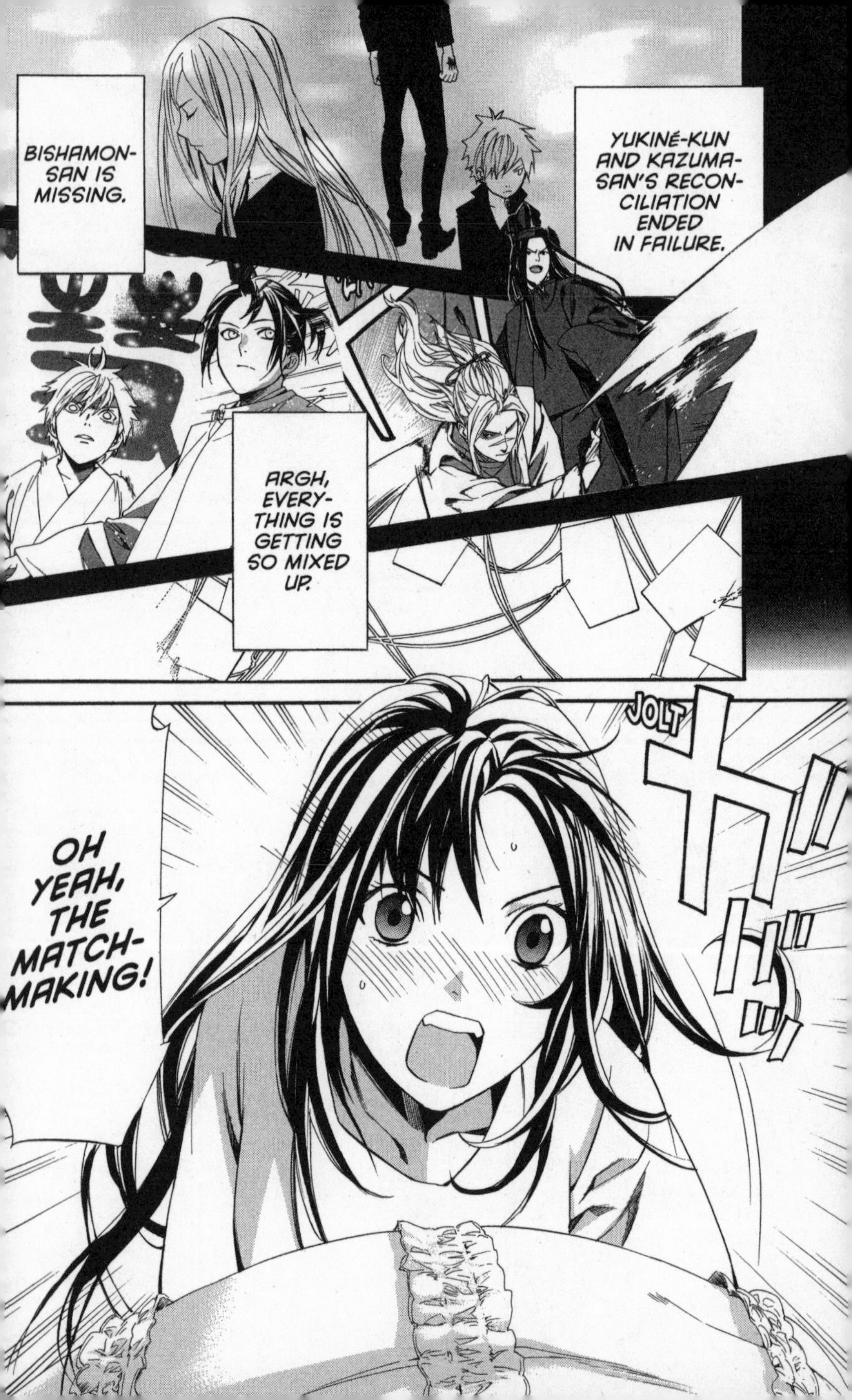
YUKINÉ-KUN AND KAZUMA-SAN'S RECON-CILIATION ENDED IN FAILURE.
BISHAMON-SAN IS MISSING.
ARGH, EVERY-THING IS GETTING SO MIXED UP.
JOLT
OH YEAH, THE MATCH-MAKING!

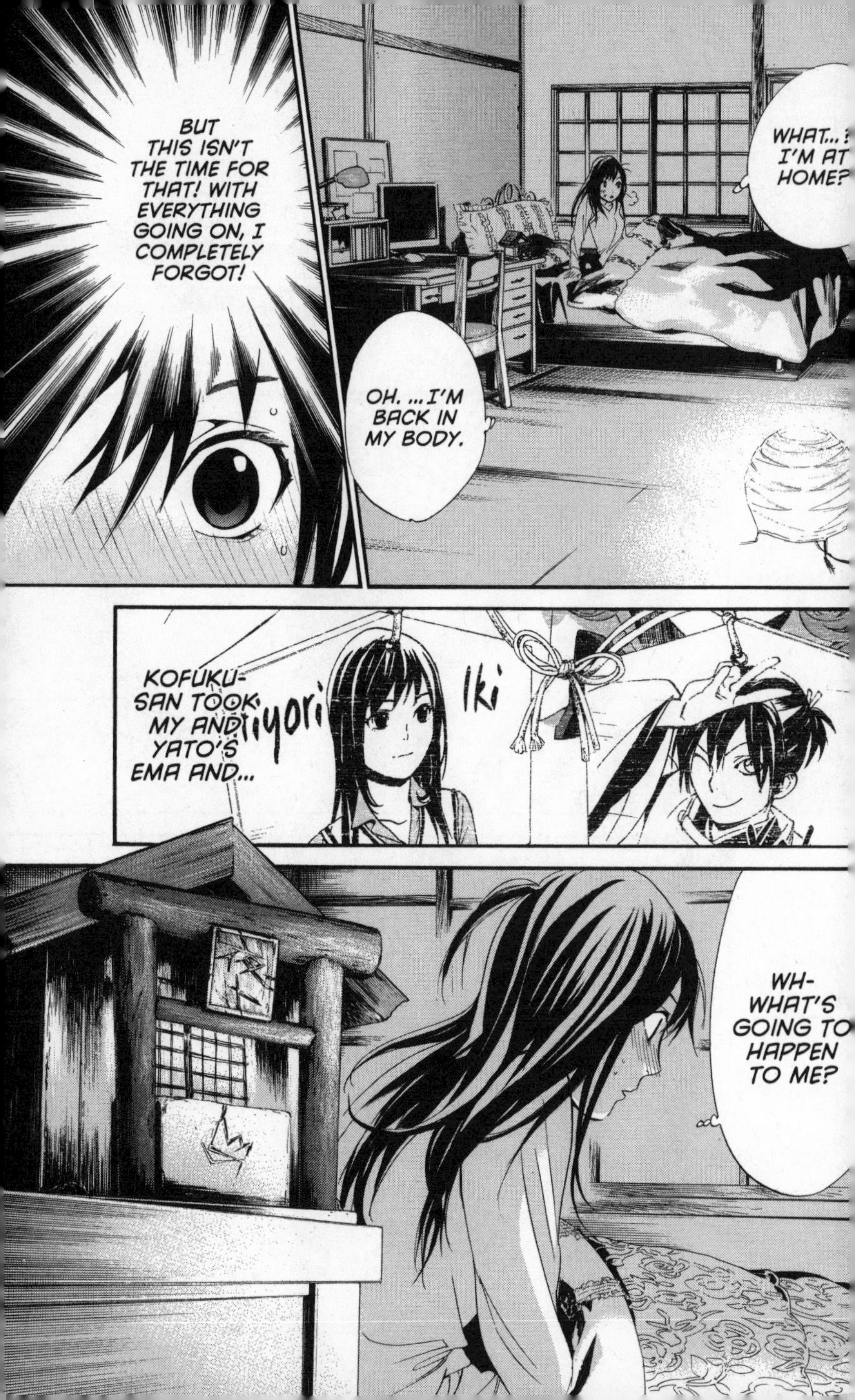
WHAT...! I'M AT HOME?
OH. ...I'M BACK IN MY BODY.
BUT THIS ISN'T THE TIME FOR THAT! WITH EVERYTHING GOING ON, I COMPLETELY FORGOT!
Iki
Hiyori
KOFUKU-SAN TOOK MY AND YATO'S EMA AND...
WH-WHAT'S GOING TO HAPPEN TO ME?

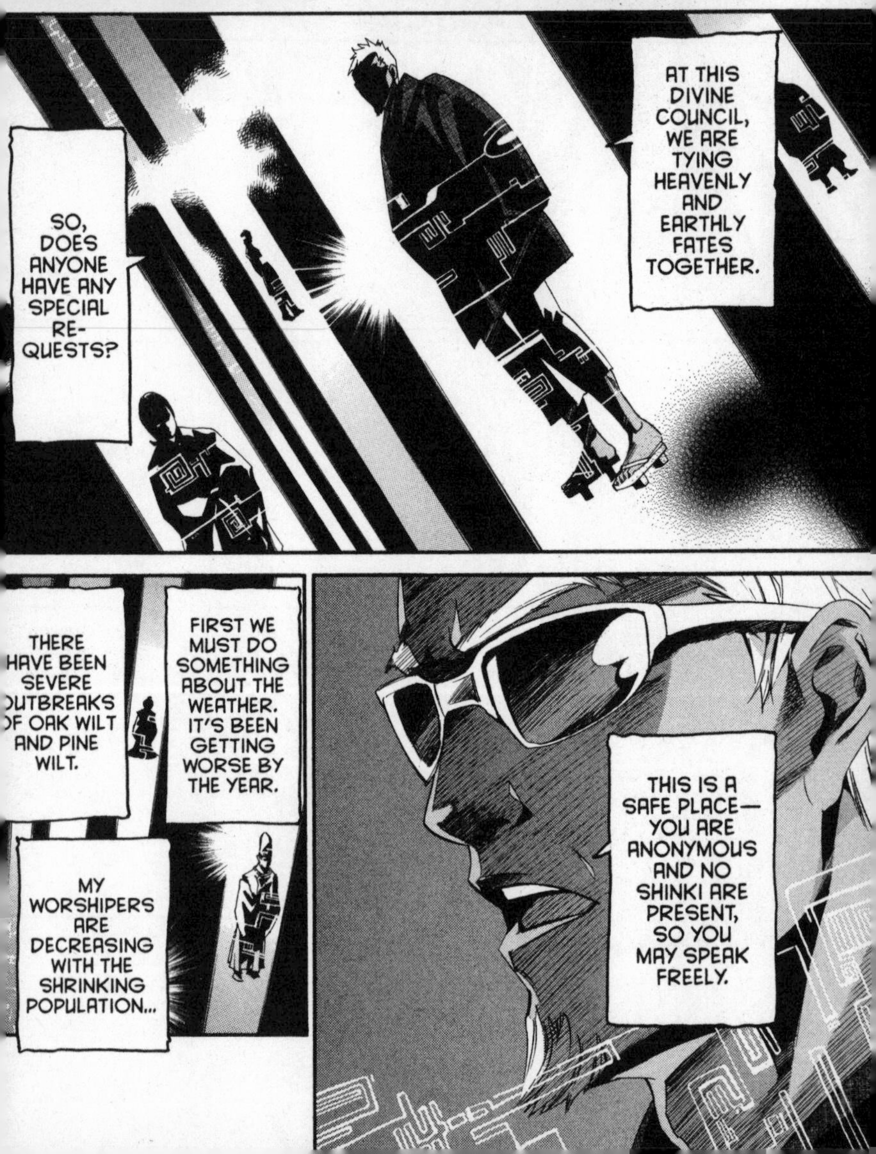
AT THIS DIVINE COUNCIL, WE ARE TYING HEAVENLY AND EARTHLY FATES TOGETHER.
SO, DOES ANYONE HAVE ANY SPECIAL RE-QUESTS?
THIS IS A SAFE PLACE—YOU ARE ANONYMOUS AND NO SHINKI ARE PRESENT, SO YOU MAY SPEAK FREELY.
FIRST WE MUST DO SOMETHING ABOUT THE WEATHER. IT'S BEEN GETTING WORSE BY THE YEAR.
THERE HAVE BEEN SEVERE OUTBREAKS OF OAK WILT AND PINE WILT.
MY WORSHIPERS ARE DECREASING WITH THE SHRINKING POPULATION...

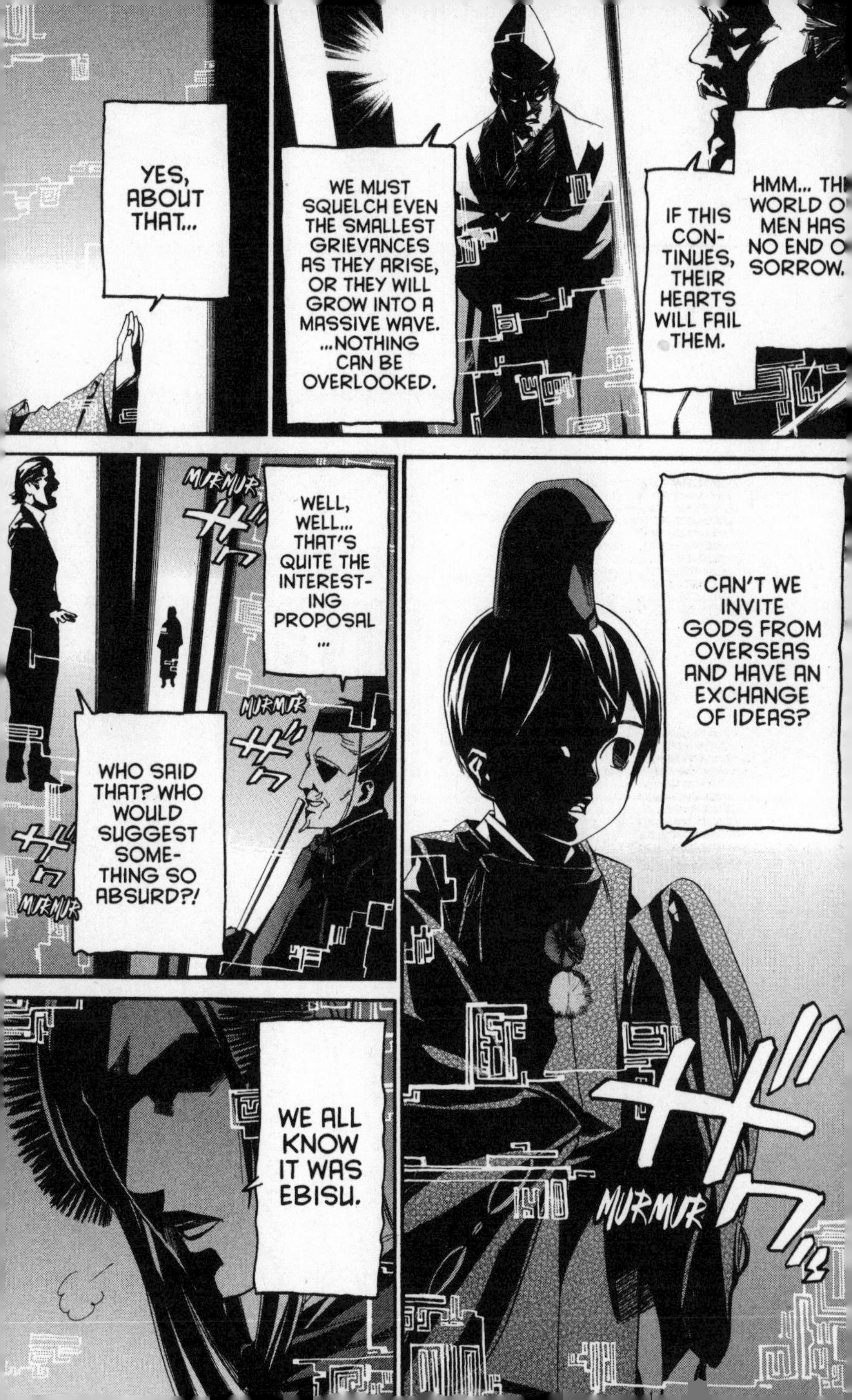
HMM... TH WORLD O MEN HAS NO END O SORROW.
IF THIS CON-TINUES, THEIR HEARTS WILL FAIL THEM.
WE MUST SQUELCH EVEN THE SMALLEST GRIEVANCES AS THEY ARISE, OR THEY WILL GROW INTO A MASSIVE WAVE. ...NOTHING CAN BE OVERLOOKED.
YES, ABOUT THAT...
CAN'T WE INVITE GODS FROM OVERSEAS AND HAVE AN EXCHANGE OF IDEAS?
MURMUR
MURMUR
WELL, WELL... THAT'S QUITE THE INTEREST-ING PROPOSAL ...
MURMUR
WHO SAID THAT? WHO WOULD SUGGEST SOME-THING SO ABSURD?!
MURMUR
WE ALL KNOW IT WAS EBISU.

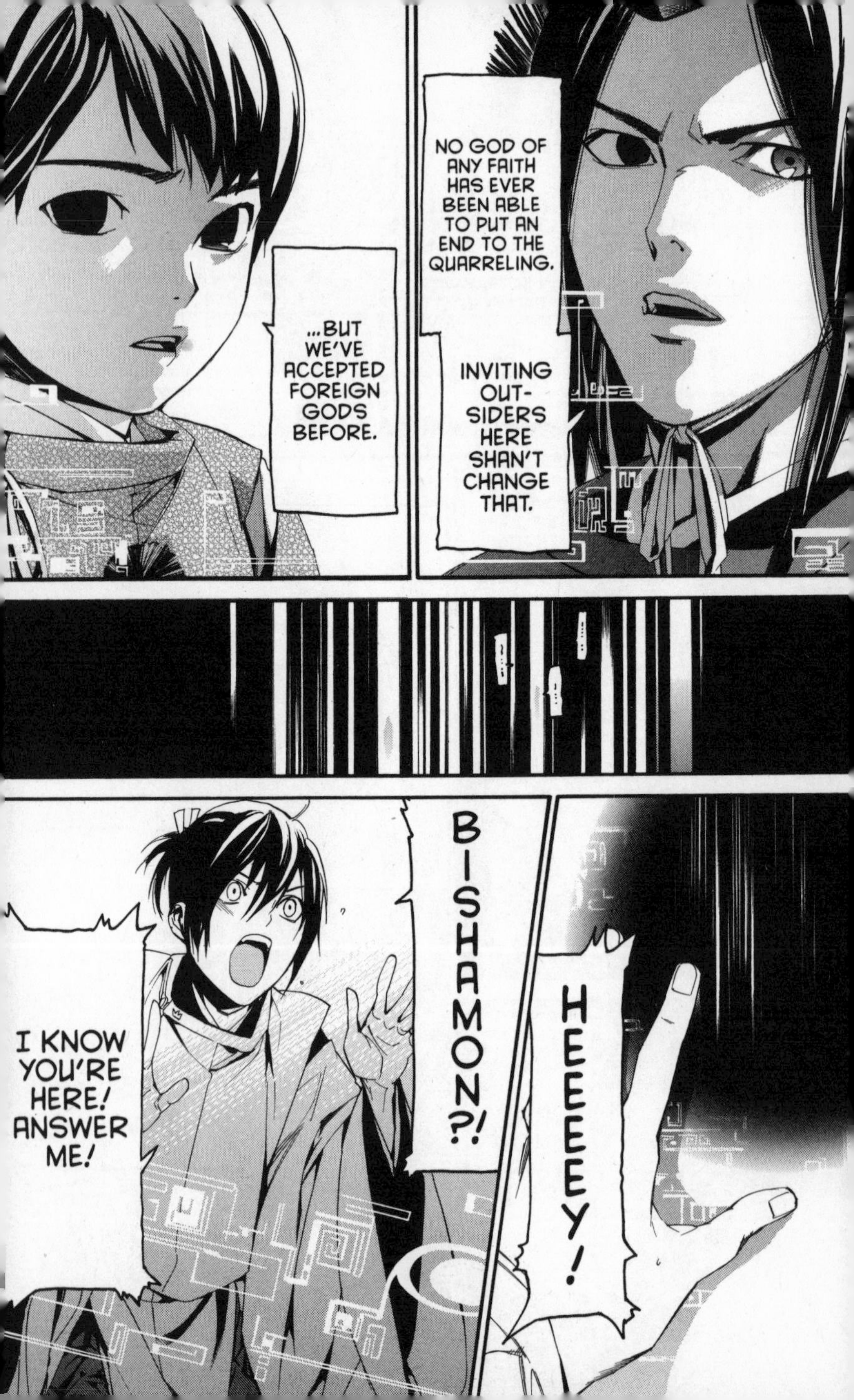
NO GOD OF ANY FAITH HAS EVER BEEN ABLE TO PUT AN END TO THE QUARRELING.
INVITING OUT-SIDERS HERE SHAN'T CHANGE THAT.
...BUT WE'VE ACCEPTED FOREIGN GODS BEFORE.
!!
!
?!
HEEEEEY!
BISHAMON?!
I KNOW YOU'RE HERE! ANSWER ME!

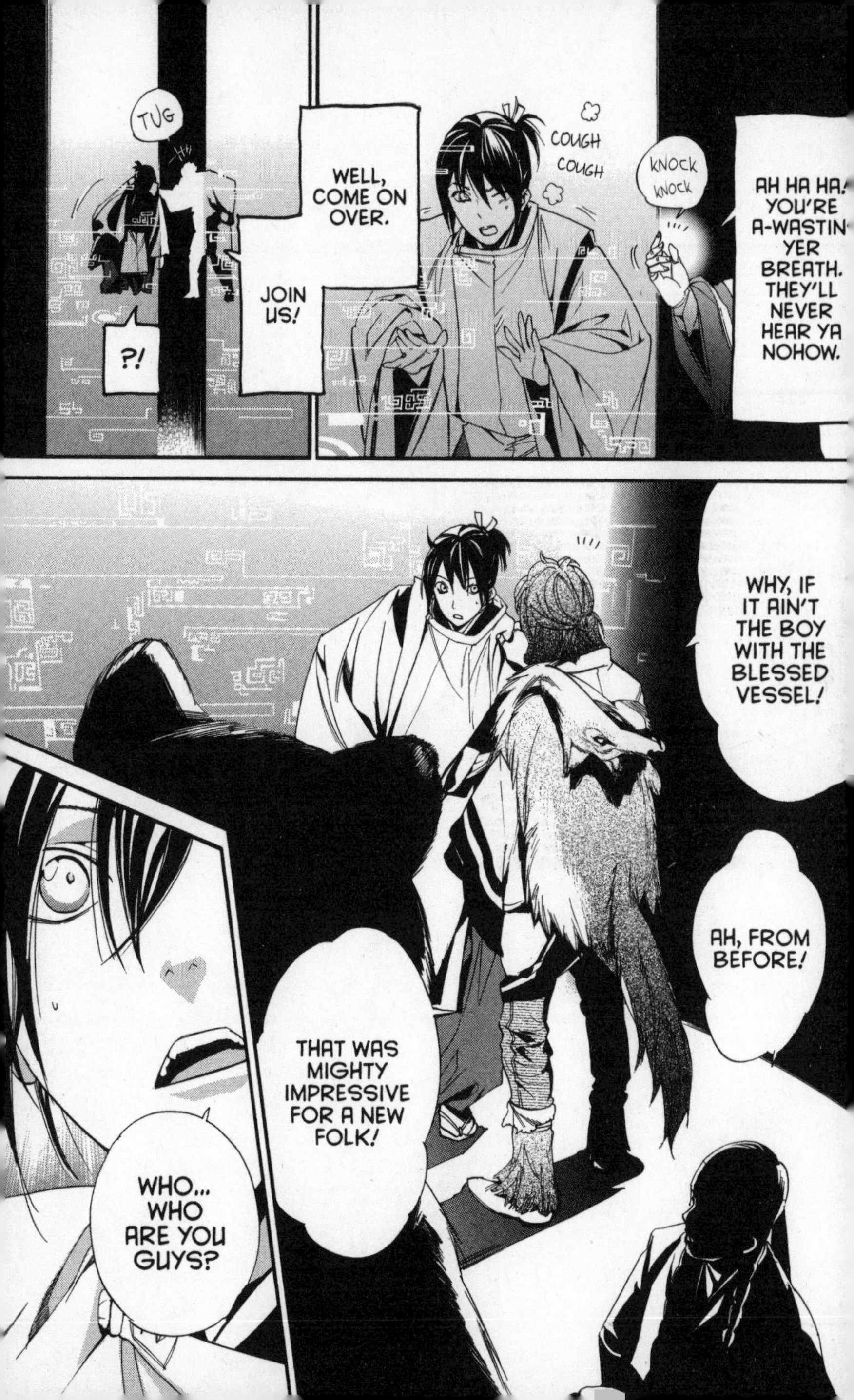
AH HA HA! YOU'RE A-WASTIN YER BREATH. THEY'LL NEVER HEAR YA NOHOW.
KNOCK KNOCK
COUGH COUGH
WELL, COME ON OVER.
JOIN US!
TUG
?!
WHY, IF IT AIN'T THE BOY WITH THE BLESSED VESSEL!
AH, FROM BEFORE!
THAT WAS MIGHTY IMPRESSIVE FOR A NEW FOLK!
WHO... WHO ARE YOU GUYS?

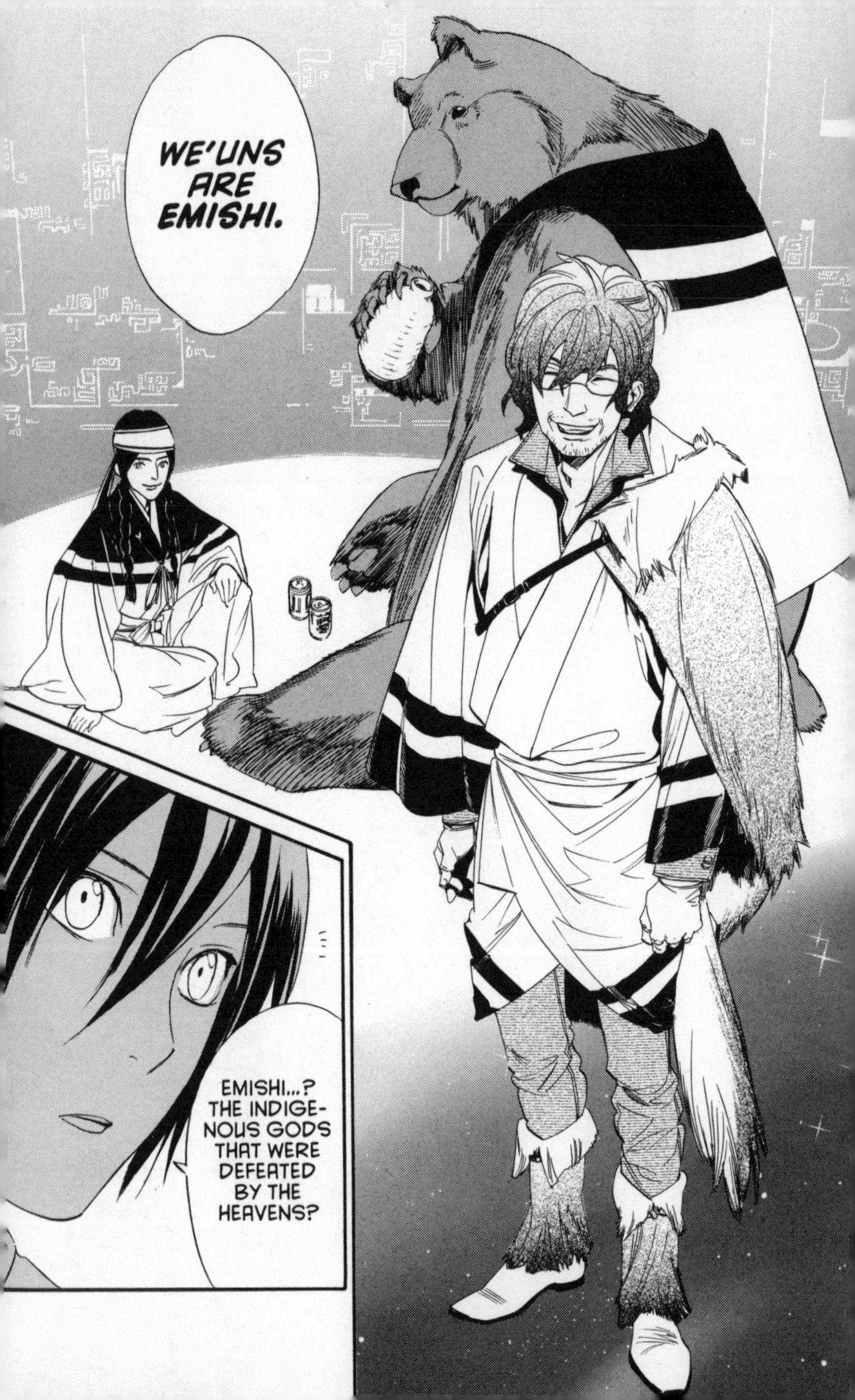
WE'UNS ARE EMISHI.
EMISHI...? THE INDIGE-NOUS GODS THAT WERE DEFEATED BY THE HEAVENS?

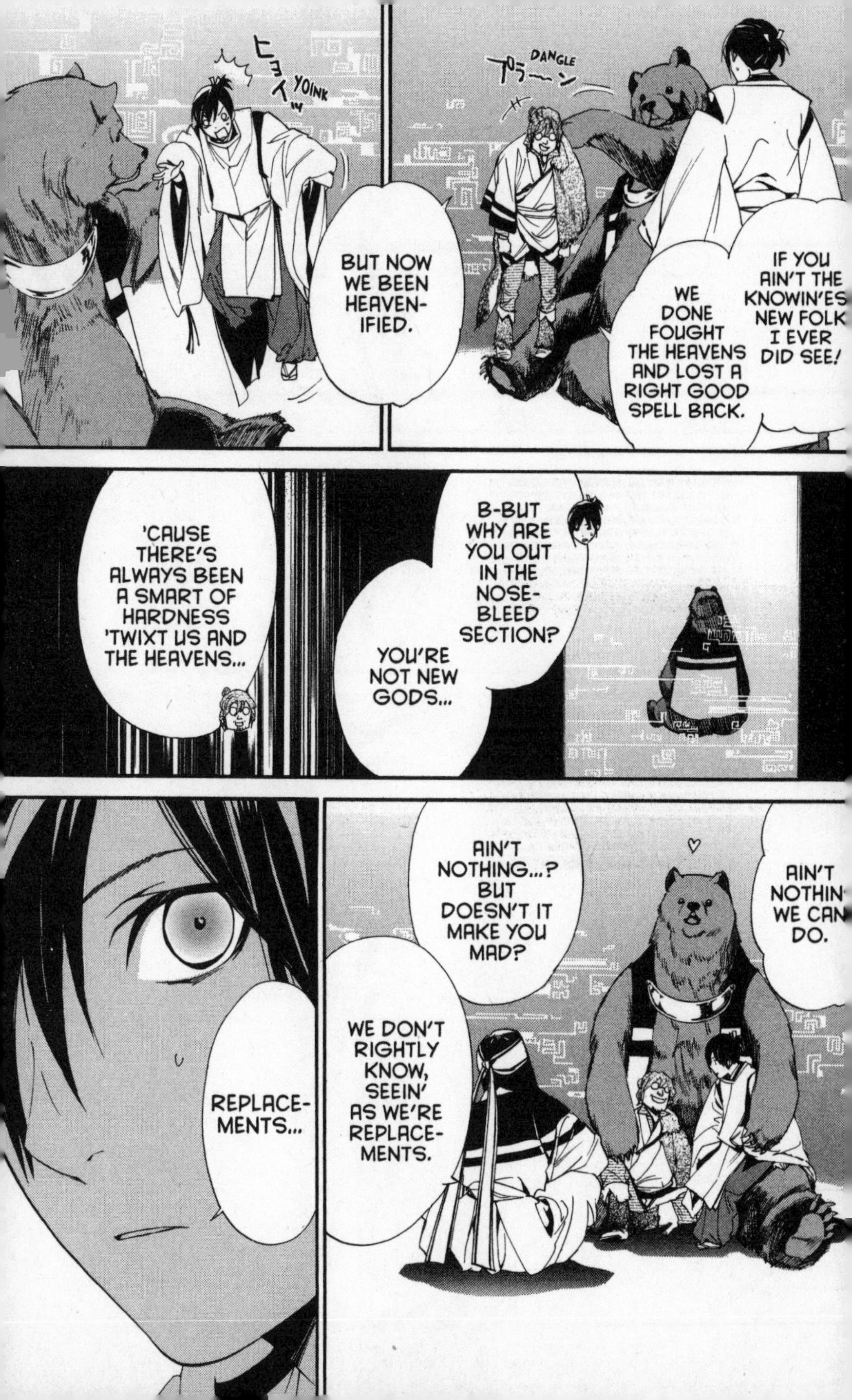
DANGLE
プラ〜ン
IF YOU AIN'T THE KNOWIN'ES NEW FOLK I EVER DID SEE!
WE DONE FOUGHT THE HEAVENS AND LOST A RIGHT GOOD SPELL BACK.
ヒョイ
YOINK
BUT NOW WE BEEN HEAVEN-IFIED.
B-BUT WHY ARE YOU OUT IN THE NOSE-BLEED SECTION?
YOU'RE NOT NEW GODS...
'CAUSE THERE'S ALWAYS BEEN A SMART OF HARDNESS 'TWIXT US AND THE HEAVENS...
AIN'T NOTHIN WE CAN DO.
AIN'T NOTHING...? BUT DOESN'T IT MAKE YOU MAD?
WE DON'T RIGHTLY KNOW, SEEIN' AS WE'RE REPLACEMENTS.
REPLACEMENTS...

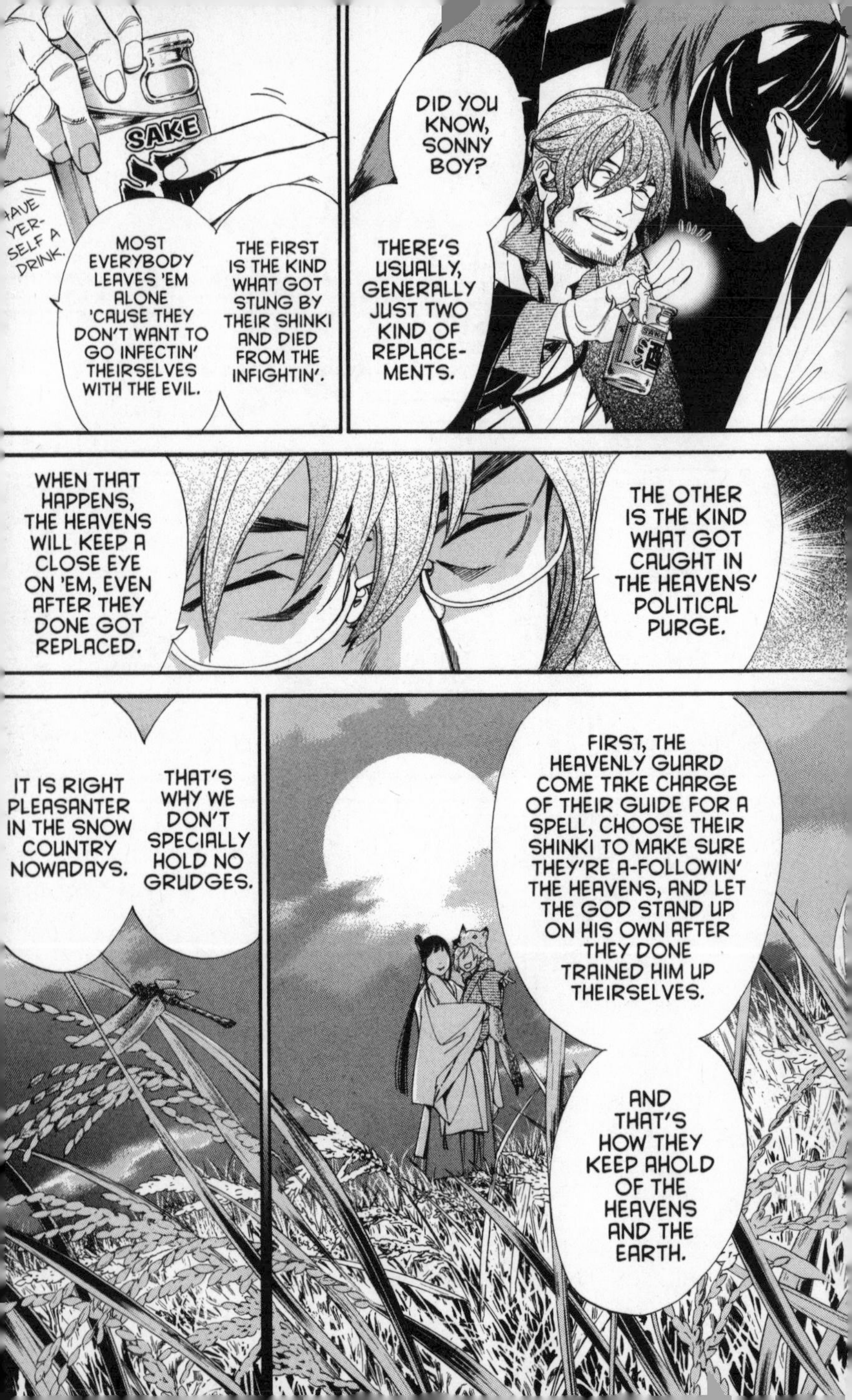
DID YOU KNOW, SONNY BOY?
THERE'S USUALLY, GENERALLY JUST TWO KIND OF REPLACEMENTS.
SAKE
THE FIRST IS THE KIND WHAT GOT STUNG BY THEIR SHINKI AND DIED FROM THE INFIGHTIN'.
MOST EVERYBODY LEAVES 'EM ALONE 'CAUSE THEY DON'T WANT TO GO INFECTIN' THEIRSELVES WITH THE EVIL.
HAVE YERSELF A DRINK.
THE OTHER IS THE KIND WHAT GOT CAUGHT IN THE HEAVENS' POLITICAL PURGE.
WHEN THAT HAPPENS, THE HEAVENS WILL KEEP A CLOSE EYE ON 'EM, EVEN AFTER THEY DONE GOT REPLACED.
FIRST, THE HEAVENLY GUARD COME TAKE CHARGE OF THEIR GUIDE FOR A SPELL, CHOOSE THEIR SHINKI TO MAKE SURE THEY'RE A-FOLLOWIN' THE HEAVENS, AND LET THE GOD STAND UP ON HIS OWN AFTER THEY DONE TRAINED HIM UP THEIRSELVES.
AND THAT'S HOW THEY KEEP AHOLD OF THE HEAVENS AND THE EARTH.
THAT'S WHY WE DON'T SPECIALLY HOLD NO GRUDGES.
IT IS RIGHT PLEASANTER IN THE SNOW COUNTRY NOWADAYS.

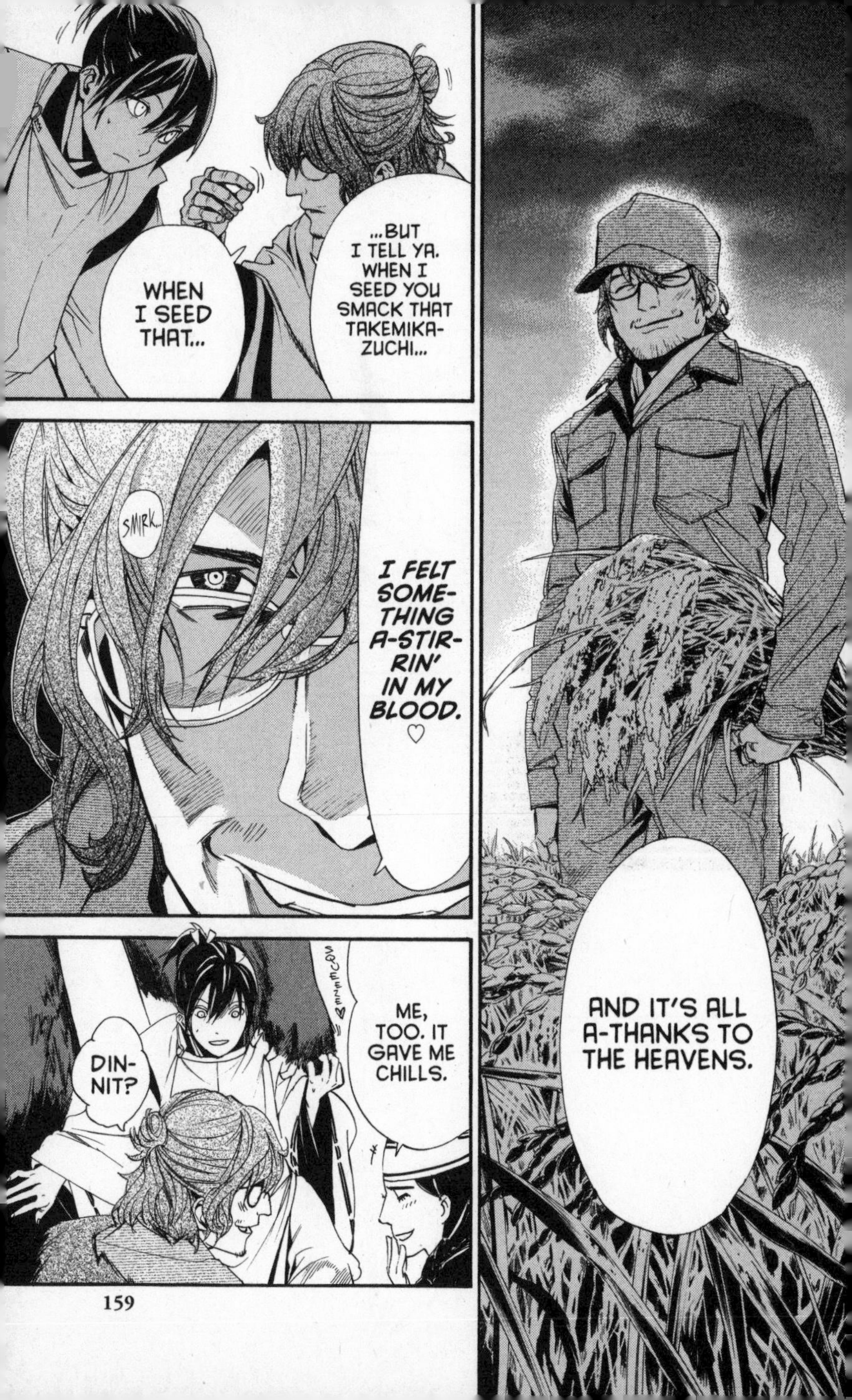
AND IT'S ALL A-THANKS TO THE HEAVENS.
...BUT I TELL YA. WHEN I SEED YOU SMACK THAT TAKEMIKA-ZUCHI...
WHEN I SEED THAT...
SMIRK...
I FELT SOMETHING A-STIRRIN' IN MY BLOOD. ♡
ME, TOO. IT GAVE ME CHILLS.
DIN-NIT?

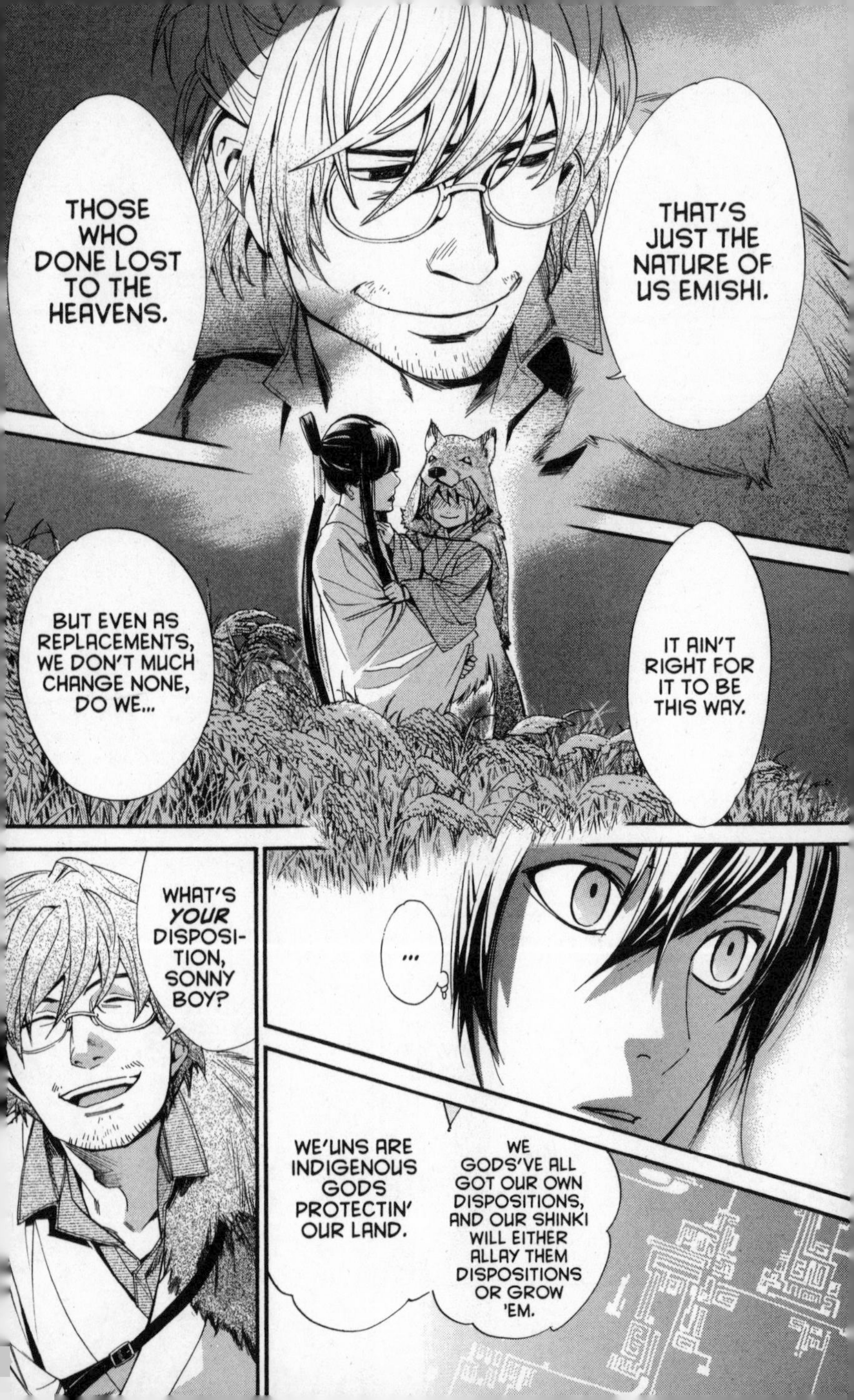
THAT'S JUST THE NATURE OF US EMISHI.
THOSE WHO DONE LOST TO THE HEAVENS.
IT AIN'T RIGHT FOR IT TO BE THIS WAY.
BUT EVEN AS REPLACEMENTS, WE DON'T MUCH CHANGE NONE, DO WE...
...
WE GODS'VE ALL GOT OUR OWN DISPOSITIONS, AND OUR SHINKI WILL EITHER ALLAY THEM DISPOSITIONS OR GROW 'EM.
WE'UNS ARE INDIGENOUS GODS PROTECTIN' OUR LAND.
WHAT'S *YOUR* DISPOSITION, SONNY BOY?

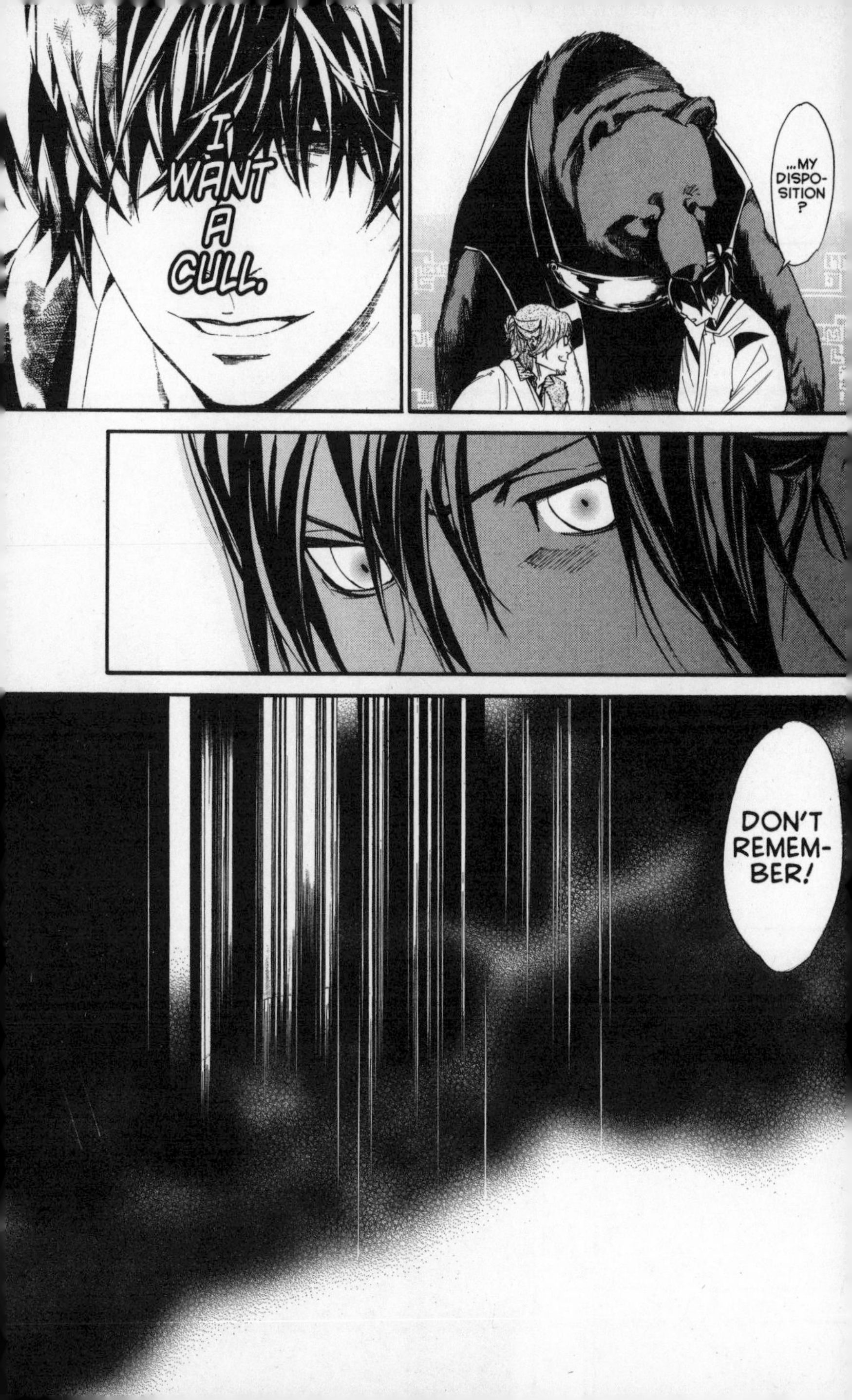
...MY DISPOSITION?
I WANT A CULL.
DON'T REMEMBER!

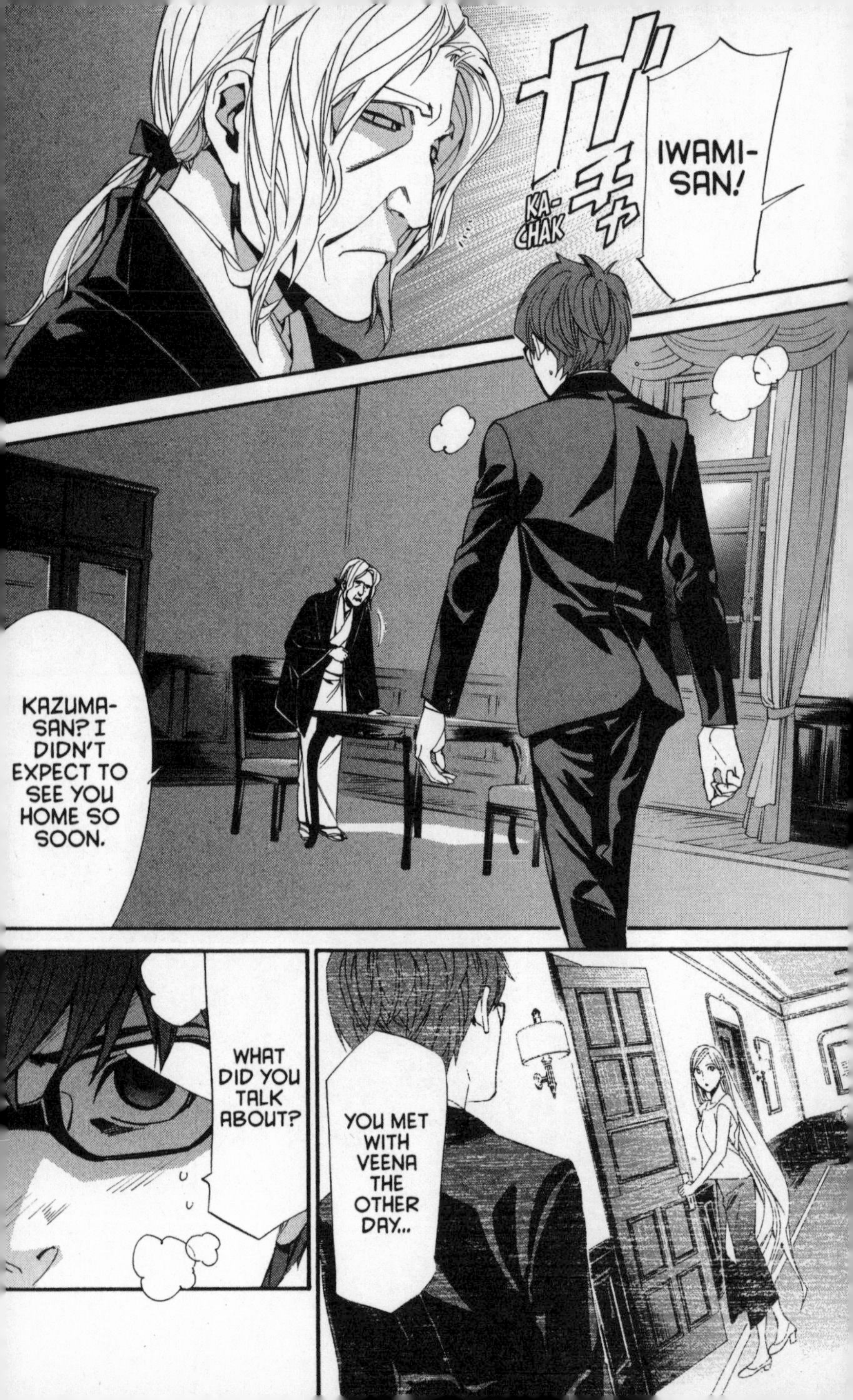
IWAMI-SAN!
ガチャ
KA-CHAK
KAZUMA-SAN? I DIDN'T EXPECT TO SEE YOU HOME SO SOON.
YOU MET WITH VEENA THE OTHER DAY...
WHAT DID YOU TALK ABOUT?

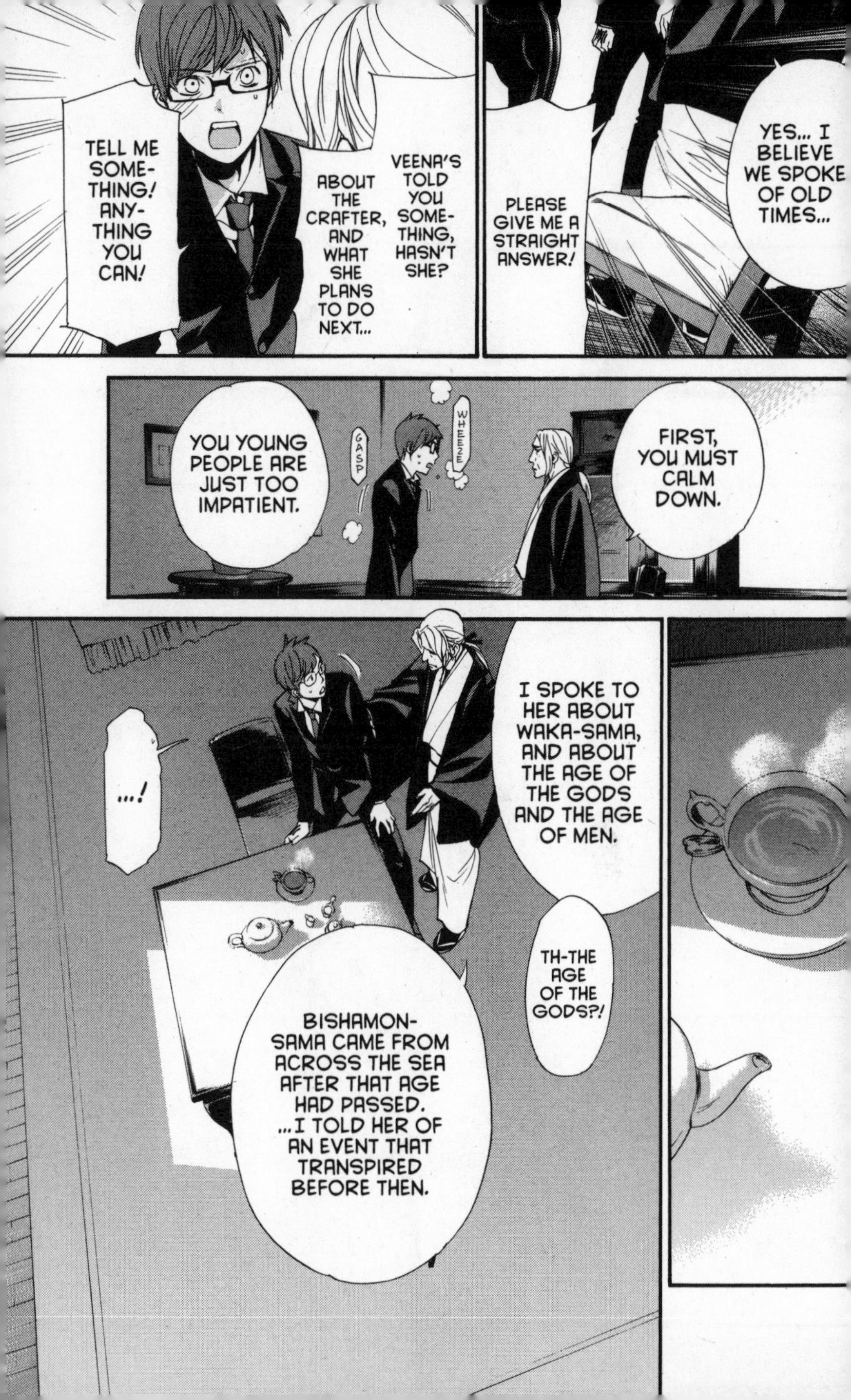
YES... I BELIEVE WE SPOKE OF OLD TIMES...
PLEASE GIVE ME A STRAIGHT ANSWER!
VEENA'S TOLD YOU SOMETHING, HASN'T SHE?
ABOUT THE CRAFTER, AND WHAT SHE PLANS TO DO NEXT...
TELL ME SOMETHING! ANYTHING YOU CAN!
FIRST, YOU MUST CALM DOWN.
WHEEZE
GASP
YOU YOUNG PEOPLE ARE JUST TOO IMPATIENT.
I SPOKE TO HER ABOUT WAKA-SAMA, AND ABOUT THE AGE OF THE GODS AND THE AGE OF MEN.
TH-THE AGE OF THE GODS?!
...!
BISHAMON-SAMA CAME FROM ACROSS THE SEA AFTER THAT AGE HAD PASSED. ...I TOLD HER OF AN EVENT THAT TRANSPIRED BEFORE THEN.

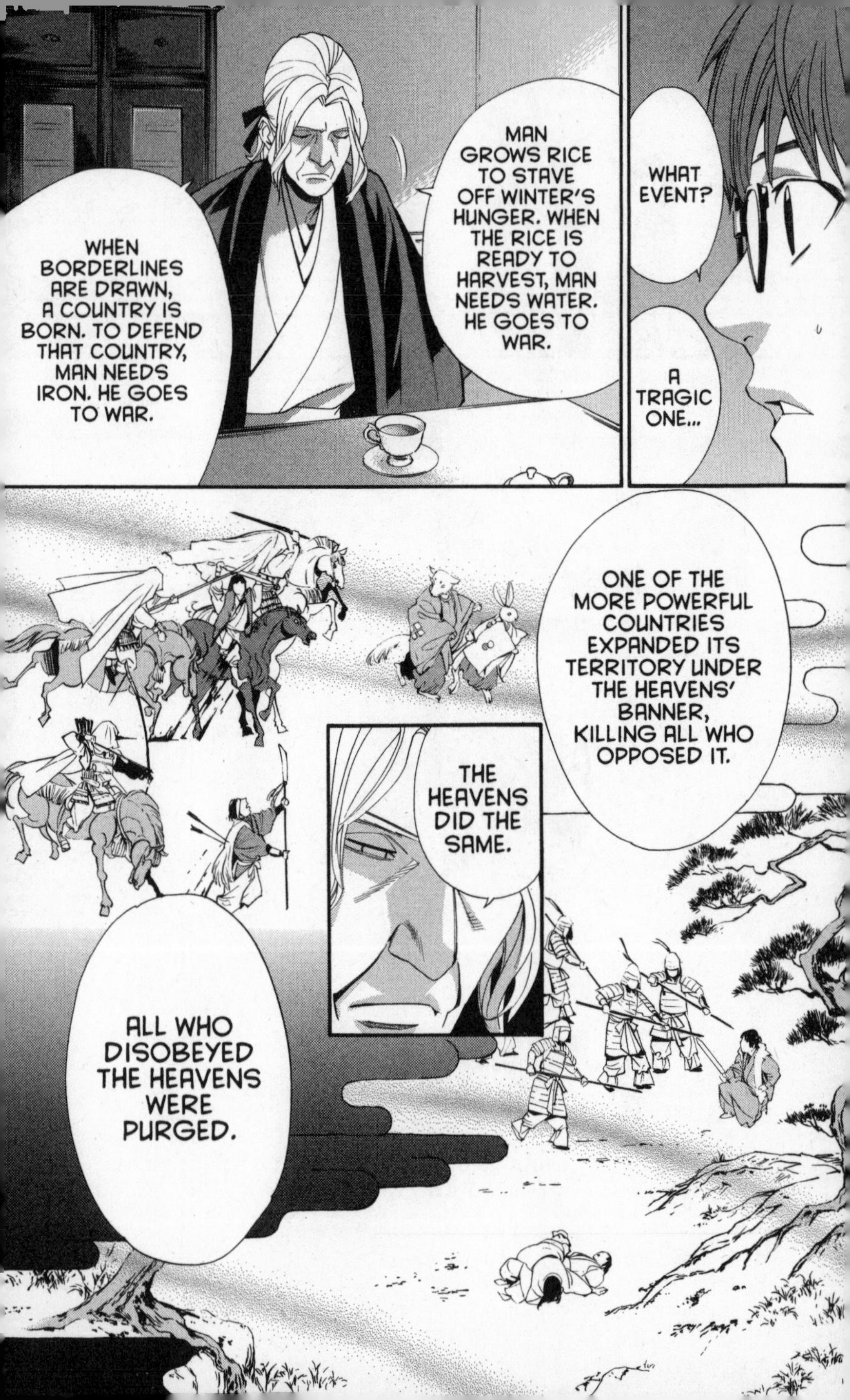
WHAT EVENT?
A TRAGIC ONE...
MAN GROWS RICE TO STAVE OFF WINTER'S HUNGER. WHEN THE RICE IS READY TO HARVEST, MAN NEEDS WATER. HE GOES TO WAR.
WHEN BORDERLINES ARE DRAWN, A COUNTRY IS BORN. TO DEFEND THAT COUNTRY, MAN NEEDS IRON. HE GOES TO WAR.
ONE OF THE MORE POWERFUL COUNTRIES EXPANDED ITS TERRITORY UNDER THE HEAVENS' BANNER, KILLING ALL WHO OPPOSED IT.
THE HEAVENS DID THE SAME.
ALL WHO DISOBEYED THE HEAVENS WERE PURGED.

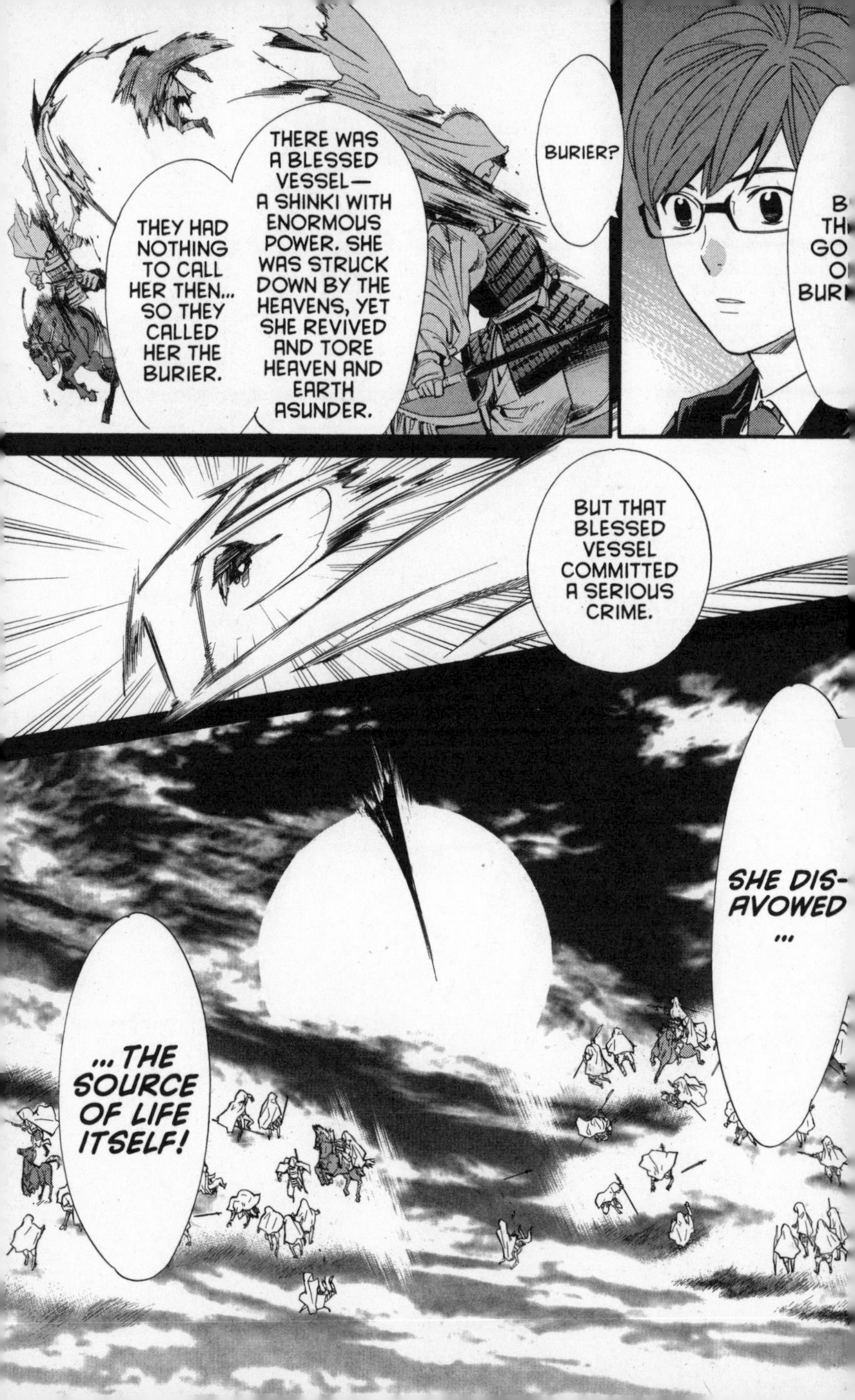
BURIER?
THERE WAS A BLESSED VESSEL—A SHINKI WITH ENORMOUS POWER. SHE WAS STRUCK DOWN BY THE HEAVENS, YET SHE REVIVED AND TORE HEAVEN AND EARTH ASUNDER.
THEY HAD NOTHING TO CALL HER THEN... SO THEY CALLED HER THE BURIER.
BUT THAT BLESSED VESSEL COMMITTED A SERIOUS CRIME.
SHE DIS-AVOWED ...
...THE SOURCE OF LIFE ITSELF!

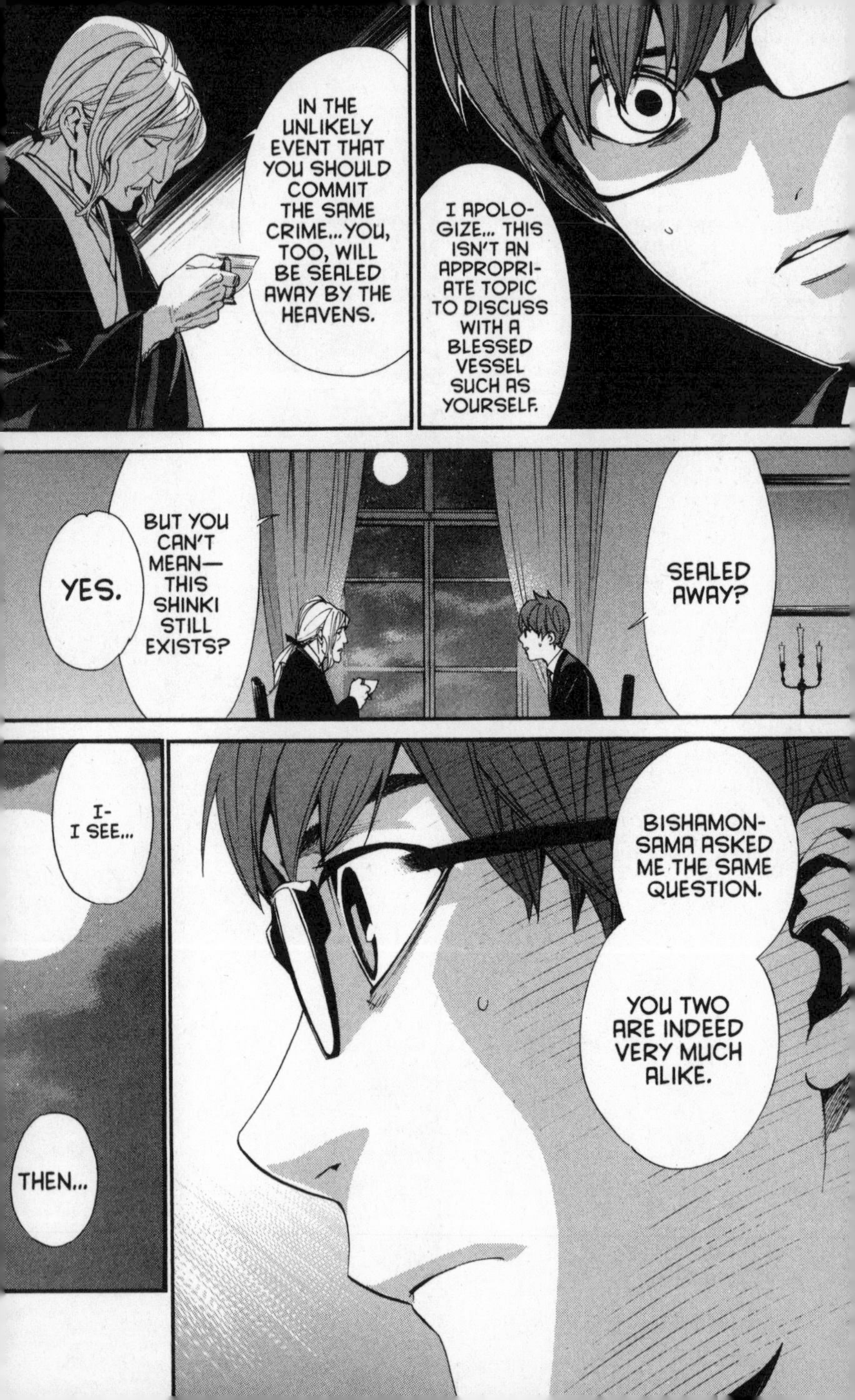
I APOLOGIZE... THIS ISN'T AN APPROPRIATE TOPIC TO DISCUSS WITH A BLESSED VESSEL SUCH AS YOURSELF.
IN THE UNLIKELY EVENT THAT YOU SHOULD COMMIT THE SAME CRIME...YOU, TOO, WILL BE SEALED AWAY BY THE HEAVENS.
SEALED AWAY?
BUT YOU CAN'T MEAN— THIS SHINKI STILL EXISTS?
YES.
BISHAMON-SAMA ASKED ME THE SAME QUESTION.
YOU TWO ARE INDEED VERY MUCH ALIKE.
I- I SEE...
THEN...

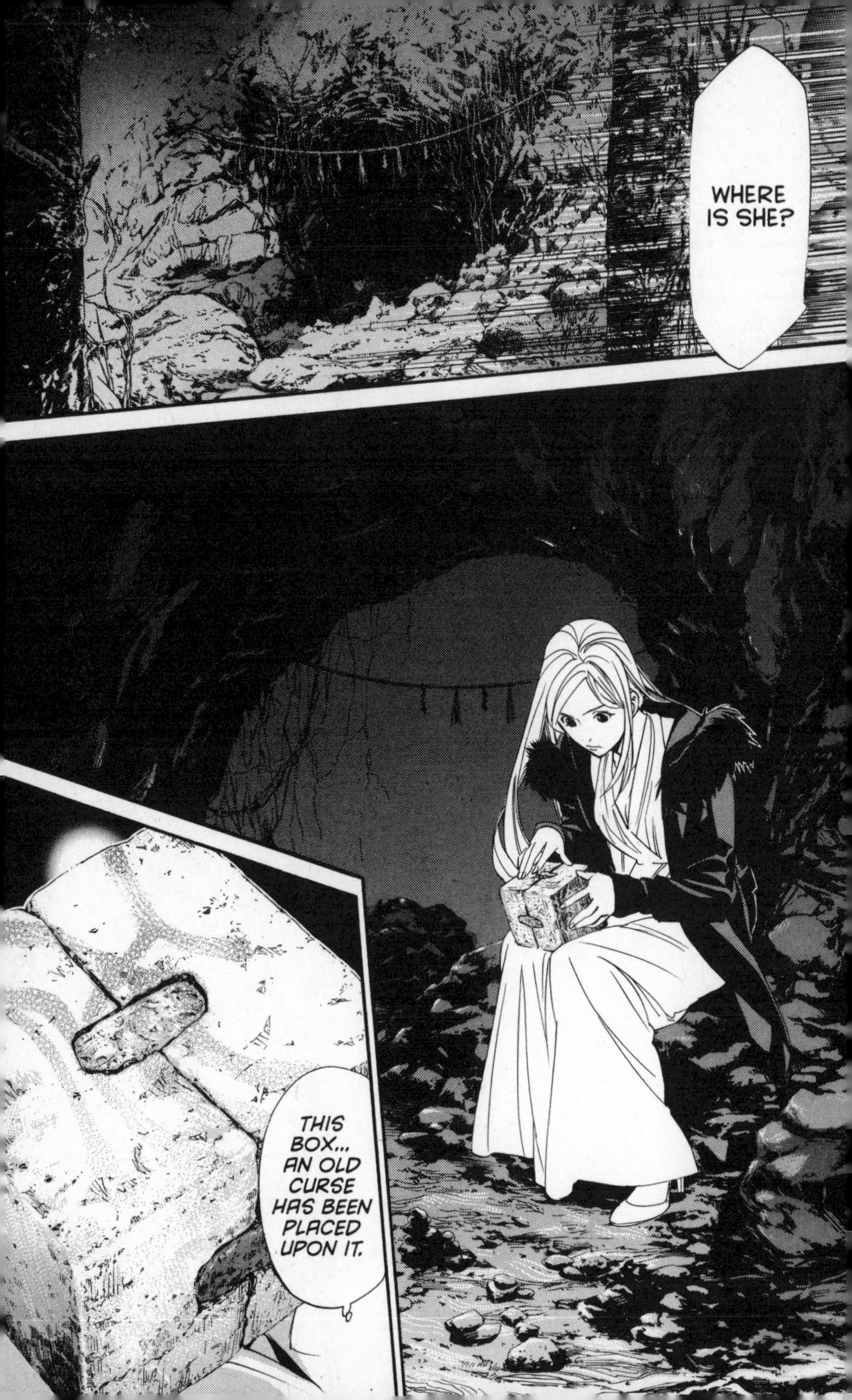
WHERE IS SHE?
THIS BOX... AN OLD CURSE HAS BEEN PLACED UPON IT.

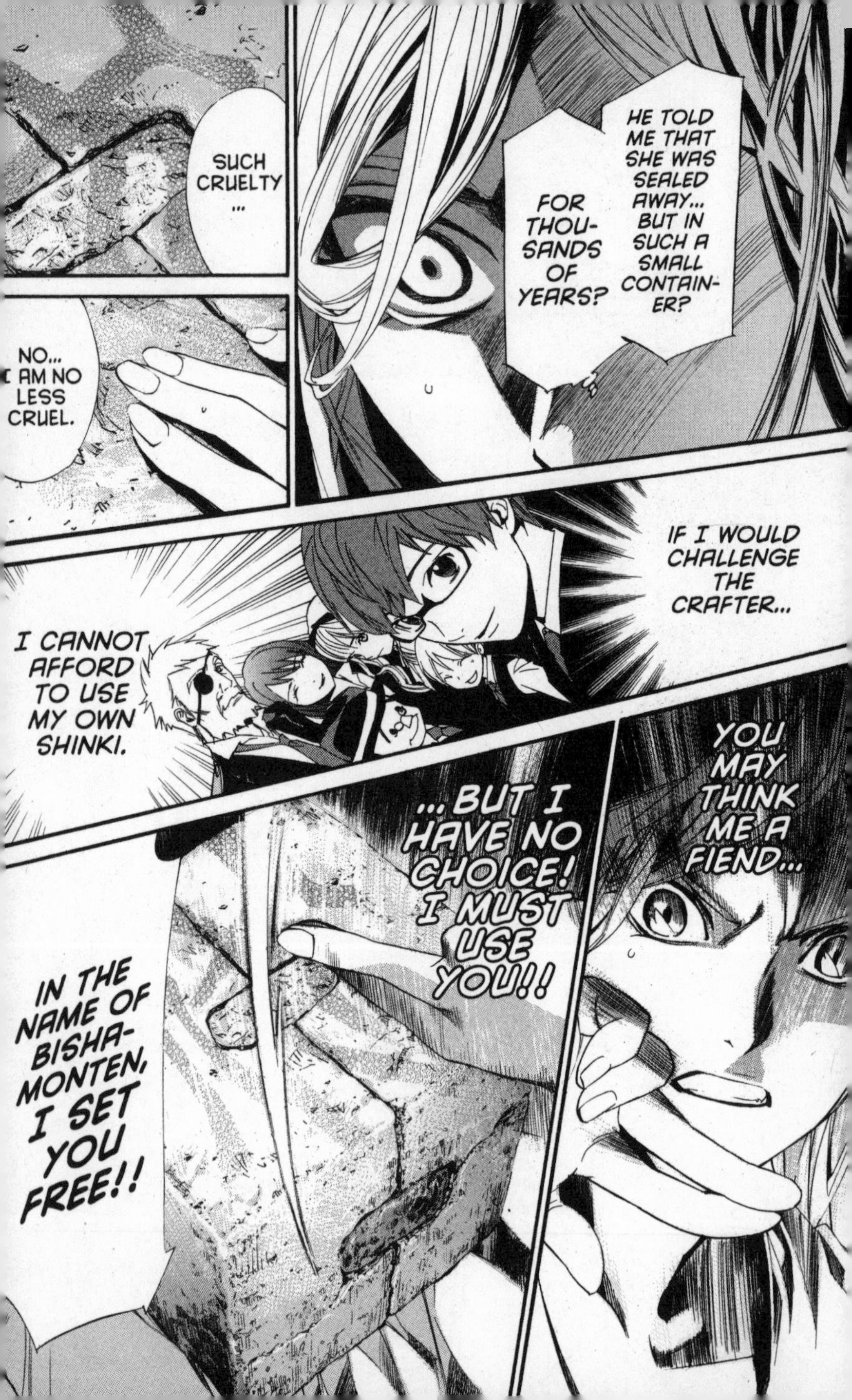
HE TOLD ME THAT SHE WAS SEALED AWAY... BUT IN SUCH A SMALL CONTAINER?
FOR THOUSANDS OF YEARS?
SUCH CRUELTY...
NO... I AM NO LESS CRUEL.
IF I WOULD CHALLENGE THE CRAFTER...
I CANNOT AFFORD TO USE MY OWN SHINKI.
YOU MAY THINK ME A FIEND...
...BUT I HAVE NO CHOICE! I MUST USE YOU!!
IN THE NAME OF BISHAMONTEN, I SET YOU FREE!!

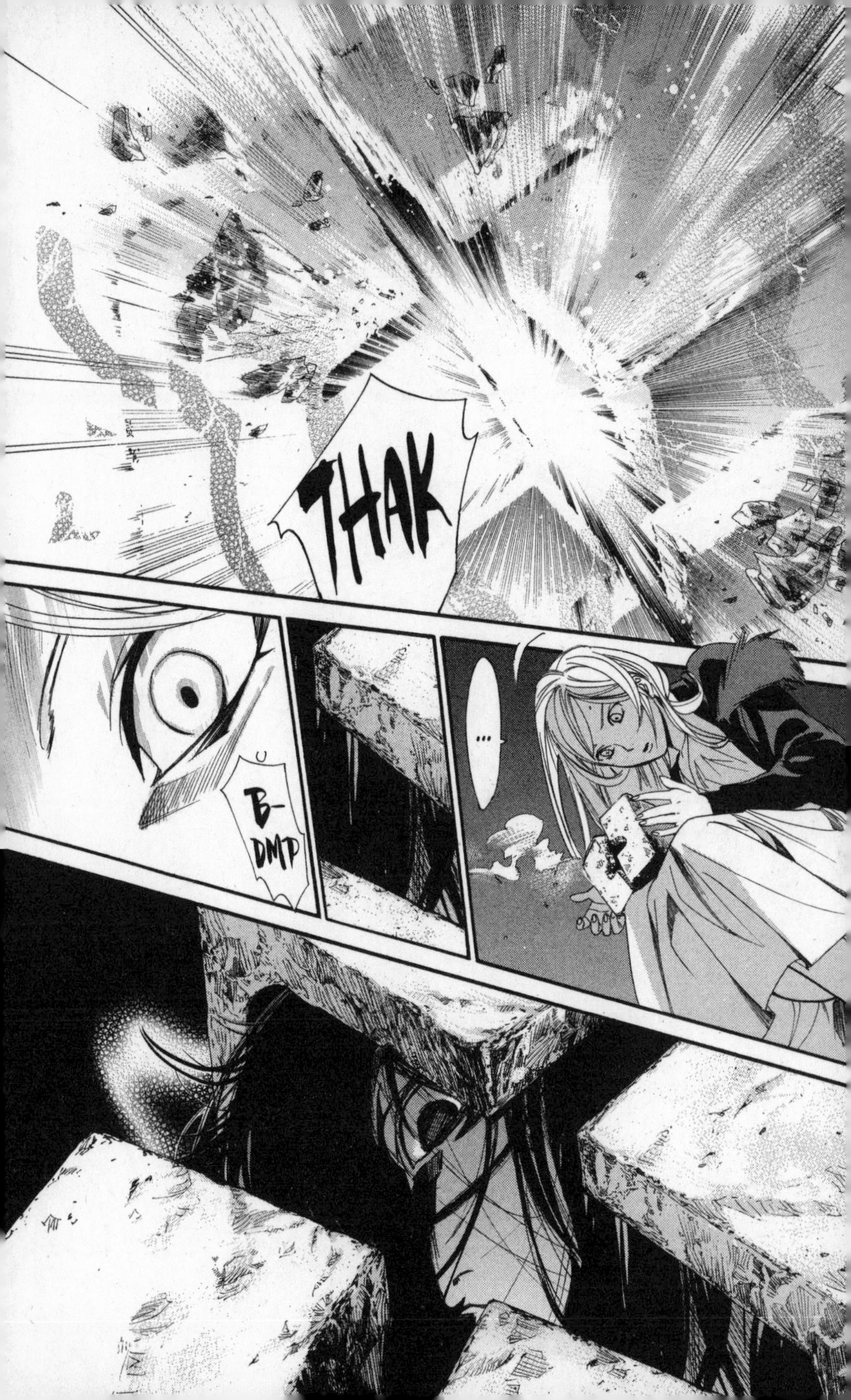
THAK
...
B-DMP

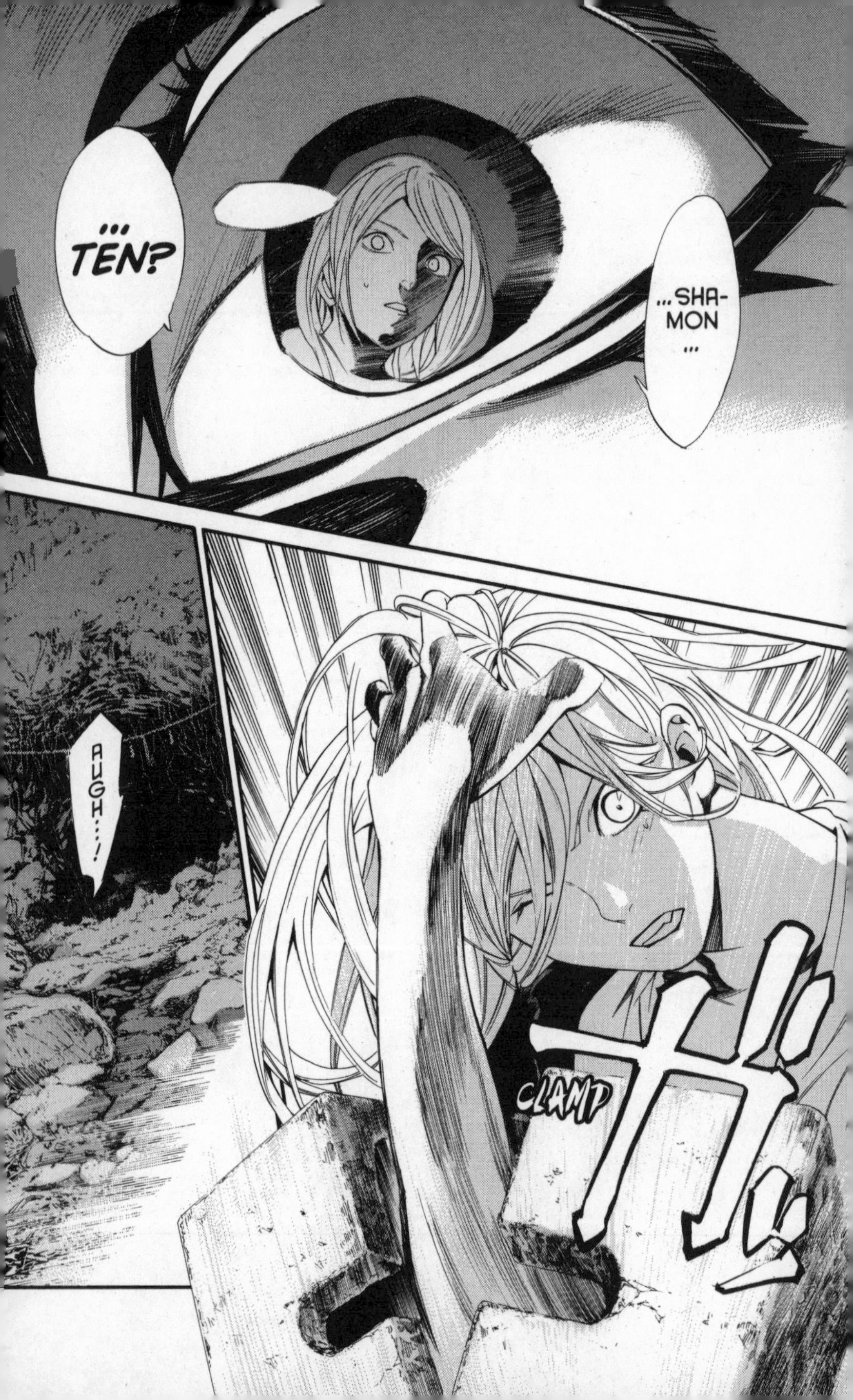
...SHA-MON...
...TEN?
CLAMP
AUGH...!

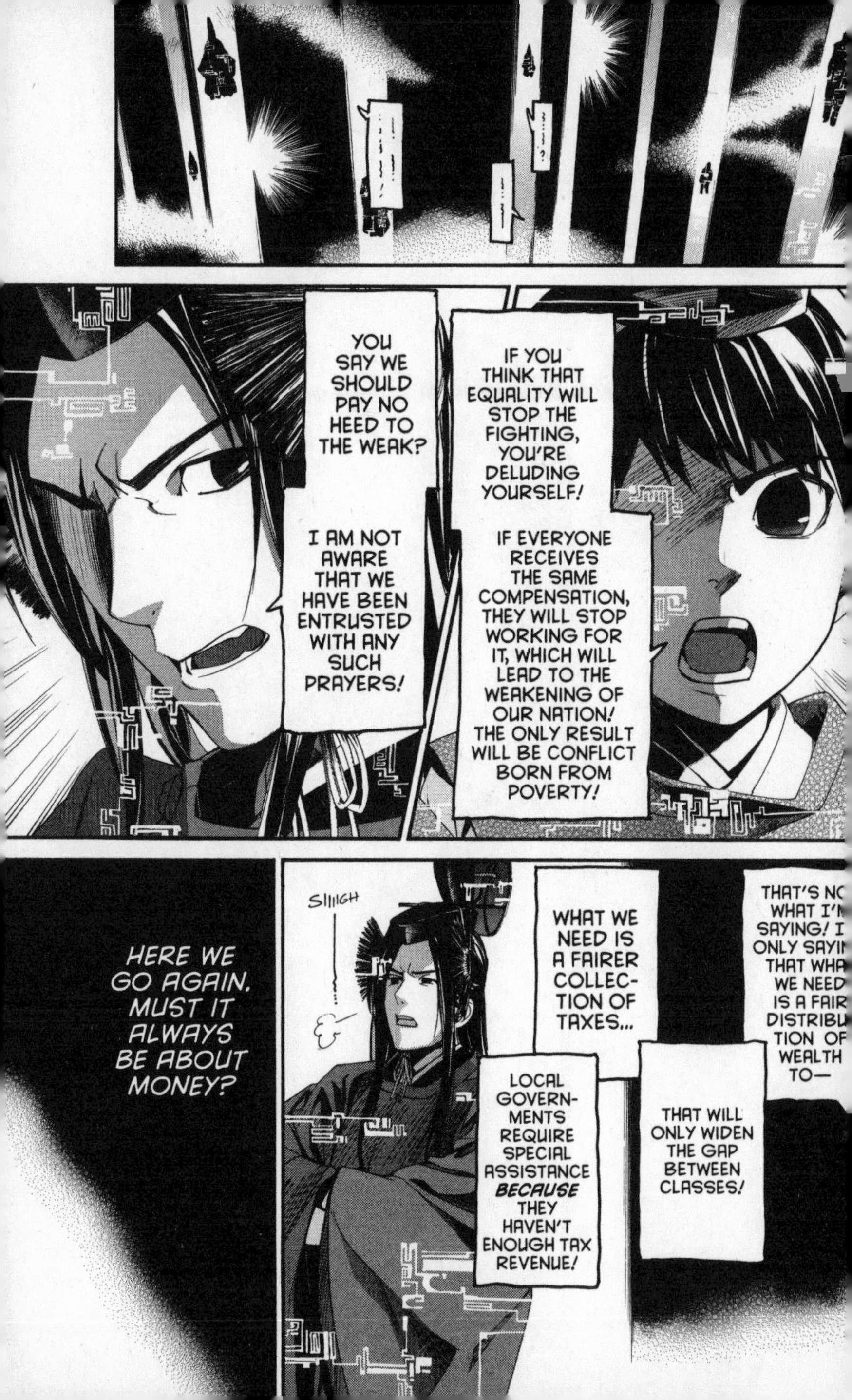
IF YOU THINK THAT EQUALITY WILL STOP THE FIGHTING, YOU'RE DELUDING YOURSELF!
IF EVERYONE RECEIVES THE SAME COMPENSATION, THEY WILL STOP WORKING FOR IT, WHICH WILL LEAD TO THE WEAKENING OF OUR NATION! THE ONLY RESULT WILL BE CONFLICT BORN FROM POVERTY!
YOU SAY WE SHOULD PAY NO HEED TO THE WEAK?
I AM NOT AWARE THAT WE HAVE BEEN ENTRUSTED WITH ANY SUCH PRAYERS!
THAT'S NO WHAT I'M SAYING! I ONLY SAYI THAT WHA WE NEED IS A FAIR DISTRIBU TION OF WEALTH TO—
WHAT WE NEED IS A FAIRER COLLEC-TION OF TAXES...
THAT WILL ONLY WIDEN THE GAP BETWEEN CLASSES!
LOCAL GOVERN-MENTS REQUIRE SPECIAL ASSISTANCE ***BECAUSE*** THEY HAVEN'T ENOUGH TAX REVENUE!
SIIIGH
HERE WE GO AGAIN. MUST IT ALWAYS BE ABOUT MONEY?

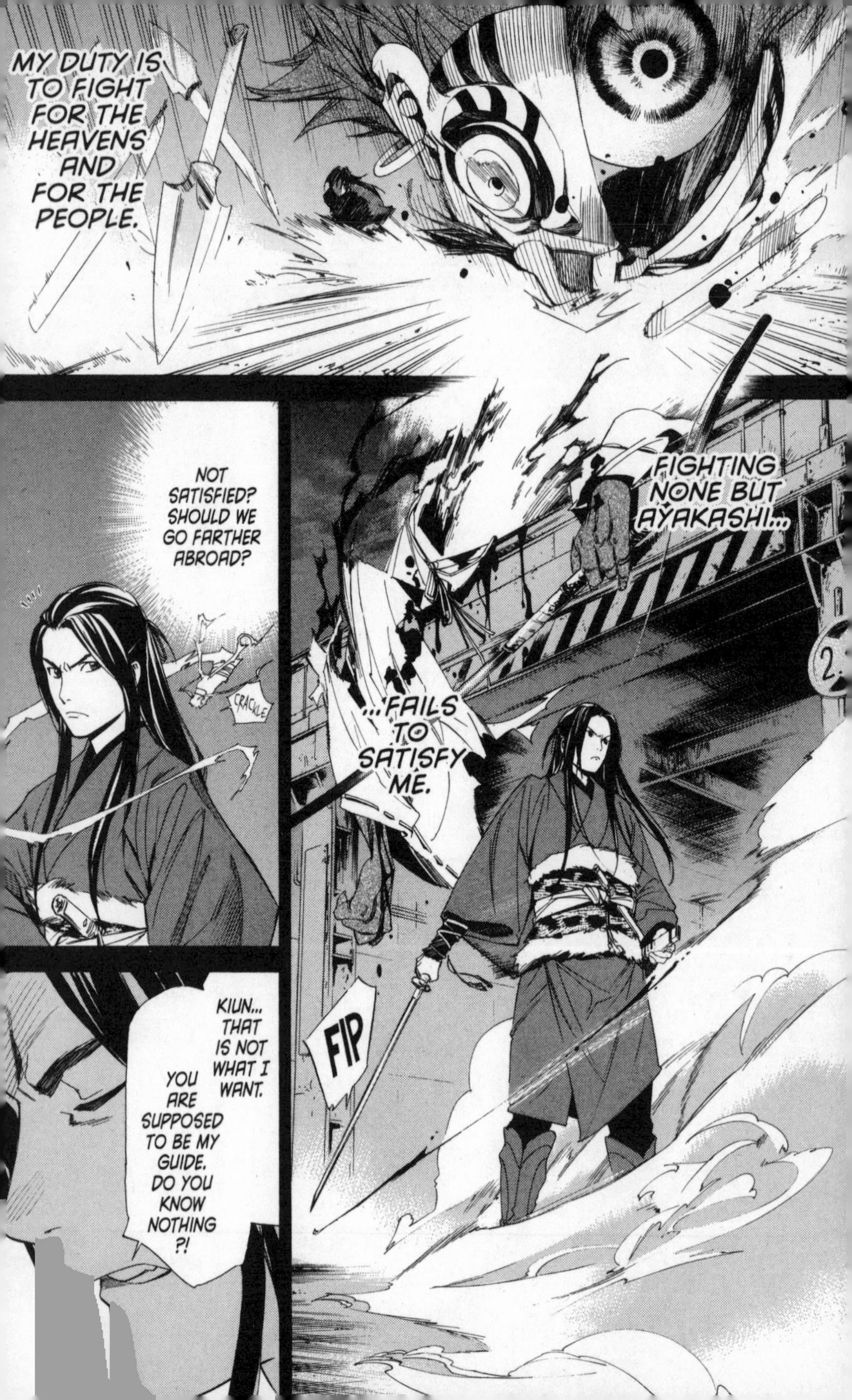
MY DUTY IS TO FIGHT FOR THE HEAVENS AND FOR THE PEOPLE.
FIGHTING NONE BUT AYAKASHI...
...FAILS TO SATISFY ME.
FIP
NOT SATISFIED? SHOULD WE GO FARTHER ABROAD?
CRACKLE
KIUN... THAT IS NOT WHAT I WANT.
YOU ARE SUPPOSED TO BE MY GUIDE. DO YOU KNOW NOTHING?!

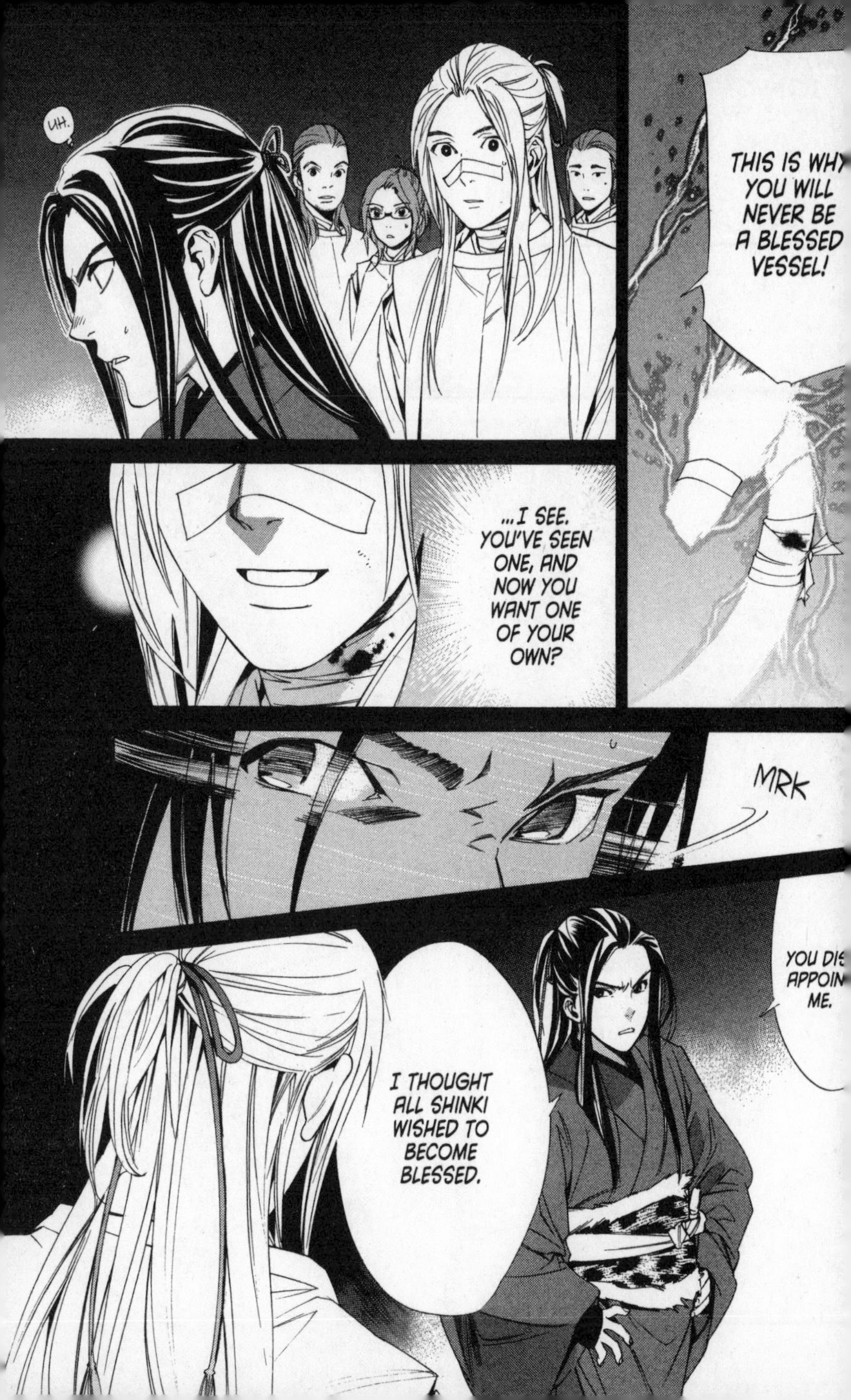
THIS IS WHY YOU WILL NEVER BE A BLESSED VESSEL!
UH.
...I SEE. YOU'VE SEEN ONE, AND NOW YOU WANT ONE OF YOUR OWN?
MRK
YOU DIS APPOIN ME.
I THOUGHT ALL SHINKI WISHED TO BECOME BLESSED.

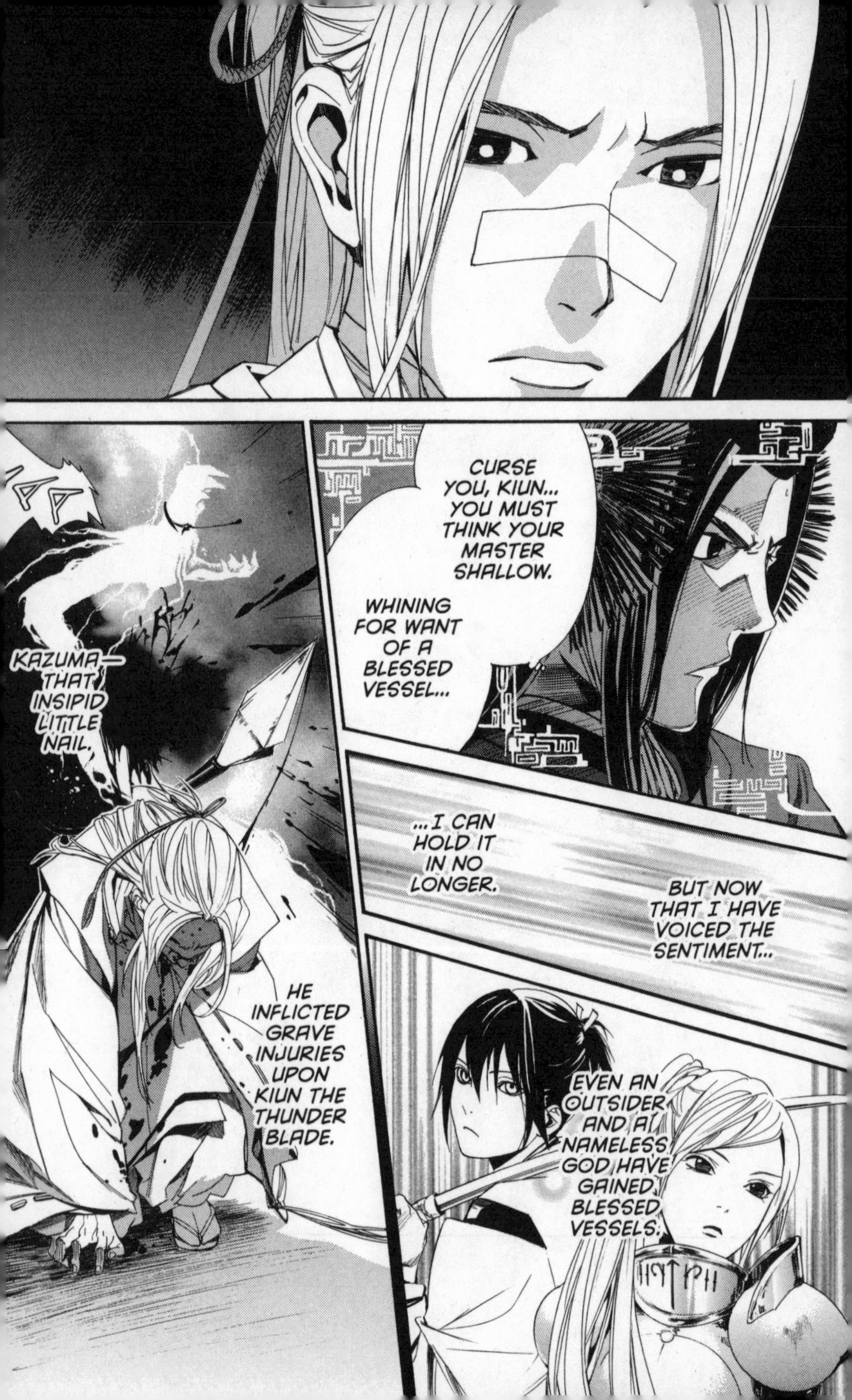
CURSE YOU, KIUN... YOU MUST THINK YOUR MASTER SHALLOW.
WHINING FOR WANT OF A BLESSED VESSEL...
...I CAN HOLD IT IN NO LONGER.
BUT NOW THAT I HAVE VOICED THE SENTIMENT...
EVEN AN OUTSIDER AND A NAMELESS GOD HAVE GAINED BLESSED VESSELS.
KAZUMA—THAT INSIPID LITTLE NAIL,
HE INFLICTED GRAVE INJURIES UPON KIUN THE THUNDER BLADE.

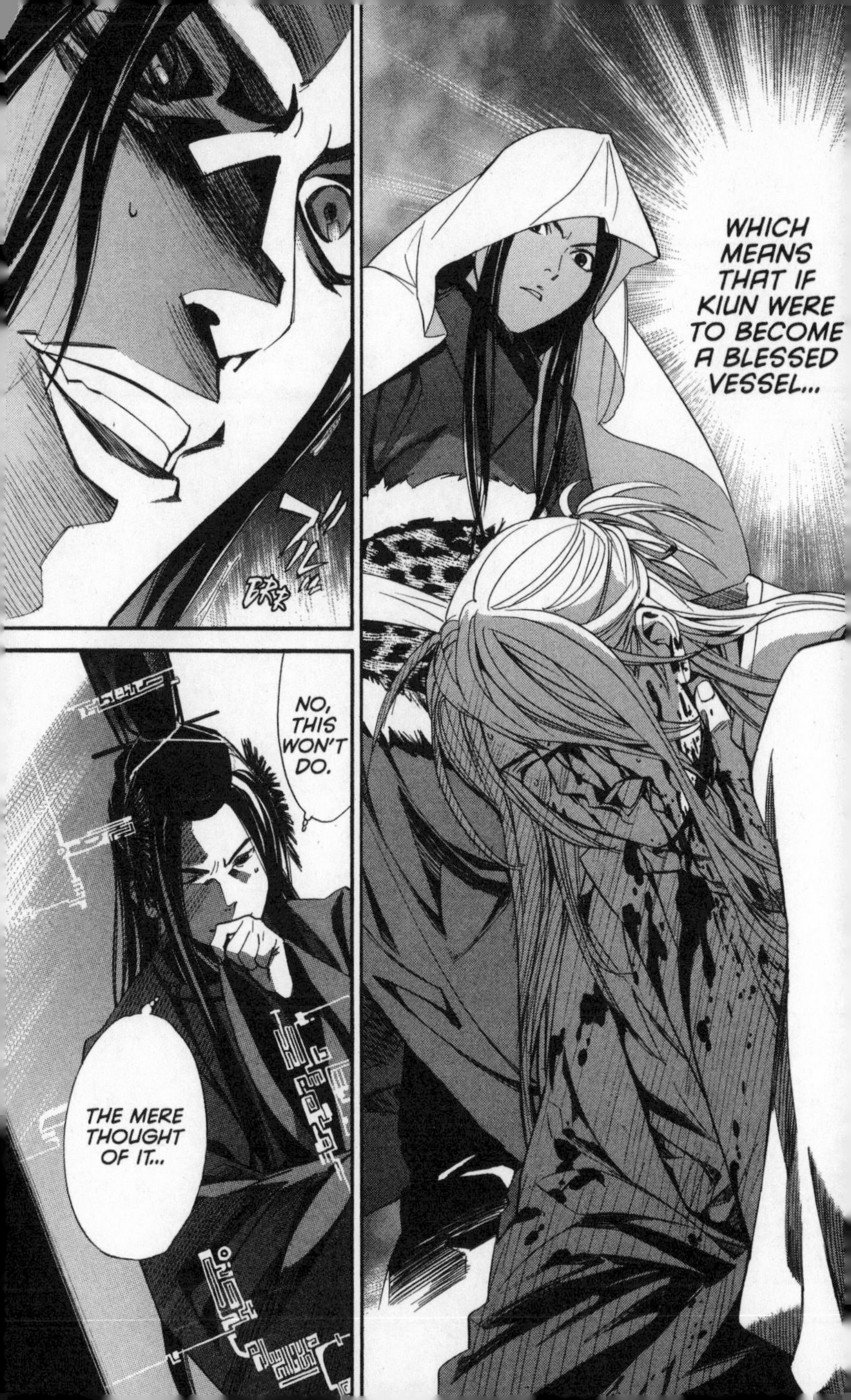
WHICH MEANS THAT IF KIUN WERE TO BECOME A BLESSED VESSEL...
BRR
NO, THIS WON'T DO.
THE MERE THOUGHT OF IT...

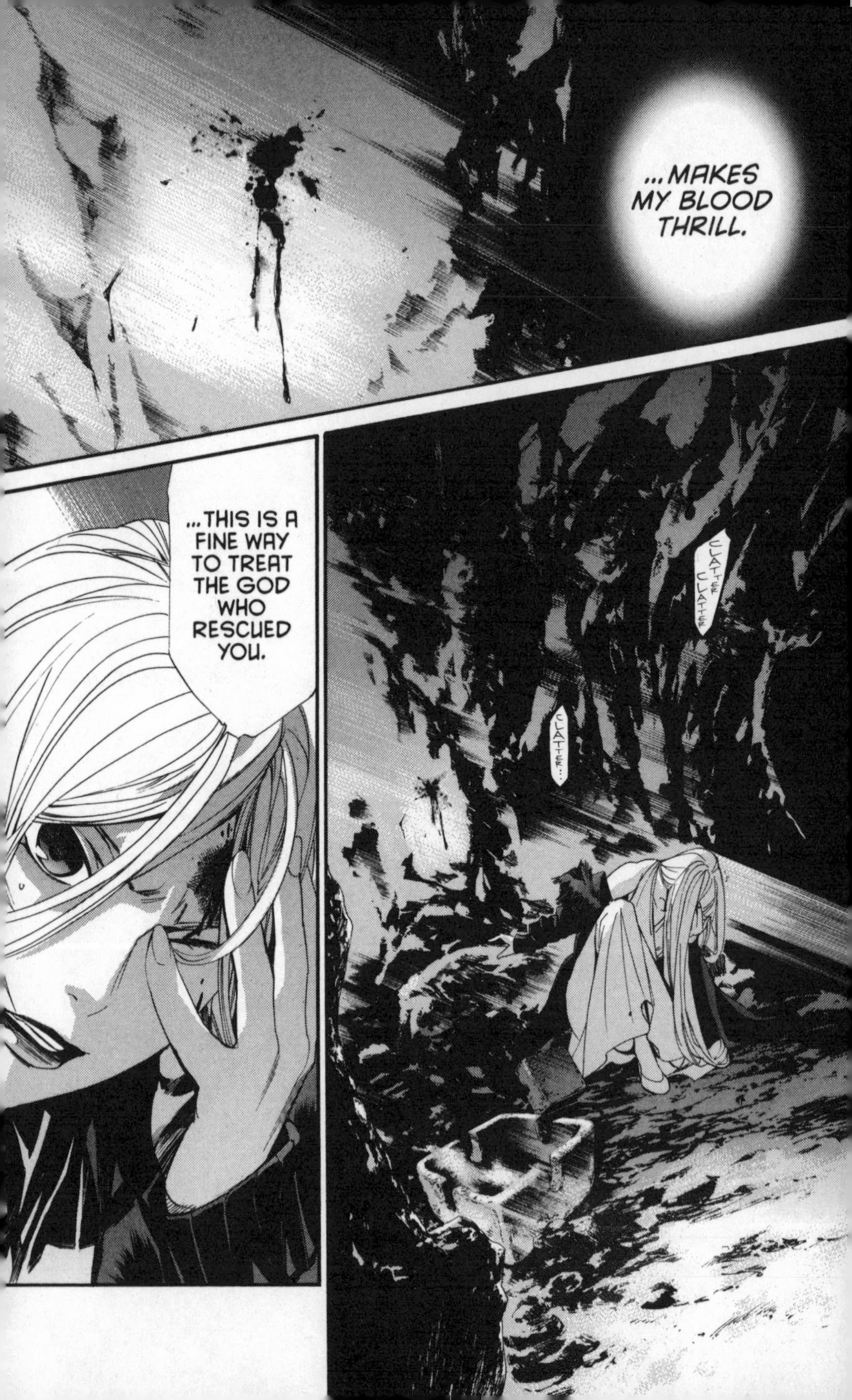
...MAKES MY BLOOD THRILL.
CLATTER CLATTER
CLATTER...
...THIS IS A FINE WAY TO TREAT THE GOD WHO RESCUED YOU.

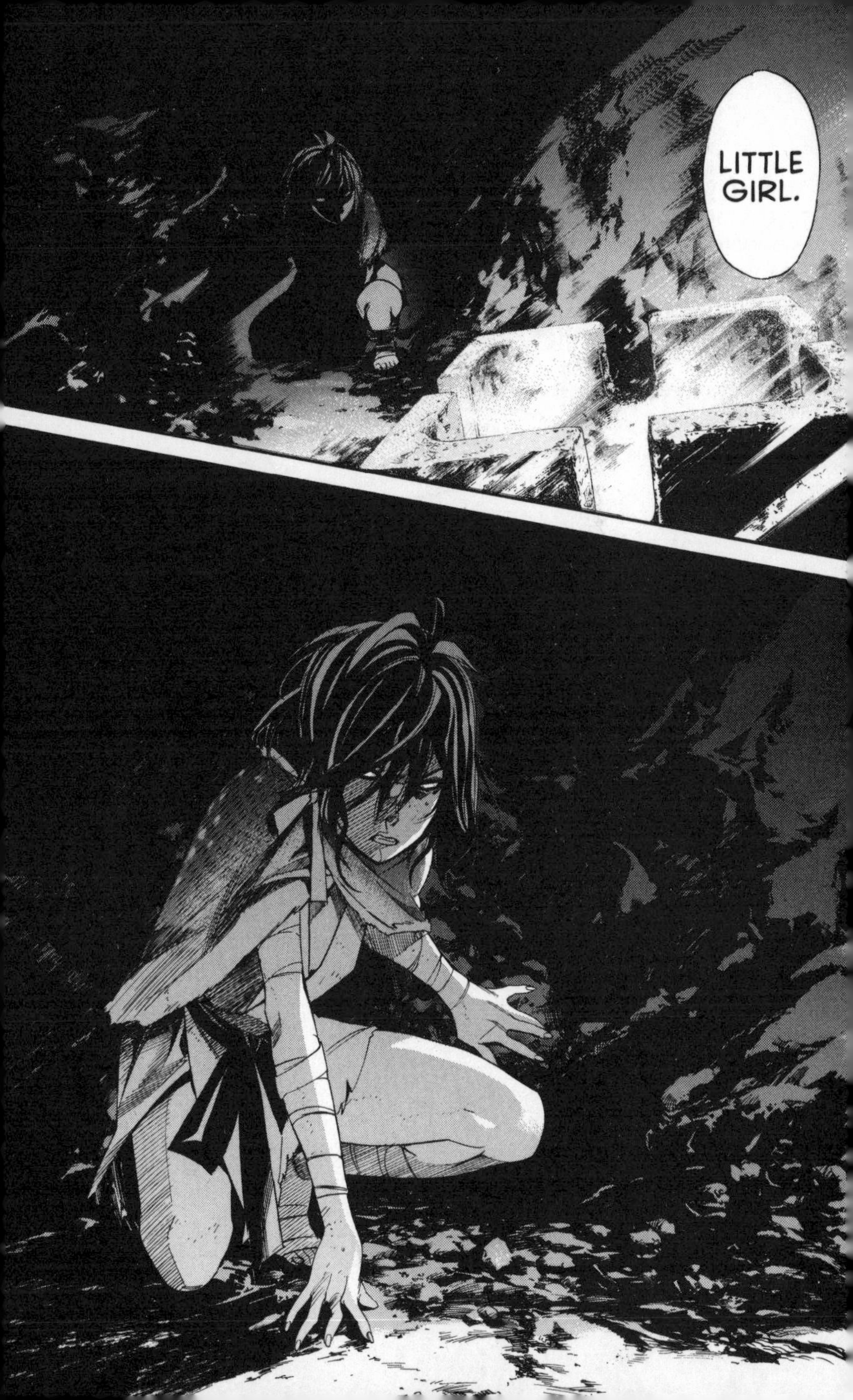
LITTLE GIRL.

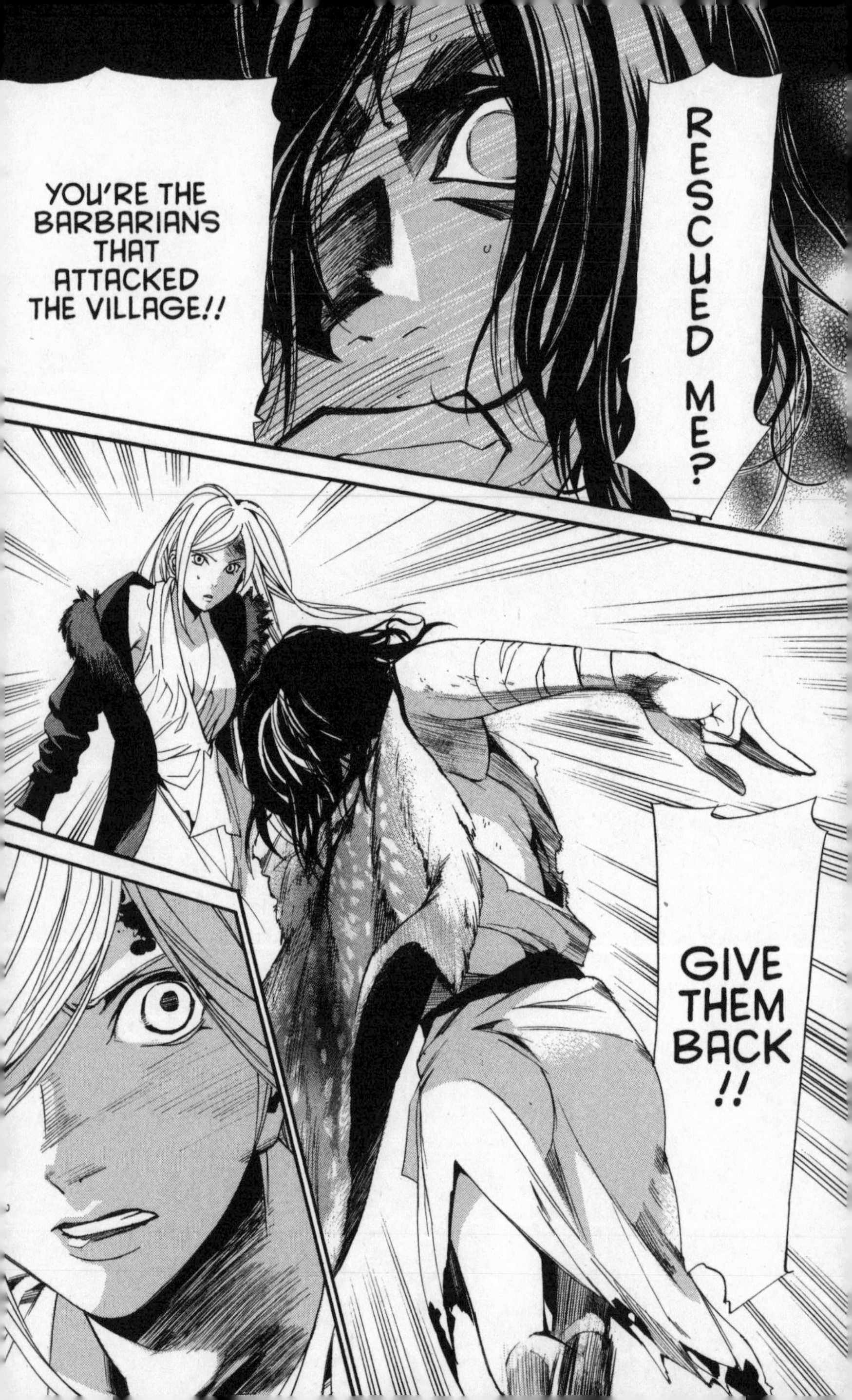
RESCUED ME?
YOU'RE THE BARBARIANS THAT ATTACKED THE VILLAGE!!
GIVE THEM BACK!!

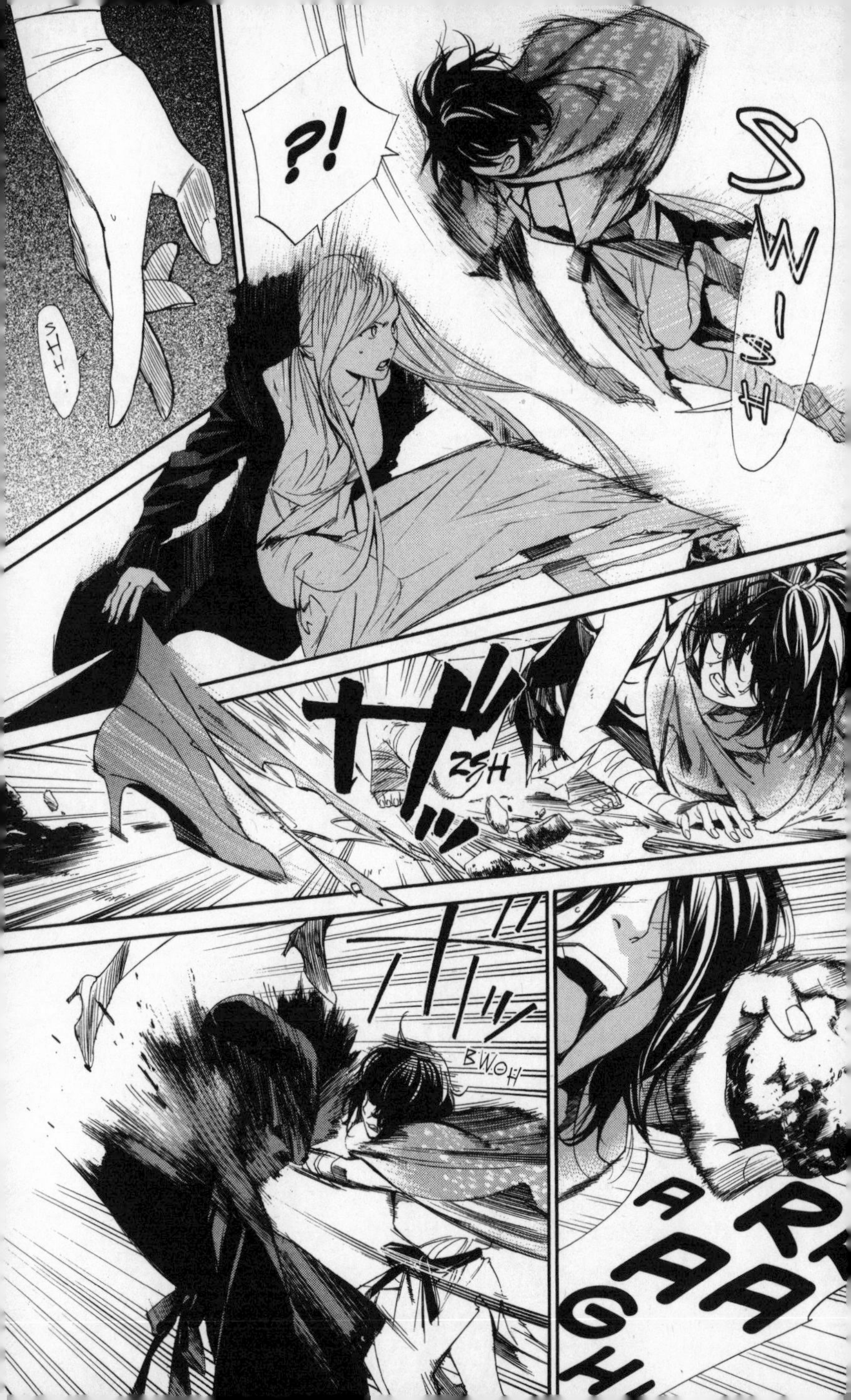
SWISH
?!
SHH...
ZSH
ARRAAAGH
BWOH

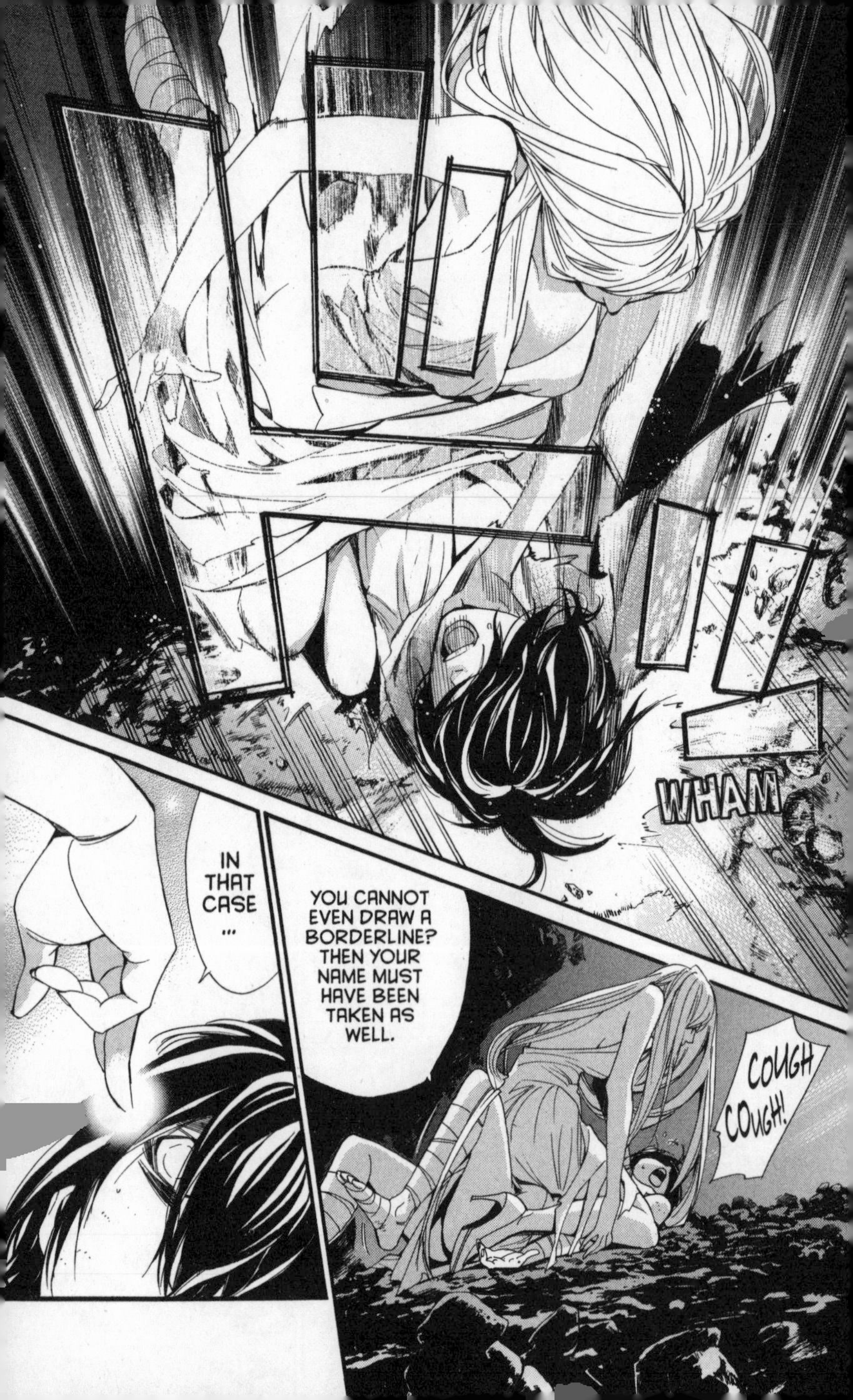
WHAM
COUGH COUGH!
YOU CANNOT EVEN DRAW A BORDERLINE? THEN YOUR NAME MUST HAVE BEEN TAKEN AS WELL.
IN THAT CASE ...

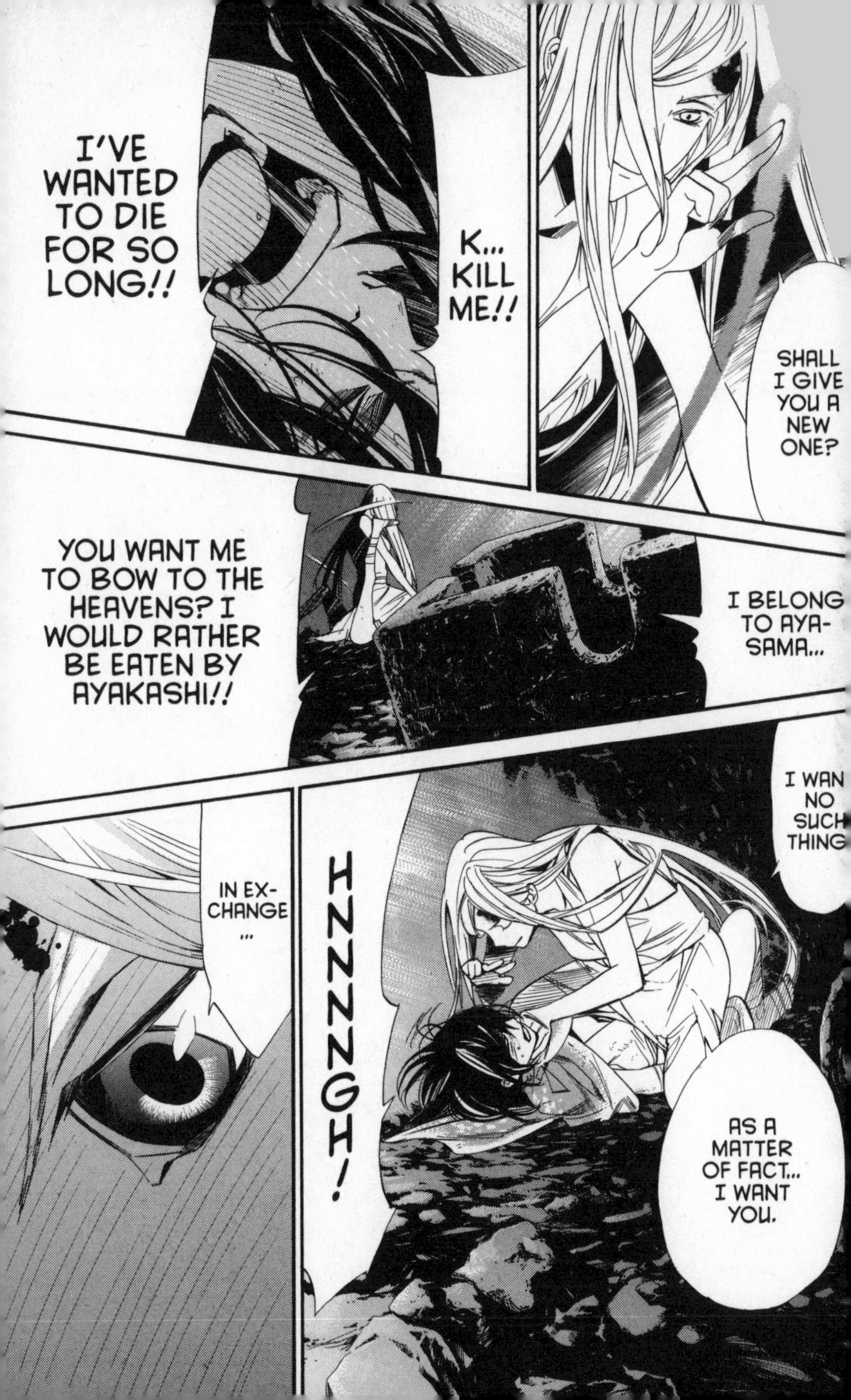
SHALL I GIVE YOU A NEW ONE?
K... KILL ME!!
I'VE WANTED TO DIE FOR SO LONG!!
I BELONG TO AYA-SAMA...
YOU WANT ME TO BOW TO THE HEAVENS? I WOULD RATHER BE EATEN BY AYAKASHI!!
I WAN NO SUCH THING
AS A MATTER OF FACT... I WANT YOU.
HNNNNGH!
IN EX-CHANGE ...

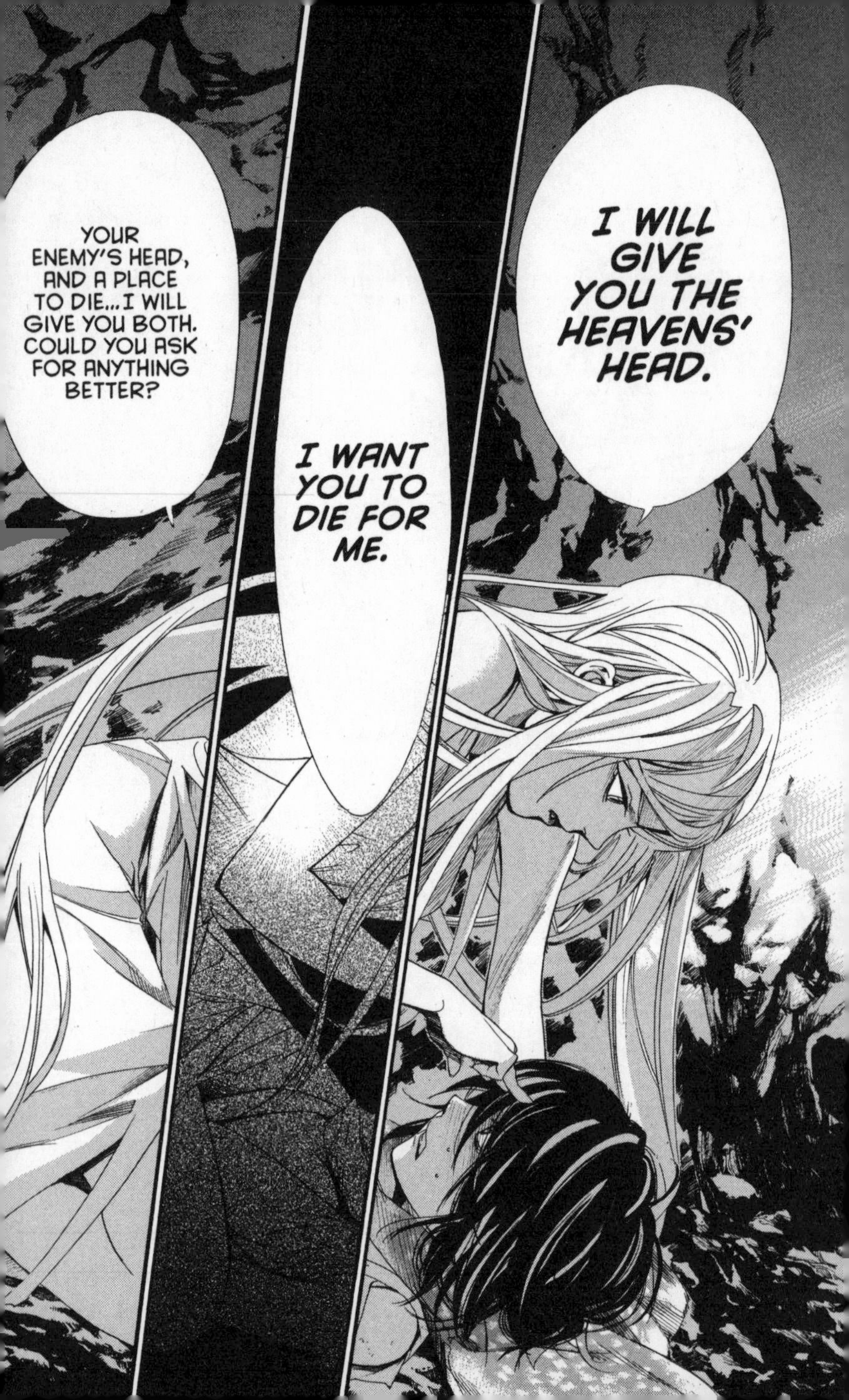
I WILL GIVE YOU THE HEAVENS' HEAD.
I WANT YOU TO DIE FOR ME.
YOUR ENEMY'S HEAD, AND A PLACE TO DIE...I WILL GIVE YOU BOTH. COULD YOU ASK FOR ANYTHING BETTER?

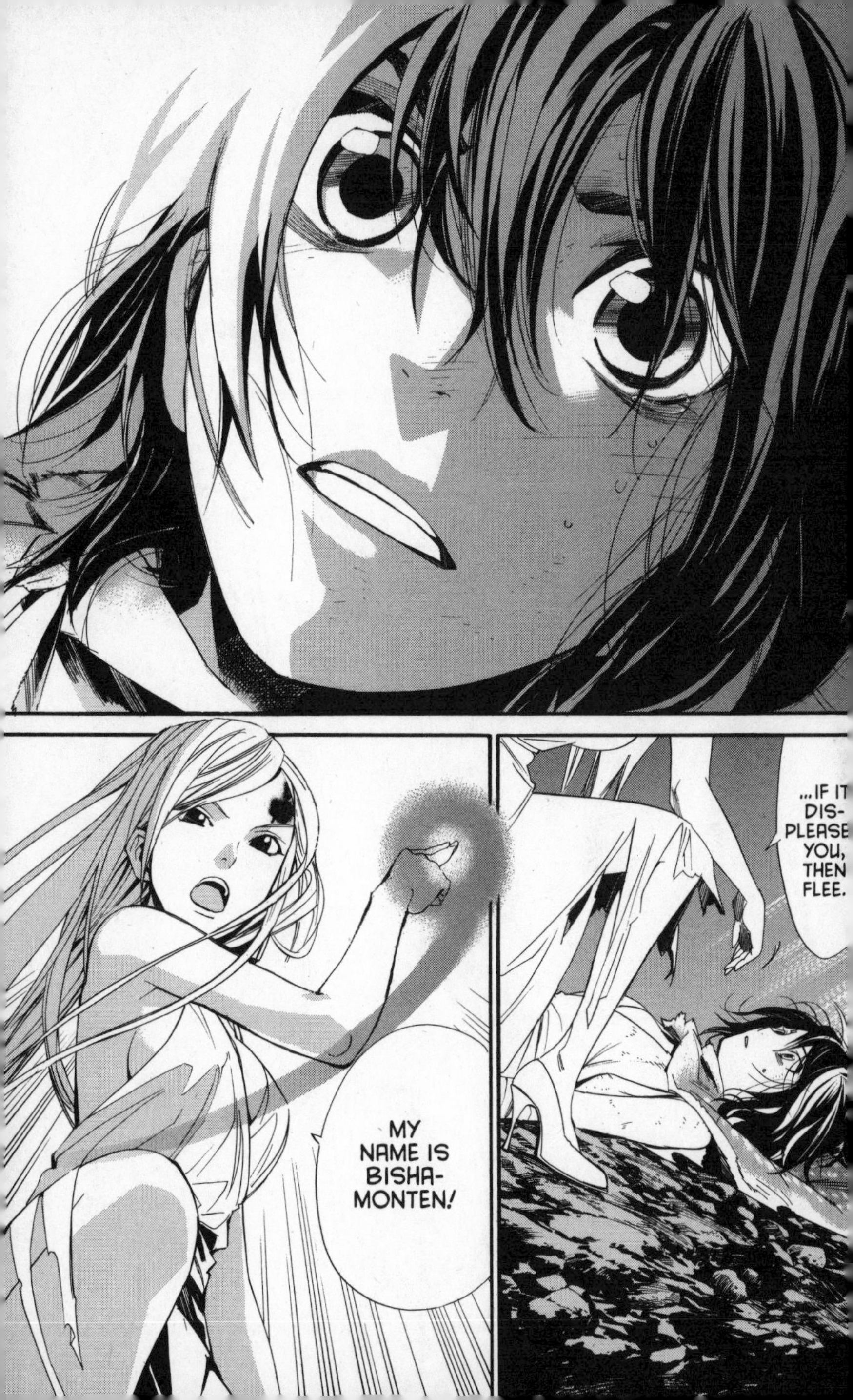
...IF IT DIS-PLEASE YOU, THEN FLEE.
MY NAME IS BISHA-MONTEN!

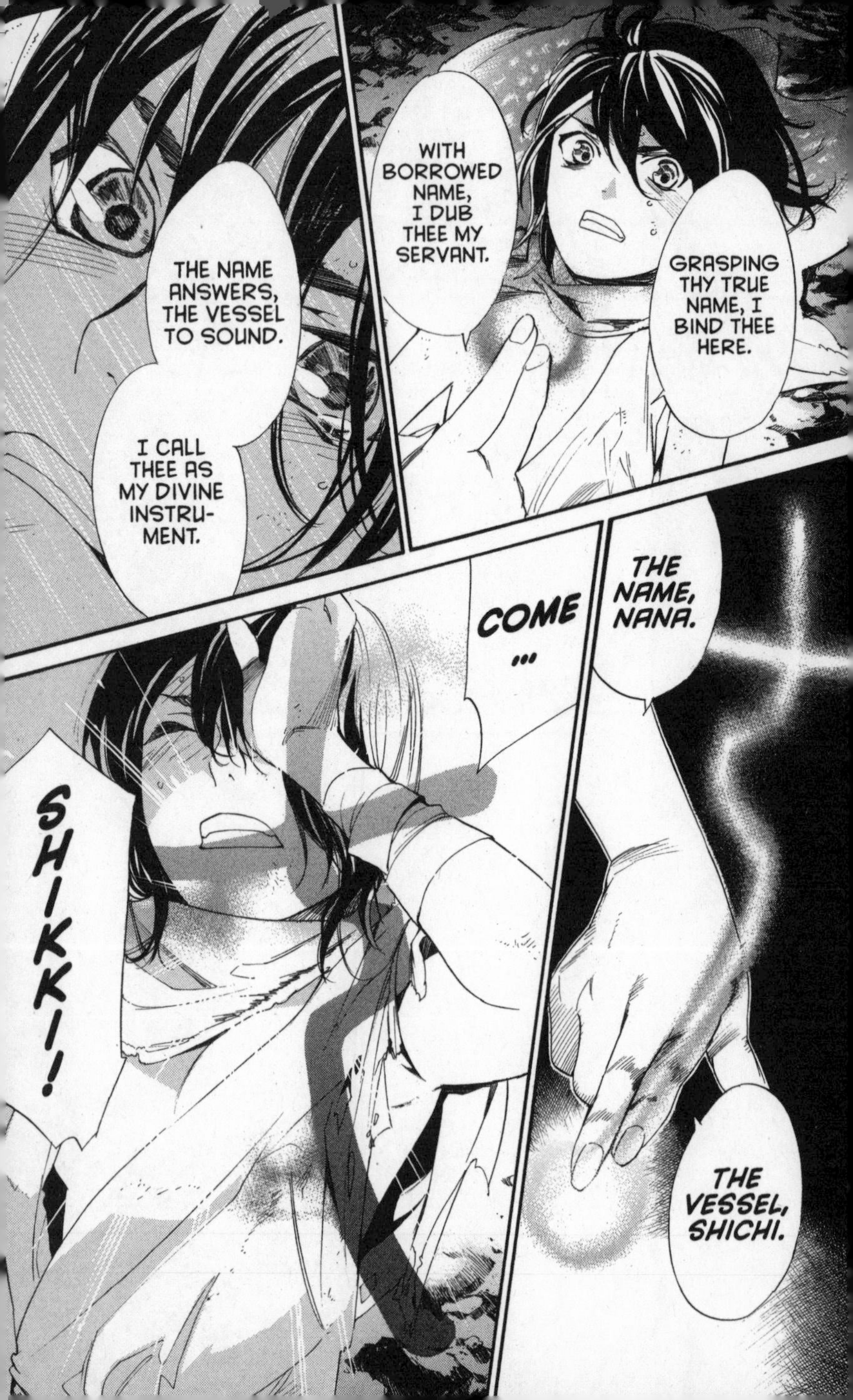
GRASPING THY TRUE NAME, I BIND THEE HERE.
WITH BORROWED NAME, I DUB THEE MY SERVANT.
THE NAME ANSWERS, THE VESSEL TO SOUND.
I CALL THEE AS MY DIVINE INSTRUMENT.
THE NAME, NANA.
THE VESSEL, SHICHI.
COME...
SHIKKI!

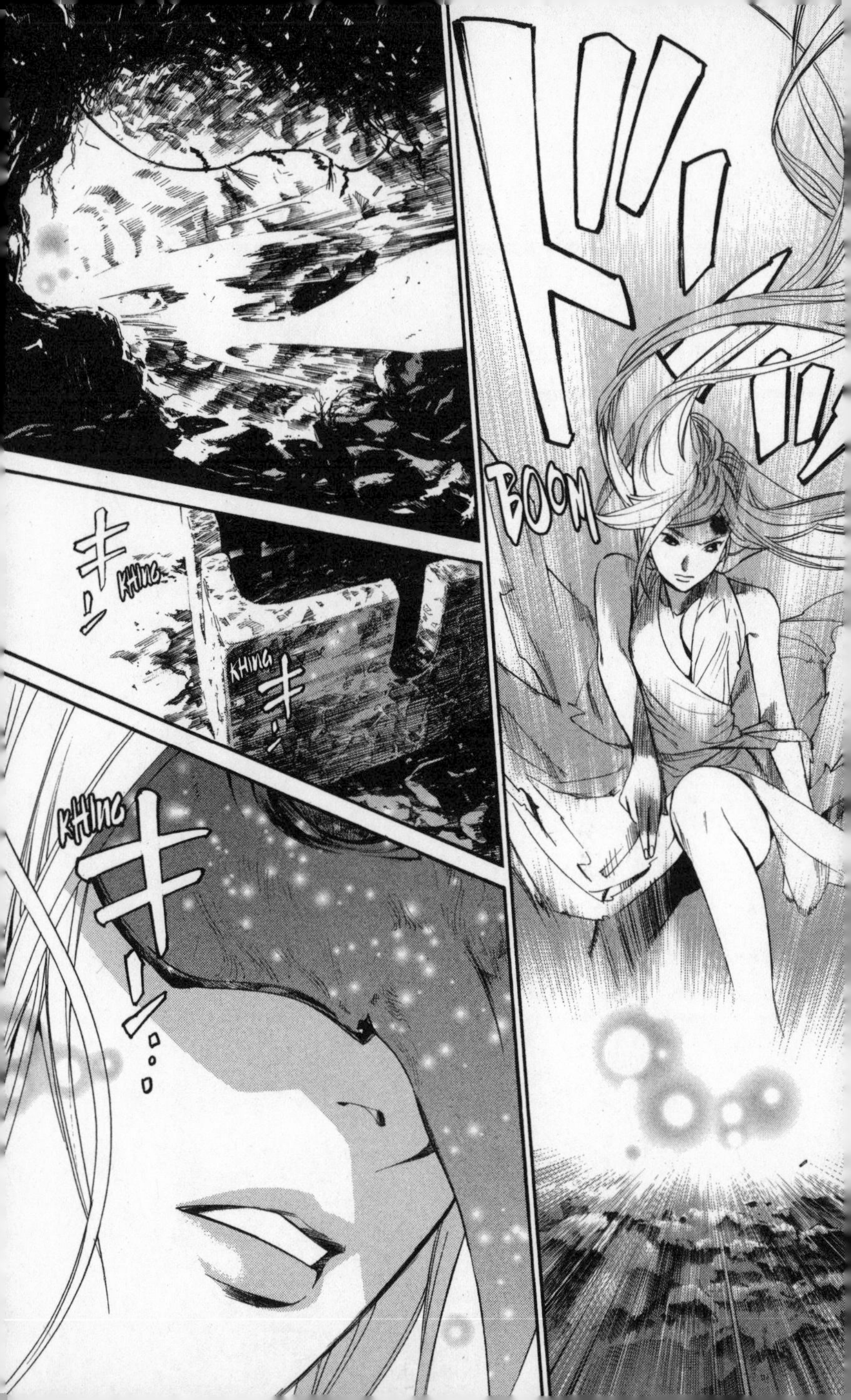
BOOM
KHING
KHING
KHING

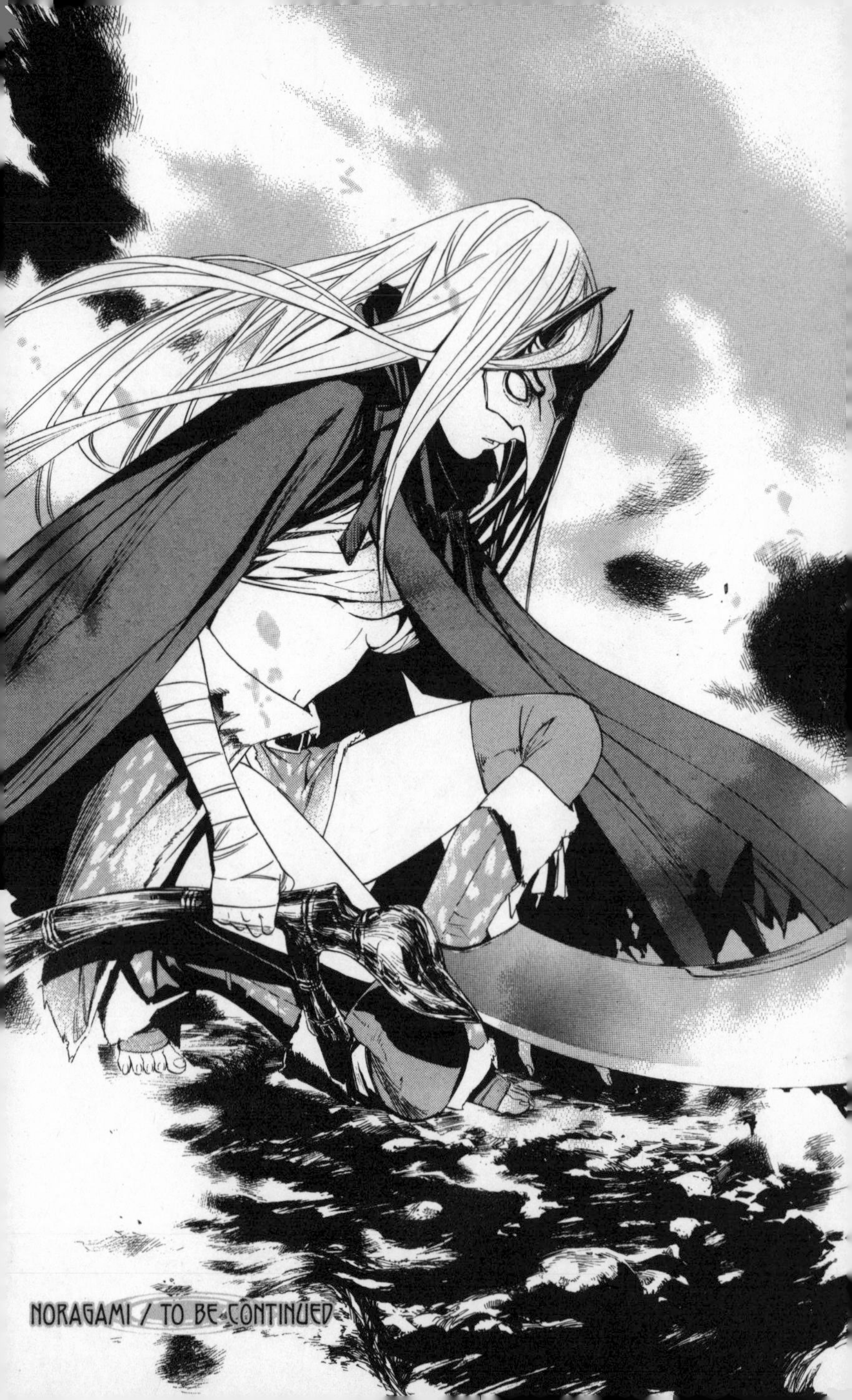
NORAGAMI / TO BE CONTINUED

野

臭

神

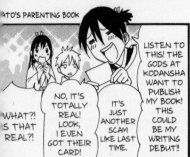

ATROCIOUS MANGA

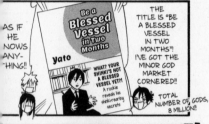

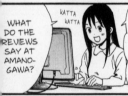

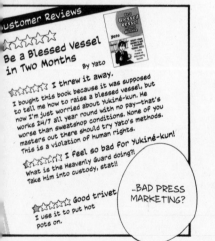

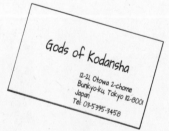

Gods of Kodansha
12-21, Otowa 2-chome
Bunkyo-ku, Tokyo 112-8001
Japan
Tel: 03-5395-3458

ATO'S PARENTING BOOK
LISTEN TO THIS! THE GODS AT KODANSHA WANT TO PUBLISH MY BOOK! THIS COULD BE MY WRITING DEBUT!!
IT'S JUST ANOTHER SCAM LIKE LAST TIME.
NO, IT'S TOTALLY REAL! LOOK, I EVEN GOT THEIR CARD!
WHAT?! S THAT REAL?!
THE TITLE IS "BE A BLESSED VESSEL IN TWO MONTHS"! I'VE GOT THE MINOR GOD MARKET CORNERED!!
Be a Blessed Vessel in Two Months
yato
WHAT? YOUR SHINKI'S NOT A BLESSED VESSEL YET?! A rookie reveals his shinki-rearing secrets
TOTAL NUMBER OF GODS, 8 MILLION!!
AS IF HE NOWS ANY-HING!!
YATO'S BOOK GOES ON SALE TODAY! I'LL BUY A COPY AND GET HIM TO SIGN IT!
KATTA KATTA
WHAT DO THE REVIEWS SAY AT AMANO-GAWA?
ustomer Reviews
Be a Blessed Vessel in Two Months
By Yato
I threw it away.
I bought this book because it was supposed to tell me how to raise a blessed vessel, but now I'm just worried about Yukiné-kun. He works 24/7 all year round with no pay—that's worse than sweatshop conditions. None of you masters out there should try Yato's methods. This is a violation of human rights.
I feel so bad for Yukiné-kun!
What is the Heavenly Guard doing?! Take him into custody, stat!!
Good trivet
I use it to put hot pots on.
...BAD PRESS MARKETING?

CATASTROPHE

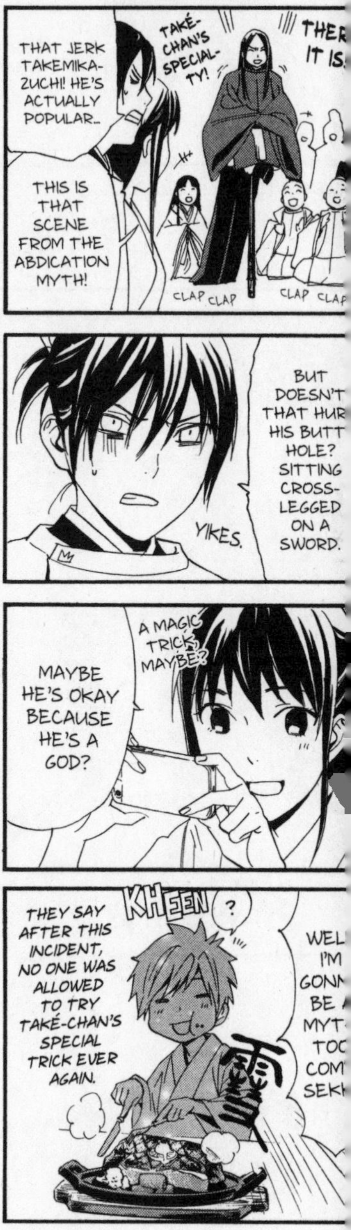
THER IT IS.
TAKÉ-CHAN'S SPECIAL-TY!
THAT JERK TAKEMIKA-ZUCHI! HE'S ACTUALLY POPULAR...
THIS IS THAT SCENE FROM THE ABDICATION MYTH!
CLAP CLAP CLAP CLAP
BUT DOESN'T THAT HUR HIS BUTT HOLE? SITTING CROSS-LEGGED ON A SWORD.
YIKES.
A MAGIC TRICK, MAYBE?
MAYBE HE'S OKAY BECAUSE HE'S A GOD?
WEL I'M GONN BE A MYT TOO COM SEK
?
KHEEN
THEY SAY AFTER THIS INCIDENT, NO ONE WAS ALLOWED TO TRY TAKÉ-CHAN'S SPECIAL TRICK EVER AGAIN.

NO MERCY FROM KIUN

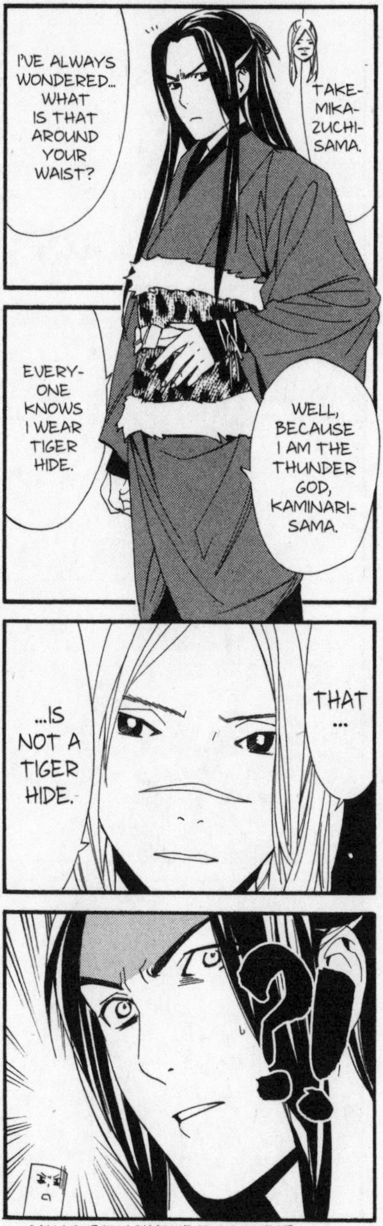
TAKE-MIKA-ZUCHI-SAMA.
I'VE ALWAYS WONDERED... WHAT IS THAT AROUND YOUR WAIST?
WELL, BECAUSE I AM THE THUNDER GOD, KAMINARI-SAMA.
EVERY-ONE KNOWS I WEAR TIGER HIDE.
THAT ...
...IS NOT A TIGER HIDE.

CAN I SUBTLY CHANGE IT TO TIGER?

MATCHMAKING

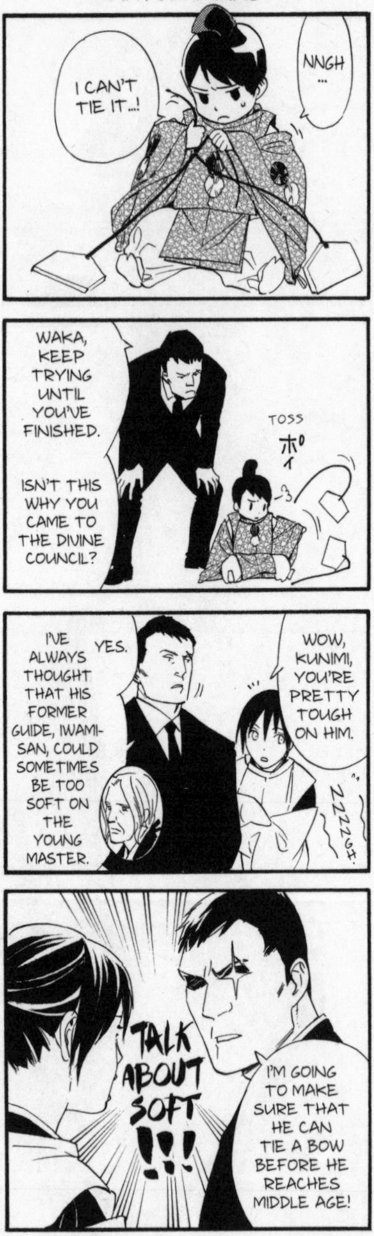
NNGH...
I CAN'T TIE IT...!
WAKA, KEEP TRYING UNTIL YOU'VE FINISHED.
ISN'T THIS WHY YOU CAME TO THE DIVINE COUNCIL?
TOSS
ポイ
WOW, KUNIMI, YOU'RE PRETTY TOUGH ON HIM.
YES.
I'VE ALWAYS THOUGHT THAT HIS FORMER GUIDE, IWAMI-SAN, COULD SOMETIMES BE TOO SOFT ON THE YOUNG MASTER.
ZZZZGH.
I'M GOING TO MAKE SURE THAT HE CAN TIE A BOW BEFORE HE REACHES MIDDLE AGE!
TALK ABOUT SOFT!!!

KUNIMI!!!!

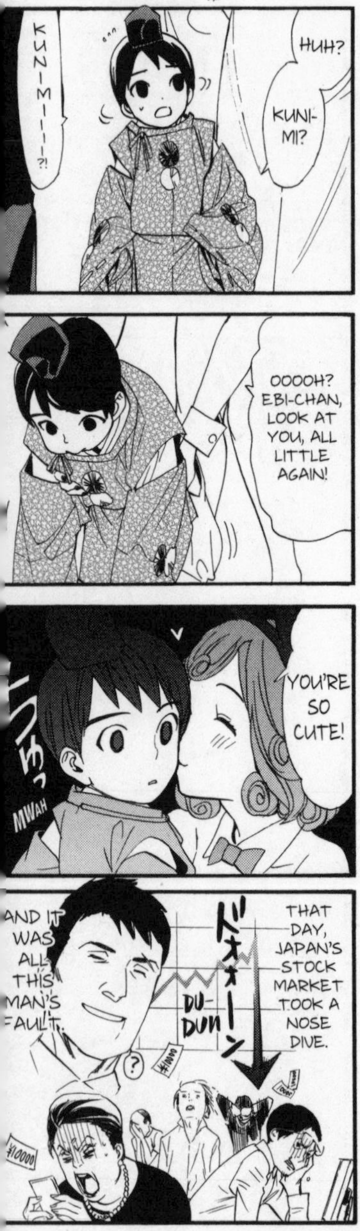
HUH?
KUNI-MI?
KUN-I-M-I-I-I-?!
OOOOH? EBI-CHAN, LOOK AT YOU, ALL LITTLE AGAIN!
YOU'RE SO CUTE!
MWAH
THAT DAY, JAPAN'S STOCK MARKET TOOK A NOSE DIVE.
ドオーン
DU-DUN
AND IT WAS ALL THIS MAN'S FAULT.

OOPS

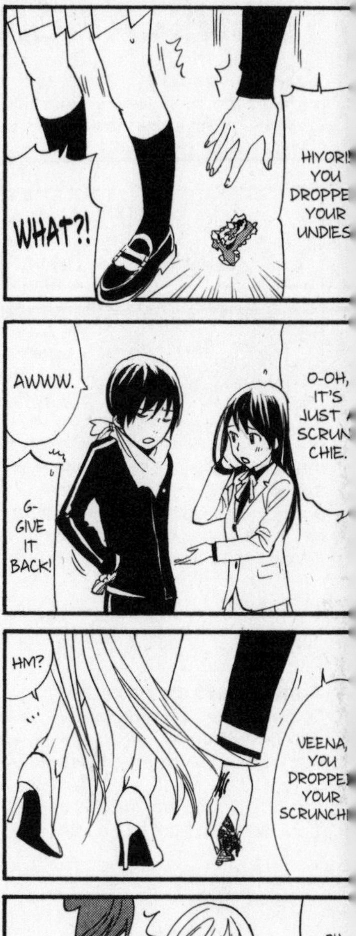
HIYORI! YOU DROPPE YOUR UNDIES
WHAT?!
O-OH, IT'S JUST SCRUN CHIE.
AWWW.
G-GIVE IT BACK!
VEENA, YOU DROPPE YOUR SCRUNCHI
HM?
OH, EXCUS ME.
THOSE ARE PANT-IES! AND YOU'RE BUCK-NAKED!!

NO MERCY FOR KIUN

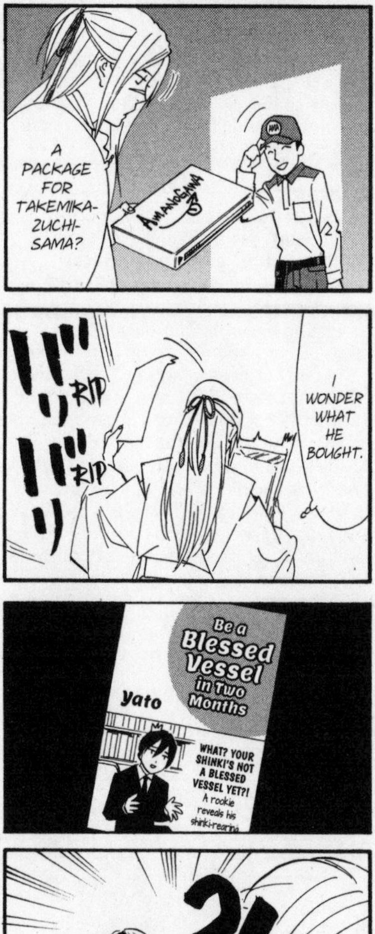
A PACKAGE FOR TAKEMIKA-ZUCHI-SAMA?
AMANOGAWA
I WONDER WHAT HE BOUGHT.
RIP
RIP
Be a Blessed Vessel in Two Months
yato
WHAT? YOUR SHINKI'S NOT A BLESSED VESSEL YET?!
A rookie reveals his shinki-rearing
?!

THANK YOU TO EVERYONE WHO READ THIS FAR!!

TRANSLATION NOTES

Japanese is a tricky language for most Westerners, and translation is often more art than science. For your edification and reading pleasure, here are notes on some of the places where we could have gone in a different direction in our translation of the work, or where a Japanese cultural reference is used.

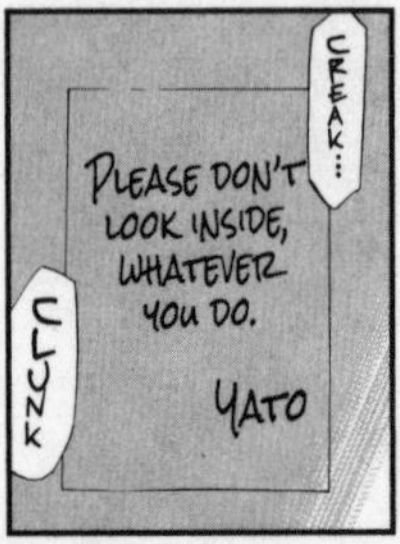
CREAK...
PLEASE DON'T LOOK INSIDE, WHATEVER YOU DO.
YATO
CLUNK

Yato the crane, page 9

There's a famous Japanese folktale called *Tsuru no Ongaeshi*, or "The Crane Returns a Favor" (also known as "The Grateful Crane"). Details of the story differ depending on the telling, but the basic version is that a man saves a crane. Later, he is visited by a beautiful young woman who asks to live with him (either as his wife or adopted daughter, depending on the age of the man in the story), and she helps earn money for her new family by providing cloth to sell. While she is weaving it, she requests that under no circumstances should anyone look inside her room. But the cloth is so wonderful, the man can't help but be curious, and eventually gives in to the temptation to peek inside. There he sees the woman, now in her true form as the crane he rescued, pulling her own feathers out of her wings to make the beautiful fabric. Because her identity has been discovered, the crane must now leave the man forever. Yato doesn't have to leave anyone forever, but his surprise has been thwarted.

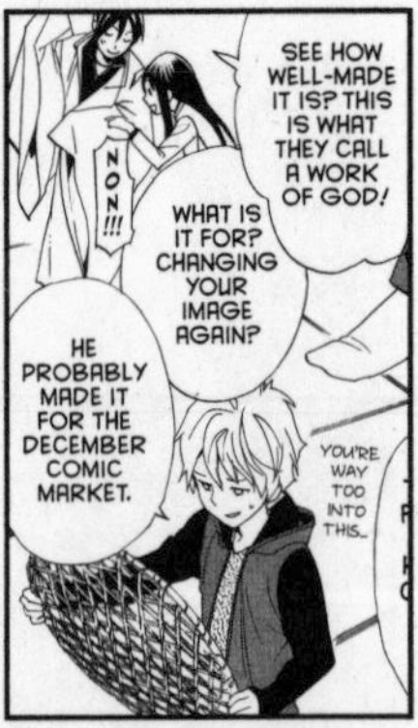
SEE HOW WELL-MADE IT IS? THIS IS WHAT THEY CALL A WORK OF GOD!
NON!!!
WHAT IS IT FOR? CHANGING YOUR IMAGE AGAIN?
HE PROBABLY MADE IT FOR THE DECEMBER COMIC MARKET.
YOU'RE WAY TOO INTO THIS...

Comic Market, page 10

Comic Market, affectionately known as Comiket, is a big convention where artists get together and sell their comics—including original comics, fan comics, and other fan art and fan works. Naturally, the convention attracts cosplayers, and a costume might be just what Tôya needs to boost sales on his own creations.

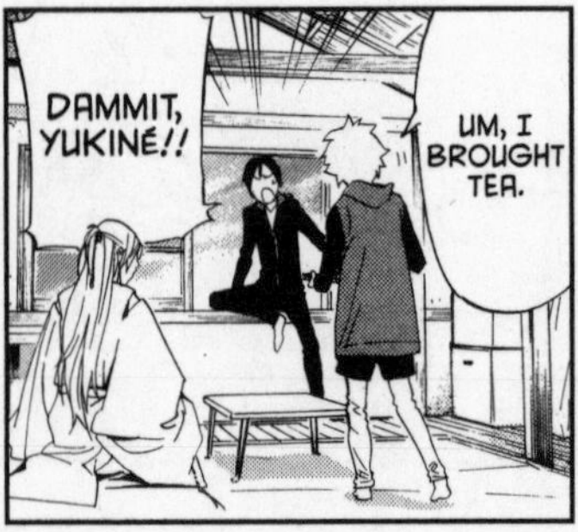
UM, I BROUGHT TEA.
DAMMIT, YUKINÉ!!

A cup of "there's the door," page 53

In the original Japanese, Yato told Yukiné to give Kiun a bowl of *bubuzuke*. In Kyoto, there's a special code to politely ask guests to leave, which is to ask them if they would like some *bubuzuke*, which is the Kyoto word for *chazuke*, a dish of rice with tea poured over it. When Yukiné points out that he couldn't be so rude as to turn Kiun away, Yato demands that he politely turn him away, by offering him some *bubuzuke* and making sure he got the hint.

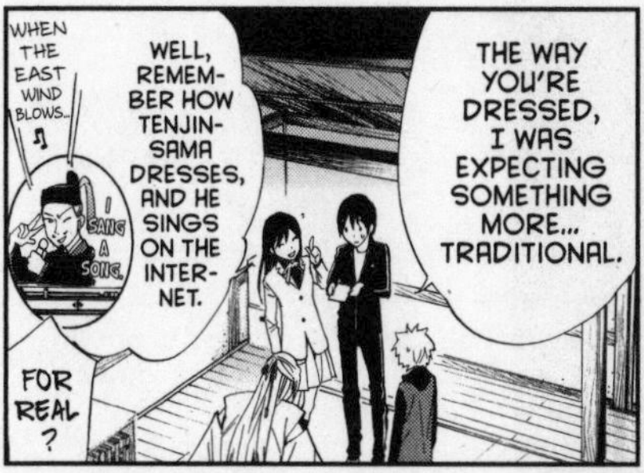
THE WAY YOU'RE DRESSED, I WAS EXPECTING SOMETHING MORE... TRADITIONAL.
WELL, REMEMBER HOW TENJIN-SAMA DRESSES, AND HE SINGS ON THE INTERNET.
WHEN THE EAST WIND BLOWS... ♫
I SANG A SONG.
FOR REAL?

Tenjin singing on the internet, page 62

In contrast to professional singers that you may see on television, known as *kashu*, there are amateur singers who upload videos of themselves singing to various streaming services, and they're known as *utaite*. Both words mean "singer." A phrase that commonly accompanies these amateur videos is *utatte mita*, which roughly translates to, "I tried singing it." Basically it means they recorded themselves singing it to see how it would turn out. Because Tenjin still dresses the way he did during his mortal life, it might surprise people to realize that he is modern enough to use the internet in such a way.

Suehiro Jinja, page 72

This is a small shrine that can be found in central Tokyo, dedicated to Bishamon and the agricultural deity Uka-no-Mitama.

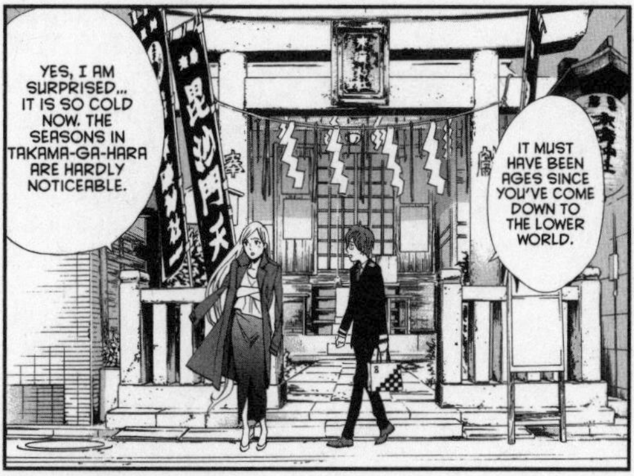
IT MUST HAVE BEEN AGES SINCE YOU'VE COME DOWN TO THE LOWER WORLD.
YES, I AM SURPRISED... IT IS SO COLD NOW. THE SEASONS IN TAKAMA-GA-HARA ARE HARDLY NOTICEABLE.

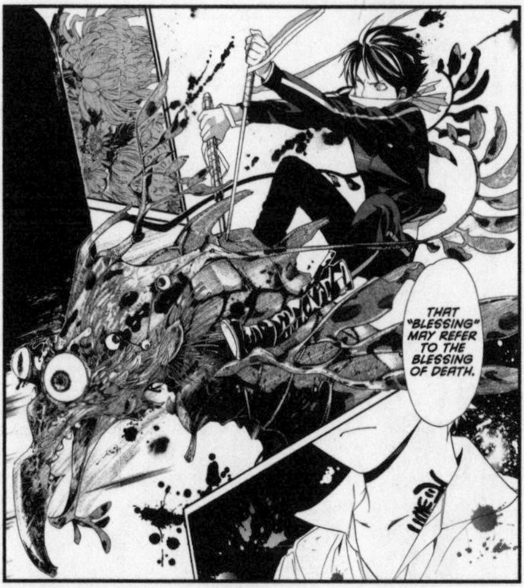
THAT "BLESSING" MAY REFER TO THE BLESSING OF DEATH.

The blessing of death, page 90

What Kiun really said is that the word *hafuri*, which means "blessed" or "blessing," can also mean "burial," as in "burying a body after death." Unfortunately, the words are not that similar in English, so the translators had to work around it. Fortunately for them, in some situations, death can be considered a blessing, either to the deceased or those left behind.

The *Raijin-zu*, page 94
The screen behind Takemikazuchi is adorned with a famous painting, the *Raijin-zu*, or "picture of the thunder god," by the artist Sôtatsu Tawaraya. Because Takemikazuchi is a thunder god, this is something like a portrait of himself.

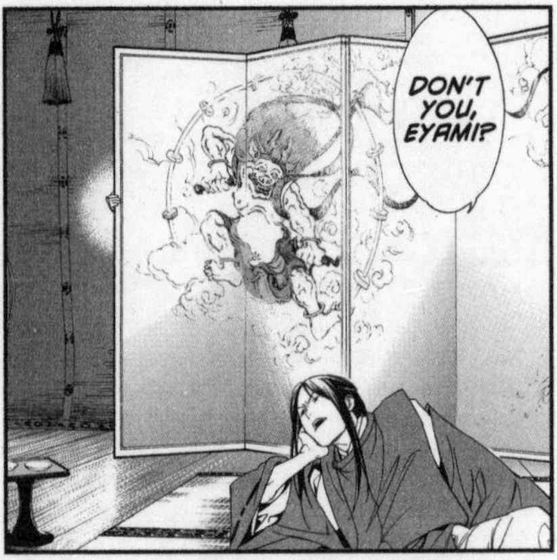
DON'T YOU, EYAMI?

Temple stamp book, page 101
Specifically, this woman is asking for him to sign her *goshuin* book, which is a book designed for *shuin*—a special kind of stamp that can be obtained at Shinto shrines and Buddhist temples. Each temple has its own unique stamp, which is stamped by a monk or priest in red ink, then written over in black calligraphy. These are souvenirs that prove you visited a certain temple or shrine, but in this case, it's more like proof that the recipient has met Tenjin himself.

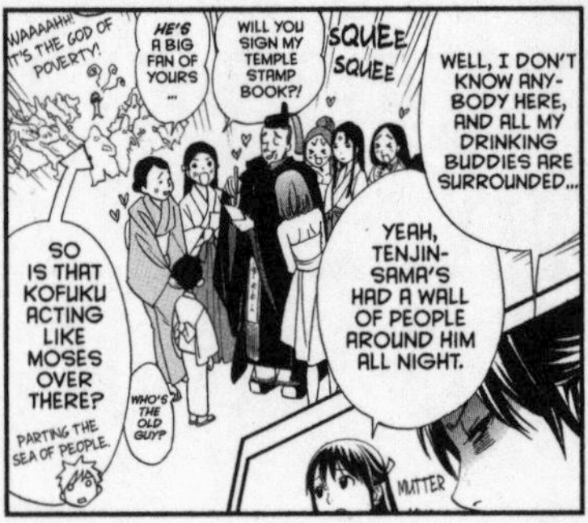
WELL, I DON'T KNOW ANYBODY HERE, AND ALL MY DRINKING BUDDIES ARE SURROUNDED...
SQUEE SQUEE
WILL YOU SIGN MY TEMPLE STAMP BOOK?!
HE'S A BIG FAN OF YOURS ...
WAAAAHH! IT'S THE GOD OF POVERTY!
YEAH, TENJIN-SAMA'S HAD A WALL OF PEOPLE AROUND HIM ALL NIGHT.
SO IS THAT KOFUKU ACTING LIKE MOSES OVER THERE?
WHO'S THE OLD GUY?
PARTING THE SEA OF PEOPLE.
MUTTER

Guarding the rest of the country, page 102
As Hiyori reminded everyone earlier, while all the gods are convened at the Divine Council, their shrines are left empty, and the land is left vulnerable. That being the case, some gods stay behind to make sure the country stays safe, and Ebisu is always at the top of this list of *rusugami*, or "caretaker gods."

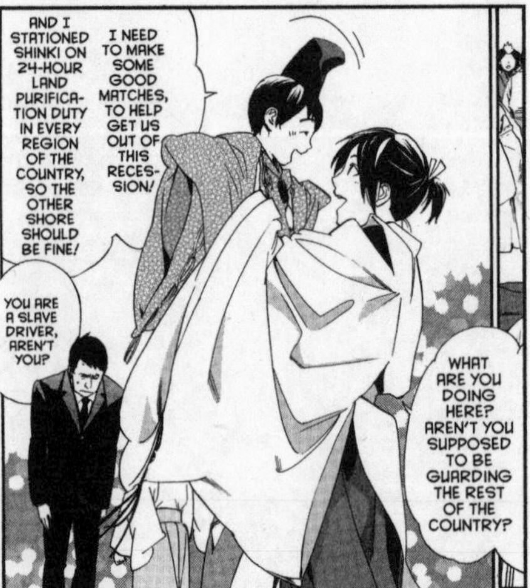
I NEED TO MAKE SOME GOOD MATCHES, TO HELP GET US OUT OF THIS RECESSION!
AND I STATIONED SHINKI ON 24-HOUR LAND PURIFICATION DUTY IN EVERY REGION OF THE COUNTRY, SO THE OTHER SHORE SHOULD BE FINE!
WHAT ARE YOU DOING HERE? AREN'T YOU SUPPOSED TO BE GUARDING THE REST OF THE COUNTRY?
YOU ARE A SLAVE DRIVER, AREN'T YOU?

Gods at the Divine Council, page 100, 108, 111

Because this is the biggest party the gods hold all year, there are several famous gods attending who haven't yet factored in to the *Noragami* storyline. The first one we hear about is Yamata-no-Orochi, who doesn't appear on the page, but whom Hiyori describes as looking like a dragon. In fact, he is an eight-headed serpent who terrorized two deities by the Hii River in Izumo by eating one of their daughters every year until he was slain by Susa-no-o, brother of Amaterasu.

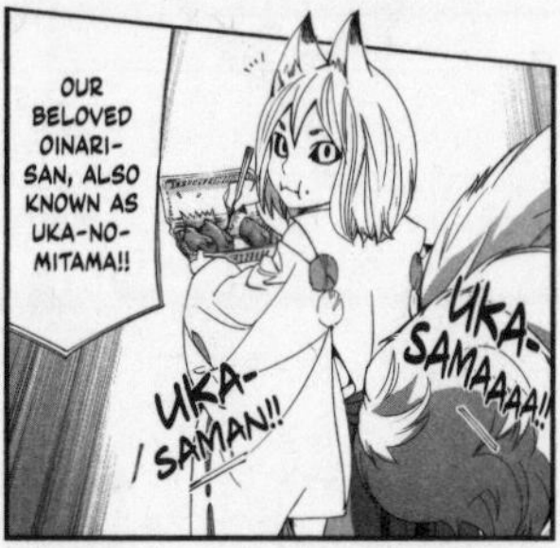
OUR BELOVED OINARI-SAN, ALSO KNOWN AS UKA-NO-MITAMA!!
UKA-SAMAAAA!!
UKA-SAMAN!!

Next we have Uka-no-Mitama, more commonly known as Inari, or the fox god and god of agriculture. Here, Uka-no-Mitama is seen with multiple tails—a symbol of age and power. The most powerful foxes have nine tails, so either some of Uka-sama's tails are hidden, or this is a younger incarnation, like Ebisu. The little fox is eating *inari-zushi*, which is rice wrapped in fried tofu, a favorite of fox spirits.

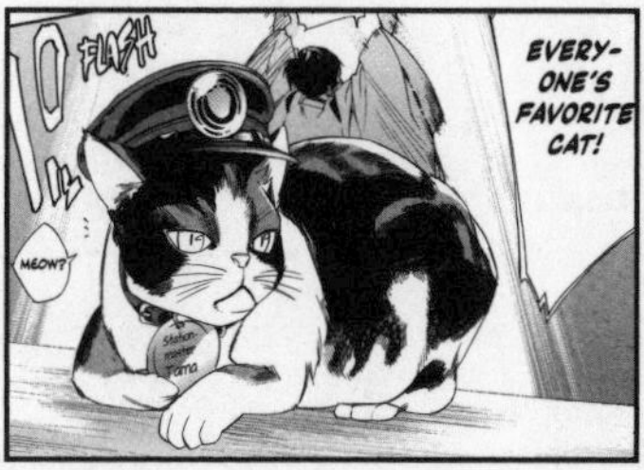
EVERY-ONE'S FAVORITE CAT!
FLASH
MEOW?

Finally, we have Stationmaster Tama. Everything that Ôkuninushi says about her is true—Tama was a cat born in 1999 and was appointed as the stationmaster of Kishi Station in Wakayama Prefecture in 2007. Her popularity was a great boon to the failing rail line, and she single-pawedly earned over a billion yen (about $10 million) for her local economy. Sadly, she passed away in 2015, but then was enshrined as a local deity.

The matchmaking song, page 114

The translators were unable to find an original source for this song, so it is likely that the gods have kept this song to themselves (meaning it's a *Noragami* original). The song does, however, use quotes from the *Kojiki* ("Records of Ancient Matters") for its lyrics. The part about meeting after going around a pillar comes from the story of Izanami and Izanagi's courtship—as part of the marriage ritual, the two of them circled a pillar, each going opposite directions. The part about flourishing like the flowers is a reference to Prince Ninigi, the grandson of Amaterasu, who married Princess Konohana Sakuya, whose name (including double meanings) means "blossoming brilliantly like the flowers of the trees." Ninigi's father-in-law's wish in giving him her hand was that their posterity would live up to their mother's name and prosper.

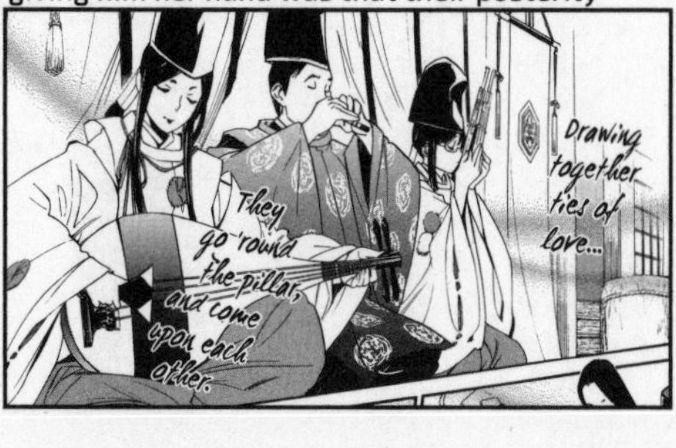
Drawing together ties of love...
They go round the pillar, and come upon each other.

The musicians are playing traditional instruments of classical Japanese music: the *biwa* (the lute seen on the left), the *hichiriki* (an oboe-like instrument played by the man in the middle), and the *shô* (the mouth organ seen on the right).

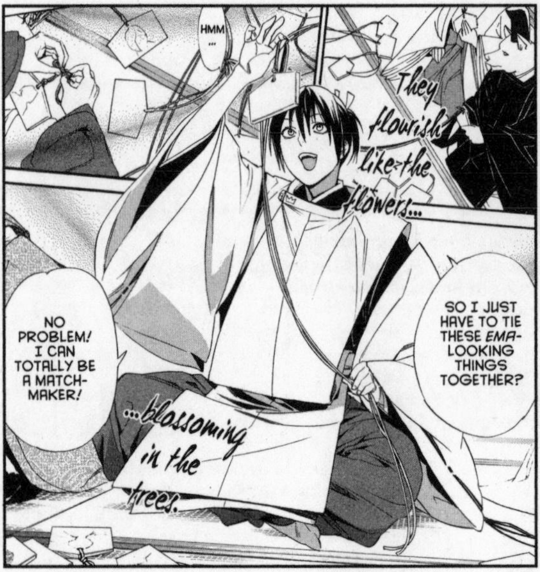
They flourish like the flowers...
HMM...
SO I JUST HAVE TO TIE THESE *EMA*-LOOKING THINGS TOGETHER?
...blossoming in the trees.
NO PROBLEM! I CAN TOTALLY BE A MATCH-MAKER!

I can totally be a matchmaker, page 114

As Hiyori mentioned much earlier in the volume, one of the main purposes of the Divine Council is to tie people's destinies together—in other words, matchmaking. The Japanese word for "matchmaking" is *enmusubi*, which literally means "tying ties." The gods are tying together people's *en*—the same *en* that means "ties" or "fate." In this case, fates tied in bonds of love—the kind that often lead to marriage.

Rabbit puns, page 115

In case the reader is wondering, the answer is no, there were not any rabbit puns in the original Japanese. However, both Kofuku and Daikoku are getting into the spirit of Kofuku's "formal" bunny girl outfit by ending some of their sentences with the word *pyon*, which is a common bunny sound effect, because it is the sound of hopping.

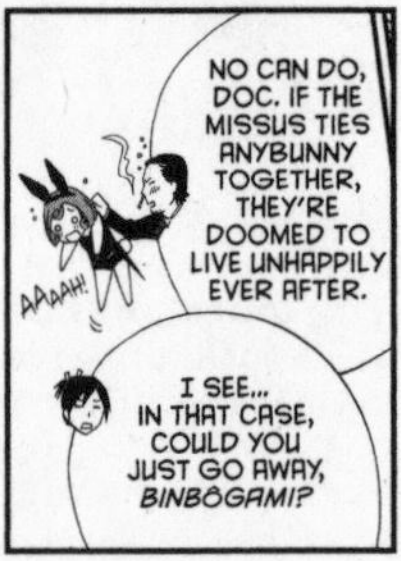
NO CAN DO, DOC. IF THE MISSUS TIES ANYBUNNY TOGETHER, THEY'RE DOOMED TO LIVE UNHAPPILY EVER AFTER.
AAAAH!
I SEE... IN THAT CASE, COULD YOU JUST GO AWAY, *BINBÔGAMI*?

Hiyori's soul mate lineup, page 120

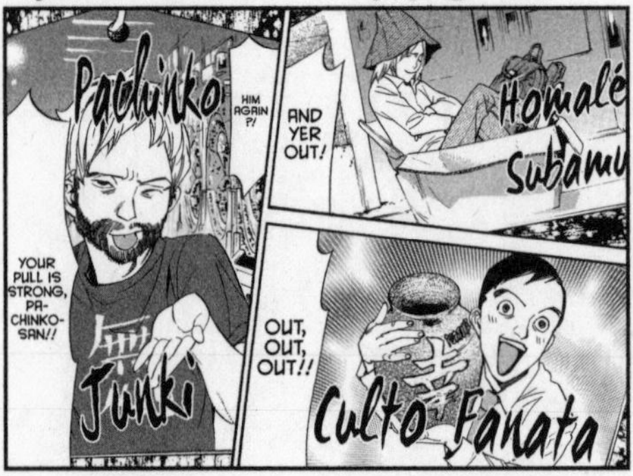
Homalé Subamu
AND YER OUT!
Culto Fanata
OUT, OUT, OUT!!
Pachinko Junki
HIM AGAIN?!
YOUR PULL IS STRONG, PA-CHINKO-SAN!!

The translators would like to apologize for the translated names of these men, which are not real Japanese names. As the reader may have guessed, the names have been changed in the hopes of making the comedy more obvious to English-speaking readers. The original names (with surname first) are Pachin Kazu, Nenashi Sôsuke, and Karuto Hamatta, meaning "pachinko junkie," "homeless bum," and "cult fanatic," respectively.

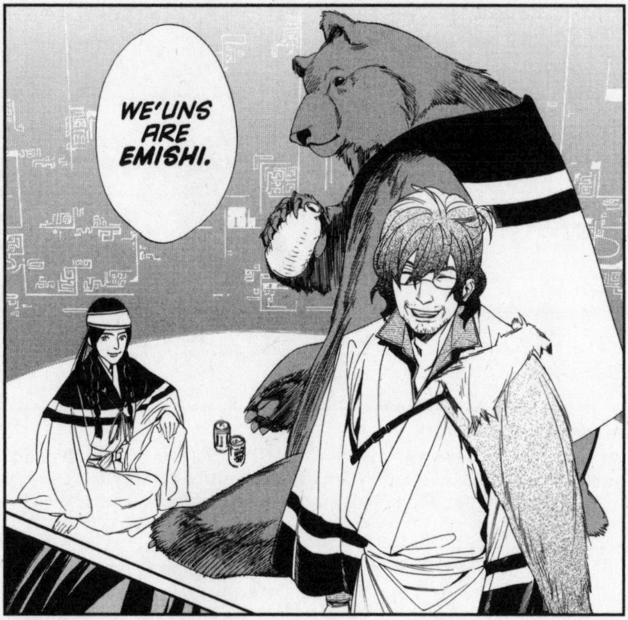
WE'UNS ARE EMISHI.

Emishi, page 156

The Emishi are the indigenous people who inhabited the northeastern regions of Japan when the Emperor came conquering under Amaterasu's banner. As Yato explains, here the term refers to those people's gods. These gods speak with the rural dialect of the regions. After some research, the translators found some similarities between the attitudes of the stereotypical natives of those regions and those of the inhabitants of the Appalachian mountains in the United States, so they attempted to replicate the Emishi's dialect by imitating the American highlanders' speech.

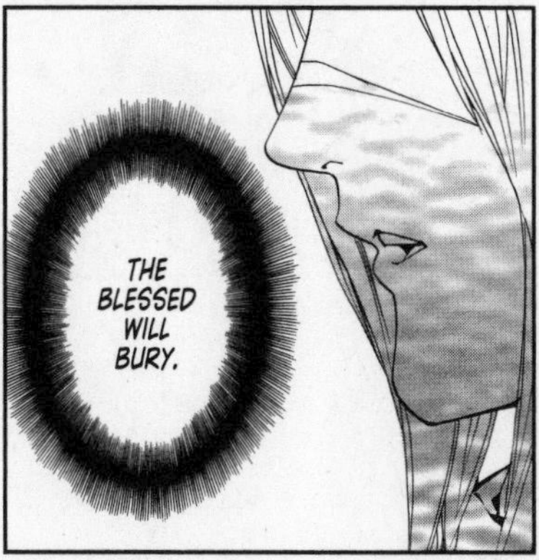
THE BLESSED WILL BURY.

The Burier, page 165

This epithet for the powerful shinki of whom Iwami speaks isn't quite as original as it may seem. She is called *hafuru-mono*, or "one who buries." As previously explained, *hafuru* or *hafuri* can mean "blessing" or "burial." When Kiun talks about the dangers of blessed vessels, or *hafuri* vessels, this is exactly the double meaning he is referring to. It remains unclear whether the positive or the negative meaning came first.

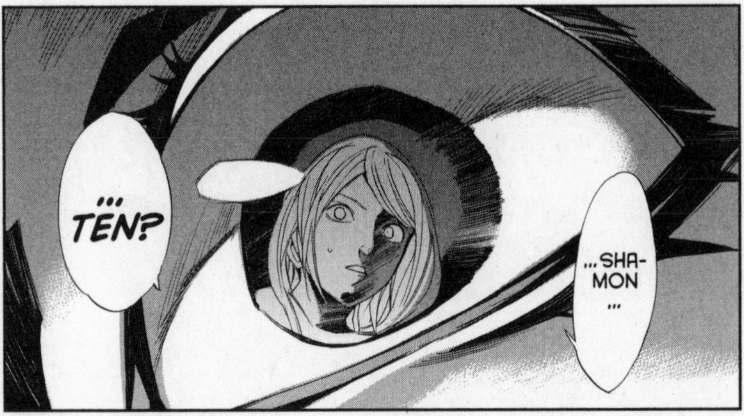
...SHA-MON...
...TEN?

Bishamonten, page 170
The final character in Bishamonten, *ten*, is written 天, and is used to denote the heavens or something heavenly. When the Burier hears this, she immediately makes the connection between Bishamon and the Heavens, and strikes.

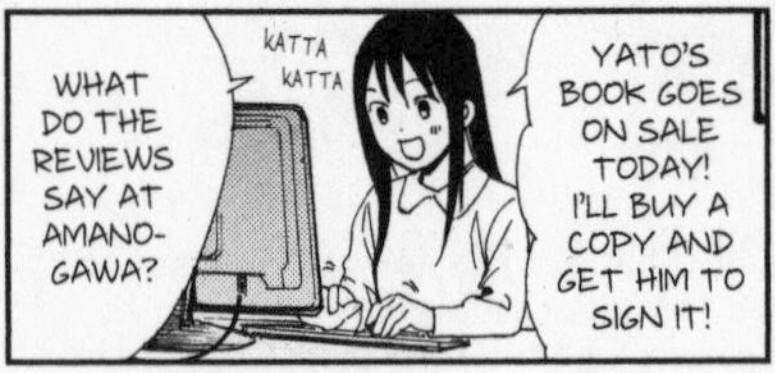
YATO'S BOOK GOES ON SALE TODAY! I'LL BUY A COPY AND GET HIM TO SIGN IT!
KATTA KATTA
WHAT DO THE REVIEWS SAY AT AMANO-GAWA?

Amanogawa, page 188
Amanogawa is the Japanese name for the Milky Way. Literally, it means "the river of heaven," so as the mortal realm has an online marketplace named after a large river, so, too, does the Heavens.

The scene from the abdication myth, page 189
Japanese mythology tells the story of how Takemikazuchi was sent to Izumo to order Ôkuninushi to relinquish the land of Izumo to the rule of the Heavens. When he and his companion arrive by sea at the beach of Izumo, they stick their swords in the waves and sit on the points while making their demands.

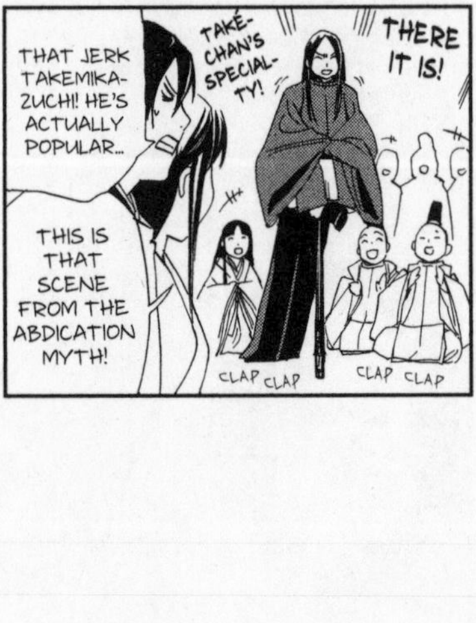
THERE IT IS!
TAKE-CHAN'S SPECIAL-TY!
THAT JERK TAKEMIKA-ZUCHI! HE'S ACTUALLY POPULAR...
THIS IS THAT SCENE FROM THE ABDICATION MYTH!
CLAP CLAP
CLAP CLAP

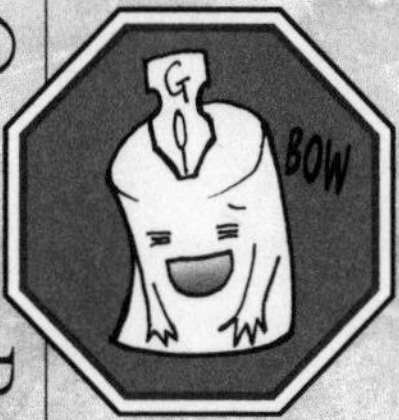
BOW

Surprise Character Trivia Part 1

Yato: He was once tricked into creating a bank account, which now occasionally has mystery money transferred into it. This is how he was able to buy a cell phone.

Yukiné: Daikoku pays him 500 yen (about $5) an hour for helping out part time at Kofuku's.

Hiyori: She basically just ignores the barrage of emails and tweets from Yato. But when Yukiné borrows Yato's phone to send her a message, she'll answer every time.

Bishamon: Underwear? Oh, I forgot...

Kazuma: He's the type of guy who can go into a lingerie store and buy women's underwear without a second thought.

Kofuku: I sleep with Daikoku!

Daikoku: He really is happy when there's a child (Yukiné) around.

Father: He wants to add Yato to his family plan, but just can't get it to work out.

Adachitoka

A Kodansha Comics Trade Paperback Original.

Published in the United States by Kodansha Comics, an imprint of Kodansha USA Publishing, LLC, New York.

Publication rights for this English edition arranged through Kodansha Ltd., Tokyo.

First published in Japan in 2015 by Kodansha Ltd., Tokyo.

ISBN 978-1-63236-256-8

Printed in the United States of America.

www.kodanshacomics.com

9 8 7 6 5 4 3 2 1

Translation: Alethea Nibley & Athena Nibley
Lettering: Lys Blakeslee
Editing: Lauren Scanlan
Kodansha Comics edition cover design: Phil Balsman